Managing National Security Policy

MANAGING NATIONAL SECURITY POLICY: THE PRESIDENT AND THE PROCESS

William W. Newmann

University of Pittsburgh Press

#51607444

Portions of this work have appeared in the March 2001 issue
of *Presidential Studies Quarterly* (vol. 31, no. 1), pp. 69–103,
© 2001 by the Center for the Study of the Presidency.
Reprinted by permission of Sage Publications.

Published by the University of Pittsburgh Press, Pittsburgh, Pa., 15260
ISBN 0-8229-4209-7

For Judy and Jeri

Contents

Figures

ABM   Antiballistic Missile

ACDA   Arms Control Disarmament Agency

ALCM   Air-Launched Cruise Missile

ANSA   Assistant to the President for National Security Affairs

CSB   Closely Spaced Basing

DOD   Department of Defense

FFPB   Friday Foreign Policy Breakfast

GLCM   Ground-Launched Cruise Missile

ICBM   Intercontinental Ballistic Missile

IG   Interagency Group

LNO   Limited Nuclear Options

MIRV   Multiple Independently Targeted Reentry Vehicles

MPS   Multiple Protective Shelters

MX   Missile, Experimental

NCA   National Command Authority

NEACP   National Emergency Airborne Command Post

NSC   National Security Council

NSC/DC   National Security Council Deputies Committee

NSC/PC   National Security Council Principals Committee

NSC/PCC National Security Council Policy Coordinating Committee

NSD   National Security Directive

NSDD   National Security Decision Directive

NSDM   National Security Decision Memorandum

NSPG   National Security Planning Group

NSR   National Security Review

NSSD   National Security Study Directive

NST	Nuclear and Space Arms Talks
PD	Presidential Directive
PRC	Policy Review Committee
PRM	Presidential Review Memorandum
SACPG	Senior Arms Control Policy Group
SALT	Strategic Arms Limitation Talks
SCC	Special Coordinating Committee
SDI	Strategic Defense Initiative
SICBM	Small ICBM, or Midgetman
SIG-DP	Senior Interagency Group Defense Policy
SIG-FP	Senior Interagency Group Foreign Policy
SIG-I	Senior Interagency Group Intelligence
SIG-IG	Senior Interagency Group Interagency Group
SIG/IRG	Senior Interagency Group / Interdepartmental Regional Group
SOP	Standard Operating Procedures
SIOP	Single Integrated Operating Plan
SLBM	Submarine Launched Ballistic Missile
START	Strategic Arms Reduction Talks/Treaty
VBB	Vance-Brzezinski-Brown Luncheon

Acknowledgments

No one writes a book by himself. Friends, colleagues, and institutions provide moral, intellectual, and financial support. Without this assistance, authors would have to crawl into a small hole with disks and a word processor, cover that hole with a rock, and emerge years later with a completed manuscript, bound, edited for grammar, and protected by a shiny dust jacket.

Niels Aaboe at the University of Pittsburgh Press has been extremely helpful and encouraging. The American Political Science Association provided an award that allowed me to make a trip to the Jimmy Carter Presidential Library. James Yancey and Mary Ann McSweeney of the library staff gave me a great deal of help, allowing me to make my way through the boxes and boxes of information I requested again and again only to find that nearly everything I was interested in was still classified.

Several former governmental officials, veterans of decision making on national security, were generous with their time and wisdom, granting me interviews that were both invaluable and enjoyable. Thanks go to David Aaron, James Baker, Zbigniew Brzezinski, David Newsom, and Brent Scowcroft.

I am grateful to James Goodby, Robert Holsworth, Scott Keeter, and David Hiley for their friendship and guidance as well as for giving me places to work and providing a collegial atmosphere while I performed this research. Paul Hammond, Bert Rockman, Michael Brenner, and Phil Williams deserve special thanks for their wisdom, patience, and eyestrain, agreeing to wade into this work even when I carried it into their offices with a forklift. Special thanks goes to Paul. Without his faith in me, not only would there be no book, but I might be doing something else for a living.

Of course, Judy Twigg has performed miracles in my life and on this book. Jeri deserves thanks as well for reading every word. She truly is the biggest miracle.

Managing National Security Policy

Chapter One

INTRODUCTION

IN THE ERA BEFORE THE ASSISTANT TO THE PRESIDENT FOR National Security Affairs (ANSA) became a permanent, often dominating, aspect of presidential decision making on national security, President Eisenhower contemplated moving the center of foreign policy making into the White House. He toyed with the idea of appointing a National Security Council (NSC) based administrator/adviser who would be the senior assistant to the president for foreign policy. Some proposals designated Secretary of State John Foster Dulles as that official, but each time Eisenhower brought the idea to Dulles, the secretary did his best to quash it. Dulles rejected the creation of a powerful special assistant for foreign affairs at the White House in any scenario, whether he or anyone else took the new position. Twice when he was instructed by Eisenhower to sound out prominent candidates to become either his replacement as secretary or the new White House assistant, Dulles made the offers (specifically to John McCloy and C. D. Jackson) so unattractive that they were refused. Eisenhower valued Dulles's role as first-among-equals adviser above all other aspects of his foreign policy process; he tolerated Dulles's bureaucratic games. No special assistant such as this was ever created.[1]

Over forty years later, in the aftermath of the September 11 terrorist attacks on the United States, the G. W. Bush administration swiftly moved to restructure its decision-making processes related to the new threats that had emerged. The new global war on terrorism loomed as a struggle that would be fought overseas and at home. The merger of foreign policy and domestic law enforcement issues called for a new style of decision making for what was soon called homeland security. The administration created a White House–based Homeland Security Council, Office of Homeland Security, and Homeland Security Adviser system based on the NSC model that had endured since the 1960s. In the face of congressional calls for a new Department of Homeland Security that would be subject to congressional oversight and directed by a Senate-confirmed cabinet office, the administration initially defended the White House system, even refusing to allow Homeland Security Adviser Tom Ridge to testify before Congress. Ridge himself summed up the notion succinctly, explaining that it was his personal relationship with the president that would give him his power and authority.[2] Eliminating that bond by forcing Ridge to become one of many cabinet officers rather than the president's personal adviser on homeland security might destroy his effectiveness.

These small tales of decision-making organization illustrate the two key themes of this work. First, presidents feel pressure to centralize decision making in the White House in an effort to gain more direct control over the policy process. Even within the White House, institutional and political pressures lead the president to streamline or create shortcuts around the system he designed to fit his own decision-making preferences. Eisenhower initiated a process to create his own personal assistant on national security affairs; G. W. Bush placed the system for addressing new national priorities as close to him as possible. Each was acting out of a desire to gain more control or establish initial control over the decision making on crucial issues. Second, the scholarly work on presidential decision making may ultimately lead to one conclusion: The key to understanding the decision-making process rests upon the study of the relationships between the president and his senior advisers. Eisenhower's relationship with Dulles was so important to him that he abandoned his plans for reorganization rather than have them jeopardize that relationship. Bush, in office less than a year and facing a new and complex war, chose a close and trusted friend to take command on his behalf. In short, all presidents feel institutional and political pressures to manipulate the decision-making process toward a more centralized, yet more informal process. Each president's relationship with his advisers, however, will determine if and how these pressures are translated into actual decision-making processes.

These basic notions provide a foundation for the examination of the changes that occur in national security decision-making processes within the senior levels of the executive branch of the U.S. government. Four questions are crucial. First, what are the causes of change in national security advisory and decision-making processes? Second, are there any distinct patterns in the way those processes change over time? Third, if there are similarities in the pattern of change over time, what are the causes of those similarities? Fourth, if there are differences in the pattern of change over time, what are the causes of those differences? These questions are answered through the development of an evolution model of national security decision making and the testing of this model with case studies of decision making on arms control and nuclear strategy by the Carter, Reagan, and Bush administrations. The key contribution of the evolution model to the study of national security decision making is its focus on the way the structure of the decision unit changes over time. Decision making is not seen as a static process, but as a dynamic one that evolves and matures in important ways during a president's term in office.

The case studies identify the similarities and differences in the way administrations' national security processes change over time. The case study evidence suggests that the structure of national security decision making begins to follow a distinct pattern of evolution over the first term of any presidential administration. Each administration begins with a standard National Security Council–based interagency process. Decision making then starts to evolve in a predictable manner—participation in the decision unit is narrowed, ad hoc and informal procedures play greater and greater roles in the process, and the standard interagency process is bypassed or streamlined more and more often. These changes represent tendencies or leanings, not a rigid linear evolution that leads all administrations toward identical structures. All administrations do seem to begin a journey in the same direction, but they do not all reach the same destination. The pressures they feel to initiate modifications in the decision-making structure are quite the same, however. These similarities stem from the pressures of the international political system, domestic political system, internal executive branch decision making, and presidential management strategies and political goals. Presidents use three structures to make decisions—a formal, informal, and confidence structure. The differences in the changes actually made within each administration, their duration, and the variation in the origins, use, and interactions between these three structures stem from the idiosyncratic leadership styles of individual presidents. The individual leadership style of each president shapes the way in which he reacts to similar pressures.

The importance of this study lies in its attention to the factors that influence the evolution of the decision unit, its identification of the tendencies toward a specific structural evolution, and its focus on the interrelationship of leadership style, political and institutional pressures. Incoming presidents designing their national security decision structures usually create systems that are the mirror image of their predecessors. In a sense, they reinvent the wheel during the presidential transition and then spend years learning how to make decisions, adjusting their decision structures along the way. Understanding the pressures on the decision unit and knowing how their personal leadership style has an impact on decision making may be essential to helping new presidents design decision structures that fit the realities of national security decision making. Although no "best decision-making process" that fits all administrations can be devised, the case studies suggest that an administration that has all three structures operating in tandem provides the best foundation for decision making. In addition, the research here makes it clear that presidents use different types of decision structures to make different types of decisions.

THE SCHOLARLY CONTEXT

Since the 1960s, foreign and national security policy decision making have been explained in two general ways. First, some scholars have argued that organizational and bureaucratic dynamics inherent in governmental decision making are the key determinants in policy making. The organizational process model contends that the government is best described as a vast conglomeration of semi-independent departments with interests and perspectives of their own; governmental policy is the output of attempts to merge those competing interests into coherent policy or the uncoordinated aggregate of decisions made by each department. The bureaucratic politics model focuses on the perceptions, interests, and ambitions of individual governmental officials. The president is often portrayed as just another player in the bureaucratic game. Governmental policy, ultimately, is the result of bargaining and compromise between individuals and coalitions of individuals. These models taken together are usually called the "governmental politics" model. Their common ingredient is the description of decision-making processes as a competition for control of policy between government officials and departments and policy choices made through negotiations among these officials and departments. In addition, they portray a process that is ruled by the institutional nature of decision making within the executive branch—separate organizations and individuals competing to see their interests become policy. Each president faces these similar institutional pressures.

Others have suggested that the role of the president, his decision-making style, and his political needs are the crucial variables. Ex-presidential advisers argue that presidents must be seen as unique individuals; each decision-making system must be tailored to the idiosyncratic needs of the particular president. Some analyses have suggested different ways of categorizing management styles; however, the purpose of the management strategy was the same in each case— gaining presidential control over self-interested departments and ambitious, often feuding officials. These management strategies are a function of a president's own decision-making theory. From his own predispositions and from the advice of scholars and practitioners, a president creates committee structures, decision-making procedures, and roles and responsibilities for specific officials and agencies. Much of the literature emphasizing the role of the president is a direct critique of the organizational and bureaucratic process models in which the president was often described as captive to the executive branch. In all of these ideas, the president is the dominant player. He manages the process to make sure that decisions are made the way he wants them made and that the policy outcomes reflect his political preferences. Within this book, these concepts will be referred to as presidential management models.

Often the governmental politics and presidential management models are seen as mutually exclusive, even competing models. Such a debate over which factors are more important can eventually grow sterile. Since the late 1960s and early 1970s these ideas have not been developed to a great extent. Both models hold more explanatory power if they are seen as complementary. Each model describes forces within an administration that shape the process. Organizational and bureaucratic actors fight for the needs of their organizations or their individual needs, respectively; presidents fight for their needs. This book argues that the internal dynamics of the executive branch and the managerial preferences of the president both influence the shape of decision-making processes.

A third paradigm that springs from the "new institutionalism" literature provides a more comprehensive framework for explaining decision making. These ideas can be adapted to include the concepts contained within the governmental politics and presidential management models. Initially the new institutionalism literature considered the structure of governmental decision making to be determined by Congress and the pressure of various interest groups; the departmental structure of the government was seen as a reflection of congressional and lobby group concerns. Further scholarship refocused the literature on the power of the presidency, suggesting that he has both the motivation and managerial advantages to win decision-making struggles with Congress, interest groups, and the bureaucracy. In this view, the president becomes the key actor in structuring decision making. Importantly, this literature adds the domestic political environment as a factor in decision making, a factor that the governmental politics and presidential management models often downplay.

These ideas originally concentrated on domestic policy making. By applying them to national security policy, the differences between domestic and national security policy are highlighted. In the latter, the president has even more of an advantage than in the domestic arena; the influence of interest groups and Congress are muted. The addition of international events as a key influence on decision making is crucial and obvious, yet often ignored.

All three models have a key limitation. They usually do not consider time as a factor in the decision-making process. There is the sense that an administration will put into place a decision-making system at the start of its stewardship over U.S. foreign policy, and maintain that structure for the next four to eight years. Time and the cumulative effects of multiple decisions on the process and personnel are not addressed. Without an inclusion of time as a factor, studies of national security decision making are handicapped. Too often one case study from an administration's tenure in office is used as a representative example of how the administration made decisions for its entire term in office. Other studies use generic anecdotal tales of how a president made decisions to characterize a president's decision-making process. This study examines the way presidents made decisions over time on a specific issue to see how and why that process changes.

A MODEL OF DECISION-MAKING CHANGE

This book uses a modified version of Walcott and Hult's "governance" model.[3] In considering the influences on decision making and White House staff structure, this model identifies three sources of decision-making structure: the political environment, the organizational dynamics/role of the advisory system, and the role of the president. Dividing the political environment further into a domestic and international political context allows this model to include all the influences on decision making suggested by the governmental politics, presidential management, and new institutional literature.

The international and domestic political environment, the internal organizational and bureaucratic dynamics of the executive branch, and the president's leadership style, management, and political strategy are all factors in shaping the process of decision making. The way in which the international and domestic political environment affect decision making seems obvious. International events, changes in domestic public opinion, and/or congressional pressure could all create new demands on an administration's decision-making process. Organizational and bureaucratic dynamics place similar pressures on standard interagency procedures. These organizational and bureaucratic forces are the basic reality of executive branch life, but can only cause changes in the decision-making process if some aspect of organizational or bureaucratic competition is settled, reshaped, or restarted because of international or domestic political pressures.

The president as an influence on decision making is more complex. His role is a function of three different factors: presidential leadership style, presidential management strategy, and political strategy. Each illustrates a different type of presidential impact on the process. The three are different enough that it is important to separate them. Their unique effects on the process help provide a clear picture of the president's place in decision making. Leadership style here is defined as the president's own choices about how deeply he wishes to participate in administration decision making and how he relates to his advisers individually and as a group. Management style refers to his preferred design for administrative decision making in terms of NSC committee structures, information flow, as well as organizational and bureaucratic roles of key agencies and officials (particularly the Secretary of State and ANSA). Political strategy is added as a factor here to emphasize that the president's policy choices are deeply dependent on his overall political beliefs, goals, and fortunes at any given point. Presidents are politicians first; national security may be a third or fourth order concern unless there is a crisis facing the United States. In many cases, national security policy may simply not even be on the president's agenda of important tasks. How those priorities change and how national security issues, in this case arms control and nuclear strategy, become issues of importance is deeply influenced by the president's overall political concerns.

This work takes a short-term focus. It examines the changes in decision-making processes in the first terms of the Carter, Reagan, and Bush administrations in an effort to isolate in a fairly detailed manner what factors account for what types of change. Changes in the international political environment and/or changes in the domestic political environment lead to changes in the organizational dynamics and presidential management and political strategies. This in turn leads to changes in decision-making structure.

The key factor in these manipulations of the process is the president. Although all four variables can lead to changes in the decision-making process, these changes are deliberately made by the president or by his key senior advisers. These adjustments in the process are responses to developments in the international and domestic political context and/or the ways in which the internal organizational and bureaucratic dynamics are affected by the changing political context. A president may also decide that he needs to make modifications in his decision-making process if he comes to perceive issues or individuals in a different way. This may not be caused by any specific event or any internal dynamics, but instead by the cumulative weight of events that might lead to a shift in presidential views. In all cases, however, changes in decision making are not inadvertent, but are conscious attempts by the president to adjust the decision-making process in ways that he feels will serve him best. How these adjustments to the process evolve also depends on the president.

The case studies suggest that the structure of national security decision making within the U.S. executive branch leans toward a distinct pattern of evolution over the first term of any presidential administration, a pattern called the *evolution model* throughout this book. Each administration begins with a similar NSC and NSC staff–based interagency process, and soon begins to make similar modifications. Narrowing takes place as the president comes to rely on fewer advisers; increased informal and ad hoc processes develop as senior decision makers turn to informal and ad hoc settings; increased bypassing or streamlining of the interagency process results as the president and a select group of advisers make decisions outside of the standard interagency process or in truncated versions of the standard interagency procedures.

Regardless of the ultimate result of these tendencies, all administrations end up using three concurrent decision-making structures as a result of the evolution of the decision unit: the initial formal interagency structure, an informal structure in which the senior officials and the president meet outside the formal structures, and a confidence structure in which the president relies on one or two advisers more than any other. The informal structure seems to evolve quickly, within the first six months in office. The confidence structure takes longer to develop.

The pattern of evolution is based upon decision-making principles of decision economy, political pressures, and learning that guide an administration's management of its national security policy process over time.[4] As time and effort constraints on the senior policy makers increase they will begin to take procedural shortcuts to economize their decision-making energies; there are identifiable and foreseeable patterns of political pressures on an administration during its term in office, as well as unpredictable pressures; and a new foreign policy team learns about the system it had originally intended to use and about working with each other. All three types of pressures, however, have the same result. They push the administration to make changes in decision-making processes as characterized above. These principles reflect a disconnect between the product of the standard interagency processes and the decision-making needs of the president as well as a subsequent incentive for the president and senior advisers to seek more decision-making control.

This desire for control leads to the evolution in decision-making structures. In the context of the variables suggested above, the influence of the international and domestic political environment, the organizational and bureaucratic dynamics, and the management and political strategies of the president lead the administration to change its decision-making process in the manner described and to develop the three concurrent decision structures. Simply put, all the stresses and strains of making national security policy lead each president in the same direction—toward narrowing participation, increased informality and ad hoc processes, and increased bypassing or streamlining of the standard interagency process.

Differences in the way these changes occur are also evident. Although the general pattern is the same, there are differences in the way the three concurrent structures develop and the way they are used by each president. Presidential leadership style is the crucial variable in explaining any differences in the way decision-making structures evolve between one administration and another. The length of time a president takes to develop the confidence structure is deeply influenced by the president's sense of his preferred role in the process. Informal structures that somewhat mirrored the formal interagency processes developed within the first six months in the Carter, Reagan, and Bush administrations. However, the development of the confidence structure, the relationships between the three concurrent structures, the president's use of each structure, and the ultimate successful operation of the decision-making process are contingent upon the president's role and his relationships with his senior advisers.

In short, although all administrations move toward similar adjustments in their decision structures, the differences in the president's leadership style produce distinct variations in the ultimate shape of that evolution.

CASE STUDIES AND METHODOLOGY

Case studies of the decision-making processes on strategic arms control and nuclear strategy during the Carter, Reagan, and G. H. W. Bush administrations offer the opportunity to examine the notion of a pattern of evolution in national security decision making. The choice of cases allows for several controls. Each administration shared a similar initial decision structure (NSC committee process), political demands for successful arms control, and nuclear strategic doctrine. A precedent had been set by the successful completion of the first Strategic Arms Limitation Talks (SALT I) and each successive president felt pressure to match that achievement. U.S. nuclear strategy stayed essentially the same as it had since the initial Single Integrated Operating Plan (SIOP) had been designed: the United States would prepare to fight a nuclear war using limited and controlled strikes on Soviet military and industrial assets.

The limits placed on the case studies are designed to focus the research for better comparison. Only first terms will be considered. This places each case within the similar context of a new administration leading the executive branch for the first time and seeking reelection for a second term. In the years since the National Security Adviser became an important player in decision making, only Ronald Reagan and Bill Clinton have finished out two complete terms. Factoring out a second term broadens the sample set to several administrations that can be candidates for comparison. In addition, preliminary study of the issue suggests that second terms are nearly completely different in their dynamics. So many other factors come into play during second terms that it seems wise to study them separately.[5] To focus the issue on the typical evolution of foreign policy as presidents and their senior advisers become acclimated to the job and each other, second terms have been excluded from this study. Similarly, choosing only one issue to examine narrows the study in some useful ways. The question of whether issue area affects the pattern of the evolution on decision making will be set aside for further research.

Choosing Carter, Reagan, and G. H. W. Bush not only allows for some continuity in the issues involved, but it also allows for some variation. The party in power in both the White House and Congress shifted during this period from unified Democratic leadership (Carter) to Republican White House/Senate vs. Democratic House (Reagan), to divided government (Bush). If domestic political factors such as the party in the White House or the nature of the relationships between the executive and legislative branch matter (divided or unified), then it should be revealed by this research design.

The end of the cold war also allows for some variation in the case studies. How do Carter and Reagan policy making on nuclear weapons and arms control during the cold war compare to G. H. W. Bush policy making on these same issues after the Soviet threat had begun to recede? If the international environment (and its impact on domestic politics) is a factor in shaping decision making, the end of the cold war will add another dimension to the utility of the case studies.

To focus the research on the cause of change, Chapter three explores the initial decision-making structures, processes, and presidential leadership styles for each administration. Each case study chapter is organized in a narrative that identifies the international and domestic political environments, the basic organizational dynamics within the administration, and the issues of presidential choice —leadership style, management strategy, and political goals. The focus on presidential choice in the case studies is specifically a focus on why, when, and how a president makes changes to his administration's decision-making process. In particular, since the evolution model suggests that all of these variables except leadership style push each president's process in the same direction, even though leadership style accounts for differences in the evolution, it is important to contrast the impact of the president's unique inputs and the environmental and institutional factors.

The dependent variable, structure of the decision unit, is examined through a "structured, focused comparison" methodology.[6] A standardized set of questions frames the analysis of each case study. This allows for a controlled comparison, and a single framework for each case. The method has been called a "process-tracing procedure."[7] In the case study narrative, these questions are not literally answered and asked; however, each case study provides an answer to these questions in its narrative of the characteristics of the decision-making process.

Given that the focus of the research is how decision-making processes change over time, single case studies of one decision in a discrete time period are not useful. It is necessary to trace the decision-making process over an extended period of time or sample the decision-making process at various intervals. The approach will depend on the quality and quantity of data. The comparison then exists on two levels. First, the set of questions are asked about each administration's decision-making process, but in an iterative manner. The analysis must be repeated in order to reveal any changes in the decision-making process. Only through asking these questions several times over the four years of an administration's term will the pattern of evolution in the process be determined. Second, this process must be repeated for all three administrations so that the pattern within each can be compared. This will isolate the basic hypothesis: Is there a single pattern in the evolution of the national security decision-making process that is apparent in all administrations? The following set of questions are those that are implicitly asked.

Initial Decision-Making Structure: What is the initial formal design of the national security decision-making unit in terms of the committee structures, the bureaucratic level and breadth included, the desired amount of presidential involvement, and the methodology for producing advice for the president and/or decisions?

Roles and Relationships: Are there prime movers of policy, individual advisers charged with directing the process or given responsibility for producing the decision? If so, does this change? If not, does the president assume this role, or are all advisers equally involved in the process? Are there new structures or additional individuals, governmental affiliated or nongovernmental, added to the decision-making process? If so, why have they been created or included, what is their relationship to the initial formal process, and what is the duration of their involvement? What is the coalition structure of the administration, the nature of alliances or coalitions or rivalries among the senior decision makers? If we use the metaphor of bureaucratic conflict to describe decision making, the question seeks to illustrate the order of battle for the administration. What is the relationship between the senior officials and the president? Who is considered loyal to the president? Who has access and who does not? How is the inner circle versus the outer circle delineated? Of course, for all these questions, does this change?

Process: Are the initial formal procedures lasting, or do more informal processes take root? If so, what are the design and the scope of responsibility of the new informal processes? What is the relationship between the formal and informal processes? Does the hierarchical level at which decisions are made change at any time? Does the breadth of departmental inclusion, the horizontal participation, change at any time? Are some departments excluded from the decision at any point? Are some departments added to the decision unit?

Political Factors: Is the political environment, either domestic or international, related in any way to the changes in the way decisions are produced by the administration?

Pattern of Change: Finally, with answers to the preceding questions, can an overall pattern of change in the administration's decision-making process be identified?

Applying these questions to each case study makes it possible to compare the patterns of national security policy change from administration to administration to identify the similarities and any differences discovered between them.

The case studies include the Carter administration's decision making for the March 1977 Strategic Arms Limitation Talks (SALT) proposal and Presidential Directive 59 of 1980; the Reagan decision-making process concerning the Eureka Proposals of May 1982, the Build-Down Proposals of fall 1983 and the Strategic Defense Initiative (SDI) speech of March 1983; and the Bush administration's decisions on the Malta Summit, the completion of the first Strategic Arms Reduction Talks (START 1), and the speeches of fall–winter 1991 that led to START 2.

CONCLUSIONS AND IMPLICATIONS

Each administration felt pressure to adapt its initial decision-making structure in the ways suggested by the evolution model. Each reacted to those pressures in ways guided by their leadership style. President Carter followed these pressures to their logical conclusions—deep centralization of the process, marked informality, and even bypassing the interagency process. He ultimately came to favor his confidence structure through a growing reliance on and relationship with Assistant for National Security Affairs (ANSA) Zbigniew Brzezinski. His administration was marked by policy inconsistencies, bureaucratic warfare, and eventually the resignation of Secretary of State Cyrus Vance.

The Reagan administration was affected by the president's hands-off style of management. From 1981 to late 1983 the administration decision-making evolution proceeded along a path similar to the Carter administration with more centralization, informality, and in some instances complete bypassing of the interagency process. The evolution was initially a response to deep philosophical divisions within the administration over policy toward the Soviet Union and a decentralized NSC process that led to gridlock in the formal interagency process. The informal structure that was created to resolve these differences and the confidence structure centering around ANSA William Clark collapsed in late 1983. President Reagan did not try to manage his decision-making process directly and allowed White House aides to sabotage and eventually destroy the new structures. By the fall of 1983, the administration had completely reversed the evolution of the first two years and was once again plagued by stalemate due to unresolved philosophical differences and mired in hostile rivalries without alternate processes designed to release the internal tensions.

In sharp contrast to the Carter and Reagan experience, the Bush administration is considered an example of a well-oiled decision-making machine. It had all three structures predicted by the evolution model. The informal structure was dominant, but it always worked in tandem with the formal and confidence structures. The process worked smoothly because the president worked hard to make sure that it did. Bush adapted his decision-making process to the institutional and political pressures, while consciously trying to maintain the advantages of his initial NSC system. Bush's previous experience in government had taught him that a well-managed policy process and good teamwork between the president and his senior aides and among those senior aides were prerequisites to good policy choices. In accordance with that belief, Bush chose as his senior advisers people he had worked with as both friends and colleagues in previous administrations. Even though these are general assessments, they are reflected in the specific cases of arms control and nuclear strategy discussed within the case studies.

The scholarly and policy implications of these findings are significant. First, in researching adaptations to existing administration structures multiple levels of analysis are necessary. The international and domestic political environments, organizational dynamics, and the president's own preferences influence the shape of decision making. However, all of these adaptations are conscious and deliberate. This means that the international and domestic political environments and organizational dynamics only cause changes in decision-making processes in tandem with a choice made by the president to modify the decision-making process.

Second, it is clear from the case studies that all three decision structures—formal, informal, and confidence—are necessary for a smoothly functioning decision-making process. However, the proper balance between the three structures is crucial. None can be allowed to dominate the process, and the informal structure should play the key role of ironing out consensus among the key decision makers. If the formal structure dominates, the decision-making process may become paralyzed by the interagency process and departmental rivalries. If the confidence structure is supreme, those advisers who feel ignored by the president may sabotage the decision-making process or resign.

In comparing the three administrations it becomes obvious that the Bush decision-making team was far more successful than the others at managing its decision-making process. This is not meant to suggest that its policies were better than those of Carter or Reagan. Such a judgment might be based on partisanship or whether idealism or realism was the guiding analytical principle. Success in this case is defined as the smooth and orderly manner in which decisions were made, and the lack of decision-making pathologies such as bureaucratic or organizational feuds that spilled out into the newspapers and television news shows.

A third issue concerns lessons that an incoming administration might take from this study. If a distinct pattern of evolution is evident within each administration, is this an identification of a generic "best" decision style that all administrations could use? Could any incoming administration use these procedures as an off-the-shelf decision-making process, rather than reinventing the wheel with each new administration? The answer seems to be yes and no. Incoming administrations can put in place a formal and informal structure on inauguration day. However, a president cannot know which individuals will fit into what parts of these structures until numerous decisions have been made in which relationships and processes are tested and the president learns which advisers he can trust. Learning seems to be the key. Presidents and senior officials enter office with theories of administrative decision making, ideas about which advisers will play what roles, who will be the most useful, and what role the president will play. They will eventually learn how right or wrong they were only after making repeated decisions over a period of time. There is no foolproof way to predict which advisers will assume what roles in an administration. However, being prepared to adjust the process through these three concurrent structures can help to make learning and implementing what has been learned a much easier task.

Fourth, this research suggests that a typology of decision-making adaptation can be developed. Each case of change can be placed into one of three categories: innovative, reactive, or opportunistic. Innovative modifications are those spurred by presidents in reaction to some political vision. Carter's Deep Cuts Strategic Arms Limitation Talks (SALT) proposal of March 1977 and Reagan's Strategic Defense Initiative (SDI) speech of March 1983 fit into this category. Reactive modifications are those made by political necessity. In particular, domestic political pressures often (but not always) in tandem with international developments cause an administration to adjust its decision making specifically to produce a certain policy. The Reagan Eureka and Build-Down decisions, and the Bush Malta Summit and START 1 decisions are such cases. Opportunistic modifications are those in which an administration modifies its decision-making process to accomplish a shift in its policy that it feels is warranted given a new development in the international political environment. They are mainly a function of presidential choice, with perhaps a nod to the domestic political considerations of a coming election year. These modifications are different from innovative and reactive modifications because the motivation for the changes has elements of both. A president may react to an international event, but he is not necessarily responding to any groundswell for changes in policy. In the case of Carter's PD-59 and Bush's speeches of fall and winter 1991, the president perceived the opening of a window of opportunity based on the domestic political (Carter) or international political needs (Bush) of the moment.

This is a reversal of the study of whether different styles of policy process produce different types of policy. In these cases, policies with differing characteristics require a president to use different styles of policy process. Policy change necessitates process change. Further study of this idea is crucial in the post–cold war era. The current U.S. national security decision-making system is a product of the cold war, designed in 1947 and evolved based on the exigencies of competing with and containing the USSR. The world after the collapse of communism was vastly different. The tragedy of September 11 revealed just how dangerous the world can be, even for a hegemon without any nation-state equals. A dangerous but familiar threat environment has given way to a dangerous, more complex environment filled with an array of more diverse and less predictable threats. The creation of the Homeland Security Council and Office of Homeland Security is a first step. The structure of decision making for national security, enshrined in the National Security Act of 1947, also needs to be reassessed. Simply put, if process is defined by policy needs, then the United States must undertake a serious review of its standard national security processes. Even in the stable environment of the cold war, the policy process was modified from time to time. In a more uncertain post–cold war world, more flexible and adaptable processes may be a necessity.

STRUCTURE OF THE BOOK

Chapter two addresses the theoretical and methodological aspects of the book. Chapter three examines the initial NSC processes of each administration as well as the leadership styles of each president to provide a context for comparisons. Chapters four, five, and six explore the Carter, Reagan, and Bush administrations' decision making on arms control and nuclear strategy, respectively. Chapter seven considers the scholarly and policy implications of the case study findings.

Chapter Two

AN EVOLUTION MODEL
OF NATIONAL SECURITY
DECISION MAKING

THE EXPLANATORY POWER OF THE STANDARD MODELS OF national security decision making—governmental politics, presidential management, and new institutionalism—are handicapped by their mutual exclusivity and their lack of emphasis on change in decision-making structures over time. The evolution model is premised on the notion that the ideas presented in the other models are accurate descriptions of the multiple and varied influences on decision making—organizational and bureaucratic politics, presidential leadership, and congressional and interest group pressures. Decision making is therefore filled with political tensions that make it inherently unstable, dynamic, and, most importantly, subject to change—an administration's initial decision-making processes will evolve with the accumulation of decision-making experience within contentious domestic and international political environments.

National security decision making has been studied from many perspectives. There are numerous approaches, from cognitive psychology, to small group dynamics, to operational codes, to the effects of stress on decision makers, to character.[1] This study is concerned with the pattern of changes in the decision-making process. For this reason, it is examined in terms of its organizational structure. Fenno's definition of decision-making structure applies best: structure is defined as the relationships among senior officials, and between senior officials and the president. Selznick calls this the "social structure" of an organization, but it is also the decision-making structure of an organization. Ultimately, what is at issue here is the structure of the advisory process and the way advice becomes government policy. Simon's premise that the terms "managing" and "decision making" can be used interchangeably is crucial to this understanding.[2] The term "structure" is used to describe both the standing committee organization of the decision-making process and the key patterns within the relationships between senior officials and the president, including the flow of paperwork, tempo of meetings, and committee relationships. Formal committee meetings and study reviews, informal networks, friendships, and conversations, debate, discussion, dissent between the senior advisors and the president, and between those officials and lower-level officials, nonexecutive branch officials, and even private citizens become a part of the advisory process in this definition. It is a broad definition of decision making that allows for inclusion of a great range of variables that might impact decisions. To focus on changes in the structure of decision making requires a breadth of this sort to capture the richness and complexity of decision making.

Since the 1980s, neorealist and neoliberal theories that focus on system-level causes of state behavior have become the dominant paradigms for studying international relations. As a result, the flood of scholarly work on state-level theories such as the governmental politics models (bureaucratic politics, organizational process) and presidential management of national security decision making that dominated research agendas in the 1960s and 1970s has been reduced to a trickle.[3] Scholars of domestic political decision making and the Executive Office of the Presidency, however, have maintained an interest in how presidents organize their staffs for decision making. This book considers both the governmental politics and presidential management models of the 1960s and 1970s debated by scholars of U.S. national security as well as the new institutionalism ideas of the 1980s and 1990s developed by scholars of U.S. domestic politics. The governance model of decision making is adapted to focus on change and is combined with elements of the other models to create the evolution model.

Four key elements of a decision-making model are used to compare all four models. These categories for comparison provide a quick way to highlight the differences in each model and any aspects of decision making that are not fully explained. First, a look at the sources of structure identifies how each model defines the influences on decision making. Who are the actors and what causes them to behave as they do? Second, a consideration of the causes of change in structure illustrates the way in which each model explains any modifications in or deviations from the initial structure of the decision unit and procedures for policy making. If the models even do consider changes in structure, what is their explanation for those changes? Third, an examination of any patterns of change identifies whether the model sees any coherent shape to the changes that occur. Finally, the character of structural change details the result of those changes, the new or modified style of decision making. Importantly, this comparison of the models highlights the contribution of the evolution model. It is the only one of the models to explicitly focus on change within the decision-making process over time.

GOVERNMENTAL POLITICS MODELS

The bureaucratic politics model and the organizational process model are often discussed separately, but should be considered as two variants of the same basic issue—the political nature of governmental decision making. Before the emergence of these models, scholars had traditionally viewed governmental decision making as the outcome of a rational and analytical process by a unified group of decision makers who based their policy decisions on cost-benefit analysis.[4] Simon and March led a reassessment of organizational decision making within the study of organization theory, while Hilsman, Huntington, and Neustadt redefined the study of foreign and defense policy decision making.[5] A second wave of studies, highlighted by the work of Allison and Halperin, refined these ideas further. These authors saw governmental policy as a political product, the output of competing interests of individuals, organizations, and institutions. The government was not a unified actor; its decisions were not analytical; policy choices were based not on cost-benefit analysis, but on struggle for power between competing decision-making participants. The upper-level decision and advisory process is a series of bargaining games among organizations, individuals, or coalitions of individuals who are more or less equal participants. The outcome of these bargaining games is a compromise policy that represents the decision of the U.S. government, but is not necessarily the first choice of any of the players or the best choice available.[6]

The organizational process model contends that the government is best described as a vast conglomeration of semi-independent departments with interests and perspectives of their own. Organizations have different views of the world, different views of U.S. national interests, and different standard operating procedures that they use to solve problems. Each hopes to be the lead organization in any policy process and implementation. This is the surest path to control over governmental policy and access to more resources. Individuals' actions are defined by the organizations to which they belong. Miles's law describes it best: "Where you stand depends on where you sit."[7] Actual governmental policy is the output of attempts to merge those competing interests into coherent policy or the uncoordinated aggregate of decisions made by each department.[8]

The bureaucratic politics model focuses on the perception, interests, and ambitions of individual governmental officials. The competition between individuals for power, input, and control of policy is a brutal one. It is not only a series of arguments over the proper policy in any given situation, but a struggle over power, influence, relevance, and career. Ambitious people who have spent a lifetime in positions of power, and who are accustomed to getting their way, face off at the highest levels of government. The winner may see a version of his or her policy enacted; the loser may see his or her career end in futility. Often scholars of this model refer to individuals playing a game; the only goal of that game is to win.[9] Importantly, the president is typically portrayed as just another player in the bureaucratic game. A variation on Miles's law can sum it up: Where you stand today depends on where you want to sit tomorrow.

The distinction between the two models is often blurred. Halperin and Kanter have provided the clearest way of illustrating the difference by classifying the actors in any decision-making process by whether their advice is based on their organizational affiliation or on their personal goals and perceptions.[10] In either case, decision making is portrayed as a contest for control of policy between competing individuals and/or organizations.

The sources of structure in the governmental politics school are institutionally defined. The division of labor between departments and agencies with specific competencies and responsibilities as well as the hierarchical relationships between officials at the multiple levels of each department and agency creates the environment for political competition. Each department and agency is trying to increase its input into policy making or control over policy implementation. Individuals do the same while also trying to ascend the hierarchical ladder. Importantly, this pattern of decision making is the same within all administrations. The institutional nature of the executive branch establishes an arena for competition. When a president is inaugurated, the struggle for control of policy begins. Scholars have often focused their study of this model on the competition between the secretary of state, secretary of defense, assistant to the president for national security affairs (ANSA), and White House staff. This competition seems to exist in any administration.[11]

The governmental politics model focuses less on change in the process than it does on describing the process. The issue of change within the decision-making process is almost implicit. Commensurate with this model's focus on power, change in the decision-making structure is a reflection of the change in power relationships among organizations and individuals. It is often linked to status and reputation. For example, Neustadt points out that as an individual's status rises and falls, his or her power to compete rises and falls.[12] The new power relationships may reshape the decision channels.

The governmental politics model does not describe any identifiable pattern of change. Since the changes in the decision-making process are a function of the changes in the power of organizations and individuals, the pattern of change reveals only the new hierarchy of power in an administration. Since changing power relationships define the structure of the decision unit, the character of structural change is simple—the most powerful individuals and organizations have the most control over the decision-making process and its outcome. Those whose power has declined are less important within the decision-making process.

Ultimately, the governmental politics models can be seen as the most chaotic or anarchic vision of national security decision making. Change and distinct patterns of change in the structure of decision making are not really the focus of scholars' attention. However, the free-for-all nature of policy making suggests that the structure of decision making may be flexible and varied over time. The explanation for those changes remains based on the shifts in the power of organizations and individuals. Unfortunately, attempting to apply this model to changes in decision making leads to a bit of a tautology. Power relationships change, and this in turn leads to changes in the power structure of the administration. Illuminating the causes of change necessitates a broader perspective on decision making.

PRESIDENTIAL MANAGEMENT MODELS

Much of the literature on presidential management emerged as a response to the governmental politics school of analysis. Rourke criticizes the "bureaucratic determinism" he saw implicit in these models as they described a weak and ineffective executive seemingly at the mercy of his advisers and subordinate departments; Krasner contends that the bureaucratic politics model is accurate when "presidential interest and attention are absent."[13] Essentially, presidents have the responsibility, authority, and ability to bring order to the process. If the president fails to perform this task, whether by negligence or inability, all hell may, in fact, break loose. Contrary to the governmental politics school, these scholars focus on the president as the central figure in the decision-making process. He is not just another player in the bureaucratic game. As Hilsman states, he is the "ultimate decider . . . coordinator . . . and persuader" in the process of decision making. Reedy's examination of the Johnson administration even argues that most of what the governmental politics school describes is actually a result of a desire on the behalf of subordinates to satisfy the personal, political, and emotional needs of the president. He compares life in the White House to life in a palace court, complete with intrigue, schemes, and vicious rivalries. The president is the king and all others compete to serve him. Greenstein even suggests that if "some higher power" had decided to create a system where one person made a huge difference, the outcome would be very much like the U.S. form of democracy.[14]

The growth of the executive branch since the New Deal has been studied at length. Corwin's and Rossiter's classic studies of the presidency both identify one of the basic functions of the president as "administrative chief." Their fundamental conclusions are that the Executive Office of the Presidency is becoming a fourth branch of government and, ironically, the president must devise ever more innovative and elaborate methods of controlling this new bureaucracy. Many presidential scholars argue that these new responsibilities are so expansive that they have fundamentally altered the nature of the presidency itself. The presidency since 1933 is considered to be the "modern presidency"; Lowi even refers to this new era as a "second American republic."[15]

Ultimately, these scholars argue that the president is the driving force in decision making and in running the decision-making process. He is not a bystander or victim bullied by his advisers or departments. He fights back, using his political and managerial resources to maintain control over the decision-making process. If this is seen as a battle for control of national security policy, then it is fair to say that, according to this model, the president wins these wars.

Two schools of thought exist. One focuses on the idiosyncratic nature of the advisory process around the president. The other examines the management strategies presidents have used to gain control of the decision-making process. They are complementary schools that emphasize different aspects of the president's role in the decision-making process.

Scholars and ex-governmental officials often emphasize the idiosyncratic nature of White House management, whether in foreign or domestic policy. They contend that each president is unique, and decision-making processes must be fit to the president's individual beliefs on management and preferred decision-making style. Each new administration must rebuild decision making in the new president's image. Scholars often make this case in the context of a criticism of the age-old search for the one best way to manage an organization such as the presidency.[16] However, retired policy makers state it most forcefully. Nixon Chief of Staff H. R. Haldeman argued that "each presidency is almost completely unique because it is under the constitution, an office held by one man, and that's all there is to the office of the president—that one man."[17] The Tower Commission, led by Senator John Tower, former Senator and Secretary of State Edmund Muskie, and former (and soon to be once again) ANSA Brent Scowcroft, which investigated the National Security Council (NSC) and NSC staff role in the Iran-Contra fiasco, was firm in its conclusions. The NSC is the "president's creature" and is "used by each president in a way that reflected his individual preferences and working style."[18] Jack Watson, head of Carter's transition staff and eventually his White House chief of staff, claimed that "one of the clearest lessons is that the White House staff organization is a personal reflection of the president and what will work beautifully for one man may not work at all for the next president."[19]

Analysts of presidential management strategies suggest that although individual presidents are unique, there is a pattern to the types of strategies they use to manage the advisory process and gain control over self-interested departments and ambitious officials. These management styles are partly a function of a president's personal leadership style. From his own cognitive or administrative predispositions and from the advice of scholars and practitioners, a president creates committee structures and decision-making procedures as well as roles and responsibilities for specific officials and agencies. Ultimately, the president hopes to make sure that decisions are made the way he wants them made and that the policy outcomes reflect his preferences. Within this paradigm scholars have suggested a range of ways to describe the various methods by which presidents structure their decisions. Johnson's model, the most widely used by scholars, identifies three management styles.[20] In a competitive management style, as used by FDR, the president pits advisers against one another and creates overlapping areas of responsibility to force senior officials to compete for influence. A formalistic management style, as used by Truman, Eisenhower, Johnson, Nixon, and Reagan, creates a committee structure and well-delineated roles for all advisers to channel the flow of information and advice to the president. Collegial management, as used by Kennedy and G. H. W. Bush and in part by Carter and Clinton, develops teamwork among senior officials and a decision-making body in which advisers debate as equals in a problem-solving environment.

While the study of governmental politics has languished since the 1970s, the study of management models has continued. Porter, Campbell, Herrmann and Preston, and Preston have all developed useful typologies of presidential management and leadership. George developed a prescriptive management theory, multiple advocacy, that calls for all relevant departments to be guaranteed a place at the table and all views to be thoroughly vetted through the decision-making process by a "custodian-manager" of the administration.[21] Importantly, the foundation of these management models is an assumption that presidents seek to create a decision-making system that will produce the types of decisions that they will find most useful. The initial decision-making structures created by incoming administrations represent a president's administrative theory—his preferred method for making decisions given his political goals and beliefs about his relationships to political appointees and the career bureaucracies.

Both the individual uniqueness argument and the management styles ideas rest on the same premise that the president is the key to national security decision making. Miles's Law can be adapted once more: Where you stand today depends on who decides where you sit tomorrow. The person who decides is the president or one of his most trusted aides.

The sources of structure are the president's own management and leadership preferences. Numerous factors influence the president's preferences in decision making. George cites three key variables: a president's cognitive style (the way an individual stores information, processes information, and judges cause-and-effect relationships), a president's sense of his strengths and weaknesses, and a president's orientation toward political conflict. Hermann and Preston add factors relating to the president's preferred level of involvement and his motivation for assuming leadership.[22] In either case, the key issue here is that the structure of the decision-making process will depend on the president's background, experience, and administrative preferences. When looking for the sources of administrative structure, look no further than the Oval Office.

Presidential management models do not often mention the possibility of change within the president's style. A president's sense of managerial design seems to be something that solidifies well before he wins the White House. His victory in the campaigns for his party's nomination and the general election may be vindications of his style of management that only cement old beliefs further. Johnson, however, does point out that policy failure could lead to changes in decision-making style. Kennedy's Bay of Pigs debacle led to subtle, but important changes in his collegial design. George and Stern have illustrated where management styles have broken down or collapsed from failures of presidential leadership or simple presidential inattention.[23] In general, however, the notion that managerial styles may evolve or change has been ignored.

Since change is not a key issue in the study of management styles, patterns of change and the character of that change become moot issues. Presidential management styles last for a president's tenure in office. He brings those administrative preferences into office with him and leaves with those same preferences.

In sum, the presidential management model focuses on the idiosyncratic aspects of the president, his policy preferences and decision-making preferences. It contrasts sharply with the governmental politics model in this aspect. While the governmental politics model illustrates the consistent pressures of organizational and bureaucratic competition that all presidents face, the presidential management model assumes that presidents rise above these pressures to control the decision-making process to make governmental processes their own.

NEW INSTITUTIONALISM MODEL

The new institutionalism model of decision making takes the structural aspects of governmental decision making head on. It moves outside the confines of the executive branch to explain decision making and the structure of the government as a result of the struggle between competing interest groups. As Moe explains, these groups push the executive and legislative branches toward creating governmental structures (departments, agencies, bureaus within departments and agencies) that will protect or further their political goals. Some interest groups win and see their priorities institutionalized in government structures; others lose this battle. They all understand that new organizations are not simply additional boxes on the organization chart. They represent the institutionalization of a perspective, a place at the decision-making table in which that interest group's ideas will be represented. This is not a new idea. Allison and Szanton's study of the U.S. foreign policy machinery saw organizational design as a clear method for the government to set priorities, "create capabilities," and "vest and weight certain interests."[24] The difference here is that the new institutionalism sees various interest groups as the initiators of organizational change. Congress responds to their needs by tinkering with the machinery of government.

These interest groups and the legislative actors involved with them through the lobbying process, financing campaigns, and overseeing governmental organization are seen as operating from a rational choice perspective.[25] Borrowing from economic theory, rational choice explains that interest groups and legislators alike are self-interested, rationally calculating strategies that will further their individual goals. Those strategies are based on maximizing their gains and minimizing their losses. However, gains and losses are always judged in a political sense; interest groups and their congressional allies duel with each other to achieve specific political goals.

While initially focused on domestic politics and the role of Congress, more recently the role of the president has become a larger part of the literature. Moe and Wilson point out that the president has distinct advantages over both Congress and the bureaucracy in determining the structure of the government and in warding off the influence of interest groups. Presidents are less susceptible to interest group pressure; the resources of the office of the presidency dwarf those of Congress in its ability to reach out directly to the American people and to a wide range of interest groups with differing and often adversarial interests. Presidents have a strong motivation to control the structure and function of the bureaucracy since they have become the personification of government policy. Presidents are also the implementers of government policy. Policy as written on paper, whether by Congress or the president, is not the same as policy when implemented. Modifications, new interpretations, and less-than-faithful translations are tools the president can use to control policy. Bureaus and organizations that have been pressured by interest groups to reorganize can be pushed aside in this way. In addition, Rockman and Aberbach argue that presidents see their elections as mandates to accomplish specific tasks. Interest group, congressional, and bureaucratic influences on the decision-making structure can become obstacles to achieving these tasks.[26] Presidents therefore hope to control the decision-making process rather than cede it to Congress or the departments/agencies of the executive branch.

Zegart adds that those advantages are even more pronounced in the area of national security policy than in domestic politics. The web of interest groups is less extensive and powerful in national security policy. The attention paid to it by Congress and the American people is less focused and intense. This notion is an extension of Wildavsky's "two presidencies" thesis, which views the legislative-executive arena in domestic and international politics as two very different environments. The president's ability to control policy in the international sphere was believed to be much greater in the domestic policy issue area.[27]

The latter conception of the new institutionalism model, when it focuses on the president, seems to blend in very well with the presidential management model. Although the presidential management model portrays a president winning a struggle with executive departments and his own senior advisers for control over the decision-making process, the new institutionalism sees the president challenged by interest groups and Congress in addition to his own bureaucracy. The president wins this battle as well. However, scholars such as Heclo and Weko argue that the president's abilities for administrative maneuvering are limited by the structure of the government as designed by Congress.[28] Presidents are temporary occupants of the White House. The institutions of the executive branch and the statutory procedures for governmental processes create, in Heclo's words, a "deep structure" that limits presidential action. In either case, there is a contest for control of the decision-making process and governmental structure that forms the foundation for governmental policy making. The sources of structure come from congressional design and redesign of the government as a response to interest group pressure. Commensurate with a democratic society, the government is structured to reflect the interests of various groups within society. The interest groups compete to see which will have the most influence; governmental structure reveals the winners and losers. However, the president may have the ability, particularly within national security, to deflect the efforts of interest groups, Congress, and the bureaucracy they have designed, and to structure the government as he sees fit.

Changes in decision making are generally seen as being based on who wins and loses each contest over redesigning governmental structure. However, Zegart explicitly addresses the evolution of national security agencies: the NSC, the Joint Chiefs of Staff, and Central Intelligence Agency (CIA). She sees change as a function of the initial agency design, the interest of the key actors (the president and the senior officials within these agencies), and international events that affect the agencies.[29]

In the standard formula the pattern of change reveals the balance of power among various interest groups and congressional coalitions. However, Zegart, using the new institutionalism literature as a starting point, comes to the same conclusions as scholars who use the presidential management model: national security decision making has become more informal and more centralized from 1947 to the present.[30]

Again, in general terms the new institutionalism does not see any permanent changes in the character of decision making aside from those that are caused by the continuing struggle for control of the policy process. Zegart does identify a distinct pattern, which again fits with most scholarly analyses of national security decision making: the formal machinery of the NSC as designed initially by Congress in 1947 has become less important to decision making. Instead, the NSC staff and ANSA have played ever increasingly powerful roles.[31]

The new institutionalism model has similarities to the governmental and presidential management models. As in the case of the governmental politics model, this literature views decision-making structure as the result of competition among different groups within society. The new institutionalism models, however, point to Congress and interest groups rather than executive departments and senior officials as the key competitors. When this literature refocuses on the role of the president it becomes similar to the presidential management model.

WEAKNESSES OF THE MODELS

These models are important elements of the study of national security decision making and decision making in general, but they have some weaknesses that have prevented them from moving to the next stage in the development of more rigorous descriptions of the decision-making process. The evolution model that will be described is an attempt to address these weaknesses by incorporating aspects of all the others and goes beyond them to focus attention on changes in decision structures over time. The intention of the following critique is not to disregard these governmental politics, presidential management, and new institutionalism models, but to build on them.

Mutual Exclusivity

Discussion of national security decision making too often becomes a dead-end dialogue about the role of the president in the process.[32] Advocates of governmental politics models focus on his weakness, while advocates of presidential management models illustrate his strength. Such a debate can go nowhere. It is more productive to view the two models as complementary rather than rivals. The president, government organizations, and individual officials all play important parts in the decision-making process. Rourke and Rosati acknowledge this. Both agree that the level of bureaucratic politics present in any administration or in any given decision situation depends upon the level of interest and involvement of the president. The more interested and involved the president is, the more he will seek control over the process and, in theory, the less power other officials and organizations will have over the direction of the policy process. Preston and 't Hart also accept this argument in their study of leadership and bureaucratic politics. Their work views bureaucratic politics as partially a function of the type of leadership the president provides, specifically the type of decision-making environment he wishes to create within his administration.[33]

If these models are seen as complementary, then the picture of decision making that is created by merging the two models is one in which there is not only a competition over the substance of policy, but also a battle over the shape of the decision-making process. The relationships between senior advisors and their relationships with the president—the essence of what has been defined as decision making in the foreign policy organization—are the product of this struggle. In this sense, there are at least two major types of influences on the structure of the decision-making process: bureaucratic/organizational forces and presidential forces. At times they can be in harmony; more often, it seems they clash. But the intersection of these forces produces a pattern of decision making, a pattern that is dynamic. The central drama of decision making within the executive branch is the president's attempt to maintain control of policy or to manage bureaucratic and organizational competition. The new institutionalism model accepts this idea as one of its basic premises.

This view allows for the possibility of changes in the foreign policy decision-making process within single administrations. These forces will produce continuous tensions within the decision-making process. Gore even refers to a "tension network" that is created as a result of all the competing forces within the organization.[34] The simplest way of viewing the tensions is to imagine a rubber band being stretched—presidential needs pulling one way, and bureaucratic/organizational needs pulling the other. By nature, then, decision-making processes are unstable and subject to change. Without this notion, both models reach a dead end. Governmental politics research identifies the tug-of-war between individuals and organizations over policy and provides case studies that illustrate the point, but does not develop the ideas much further. Presidential management models create new categories to describe the ways presidents make decisions, but often fail to consider categories created by other scholars.[35] Attention to the complementary nature of the models gives them new life.

Time and Change

The greatest weakness of these models is their static nature. The effect of time on a decision-making unit is rarely explored and the potential for change in the decision-making process as well as the search for patterns in that change are equally ignored by most scholars. Governmental politics models have been criticized for being event centric.[36] Research on governmental politics usually consists of very focused case studies of specific foreign policy events. The elements of the governmental politics model are then derived from these events and it is then assumed that this is an accurate picture of decision making in all cases. Allison's breakthrough work on the Cuban missile crisis is a prime example.[37] He uses a case study of crisis decision making to develop propositions about routine governmental policy making. However, scholars of crisis decisions point out again and again that the nature of decision making during a crisis is very different from decisions made during the normal everyday flow of policy.[38] These case studies suffer in that they are detailed snapshots of an administration's decision-making process at a specific period in time. The possibility that this picture of decision making may be accurate only for that moment or that the decision-making processes during an administration's first six months in office may differ from decision-making processes in its last six months is not a factor in the research. The effects of time and the possibility of change are not issues.

Presidential management models suffer from similar problems. The vast literature that places president's decision styles into categories does not consider whether presidents might alter their styles during their tenure in office. The styles themselves are often derived from very focused case studies that draw conclusions about a president's general style of decision making from the evidence of the case studies (which are often crises).[39] The styles may also be derived from a general examination of the way a president makes decisions, usually based on anecdotes. This general style is then used to explain how a president makes decisions in any foreign policy situation.[40]

Some analyses of national security decision making have addressed these issues. Kohl and Rosati suggest that different types of decisions will be made through different types of decision-making processes. Rockman accepts the notion of change in decision-making structures by arguing that decision-making units such as the NSC staff that are more adept at handling unusual circumstances can increase their role in decision making. Crisis decision-making theories are premised on the idea that decision structures will change depending upon the types of situations an administration faces. Best and Pearlmutter contend that, in general, the relationships between the president and his senior advisers will change over time as a function of the challenges they face, their preferred styles of decision making, and what they learn about each other in the course of repeated interaction.[41] However, study of how decision-making structures change and why they change is underdeveloped.

This does not imply that the research on governmental politics or presidential management is without merit. On the contrary, it is crucial research that can help both scholars and policy makers understand how decisions are made and hopefully how better decisions can be made. However, without a focus on the potential changes in decision making over time and without a more systematic research methodology that examines the nature of decision making at several periods of time during an administration's term in office, these approaches are limited.

Ponder's study of domestic policy making suggests that the use of staff and the amount of centralization varies from issue to issue. Zegart's work on the evolution of the NSC, CIA, and JCS is the first to truly place the evolution of national security decision making in a theoretical context that includes the notion of change over time.[42] Using the new institutionalism theories as a base, Zegart adapts the model to the context of national security decision making. However, her work examines the evolution of these institutions over a period of decades. The evolution model, as described below, takes a shorter-term perspective, examining changes in decision-making processes that occur during the term of a single administration and comparing the changes within several administrations (Carter, Reagan, and G. H. W. Bush) in an effort to reveal patterns of change, similarities, and differences.

THE EVOLUTION MODEL

The evolution model draws ideas from all three of the models just described. It accepts the notion that presidents attempt to manipulate the decision-making process (presidential management and new institutionalism). The model views decision outcomes as a function of competition and bargaining among senior officials and departments (governmental politics). The actions of senior officials, executive departments, and the president are crucial to understanding decision making. Each must be considered a factor in the decision-making process. The evolution model also adds the international environment and the domestic political environment as influences on decision-making structure. It does not assume that these independent variables are mutually exclusive. On the contrary, it accepts that all of them play a role in changes in decision-making structure.

These multiple sources of change allow for a more inclusive model and an evaluation of the impact of each independent variable. The new institutionalism and governmental politics models often imply that the nature of governmental decision making creates similar pressures on each president. As a result, decision making from administration to administration is essentially the same and comparisons of decision making within different administrations will reveal more similarities than differences. The presidential management model argues the opposite. Presidents are all unique actors and decision making from administration to administration exposes the idiosyncratic and personal nature of the decision-making process. The inclusion of institutional variables and more idiosyncratic variables relating to presidential leadership creates a test in which the impact of these variables in different situations can be assessed. When are institutional pressures decisive? In what types of situations do presidents have more control over the process? With the addition of political factors from the international and domestic environment, this framework begins to answer the questions posed at the beginning of this book.

A model of change in decision-making structure can be developed. Figure 2.1 illustrates the evolution model. The independent variables are the international and domestic political environments that influence the ongoing relationships between the president and his senior advisers within the executive branch. The president's actions are defined by his leadership style, management strategy, and political strategy. The decision-making structure is produced by the interaction of these intra-administration dynamics as influenced by the international and domestic political environments. Change is represented at the bottom half of this figure, in which for time T_1 changes in the political environment and/or changes in the domestic political environment have an effect on the organizational dynamics within the administration. Changes in the international environment can lead to changes in the domestic environment. The organizational dynamics within the administration change as well. The president may also decide to adjust his management and political strategy. The only variable that remains the same is the president's leadership style.

The dependent variable illustrates the impact of these changes. The president decides to modify the existing decision structure, obeying consciously or uncon-

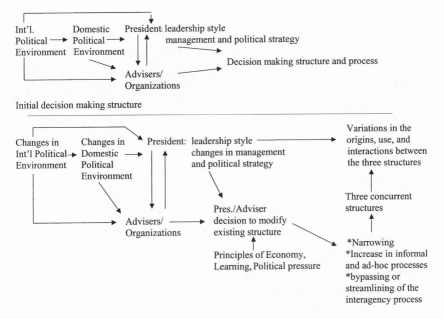

Int'l.   Domestic   President: leadership style
Political → Political →   management and political strategy
Environment Environment

                                Decision making structure and process

                    Advisers/
                    Organizations

Initial decision making structure

Changes in   Changes in   President: leadership style   Variations in the
Int'l Political→ Domestic →   changes in management   origins, use, and
Environment   Political   and political strategy   interactions between
             Environment   the three structures

                                              Three concurrent
                        Pres./Adviser   structures
                  Advisers/ → decision to modify
                  Organizations   existing structure
                                        *Narrowing
                      Principles of Economy,   *Increase in informal
                      Learning, Political pressure and ad-hoc processes
                                      *bypassing or
                                      streamlining of the
                                      interagency process

Decision Making Structure at T_1

FIGURE 2.1. The Evolution Model of National Security Decision Making

sciously the impact of the ideas categorized here as the principles of economy, learning, and political pressure. He will then have a tendency to narrow the range of participants in the decision-making process, move toward more informality and additional ad hoc processes, and begin to bypass or streamline the interagency process with increasing frequency. These changes start to occur in every administration, but individual presidents may not carry them through to their logical conclusion—an informal, centralized process that typically bypasses the interagency process. In any case, presidents will begin to develop three different structures for their decision-making process: the formal interagency structure, an informal structure, and a confidence structure. The relationships between the three structures, their origins (particularly the pace of development of the confidence structure), and their use differ from administration to administration depending on how presidents react to the natural pressures for centralization, informality, and ad hoc decisions. This presidential choice is based on the leadership style of the individual president.

Walcott and Hult's governance model provides a partial framework for understanding the influences on decision-making structure. Adapting and expanding this model is the first step in examining the evolution and modification of an administration's national security decision-making process. They identify three different sources of structure: the political environment, presidential choice, and organizational dynamics.[43] The following discussion elaborates and expands on the model of Walcott and Hult, focusing attention on how these influences impact decision structures over time.

Variables Influencing Policy

Obviously, when it comes to national security policy the international political environment plays a large role in determining the substance of policy. Outside of crisis decision making, the role of international and domestic political pressures is often downplayed in the study of decision making. Internal executive branch competition and presidential leadership are the usual focus. However, the external environment is crucial. This includes public opinion, domestic and international political actors, and the technology of governing in the modern age. The study of organizational behavior has a more well developed body of literature than does political science when it comes to studying the way in which organizations interact with their environments. Borrowing from this literature allows the executive branch and the national security decision-making process to be seen as "open systems."[44] Their decision-making characteristics are deeply influenced by environmental stimuli, and one of the overriding concerns of these open systems is adapting to uncertainty in their environment. The literature on organizational behavior often focuses on how corporations adapt to the market within which they operate. Similarly, public institutions operate within a political market. Presidents certainly understand this. Just as corporations are judged by the quality and price of their products, presidents will be judged by the quality of their policies. Poor products left on the shelf can lead to a company's bankruptcy; poor policies without public support will lead a president to electoral failure or a stained legacy. Structural contingency theory hypothesized that management systems are dependent upon the environment within which they operate and that the first task of any organization is to design itself to deal with its environment and the challenges it may pose.[45] In the context of organizational change, national security decision-making processes must adapt to changes in the domestic and international political environment.

The impact of the international environment has been recognized by proponents of the governmental politics (Halperin and Kanter), presidential management (Rosati and Rourke), and new institutionalism (Zegart) models. However, there has been no real systematic investigation of the impact of the international environment on the structure of the decision-making process. A basic premise of the new institutionalism model is the role of the domestic political environment in the form of Congress and interest groups. Burke and Greenstein and Art also emphasize the domestic political environment in their study of foreign policy decision making.[46] Obviously, in any discussion of national security policy, the international context must be considered. However, the domestic political environment is equally important. The impact of the international situation on the political fortunes of presidents and their opponents cannot be underemphasized.

The second variable is presidential choice. Walcott and Hult define it as the president's political objectives and strategy for achieving those objectives.[47] However, the presidential management literature needs to be considered here as well. The impact of the president is a function therefore of three issues: presidential leadership style, presidential management strategy, and presidential political strategy. Leadership style refers to the ways in which the president involves himself in the decision-making process and how he relates to his advisers as a group or individually. Importantly, both the informal and formal aspects of this are crucial.[48] Presidents may delegate, they may become deeply involved in the process, or they may rely on one or two advisers or use all their advisers equally.

Management strategy refers more directly to the overall design of the administration's decision-making process. The key issues here are the NSC committee structures, the procedures for reviewing policy and creating policy options, the method of making final decisions (consensus, command, large groups or small), and the roles and relationships of key officials, particularly the secretary of state and ANSA.

A president's political strategy is obviously a determinant of his policy choices, but it is also a factor in his choices about how to structure the decision-making process. The organizational behavior literature provides depth to this concept. In strategic choice theory, a linkage of structure, environment, and choice, Chandler argues that "structure follows strategy." An organization's response to its environment is not like a leaf turning toward the light. Child emphasizes that it is a measured and calculated response to environmental stimuli based on a reassessment of strategic goals and tactical actions. Importantly, presidential strategy is seen here as a reaction to the political environment. Presidents may feel that the proper political response to international and domestic political events can only be achieved through a modification to their decision-making processes.

Lake and Powell, in an application of strategic choice to international relations, suggest that the crucial variable is the interaction between actors' preferences (nation-states, political leaders, or political organizations) and the international system.[49] Their work does not deal with decision-making structure, but it does emphasize the interrelationship between strategy and the environment. Structural changes in national security processes are partially dependent on the changes in a president's strategy for dealing with a given political challenge.

The third structural factor is organizational dynamics. Once an administration takes office, an initial decision-making structure is put in place. These procedures, committee structures, and delineated roles and responsibilities for senior officials influence the way decisions will be made in the future and the way in which the structure of the decision-making unit will evolve. At first glance, this aspect seems to lean toward tautology. Walcott and Hult focused on three dependent variables in their work: emergence of White House structures, stability of those structures, and differentiation within those structures. Suggesting that organizational dynamics affect structure is almost like saying that structure is an influence on structure. However, the cause-effect dilemma is less problematic if the nature of decision making is seen in the context of competing forces and as a function of time. Organizational dynamics, in this sense, refers to the interaction of organizational and bureaucratic actors with each other and with the president over an extended period of time. Today's interactions affect tomorrow's interactions, which will have an effect on interactions next week, next month, and next year. These interactions are a constant factor in the evolution of a decision-making process. Organizational dynamics is the essence of the governmental politics model and a key part of the presidential management and new institutionalism models.

This study emphasizes three crucial assumptions that can be added to the Walcott and Hult model to allow it to be applied to changes in a decision-making process. First, the evolution model assumes that the president is the agent of change. He makes a concrete decision to alter the structure of decision making. Changes in the decision-making process are deliberate. The president's decision to alter the decision-making process is dependent on the international and domestic political environment, organizational dynamics, and his own leadership style, management strategy, and political strategy. However, the changes are not inadvertent; they are deliberate and calculated adjustments.

Second, decision-making processes are inherently unstable. If structure is defined as the relationships between the president and his senior advisers and the relationships among the senior advisers, then the design of any administration's decision-making process represents the way in which presidents order these relationships. A look at several aspects and weaknesses of the presidential management model, the model that most comprehensively focuses on decision structure, illustrates the point. Kohl, Porter, Thompson, and Walcott and Hult accept the notion that more than one management style can exist within a single administration at any given time. Burke and Greenstein are even skeptical about the use of a classification scheme for decision-making styles.[50] Both of these points highlight a key weakness in these structural models of decision making. They are too static and do not account for evolution or change in the structure of decision making. Even with caveats from the authors of articles and books dealing with management styles about the limited utility of these models, they have become a standard shorthand for judging presidential decision making.

A more accurate way of viewing decision-making structure or management styles is to see them as inherently unstable. These models are best seen as starting points for any administration. They represent the initial design of the administration's decision method. As more and more decisions are made within this process, the process begins to evolve. The three decision-making models described—governmental politics, presidential management, and the new institutionalism—can be seen as three sides of the same issue, models that focus on the competing forces that affect any administration. The governmental politics model describes the role organizations and individuals play in decision making as they compete for responsibility, authority, and resources. Presidential management models illustrate the president's attempts to control these forces and gain control over administration decision making. The new institutionalism adds Congress and domestic politics into the equation. The clash between these forces never ends. A decision-making structure is evident; assigned roles and responsibilities and committee procedures are defined. However, a closer look at the process will reveal that this structure is like the topography of a battlefield. It is where combatants must fight, adapt to the terrain, and seek advantage within the given geographical context.

Third, decision making changes over time. Accepting that organizations, officials, and the president fight repeated battles leads directly to the notion that any decision-making structure will be unstable and subject to modification and significant change. Any picture or analysis of administration decision making will therefore depend on when that snapshot is taken. Any examination of national security decision making at a single moment will not reveal an accurate portrayal of the nature of the administration's decision-making process or how that decision-making process changes and evolves over time. An understanding of the process must be based on an observation of the decision-making process over a specific period of time.

Sources of Structure and Causes of Change

The evolution model considers the international and domestic political environment, the internal organizational dynamics of the administration, and the choices made by the president (leadership style, management strategy, and political strategy) to be the key factors in the shape of national security policy making. Though Congress has the statutory authority to design the executive branch, as in any instance, the actual legislation is a compromise between the two branches. (The initial design of the executive branch machinery for national security, both in terms of the National Security Act of 1947 and each subsequent administration's version of that basic design, are discussed in the next chapter.)

Changes in the international and domestic political environment, the organizational dynamics within the administration, management strategy, and political strategy may result in changes in an administration's decision-making process. The initial administration design for national security policy making is based on a pre-inauguration or early term evaluation of the decision-making needs of the administration, given political context, the realities of the executive branch, and the president's preferences. However, if these change, presidents and/or their senior advisers may see the need for modifications in these initial decision-making processes. The mechanism for change is the key element in the process—the president deliberately decides to modify his decision-making process. The real question is why presidents may feel that the initial process must be adapted.

Changes in the decision-making processes seem to be based upon three principles: the economy principle, the learning principle, and the principle of political pressure. Importantly, this study hypothesizes that these principles and the decision-making pressures they represent are the same in any administration and lead the president and his senior advisers toward manipulation of the decision-making process in the same manner. In assuming that presidents are the ones who shape and reshape the decision-making process, these principles fall in line with the ideas within the presidential management and new institutionalism models—presidents have both motivation and ability to structure and restructure decision-making processes. The principles are also based on the notion that the president does have to fight for control of the decision-making process. Challenges to his control of the process come from his own executive agencies and senior advisers, Congress, interest groups, as well as the domestic and international political environments, which may give him new and unexpected hurdles to jump from time to time. These principles explain why presidents attempt to order and reorder the decision-making process. The discussion of the long-term evolution of the NSC process and presidents' often rocky relationships with their own executive branch structures for making national security decisions in chapter three adds depth to the principles presented here. These principles can be seen as ones that are applicable to both domestic and national security policy (and even to the private sector with some modifications).

The economy principle suggests that the president and his senior advisers may feel pressures to reduce the amount of time and effort they have to put into the decision-making process. Though presidents would like to see their initial decision-making process run smoothly, they may feel that managing that process and making it function the way they would like to see it function is simply too time-consuming and energy intensive. A deliberately designed decision-making system is inaugurated at the beginning of an administration's term in office with specific goals in mind. Committees are created; areas of responsibility and authority are delineated; the flow of paper through the bureaucracy and back and forth between the bureaucracy and the president is charted.[51] Usually this system is designed to include all relevant departments in an interagency process that will allow for a broad and diverse range of inputs into policy making. Presidents want to make the best decisions possible and wish to use the full resources of the executive branch to that end. However, the time constraints placed on the president and senior decision makers are enormous.

At least in the first term of any administration, the demands on senior decision makers' time are continuously expanding. The emphasis in decision making may shift from achieving diversity and inclusivity, the purposes underlying the initial decision-making structure, to meeting some policy timetable or conserving the time and effort it takes the president and senior advisers to make decisions. In essence, making decisions based on the most thorough method of staffing out an issue may eventually be less important as timely and/or efficient decision making. A more crude way of putting it is to say that making the best decision becomes less a priority than making the swiftest decision or the least bureaucratically complicated decision. This is an analog to March and Simon's notion of "satisficing"—choosing a policy that is good enough, rather than a policy that is optimal.[52] Decision makers may feel the need to cut corners and de-emphasize the formal process. The decision-making process is then downsized or streamlined for the sake of freeing up time and energy that senior officials may use to carry out their other responsibilities.

The principle of political pressure accepts that national security is a political phenomenon both in process and policy. Analyses of national security decision making, such as the organizational process, bureaucratic politics, and presidential management models, assume that the internal dynamics of decision making is a political process. However, it is crucial to remember that the milieu within which national security decisions are made is also a political context. Both the domestic and international environments are constant sources of pressure upon the administration, pressure that has an impact on the structure of the decision-making process. These ideas are not new. However, the notion that domestic politics as well as international events can have a substantial impact on the way an administration makes decisions has been neglected by scholarly analysis. Crisis decision making, in which events cause distinct changes in the size, shape, and behavior of the decision unit, is an exception; however, these changes are considered to be temporary. The changes described here are more permanent.

Two types of pressure can be identified, anticipated and unanticipated. Anticipated pressures are related to a president's ability to achieve his policy goals over his years in office. A president's political power, and therefore his potential for success, is not the same in his first few months in office as it is in his last few months. Neustadt linked the notions of presidential power to the years of a president's term. Presidents spend their first eighteen months on the job learning their way around the executive branch and Washington, D.C. They have the most chance of accomplishing their agendas in their third year in office, while in their fourth year their actions are dominated by the quest for re-election. Light expanded on Neustadt's ideas by suggesting that there is a finite amount of political capital a president is given upon election that decreases over time whether a president uses that capital or not. In terms of timing then, a president must act quickly to implement his domestic policy agenda or lose that opportunity as mid-term elections or re-election end that opportunity.[53] Both authors suggest that there is a political timetable that frames the four years of a president's term in office.

This idea can be expanded to consider decision-making structures. The initial honeymoon, which gives a president a limited period of good will before his opponents may attack him vigorously, the midterm elections during which partisanship may increase, and re-election that may shift the emphasis on policy making from solving problems to satisfying constituencies are well-identified political pressures. Additional pressures exist. The need of a president to immediately differentiate himself from his predecessor is a major factor in the early days of an administration. The political pressure to fulfill precedents set by past administrations can also weigh heavily on an administration. The congressional budget process itself sets a political timetable for decisions related to appropriations. Presidents are expected to satisfy many political responsibilities related to public opinion and the legislative process. These pressures will influence the decision-making structure. Importantly, a president can anticipate them. Whether a president can anticipate how his decision-making process must be adjusted in response to these pressures is a subject addressed in the concluding chapter.

Unanticipated pressures, obviously, are only predictable in the sense that ex-presidents can remind their successors that any number of issues will become key chapters in the tale of their presidencies in ways no one would have predicted. Crises will have effects on the decision-making process that remain after they have ended. General international and national trends in key countries can also create pressures on an administration that reshape decision making as an administration attempts to develop and follow through on new policies.

The point here is that these pressures—both anticipated and unanticipated—from within the domestic and international political arena also push an administration's decision-making structure in the direction predicted by the evolution model. Every anticipated deadline in the political "schedule" an administration must meet and every unanticipated event is an invitation for organizational and bureaucratic conflict and bargaining. It is also an impetus for the president or key senior advisers to manage the decision-making process to maintain presidential control.

The learning principle considers that the literature on learning in regard to foreign and national security policy often focuses on how policy makers learn about the international environment. Leaders may see more complexity in the international environment or they may change their beliefs about specific nations and the tools of diplomacy and coercion or use the lessons of the past to guide future policy in new ways.[54] In particular, presidents who have been elected based on domestic political considerations learn about the complexities and dilemmas of international politics. However, for this study the most important aspect of learning is that presidents learn how to make decisions. Henry Kissinger, scholar of decision making as well as secretary of state and ANSA in the Nixon and Ford years, emphasized just that point in his memoirs.[55] A first-term president by definition has never been president before. With some exceptions, his most senior advisers are also starting new jobs unlike any they have ever held. In addition, they have not worked together as a team before inauguration day. The process of policy making becomes a learning experience for all of them. They learn about a number of things: the dynamics of the relationships between this particular group of people, their decision-making needs given the positions they hold within the government, and the strengths and weaknesses of the decision-making system they had initially installed.

Most importantly, as Seidman and Best emphasize, the president learns about the advisers he has chosen.[56] This new understanding about the decision-making process can lead to modifications of that process. In short, the initial decision-making process represents the president's theory about what he will need to make high-quality decisions. Actually making those decisions tests that original theory. Presidents who find that their theoretical design is not adequate to handle the realities of policy making will begin to make adjustments. These adjustments represent learning in the broadest sense of the word—officials within the administration feel that they have learned something about their political environment, their fellow decision makers, and/or the administration's decision-making processes.

All three of these principles are intimately related. For example, pressures related to submitting a budget request may create the need for a swifter decision-making process. A president then may decide which advisers can speed up that process, something he has learned during repeated iterations of the decision-making process. Most importantly, all presidents seem to push the decision-making process in a similar direction.

Pattern and Character of Change

The evolution model suggests that any administration's decision-making process will begin to evolve in similar ways over its first term in office. Narrowing, an increase in informal and ad hoc processes, and growing instances of bypassing or streamlining of the interagency process characterize the changes that occur.

Over time presidents will begin to narrow the range of participation in the decision-making process. In crucial meetings, particularly the more informal forums and postmeeting gatherings with the president, presidents will begin to listen to some advisers more than others. All advisers may still have the ability to speak their minds, but the president will seriously consider the advice of a smaller number of them than he did at the beginning of his term. Presidents have a number of advisers at their disposal. In theory, a president desires to make decisions with as much input as possible from the men and women he has chosen for advisory roles. However, certain advisers may come to be seen by a president as too wedded to their organization's perspective, or too personally ambitious, or too burdened by political or perceptual burdens, or too willing to challenge the president's views, or even too often wrong. An adviser may be perceived as performing all his or her tasks except that of serving the president's needs. Ultimately, as part of a process of reconciling these differing interests, presidents will come to rely on fewer advisers, selecting a handful or even one to be first among equals within the administration.

Each administration begins its time in office by attempting to outline a specific formal method of national security decision making, usually centered around the National Security Council and including supporting committees and specific written methods of assigning interagency review and communicating presidential decisions. As an administration's tenure continues it will have a tendency to skip these formal committee and paperwork procedures in favor of informal meetings, ad hoc reviews, and more spur-of-the-moment decision making. The formal process may begin to be viewed as too unwieldy or slow. New ways of making decisions become a shortcut to quicker decisions and, importantly, decisions that the president will have more control over, both in terms of content and timetable.

Initially the president attempts to make full use of the vertical depth and horizontal range of the executive branch's institutional resources through the creation of an elaborate interagency process. However, this may be followed by a reduction in the bureaucratic depth and breadth of participation. The formal interagency process is not completely jettisoned. It is instead bypassed in favor of informal or ad hoc committees and processes when seen necessary by senior administration officials. In other cases the interagency process is streamlined. Key officials may meet in truncated versions of the interagency process, without staff and the standard staffing procedures, as a method of conserving time and energy. After numerous decision opportunities a president has a good understanding of his administration and its senior officials. He knows the administrative order of battle—the coalitions, the feuds, the officials and organizations willing to compromise and those who would rather have gridlock than policies of which they disapprove. Bypassing the interagency process may be the result of a desire to exclude specific officials or departments. The inclusiveness and diversity of the formal interagency process may be seen in many instances as weaknesses rather than strengths of the decision-making process. Streamlining the process may be a strategy to save time and effort among the senior officials and the president.

These are patterns of evolution. They are nonlinear in the sense that they should be seen as general tendencies within the decision-making process and may change in fits and starts, reversals and counter-reversals. They are not hard-and-fast rules, but identifiable leanings. The relationships among senior administration officials and between those officials and the president—defined here as the structure of decision making—is far too fluid to be described by rigid frameworks. Presidents will begin to move their administrations in these directions, but may not ultimately maintain these new patterns of decision making.

The pattern of change can be restated to identify the structural nature of that change. All administrations seem to develop three concurrent or simultaneously operating decision-making structures after some time in office: the initial formal interagency structure; an informal structure in which the senior officials and the president operate within a smaller version of the National Security Council; and a confidence structure in which the president relies on one or two advisers more than any other. The formal interagency structure is the one created at the inception of the administration's tenure. The other two represent the evolution of that structure as explained above; each structure represents a narrowing in participation, an increase in informal and ad hoc decision making, and an increase in instances of bypassing or streamlining of the interagency process. The informal structure is more narrow in participation than the interagency process. It contains more informality and more ad hoc processes. It bypasses or streamlines the interagency process in significant ways. The confidence structure is narrower still, even more informal and ad hoc, and almost defiantly outside the formal interagency system. The three structures complement each other and are related in complex ways. They can be supplements to each other—concurrent structures working together. They can be rivals to each other—concurrent structures that compete for power over various decisions. They can be indifferent to each other—operating as if the other structures do not exist.

The informal process develops as an adjunct to the formal structure. The informal structure is created because the president and his senior advisers feel the NSC is too large, too slow, too leaky, or too impersonal a forum for serious consideration of crucial policy issues. Informal forums can be used as replacements for the formal structure or as supplements. The confidence structure is based on the notion that the president learns to trust some advisers more than others, a key element of the presidential management model. The president will implicitly or explicitly arrange his advisers in a hierarchy. There will be a first-among-equals adviser who has a unique relationship with the president, other important advisers often included in the informal structure, and another layer of advisers who may be NSC participants but not part of the informal structure.

The case studies presented in this book suggest that all three structures seem to be necessary for a smoothly functioning national security policy process. The interagency process is the backbone of presidential decision making, a super-structure that connects the president's brain trust to the eyes and ears, arms and legs of the departments and agencies. To control the executive branch for the sake of implementation and to stay on top of world developments, that backbone cannot be eliminated nor separated from the top decision makers. The informal process and the confidence structure provide that brain trust, that most basic level that determines mission, purpose, and agenda. The informal process serves to filter out much of the noise and sensory information collected by the entirety of government—intelligence and lower-level analysis—enabling the principals to focus on an issue. The confidence structure helps order that informal structure, establishing a pecking order. Everyone in the informal structure understands that for the toughest decisions, the last action a president may take before making up his mind will be to turn to one specific adviser and ask, "What do you think?" As time drags on a president relies more and more on that ultimate resource, a specific official whose judgment he trusts.

The origins, relationships, and presidential use of the three structures vary depending on the leadership style of each president. The above discussion seems to suggest that the pressures placed on each administration and the results of those pressures are the same in any administration. If true, all the decision-making processes within each administration will come to resemble each other. This, however, is not the case. The evolution of the informal and confidence structures and the relationships between the informal and formal structures vary between the Carter, Reagan, and G. H. W. Bush administrations because of the different leadership styles each favored while in office. Generally, presidents do seem to lean toward making more decisions in the latter two structures, but their definitions of their own role in the process affects this. In theory, a president wants a proper balance between all three structures; each has a unique and important role to play. Yet presidential leadership styles may allow one structure to overshadow the others or prevent one from fully developing. The case studies will explore this issue.

The time frame for this evolution is a key issue for this study. Most scholars see the first two years as the period during which presidents learn on the job. Rockman states that presidents learn to whom they should listen and whom they should ignore by the midpoint of their first term. Destler contends that the NSC process itself evolves over the first two to three years of an administration's tenure in office.[57] However, the case studies that follow suggest that the informal structure is created within the first six months of an administration's term in office. The confidence structure may take up to two years to develop. Again, however, these structures may never fully stabilize. They represent general trends.

Chapter Three

THE PRESIDENT,
THE NATIONAL
SECURITY COUNCIL,
AND THE STANDARD
INTERAGENCY PROCESS

THE DEVELOPMENT OF THE NSC STAFF AND THE ANSA INTO THE president's own personal bureaucracy is the central fact of postwar decision making for foreign and national security policy.[1] Robert McFarlane, ANSA in the Reagan administration, sees this as a function of the "failure of the cabinet to meet the politician president's need for accomplishment within a four-year period of time." Colin Powell, a man with long experience at top levels of government as ANSA (Reagan), chair of the Joint Chiefs of Staff (G. H. W. Bush and Clinton), and secretary of state (G. W. Bush), sees it as the duty of the NSC staff "to mold themselves into the personality of the president."[2] The following discussion of the general evolution of the NSC process flows from these two ideas. First, the explanation of the long-term institutionalization of the NSC process arises out of the contrasting needs of the interagency process and the president. The NSC staff becomes a personal tool of presidential power as presidents become dissatisfied with the inability of the interagency process to satisfy their needs. This idea fits in well with the governmental politics and new institutional models as well as most aspects of the evolution model. In another sense, the NSC is a reflection of the president, an explanation found in the presidential management model and the leadership style aspects of the evolution model.

The evolution model itself is a short-term analog of the long-term trend toward centralization within the NSC staff. Each new president waxes poetic about a return to cabinet government, a reversal of the centralization of his predecessor's decision making, and a return to prominence of the secretary of state, with a commensurate reduction in the role of the ANSA. Yet each president moves toward centralization in ways the evolution model describes because of his dissatisfaction with the standard interagency process. This dissatisfaction lays the foundation for the principles of decision making, economy, political pressure, and learning introduced in the preceding chapter.

An understanding of the changes in national security processes requires an exploration of these ideas through two contextual guideposts, an overview of the general evolution of the National Security Council (NSC) interagency process itself from 1947 to the Carter administration and an explanation of the initial design of each administration's decision-making process. Before national security decision making within the Carter, Reagan, and G. H. W. Bush administrations can be examined, the overall context of the ANSA and NSC staff role must be illustrated. A third task remains before the case studies can begin. Implicit in the study of change is the notion of a starting point. The initial standard interagency NSC machinery of the Carter, Reagan, and Bush administrations are compared to provide a reference point for the case studies that follow. The structured, focused comparison of the changes in the decision-making processes of these administrations cannot be accomplished without a clear understanding of how each administration made decisions in its early days, or at least how each administration believed it would make decisions. Three aspects of that initial process are crucial: the leadership style of the president, the management strategy of the administration (committee structures and paperflow), and the organizational dynamics within the administration. In addition, this section touches upon the initial evolution of the decision-making unit through the creation of an informal process to supplement the formal process. Since this informal process was not explicitly created for decision making on arms control and nuclear strategy but became an important part of the process for these issues, it is necessary to see how it operated in general before examining its specific role in each case study. If the changes in an administration's decision making represent a journey toward a modified process, a description of the initial interagency NSC process represents the starting place.

Interestingly, all three administrations began with a similar decision-making structure of hierarchically connected interagency committees working under the NSC. Carter, the amateur, Reagan, the delegator, and Bush, the professional, initiated similar systems at the beginning of their terms in office. The key difference in the nature of decision making that followed these original designs was the personal leadership style of each president.

THE NSC AND THE INTERAGENCY PROCESS

The interagency process is the basic structure of executive branch decision making. Policy making, particularly for national security, is designed to be an interagency process for a number of reasons. First, the size of the executive branch, its ever-growing responsibilities (even in an age when the trend is to decrease the size of government), and the diverse range of those responsibilities necessitates that it be composed of numerous agencies with specialized competencies. However, the division of labor is ill defined in most instances. Very few governmental activities can be performed by one department or one agency alone. Second, the NSC was designed initially as a method of creating inclusivity, diversity, and coordinated national security policy.[3] Inclusivity of agencies and departments allows participation in decision making for those agencies and departments that have important roles in implementation. This is related to the need for diversity. One of the essential premises of cabinet government, the ultimate interagency committee, is that a wide range of views is necessary to make the best decision possible. All agencies and departments with implementation and analytical responsibilities on a given issue can, in theory, bring a unique perspective to problems and solutions. To make sure that U.S. government policy is truly national policy and not simply the outcome of organizations undertaking disconnected tasks that may be operating at cross-purposes, interagency decision making is necessary. Not only must the left hand know what the right hand is doing, but the hands should be working together. This can be seen as a basic necessity of operating a mammoth organization with responsibilities ranging from delivering mail to delivering nuclear missiles. The NSC is the expression of this search for coordination within national security affairs.

The NSC process is still based on the National Security Act of 1947 and constructed around the NSC, which includes as statutory members the president, vice president, secretary of state, and secretary of defense, and as statutory advisers, the director of central intelligence and chairman of the Joint Chiefs of Staff. Others are added at the discretion of each president. Underneath the NSC is a series of committees representing levels of bureaucratic hierarchy (at least down to the assistant secretary level). Each committee has horizontal participation from departments and agencies with intelligence, analytical, and implementation responsibilities over a given issue. These committees are embedded within a vertical hierarchy of committees reporting to more senior committees and ultimately to the NSC. The policy process begins with an NSC request for information and analysis that is transmitted down to a specific interagency committee or committees. The subordinate committees refine the analytical output they desire and request information and analysis from the departments and agencies represented on those committees. When the interagency committee receives the output of the departments and agencies, it is reviewed with the intent of coordinating the diverse views of the departments and agencies. Reports are written and transmitted up the hierarchy of committees toward the NSC. The ultimate purpose of the review process is to generate options, analyses, and recommendations for presidential decision.

This formal description does not really tell the tale of the NSC or its staff. Though the National Security Act of 1947 hoped to enshrine cabinet government in the conduct of national security policy making, presidents have bypassed the NSC itself, using the professional NSC staff as a personal national security bureaucracy. Crucial to this process is the evolution of the ANSA position. Theoretically the secretary of state is the president's senior adviser on foreign policy and the secretary of defense plays that role in the realm of defense policy. The statutory design of the NSC gives them these roles formally. When a president makes decisions on foreign policy, their voices are supposed to be the most prominent the president hears. By the early 1960s, however, the ANSA and his NSC staff had become a personal presidency-based analog to the executive branch machinery for national security and foreign policy. The ANSA and the NSC staff have come to be seen by presidents as the antidote to the problems of bureaucracy, organizational parochialism, and interagency pathologies. Their status as presidential staff means they are loyal to the president, absent of departmental responsibilities, and shielded to a great extent from congressional scrutiny. A rivalry between the ANSA and the secretary of state and to a lesser degree the secretary of defense has become a central feature of all administrations.

This is part of an overall trend in governmental policy making in which presidents create more and more capability within the Executive Office of the President and White House Office to essentially run the government without the rest of the executive branch.[4] The Office of Management and Budget mirrors the Department of the Treasury; the Office of the U.S. Trade Representative mirrors the Department of Commerce; and the NSC staff mirrors the State Department, DOD, and CIA. These are long-term trends. This book focuses on the short-term trends within single administrations.

The long-term trend provides an important context. Though he signed the bill that created the NSC itself, Truman mostly ignored it until the North Korean invasion of South Korea in June of 1950. He thereafter used it as an advisory cabinet for foreign affairs. Eisenhower truly institutionalized the NSC in a way that would have made its creators proud. Since Eisenhower institutionalized the NSC process, every president except Kennedy has designed his NSC interagency process in a similar manner.[5] Through the Planning Board and the NSC itself Eisenhower used the process to generate policy on a firm interagency basis through a formal and rigorous process. Kennedy abandoned this formal process in favor of informal structures. At this point, the NSC staff under ANSA McGeorge Bundy became the president's personal advisers and Bundy eclipsed Secretary of State Dean Rusk. Bundy and his successor, Walt Rostow, remained the equals of Rusk during the Johnson administration. The Johnson administration resurrected and reformalized the basic Eisenhower NSC structure during the reorganization of 1966, creating the senior interdepartmental group/interdepartmental regional group (SIG/IRG) system. Under the Nixon administration, this centralization reached its logical extreme. ANSA Henry Kissinger became the single most important adviser to the president at the near exclusion of the secretaries of state and defense. Kissinger was so prominent that from September 1973 to November 1975 he occupied the positions of ANSA and secretary of state. President Ford's decision to relieve Kissinger of his ANSA post reversed that trend slightly. Kissinger became a powerful secretary of state, and Brent Scowcroft, a protégé of Kissinger and Deputy ANSA, was named ANSA. However, Kissinger's power had originated while in the White House close to the president. It was that power he transferred to the State Department. The trend had clearly been set by the arrival of the Carter administration.[6]

These events suggest a linear evolution of the NSC process over a period of decades, a slow but inexorable movement of the NSC staff from clerks and typists to professional advisers ruled by an ANSA who has the president's ear. This is too broad a view, however. While true, its long-term focus prevents it from addressing some of the theoretical aspects of decision making. In particular, it is too blunt an idea to capture the dynamics of that evolution as it occurs in each administration. In particular, it factors out each president's attempt to create a cabinet-style NSC process and the particular leadership styles of presidents.

This notion of inevitable centralization seems to contrast with the more idiosyncratic judgment that, as the Tower Commission argued, the NSC staff "is the President's creature, molded as he sees fit, to serve as his personal staff for national security affairs."[7] The more idiosyncratic aspects of the presidential management suggest a more personalized shape of the NSC staff. This paradox is reconciled by this study. Institutional forces, as described by the governmental politics and new institutionalism models, create an incentive for the president to centralize decision making in the NSC staff. However, the specifics of how the NSC process, the NSC staff, and the relationships among the senior advisers can differ depend on the president's leadership style. Again, the issue is not whether bureaucratic and organizational gamesmanship or the president's own power defines the process. It is the interaction of these forces that determines the shape of the decision-making process.

THE PRINCIPLES OF DECISION MAKING AND THE NSC PROCESS

The centralization of the advisory process within the NSC staff under the direction of the ANSA can be expressed in more detail as narrowing in the range of participants, an increase in informal and ad hoc processes, and an increase in instances in which the standard interagency process is bypassed or streamlined. The model does not see centralization as a clear-cut decision by a president to favor the ANSA/NSC staff combination at the expense of the departmental bureaucracies. Rather the evolution model suggests that the president picks and chooses which officials and procedures of both the executive departments and the NSC staff he wishes to include in decision making at a given time. As time goes on he sees the full interagency process as a less advantageous way to make decisions. He may then rely on the ANSA/NSC staff for many decisions, but he does not completely discard the bureaucracy. All presidents develop the three concurrent structures because of dissatisfaction with the standard interagency process. The balance of use between them and their maturity depends on the leadership style of the president. To understand why, in general, the interagency process pushes the president toward modifying his NSC process and how this relates to the evolution model, it is necessary to take a deeper look at the decision-making needs of the president and the weaknesses that presidents perceive in the interagency process. It provides a generic context in which the discussion of individual presidents' leadership styles and standard interagency processes can be set. The discussion that follows also adds weight to the three decision-making principles.

The basic structure of the interagency process is the one thing that all the administrations studied here have in common. The particular difficulties a president encounters when making decisions within an interagency environment give rise to the principles of decision making. The similarities in the initial processes, the decision-making dilemmas, and the strategies for overcoming these dilemmas account for the similarities in the way the decision-making processes in each administration evolve. The decision-making principles arise because of a frequent disconnect between the realities of the interagency process and the decision-making needs of the president. This is, of course, one of the most basic premises of the study of presidential decision making—the inability of the president to get the bureaucracies to work for him.

In theory, the NSC-based interagency process forces the organizations and individuals to work together for a common purpose, alleviating in some respect the difficulties that are illustrated by the organizational process and bureaucratic politics models. However, presidents have found that the interagency process itself presents new problems, even as it attempts to solve others. These difficulties are described throughout the literature on governmental politics, presidential management, and the new institutionalism.

Presidents and advisers at the senior levels of the administration lament the departmental bureaucracies for numerous reasons. The slowness of the bureaucracies is a common feature of all literature on decision making. The endless revisiting of a given issue as each department and agency desires an opportunity to review any policy change contributes to the perception of the glacial pace of interagency decision making. Officials who act as spoilers are another problem. As consensus is generated and a critical mass on a given issue nears, the inclusion of opponents of that decision can give those opponents a unique ability to block final decisions. Too often interagency committees produce policy that is simply a watered-down compromise of each agency's standard operating procedures (SOPs). This lack of innovation is a particular headache for incoming presidents with bold agendas. In addition, the bureaucracies have difficulty accepting presidential guidance. Presidents may want to use the expertise of the departments to staff out a specific agenda item. They may discover, however, that the permanent occupants of the executive branch are not interested in this new guidance. They may have their own agendas, and/or ties to Congress and interest groups. In particular, the political success of the president, as marked by his ability to implement campaign promises, may not be on that agenda.

These items are often considered weaknesses of the interagency process in the eyes of the president.[8] The problem is one of a disconnect between what the interagency process produces, as described by its weaknesses above, and what the president wants from his decision-making process. Presidents want their decision-making process to produce certain types of decisions. Presidents want timely decisions. Whether motivated by congressionally imposed mandates, budget cycle imperatives, or windows of opportunity opened by domestic and international events, presidents may desire policy decisions on an often brutal timetable. Specific analyses and implementation plans are also crucial for a president. If a president wants to implement his agenda or pet ideas, what he may desire from the interagency process is an honest review of those ideas with a priority on finding ways to make them practical. Presidents also want creativity, new and bold ideas that will distinguish this president from his predecessors. Most importantly, presidents want politically feasible and useful ideas. Though presidents operate within both a policy and political environment, their expertise is usually the political environment, so they often focus their attention on whether policies can pass the test of Congress and public opinion.

The basic disconnect between what the interagency process produces and what the president wants becomes obvious. The bureaucracy has a reputation for being slow, and the president often desires policy making on a demanding deadline. The president wants new and bold departures from the past, whereas the bureaucracy may be unable to make a decision or, if it does, that decision may be only a slight modification of the existing policy. Presidents want to steer the government in specific directions, but the bureaucracies and other individuals want to keep their hands on the wheel. Presidents think in terms of their political needs, while the bureaucracies may be thinking of their own needs.

Importantly, as the presidential management and new institutionalism models suggest, this creates the motivation for a president to gain more control over his own decision-making process. He will try to manage the process to make it more able to satisfy his decision-making needs. A president will desire more control over four aspects of the decision-making process: the pace of the decision, the content of the policy, the range of participants, and the timing of public release of the policy. The case studies in the following chapter illustrate how each president attempted to gain control of these aspects of his decision-making process.

The case studies also explain how this basic interagency-president disconnect relates to the principles of decision making. In general, however, the relationship becomes clear. The economy principle places a premium on swift and efficient decision making in many instances. The interagency process may not be able to speed itself up or manage itself effectively, and particularly without direct presidential effort. The learning principle posits a steep learning curve for the president and his advisers. The interagency-presidency disconnect may seem obvious to scholars and experienced executive branch policy makers, but incoming presidents are usually neither.

Even if they are experienced politically, their own administrations have never made decisions before; their administrative context is new. Answers to key questions simply do not exist. How effective will the administration's initial decision-making processes be in managing the interagency process? Who are the spoilers? Where is the consensus or lack thereof for each given issue? When will windows of opportunity open and how swiftly will they close? These questions can only be answered over time. The political pressures placed on the president are also uncertain. The politically feasible ideas of today may be the impossibilities of tomorrow, or the reverse may be true. Presidents may come to see the departments and agencies of the executive branch as ponderous black holes from which innovative ideas, opportunities for policy shifts, and political success cannot escape. At that point, they begin to contemplate changes in their decision-making processes.

CARTER, REAGAN, AND BUSH: LEADERSHIP, MANAGEMENT STRATEGY, AND ORGANIZATIONAL DYNAMICS

The crucial aspects of the initial standard interagency processes of the Carter, Reagan, and Bush administrations are each president's leadership style, the management strategy of each administration, and the organizational dynamics among their senior advisers. On the surface, Carter, Reagan, and Bush had somewhat similar views of the way foreign policy decisions should be made. In terms of management style, each believed in a collegial process within which advisers could speak freely and debate issues while advising the president, and each talked of a strong secretary of state, firmly in charge of U.S. policy making. However, their leadership styles and their methods of dealing with organizational dynamics differed greatly. Carter and Bush wanted to be deeply involved in the process, while Reagan delegated tasks to his senior cabinet officials. The organizational dynamics also varied. Carter and Reagan were handicapped by vicious infighting, while Bush benefited from a collegial process among old friends.

Another key issue must be mentioned at this point. Each incoming president desires to differentiate himself from his predecessor in terms of both policy and process. This is an often deliberate factor in the design of new administrations. In particular, Carter followed administrations dominated by Henry Kissinger as ANSA and secretary of state and desired to reinstate cabinet government. Reagan entered office on the heels of foreign policy crises that led to the resignation of Secretary of State Vance and a generally unfavorable public review of Carter's foreign and national security policy and process. Though a part of the Reagan team, Bush entered office seeking to reenergize a policy process that had fallen victim to extremes of competition and the Iran-Contra crisis. The Bush team was successful enough that the Clinton administration maintained the Bush administration structure.[9] All three administrations had a reason to take the policy process seriously.

Leadership Style

Each president brings with him into office his own administrative personality. It is his preferred way of receiving information and advice, making decisions, and involving himself in the process. It may be based on cognitive style, or the shaping of his character during childhood, or lessons of success and failure in past governmental experience.[10] The roots of these leadership styles are beyond the scope of this book. In any case, as stated in chapter two, one of the premises of the presidential management model is that an incoming administration is tailored for the decision-making characteristics of the incoming president. Carter, Reagan, and Bush had very unique, even archetypal leadership styles that account for the differences in the evolution of their administrations.

Jimmy Carter

Carter made it clear that his administration's decision-making machinery was an advisory process only. He would be the decision maker. Senior cabinet officers were advisers to the president, and the NSC staff served as the president's personal national security policy staff. Carter's system was designed with one goal in mind—to give the president the tools to make the best decision possible. There were to be no rivals to the decision-making power of the presidency, no "lone ranger" diplomacy, as Carter called it. At its most basic, Carter was explaining that his decision-making process would not and did not resemble predecessors, Nixon and Ford. Carter intended to reverse the trend of NSC staff as a replacement for the foreign and defense policy bureauci hoped to build a collegial decision-making process in which the expe experience of senior national security advisers could be used to his ad diverse opinions, rigorous debate, and the resources of the existing national security machinery would guarantee that no viewpoints were ignored, no options were left unaddressed, and the best possible decision had been made.[11]

This style reflects Carter's sense of the purpose of presidential decision making. Presidents should base their decisions on what is right, not what is politically expedient or popular. This is an engineer's approach to government. Policy making was a matter of cost-benefit analysis and problem solving, not political calculation.[12] It also reflected an attempt by Carter to create a more open national security policy process, a clear reaction to the secrecy, lack of credibility, and criminality of the Johnson and Nixon administrations. His legendary attention to detail and often extreme hands-on approach left him acting almost as if he were Assistant Secretary of State for the World. His senior advisers realized within the first months of the administration that Carter would read all the paper that came across his desk. They soon adjusted the paper flow to limit the amount of departmental analyses and studies that would reach him in nonsummarized forms.[13] As Carter gained more confidence in his advisers, he delegated more authority to them.[14]

Ronald Reagan

Discussions of the Reagan administration's decision making usually start with explanations of Reagan's leadership style. Memoirs of senior administration policy makers, newspaper accounts, and scholarly analyses all paint essentially the same picture. Reagan was a "detached" and "hands off" president who preferred to set overall policy themes—the "big picture"—then delegate both tactical decisions and implementation details, leaving an unusually large amount of power in the hands of his senior advisers.[15] Although Reagan did set general policy guidelines, his approach to making sure that current policies fit those guidelines was the opposite of Carter's. Whereas Carter was notorious for diving headfirst into the details of any policy, Reagan seemed to shy away from the details of policy or its implementation.[16]

This raises questions of who was in charge within the administration and how involved the president was in his own policy-making process. The two most complete journalistic accounts of the Reagan presidency describe an administration in which often the president was merely the spokesman for the senior decision makers within the administration. As president, Reagan's main function was to represent to the American public a series of political beliefs and their attendant policies. He was the salesman, an actor playing a role. Journalistic accounts and memoirs of the administration suggest that many officials felt that Reagan would agree on policy matters with the last person to whom he had spoken. Secretary of State George Shultz (1982–1989) noticed this as well and commented in his memoirs that the president "allowed himself to be deceived . . . sometimes almost knowingly." The president's lack of knowledge about his own policy and his willingness to accept that lack of knowledge and rely on subordinates was a serious problem.[17]

One scholar suggests that the overall dilemma of the Reagan administration was the problem of creating decision-making structures for a "committed presidency and a detached president." Some analyses suggest that the administration never solved this problem. Reagan's lack of attention to the process allowed the administration to descend into chaos.[18] The chaos manifested itself in continuous battles between senior advisers, resignations, and repeated process redesign.

George Bush

In terms of national security philosophy and presidential leadership Bush has often been criticized for being too cautious, too pragmatic, or an incremental problem solver in an era where grand designs were necessary as the cold war ended. His lack of a strategic mission for his presidency or, as he put it, "the vision thing," caused him to be a reactive decision maker according to some analyses. His realism guided him toward status quo, supporting policies as the bipolarity in Europe collapsed and the basis of U.S. national security since the end of World War II shifted.[19] Even if Bush's response to Iraq's invasion, his hailing of a "New World Order," and his use of military force to end the starvation in Somalia in 1992 are considered, Bush national security is often seen as a series of reactions to crises, rather than preventive steps or policy innovation.

Policy leadership aside, it is difficult to discuss Bush's process leadership without setting it in the context of his overall foreign policy team. The Bush team had more experience in upper-level executive branch decision making than arguably any president since FDR. Bush had been U.S. ambassador to the United Nations (1971–73) and chief of the U.S. Liaison Mission to China (1974–75) before becoming director of Central Intelligence in 1976. As Reagan's vice president, he was unusually powerful, holding roles as the permanent chair of the Special Situations Group, the Reagan crisis management committee, as well as serving as ad hoc chair of the NSC and National Security Planning Group (NSPG) on many occasions. A consummate professional in foreign affairs and a serious student of process as well as policy, he chose similarly experienced men as his advisers. James Baker, the new secretary of state, had been an undersecretary of commerce in the Ford administration, Reagan chief of staff, and secretary of the treasury. Dick Cheney, Bush's secretary of defense, had been Ford's chief of staff. Brent Scowcroft, the new ANSA, had already served in that position during the Ford administration. General Colin Powell, who replaced Admiral William Crowe as chairman of the Joint Chiefs of Staff in October 1989, had been Reagan's ANSA from 1987 up until the end of Reagan's second term.

All of this experience suggests that this team would have strong beliefs about the proper way to make decisions for foreign affairs. Above all else Bush stressed that all decisions were to be made on an interagency basis. No departments or points of view were to be excluded. This meant that the first rule of administration decision making was that each of the principal decision makers had access to the president. The overall atmosphere was informal, with senior advisers and staffers interacting directly with the president as a matter of standard procedure.[20]

The atmosphere came directly from Bush's personal style. The contrast with President Reagan could not have been sharper. Bush was a hands-on, detail-oriented decision maker with vast experience in foreign affairs. He wanted to be both the final word on any issue and a policy analyst; one senior administration official commented that Bush often acted as his own chief of staff and his own intelligence analyst.[21] Bush was more like Carter than Reagan in his approach to decision making, but he was a Carter with executive branch experience and a perspective on the way the world worked. His specialty was foreign affairs and he set up a system that channeled national security information toward the Oval Office. Ultimately, he made the final decisions after consultation with his advisers. The real question for Bush as his term began was how he planned to use his advisers.

Management Strategy

Management strategy considers the initial formal committee structures and procedures for policy review as well as the roles and responsibilities of the key advisers, in particular, the ANSA and the secretary of state. Every president enters office with a theory about how to make decisions. The initial design of the

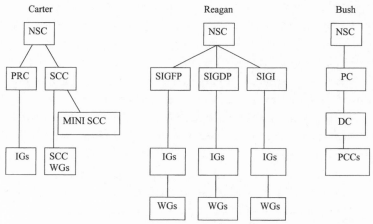

Key: NSC -- National Security Council   IGs -- Interagency Groups   PC -- Principals Committee
     PRC -- Policy Review Committee   WGs -- Working Groups   DC -- NSC Deputies Committee
     SCC -- Special Coordinating Committee   SIGI -- Senior Interagency Group-Intelligence
     PCCs -- NSC Policy Coordinating Committees   SIGFP -- SIG-Foreign Policy
     SIGDP -- SIG-Defense Policy

FIGURE 3.1. Comparison of Initial Formal Interagency Processes

NSC process is that theory put into practice. The Carter, Reagan, and Bush NSC designs were somewhat similar. Figure 3.1 illustrates the standard committee structures of each administration.

Committee Structures

As codified in Jimmy Carter's Presidential Directive 2 (PD-2), the NSC consisted of two senior-level interagency committees that would provide support for the statutory NSC itself: the Policy Review Committee (PRC) and the Special Coordinating Committee (SCC). Attendant to the PRC were lower level Interdepartmental Groups (IGs). The IGs were the working level of the PRC process and operated at the undersecretary or assistant secretary level. Which department provided the chair of the IG depended on the issue area. Importantly, the SCC was always chaired by the ANSA, Zbigniew Brzezinski. This was Brzezinski's committee, and in his absence his deputy David Aaron chaired the committee. The SCC also had what was called a "mini-SCC" chaired by Aaron that assisted the SCC in managing foreign policy. The SCC was designed to deal with shorterterm problems that were interdepartmental by nature such as intelligence, arms control, and crisis management. The SCC contained within it subcabinet-level working groups chaired by NSC staffers. The membership of both the PRC and SCC was cabinet secretary level and included statutory NSC members and whoever else was needed.[22]

The Reagan NSC was one of eight issue-specific cabinet councils within the administration that served as a replacement for a full cabinet meeting in which the secretaries of all cabinet departments would gather regardless of the issue. Each cabinet council had a specific jurisdiction and membership and a lead department.[23] Within the NSC a decentralized structure was created. Reporting to the full NSC were three main senior interagency groups (SIGs) for foreign policy (SIG-FP), defense policy (SIG-DP), and intelligence (SIG-I). Additional SIGs for other issues were added as needed. The SIGs were staffed by cabinet-level officials and chaired by the cabinet officer whose department had the most direct jurisdiction. Supporting each SIG were a number of interagency groups (IGs) chaired and staffed at the assistant secretary level. This system was put into place in an ad hoc manner in 1981, but not codified as National Security Decision Directive 2 (NSDD-2), "National Security Council Structure," until 1982 during the tenure of Reagan's second ANSA, William Clark. Reagan's initial ANSA, Richard Allen, was hamstrung by a structure that rendered him subordinate to Edwin Meese, counselor to the president, whose priorities lay in domestic affairs. The management of national security during Reagan's first year in office was often an afterthought or the haphazard result of a tug-of-war between Secretary of State Alexander Haig, Secretary of Defense Caspar Weinberger, and Meese. Clark took charge in early 1982, formalized the system, and elevated the NSC staff to its more typical role in national security—coordination of the SIG-IG interagency process and a steady drift toward controlling the policy-making process.[24]

The Bush system codified in National Security Directive-1 (NSD-1) was much more centralized than the Reagan administration and slightly different, though conceptually the same, as the Carter system. The NSC was supported by the Principals Committee (NSC/PC), a cabinet-level committee composed of NSC members minus the president and vice president and chaired by the ANSA (Brent Scowcroft). Supporting the NSC/PC was the Deputies Committee (NSC/DC), chaired by the deputy ANSA (Robert Gates). Its members were the principal deputies to the cabinet officers on the NSC/PC or key undersecretaries. Both committees added additional officials from the appropriate levels as needed. Below the NSC/DC were regionally or functionally differentiated interagency committees called Policy Coordinating Committees (NSC/PCCs), each chaired by an assistant secretary from the department whose expertise was most crucial to the issue. The NSC/PC was the key advisory body to the president, setting agendas and preparing issues for presentation to the full NSC. The NSC/DC actually ran the day-to-day operations of foreign policy, tasking the NSC/PCCs and the departmental bureaucracies.[25]

Paper Flow

The formal paperwork of the NSC process in each administration was similar, consisting of a review and directive process. For Carter, it was the Presidential Review Memorandum (PRM), Presidential Directive (PD) system. Under Reagan, National Security Study Directives (NSSDs) and National Security Decision Directives (NSDDs) comprised the formal paperwork of the system. For Bush, it was dubbed the National Security Review (NSR), National Security Directive (NSD) system. PRMs, NSSDs, and NSRs were study papers. Once the president or cabinet-level NSC committees had decided that there was a specific issue or existing policy that needed further study, the ANSA or deputy would draw up a PRM, NSSD, or NSR that would provide instructions for the interagency policy review. Those instructions contained process and policy guidelines. The document mapped out a bureaucratic route for the review along with a timetable for the review process. These reviews were the basic method of staffing out policy analyses that were important enough to be elevated from the normal routines of bureaucratic standard operating procedures. Once the interagency study had been completed it would be addressed by the upper-level NSC committee for debate and discussion.

While the Carter SCC and PRC did the heavy lifting at this stage, the Bush NSC/DC attempted to hammer out a consensus, ordered more reviews, or documented policy gridlock within a review before an issue was sent up to the NSC/PC. Within the Reagan administration the policy might go to the SIGs or directly to the NSC or the more informal cabinet-level National Security Planning Group (NSPG). At this level the study might be revised by the cabinet secretaries or formally given to the president, whether consensus or disagreement was the result. This process allowed the president to understand where agreements or disagreements among his senior advisers lay. If the issue was serious enough to merit a specific presidential guideline, a directive (PD, NSDD, or NSD) was drawn up by the ANSA for the president to sign, providing official presidential guidance on the policy. [26]

Roles of Principal Committees and Advisers

A brief assessment of the roles of committees and the principal advisers provides a glimpse at the power relationships within the administration at the beginning of its term in office. Assigning roles and responsibilities to specific committees or advisers is a process through which a president consciously or unconsciously delegates some of his power. No president makes decisions alone. Even actively involved presidents such as Carter and Bush parcel out a significant amount of power to key players in their administrations. In particular, the roles and responsibilities of the secretary of state, secretary of defense, and the ANSA are crucial.

During the Carter administration the NSC process was designed by Carter and Brzezinski; neither Secretary of State Cyrus Vance nor Secretary of Defense Harold Brown was part of this decision. The ultimate structure reflects this. The ANSA chaired the SCC permanently, while the secretaries of state and defense were among a number of cabinet officers who could be picked by the president to chair a PRC meeting on a given subject. Carter and Brzezinski decided together which committee handled which issues, as well as which senior cabinet official would chair the PRC process for that issue. The NSC staff wrote all PRMs that fell under SCC jurisdiction, while PRMs were written by the department chosen by Carter and Brzezinski to lead the study. There was keen competition between the executive departments to lead studies and write final drafts of PRMs. Completed PRMs were passed on to the president accompanied by the ANSA's cover memo summing up his thoughts on the PRM. If the president requested that a PD be issued, Brzezinski had the drafting responsibility. Importantly, whether there was consensus or not within the PRC or SCC on the issue, once a draft PD was drawn up it would not be reviewed by the SCC or PRC before it was given to the president. Vance had protested this process unsuccessfully, for it gave Brzezinski the final say over all official policy directives.[27]

This entire system gave Brzezinski significant and unchecked ability to influence presidential decisions. He was deeply involved in designing the policy process and had the ability to put the final spin on each PD. Brzezinski was Carter's eyes and ears in the decision-making process. He was to act as Carter's surrogate, both managing the process and steering it toward desired policy outcomes. The repercussions of this were enormous in terms of bureaucratic rivalry and Brzezinski's ability to become the dominant figure in the administration's foreign policy at the expense of the secretary of state and secretary of defense.

In the Reagan administration, even though the president was technically chair of each cabinet council, at meetings he was usually represented by Counsellor to the President Edwin Meese and Chief of Staff James Baker. This meant that Meese and Baker had real control over all the councils as surrogates for the president. Along with Michael Deaver, the deputy chief of staff, Meese and Baker formed the "troika" that controlled policy, process, and public relations within the administration.[28]

The NSC was the only one of the councils that did not have a permanent lead department. The decentralized SIG-IG structure of the NSC was based on informal discussions among the senior foreign policy advisers, but was ultimately designed by Meese. The SIG for foreign policy (SIG-FP), chaired by Secretary of State Haig, had jurisdiction over issues related to international and regional affairs. The SIG for defense policy (SIG-DP), chaired by Secretary of Defense Weinberger, had jurisdiction over issues that primarily dealt with U.S. armed forces. The SIG for intelligence (SIG-I), chaired by Director of Central Intelligence William Casey, held jurisdiction for intelligence matters (counterintelligence and intelligence countermeasures). SIGs and supporting IGs proliferated. The administration itself put the number at 25 SIGs and 55 IGs that had been created, though others have suggested that the number of SIG- and IG-level committees reached 200.[29]

This extra layer of committees decentralized the power of the NSC itself and left overall coordination of foreign policy uncertain. The decentralization had two results. First, the vacuum created by the lack of a decisive presidential presence or single powerful committee allowed Meese to become the most powerful Reagan adviser on foreign affairs. Haig, though secretary of state, was never allowed to become the president's key adviser on foreign policy. Meese, Baker, and Deaver saw his efforts at becoming a secretary of state on the order of Acheson or Dulles as a threat to White House dominance of policy content and process. Meese also downgraded the role of the ANSA and the NSC staff. Neither Haig nor the administration's first ANSA, Richard Allen, had direct access to the president. Allen and the NSC staff clearly worked under Meese's direction.[30] The troika or the domestic policy staff was Haig and Allen's conduits to the president.

Second, the committees were stifled as well. The SIGs were mired in jurisdictional battles, while Meese, Baker, and Deaver had unlimited access to the president. Meese had constructed a system in which only he would be allowed to play the role of dominant ANSA. However, he had neither the interest nor the expertise. The ANSA and the NSC staff functioning as the president's personal foreign policy bureaucracy was ended. Instead, a more free-form cabinet system developed out of the decentralized NSC process. One staffer refers to it as Reagan's "foreign policy directorate." The real structure is described as Reagan simply consulting with his senior advisers informally, then making a decision. Notably, that team included Vice President Bush, Haig, Weinberger, Casey, Allen, Ambassador to the United Nations Jeane Kirkpatrick, Meese, Baker, and Deaver.[31]

The Bush administration document National Security Document-1 (NSD-1), "Reorganization of the National Security Council," set out a division of labor among committees with clear and well-developed vertical and horizontal committee relationships. The NSC/PCCs allowed the bureaucracies to fight their traditional bureaucratic and organizational battles over policy as they developed interagency policy proposals. The NSC/DC supervised those battles and ironed out the differences. Most importantly, the NSC/DC served two functions. First, it was the place where the administration hoped to create a consensus among the foreign policy bureaucracies. Its second function stems from the first. The NSC/DC insulated the principals from bureaucratic battles within the administration so they could develop collegiality at the cabinet level. Robert Gates, the deputy ANSA, in his role as chair of the NSC/DC, managed the process that developed policy options, contingency plans, long-term policy reviews and recommendations to the NSC/PC, advised the president, and sat in on the NSC/PC meetings as the link between the NSC/PC and NSC/DC.[32] His daunting responsibilities allowed Scowcroft to concentrate on his role as adviser to the president and "honest broker" between the principals. If the NSC/DC was a shock absorber for the principals, it was Gates's role to make sure the ride was smooth, but the senior officials at the wheel knew how rough the road actually was. This was a process of insulation, not isolation, and allowed for the development of collegiality at the top level.

The most important decision concerned the roles of the secretary of state and ANSA. For secretary of state, Bush chose Baker, one of his oldest and closest friends who also happened to be a former chief of staff and secretary of the treasury. Bush saw it as an easy choice. He was adamant about avoiding the type of bureaucratic warfare he had seen in the Nixon and Reagan years. The secretary of state was assigned the role of "chief action officer" and number one adviser.[33] Baker, not ANSA, implemented U.S. foreign policy on the president's behalf. There were to be no rivals to the power of the secretary of state in foreign affairs. In a unique situation, Bush had picked his best friend as his secretary of state.

The Bush-Baker relationship was a solid one. The question was whether the Bush-Scowcroft relationship might come to rival or surpass it. As indicated above, Bush saw Scowcroft as the quintessential ANSA. He saw the ANSA as an official who would "objectively present the views of the various cabinet officers across the spectrum," and who commanded such respect from the other advisers that he could eliminate a significant amount of the natural rivalries and organizational disagreements that are the nature of governmental decision making. Though Bush considered Scowcroft for both director of central intelligence (DCI) and secretary of defense, he ultimately decided that the administration was best served by Scowcroft in the ANSA role. Scowcroft and Bush were also friends from their days in the Ford administration. Scowcroft as ANSA was in effect DCI Bush's superior within that administration, and Bush was granted access to the president through Scowcroft. A relationship this close could have been a danger to the Bush-Baker relationship and Baker's role as secretary of state. It never became a major problem for three reasons. First, no matter how close Bush and Scowcroft were, Bush and Baker were always closer. Second, Baker and Scowcroft were also friends, veterans of the Ford administration who had been tested under fire together. They had been witnesses to terrible infighting between the NSC staff and the State Department and were determined not to let that happen again.[34]

The most important reason may have been simply that Scowcroft understood the proper role of an ANSA as a process manager and presidential adviser who should never overstep his role and become a rival to the cabinet officers. Description after description of Scowcroft's role as ANSA portray him as an "honest broker" with no "private agenda," a man with "a lack of ego" who genuinely felt his role was not to block other advisers' ideas from getting to the president, but to make sure that the president was exposed to the widest range of opinions and analyses. Scowcroft saw his role as making sure that the president had the information and ideas necessary to make the best decision possible. The less publicity he received and the fewer of his fingerprints that were left on the policy the better. Deferential to Baker, Scowcroft never challenged Baker's role as the public face of U.S. diplomacy to the American people and the world. According to some subcabinet officials, the only serious tensions between Baker and Scowcroft occurred over the "Two plus Four" talks over the reunification of Germany.[35]

Organizational Dynamics

This section briefly examines the general rivalries between departments and senior officials that shaped the contest for control over policy. In some ways, this is the order of battle for the bureaucratic war over policy and power that is highlighted in governmental politics models. Though the case study chapters examine changes in the organizational dynamics, the initial relationships between the senior advisers and departments and the way in which they evolved in general create a context within which to assess those dynamics as they played out in decision making on arms control and nuclear strategy.

In the Carter administration, Carter's leadership style led him to deep involvement in the substance and process of each decision; he viewed each of the principals as his advisers, not as co–decision makers. The NSC staff was his national security staff, and Brzezinski was to play the role of "honest broker" and manager of the process. If the president acted as his own secretary of state, Vance was left in a somewhat precarious position. He used his ability to implement policy as a way of influencing policy. Brzezinski eventually combined the management role and an advocacy role to become nearly Kissingerian in his dominance of the policy process and intellectual influence over U.S. policy. Though Brzezinski did start out as a neutral process manager, his access to Carter and the president's desire to control national security naturally gave him the ability to expand his role.

Neither Secretary of Defense Harold Brown nor CIA Director Stansfield Turner was close to Carter. The bureaucratic rivalry was between Vance and the state department, and Brzezinski and the NSC staff. Although Carter did not encourage the rivalry deliberately (as FDR had done with his advisers), he did not put a stop to the rivalry as it began. He attempted to create a compromise policy based on the competing advice of his advisers, rather than choosing between them on an issue-by-issue basis.[36] Carter allowed Brzezinski to publicly disagree with Vance and also designed an NSC paper flow that gave Brzezinski the last word on all issues. Vance did provide Carter with a daily memo on national security developments. Brzezinski, however, had immediate access to Carter. As in other administrations, the advantages of the ANSA and NSC staff allowed Brzezinski to end his neutral role and expand his influence. By the time the bureaucratic and philosophical disagreements between Vance and Brzezinski became a feud in 1978 and 1979 it was easy for Brzezinski to quickly assume the role of first among equals in the decision-making process.[37]

The natural secretary of state–ANSA rivalry was exacerbated by fundamental disagreements on policy. Vance leaned toward idealism as a philosophy, negotiation as the preferred tool of diplomacy, a foreign policy based on human rights, and the maintenance of detente with the USSR as the overriding national security goal. Brzezinski tilted in the opposite direction as a realist in philosophy, a believer in the utility and necessity of coercive diplomacy, and a skeptic concerning detente and human rights policies that might weaken containment. He often preferred to rely on the balance of power and the "China card" rather than summitry and treaties with Soviet leaders. Carter's inexperience in foreign policy allowed this ideological debate to become a real struggle for Carter's foreign policy soul between these two. Each adviser felt he could teach the president that his view was the correct one. Their competition and rivalry grew partly on this basis.[38]

The issue that ultimately destroyed the relationship between Vance and Brzezinski was the question of linkage. Should the U.S. link Soviet behavior in the Ogaden war between Somalia and Ethiopia on the Horn of Africa or Afghanistan to detente and progress in SALT II? Vance was against this linkage. SALT II, in and of itself, enhanced U.S. security; linkage would hurt the U.S. as much as it would hurt the USSR. Brzezinski saw it as a useful tool to punish the USSR for its expansionism. Firmly blaming the USSR for the collapse of SALT II, Brzezinski stated that "SALT lies buried in the sands of Ogaden." Carter wavered until the invasion of Afghanistan, then fell firmly on the side of Brzezinski, calling the Soviet invasion of Afghanistan "the most serious threat to world peace since the second world war." He then withdrew SALT II from Senate consideration and pledged, in his State of the Union address of 1980, to defend the Persian Gulf with military force if necessary.[39] Vance saw his relevance decrease to a low point in April of 1980. The administration made the decision to rescue the U.S. hostages in Iran while Vance was out of Washington. The timing was deliberate to avoid Vance's dissent on the rescue mission. He resigned soon after and was replaced by Edmund Muskie, the senator from Maine.[40]

Deep and fundamental differences in the foreign policy philosophies of Reagan's senior aides were apparent from the first day of the Reagan administration. Meese himself considered the administration, in total, to be a "coalition government."[41] Reagan's advisers represented a mix of the conservative and moderate groups of the Republican Party. The conservatives were descendants of the old nationalist or isolationist wing of the party, with roots in Senator Henry Cabot Lodge's campaign against Woodrow Wilson's League of Nations, and Robert Taft's more modern isolationism. It had developed the rabid anti-communism of the 1950s that lay in remission, it seemed, until Carter was elected. It had resurfaced, full force, as the Committee on the Present Danger (CPD), an organization dedicated to warning the American people about the growing threat of Soviet power. The conservatives came to power in the form of the Reagan administration. The moderates within the Republican Party, heirs to Eisenhower's and Senator Arthur Vandenberg's more balanced anticommunism, were represented in the administration by many veterans of the Nixon and Ford administrations.

These divisions were real and institutionalized within the departments. In particular, the State Department, whether under Haig or his successor George Shultz, was the home of the moderate wing's pragmatists, while Weinberger's DOD, and to a lesser degree, Casey's CIA and the Arms Control and Disarmament Agency (ACDA) were the headquarters of the conservative wing's hardliners. The White House itself was also divided. Meese's staff was filled with alumni of Reagan's days in California, hardliners to the core, while Baker's staff was composed of Nixon and Ford era pragmatists.[42]

The philosophical differences between these groups, particularly over policy toward the USSR, were great. The pragmatists certainly were anticommunist, but their preferred method of dealing with the USSR was rooted in Nixon's detente strategy. The best way to contain the USSR was to draw it into ties with the West that provided better leverage to manage U.S.-Soviet relations and Soviet activities around the globe. Trade with the USSR and arms control were key elements of this balance of power strategy. Following the invasion of Afghanistan, the collapse of SALT II in the U.S., and the faceoff over the Solidarity movement in Poland, the hardliners were in ascendance in the Republican Party. Their view was more rigid, more absolute, and often described in moral terms. The USSR was evil; detente was a fool's game; negotiations on arms control with notorious liars were a prelude to unilateral disarmament. The result of these divisions was a bitter bureaucratic rivalry.

On top of all these tensions was a rivalry between the White House troika —Meese, Baker, and Deaver—and the executive departments themselves. The troika had attempted to run every aspect of Reagan's domestic and international policy. However, by the fall of 1981, they had decided that repeated foreign policy missteps necessitated a change. The troika engineered the removal of Allen and the shift of Deputy Secretary of State William Clark to a more powerful ANSA position.[43]

Clark reorganized the NSC process immediately. Though he codified the SIG-IG system in NSDD-2, "National Security Council Structure," of 12 January 1982, he and the NSC staff became the primary initiators and authors of all NSSDs and NSDDs. Overall, Clark's role was in the model of the previous ANSAs. He was the president's personal national security policy adviser, organizer of the president's national security policy staff, manager of the process, and mediator between the senior officials in the administration. Clark was particularly well suited to the mediator aspect of this role. Not only was he a loyal friend of the president, but he also got on well with most of the other principals. Clark's power, however, was soon seen as a threat to turn the troika into a quartet.[44]

Secretary of State Haig was a casualty of Clark's new power. Clark and Haig renewed the secretary of state–ANSA feud. Clark joined the troika in resenting Haig's attempts to become the president's chief adviser of foreign affairs. Haig finally resigned under pressure in June of 1982. The appointment of George Shultz as his successor was no remedy. Shultz, a pragmatist, renewed a rivalry with Weinberger dating back to their days in the Nixon administration and developed new ones with Clark and Meese as well as other hardliners. The tensions as well as a growing rivalry between the troika and Clark resulted in Clark's shift to the post of secretary of the interior. The choice of Clark's successor illustrated the depth of the disagreement in the administration. Pragmatists and hardliners fought to such a degree over who would replace Clark that the president simply elevated Clark's deputy Robert McFarlane as a way to end the feud over this appointment.[45]

The story of Reagan foreign policy can be told as a tale of a series of battles between these factions. The head-to-head conflicts were numerous: Haig vs. Allen; Haig vs. Kirkpatrick; Haig vs. Weinberger; Clark vs. Shultz and Baker; and ultimately the longest rivalry, Shultz vs. Weinberger.[46] No faction ever won, and Reagan never chose a winner. Before the war within the administration had ended, the cold war itself ended and the points in contention were moot.

The Bush administration decision-making process worked well and suffered no breakdowns because of the friendships among the senior advisers and the ideological homogeneity of their beliefs on international affairs. For Bush, personal friendships were a philosophy of life. Bush's use of personal relationships with world leaders through frequent telephone calls, letters, or get-acquainted summits as an adjunct to U.S. diplomacy is well documented. This was his personal style for making decisions within the administration as well. Journalistic accounts of the decision-making process and memoirs all point to the important role of the friendships among the senior decision makers and their loyalty to each other and to Bush. Scowcroft called it a "deep camaraderie" that existed at the senior level. These relationships were as deep and intertwined as might be expected from veterans of three Republican administrations. The unique aspect of this was that they all seemed to come away from their experience as friends, not rivals.[47]

Whereas the Reagan administration was plagued with philosophical differences among the senior advisers as hardliners fought pragmatists for every inch of the Reagan foreign policy platform, the Bush administration was composed almost exclusively of pragmatists at the senior levels. All of them were realists in their orientation toward the world, supporters of détente in the 1970s, and skeptics as they viewed the deep changes in the USSR in the 1980s. Only Vice President Dan Quayle can be seen as a hardliner in the mold of the Reagan-era hardliners. When it came to foreign policy advisers, however, Bush chose not only friends, but people whose outlook on the world and in particular the USSR matched his own.

Informal Structures

An informal process develops within the first six months of any administration's tenure in office. This section addresses that process to provide a context for the case studies since it grows as a general part of the decision-making process independently of any specific issue area. This informal structure, one of the three concurrent structures of the evolution model, becomes an important feature of the administration. Presidents and their senior advisers create it to control and direct the formal interagency process. Even the most streamlined and well-organized NSC system can be cumbersome given the enormous amount of horizontal and vertical bureaucratic participation involved. The constant pressure from all quarters for involvement in the top-level decision-making committees never stops. The establishment of these informal structures reflects the principles of decision making as discussed above and in the preceding chapter. They also illustrate the narrow, informal, ad hoc bypassing or streamlining of the interagency process that the evolution model suggests. All the competition described by the governmental politics and new institutionalism models was met by a presidential management response.

As the evolution model suggests, the responses of each administration were the same—creation of an informal process that included a narrower range of senior advisers and less formal procedures as a deliberate way to bypass or streamline the formality of the standard NSC process. However, the ultimate use of

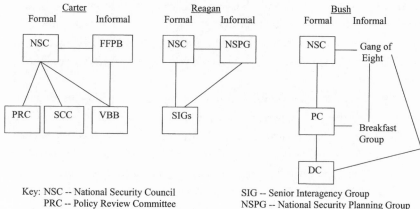

FIGURE 3.2. Comparison of Informal Processes

these informal groups was dependent on the differences in the ultimate role of the informal processes stemmed the president's leadership style. In all cases, the president had decided that he had learned something: the NSC process was more formal than he desired for certain decision-making tasks. It was often too slow and effort-intensive, and it could not always respond with the political dexterity necessary for presidential policy making. The use of these informal structures in the specific area of arms control and nuclear strategy are addressed in the case study chapters. The concluding chapter compares the informal structures in terms of how their use, origin, and relationship with the formal and confidence structures were affected by each president's leadership style. Figure 3.2 illustrates the informal structures in each administration.

Carter Administration

The Carter administration's informal processes developed by March of 1977.[48] The Vance-Brzezinski-Brown (VBB) lunches and the Friday Foreign Policy Breakfasts (FFPB) were created by the principal decision makers as adjuncts to the NSC committees, a streamlining of the process. Carter and Brzezinski saw the small groups as useful for gathering the best minds outside of formal settings where they could concentrate on the big picture uninhibited by the presence of staff. A small group of only the most senior people, without staff, was considered necessary to deal with overall policy guidance and the most crucial issues.

The VBB group held lunchtime meetings during which Vance, Brown, and Brzezinski could discuss pending issues outside of the NSC, PRC, and SCC. Both Vance and Brzezinski felt that the NSC process was too formal and too staff-filled a forum for real collegial and far-reaching discussions where each principal felt free to speak his mind. During the VBB lunches the principals could develop unified stands to present to the formal NSC committees. Though Carter wanted collegiality, the NSC process channeled that collegiality through a formal process. The informal lunches allowed debate, even brainstorming, on key issues without initiating bureaucratic action either intentionally or unintentionally. Brzezinski saw these meetings as ways to enhance the effectiveness of the NSC process, not supplant it.[49] Through this venue, the decision-making process might flow more smoothly and proceed more quickly.

The FFPB allowed for the same type of dialogue among a slightly larger group that would, importantly, add the president. With a VBB meeting on a Thursday, the principals would continue their discussion with or present the results of their discussion to the president on Friday mornings. The membership of this group is revealing. Initially, the meetings included Carter, Vice President Walter Mondale, Vance, and Brzezinski. Hamilton Jordan, a special assistant to the president who performed the duties of a chief of staff (and would later have that title), and Brown were added to the group in 1978. Clearly, Carter wanted to keep this as small and unobtrusive as possible. No aides were present; Carter even resisted setting an agenda. The value of the meetings for the president was in the freewheeling nature of the VBB-FFPB process and its role as a type of shortcut to decisions. Carter felt that this was where he could make final decisions and make them stick. The VBB-FFPB process itself evolved over time into a more formal decision unit with agendas and implementation planning.[50]

Reagan Administration

The Reagan administration added an informal process in July of 1981. The National Security Planning Group (NSPG) was created as an adjunct to the NSC process. The NSPG was scheduled to meet three mornings a week on Mondays, Wednesdays, and Fridays. These meetings included the president, Vice President Bush, Haig, Weinberger, Casey, Allen, Meese, Baker, and Deaver. Though these same people made up the core of the NSC, these meetings included fewer staff assistants. There were not necessarily set agendas for these meetings, nor did they meet on a regular schedule as originally planned. Working groups within the NSPG were also set up to consider specific issues.[51]

Attendance at NSC meetings had grown to such an extent that it was becoming an obstacle to open policy debate. A smaller group, essentially the principals and Reagan's most senior White House staffers, had a better chance of building the collegiality and coordination that is seen as crucial to a strong national security team.[52] In this sense, the NSPG was similar to the VBB-FFPB system of the Carter administration. The difference in the actual functioning of the NSPG in relation to the NSC and the overall NSC process is unclear. Clearly, the reduced size and the lack of a set agenda rendered it a better place to hash out differences in a more informal way in preparation for NSC meetings where decisions might be made. Scholarly research, however, including the case studies that follow, shows no real difference in the role played by the NSPG and NSC. The two committees seem to be interchangeable.[53] Some issues were discussed in the NSPG on one day and in the NSC on the next. No reason for using one decision group over the other seems evident except scheduling. The relationship between the NSPG and the SIGs is also unclear. Sometimes a policy traveled up through the SIG-IG process to the NSPG; other times it went to the NSC; still other times issues were discussed in the NSPG, then the NSC. It may have been a simple matter of using the NSC when a meeting was scheduled and the NSPG in other instances. The NSPG did not solve the problem of administration feuds, nor did it bring Reagan deeper into the decision-making process. With the NSC, the growing number of SIGs, and the NSPG, the senior national security advisers to the president had the opportunity to argue in a number of forums. As the case studies will show, the NSPG became part of the formal paper flow of the NSC process, essentially captured by the formal process. Neither Reagan nor his ANSAs attempted to isolate this informal process from the formal one.

A second attempt to build small-group collegiality was made late in the first term. Reagan, Shultz, and McFarlane began to meet Wednesday and Friday afternoons. Interestingly, Weinberger was excluded from these meetings. In November 1984, Shultz suggested that the principal advisers should meet once a week in an attempt to smooth over their differences. Wednesday morning meetings, called Family Breakfasts (after the meeting place, the family dining room of the White House), included Shultz, Weinberger, Casey, and McFarlane and began in the second term.[54]

Bush Administration

The evolution toward more informal decision making came swiftly for the Bush administration. Their experience in government allowed them to learn faster than more inexperienced decision makers would have. Though the NSC system was based on those experiences, they learned that even deeper collegiality could be developed with a more informal process. The core group of decision makers narrowed down to what has been called the Gang of Eight—Bush, Baker, Cheney, Scowcroft, Crowe, then Powell, Gates, Chief of Staff John Sununu, and Quayle—as well as a narrower Breakfast Group of Baker, Cheney, and Scowcroft. This Gang of Eight became a regular feature of the administration by March of 1989. The Breakfast Group began even earlier. If these advisers are seen as Bush's "brain trust," then the cabinet and the "kitchen" cabinet had been merged in the Bush administration.[55] The role of the NSC/DC in enabling the Gang of Eight to operate by maintaining the smooth functioning of the formal process cannot be understated.

There were numerous reasons to develop the informal process. It began shortly after Scowcroft suggested a principals-only meeting to consider the current developments in Europe. Bush liked the idea and the result so much that he decided that such meetings should be held as often as possible. Baker and Gates both contend that a major reason for the move toward a Gang of Eight was the inability of the bureaucracies to deal creatively and innovatively with the revolutionary changes taking place in the world. Scowcroft states that he began questioning the ability of the full NSC to make quality and timely decisions as early as March of 1989. The administration's rule for inclusion at NSC meetings was that if the decision affected a specific department, the senior person from that department was included. This could increase the size of meetings. To Scowcroft, the size of the meetings and the vast range of people included and who wanted to be included meant that the NSC became no place for a "no-holds-barred discussion among the president's top advisers." These advisers were "inhibited" by the size of the group.[56] Since horizontal inclusion of all relevant agencies was a basic part of the Gang of Eight, the senior decision makers saw this group as an aspect of the formal process, even though it was by its nature informal.[57]

Bush's leadership style was also a factor. Bush wanted meetings of the NSC and cabinet to be as small as possible and called only for major decisions, particularly to limit leaks.[58] NSC meetings included staffers and the formal recording of minutes. Both of these were avenues through which information could trickle through the executive departments and make a large splash in the next day's morning newspaper. The informal committees helped eliminate this problem.

The decision making of the Gang of Eight did not replace that of the full NSC. However, as the Gang of Eight decision making became a more regular feature of Bush decision making, NSC meetings became less frequent. Scowcroft states clearly in his memoirs that the "informal group became the rule rather than the exception for practical decision making." [59]

Although the formal NSC had its informal analog in the Gang of Eight, the NSC/PC was also in effect shadowed by a weekly breakfast meeting between Baker, Cheney, and Scowcroft. [60] These breakfasts were similar in concept to the Vance-Brown-Brzezinski (VBB) lunches of the Carter administration and the attempts at such meetings during the Reagan years. This was the ultimate place for ironing out the differences between the bureaucracies at the State Department, Pentagon, and NSC staff. If the rivalry between these institutions is seen as a permanent fixture of life in the government that will outlast any administration, then the problem of an incoming administration is to prevent those animosities from bubbling up to the top and affecting the harmony of the new team that surrounds the president. The Breakfast Group was designed to do just that —maintain harmony at the senior level, and shield the president from bureaucratic and organizational warfare. In addition, the breakfast meetings allowed Baker, Cheney, and Scowcroft to create a consensus among themselves in preparation for NSC/PC and NSC meetings. If these three created a common stand, no other coalition of advisers would be able to win the argument. These meetings also provided a place to consider which issues were brought to the president and which stayed at the cabinet level. This was one of the functions of the NSC/PC that may have been usurped by the informal committee.

General Assessment

The Carter, Reagan, and Bush teams initially put into place similar styles of national security decision making. Their leadership styles, however, were significantly different. At this point, it is useful to address briefly some general points about each administration.

As judged by scholars, by journalists, and by the U.S. public in November of 1980, Carter was an unsuccessful president. His national security process is often seen as the antithesis of a well-oiled machine. Supporters and critics alike lamented the confusion, chaos, and inconsistency of Carter's decision making.

These problems may have as their root cause a decision-making process designed around a president who lacked national security experience. As a neophyte in national security Carter had no solid, well-developed worldview, and a president whose belief systems on national security are still in their formative stages cannot design mature policy guidelines for his administration to follow. Carter was never able to achieve a consensus on his shift of U.S. foreign policy toward human rights and away from containment. He underestimated the need for creating a consensus within the American polity, between the president and Congress, and within the administration.[61] Ultimately Carter's human rights policy foundered on a perceived decline in U.S. strategic power and renewed Soviet aggression. Inexperience became inconsistency.[62] This was a particular problem in a system in which Carter played the key role. In Carter's defense, however, one could argue that he suffered from bad timing. Carter was the first post–Viet Nam, post-Watergate, post–oil shock president. Operating in a nation without a foreign policy consensus and faced with growing Soviet assertiveness, Carter might not have succeeded in creating consistent, strategically sound, and popular national security policies even if he had been an expert in foreign policy with the best national security system imaginable.

In a general sense, the Reagan administration policy process is often seen as a mirror image of the Carter process. If Carter could not see the forest for the trees, Reagan has often been accused of not knowing that the forest was made of trees. However, there are similarities between both presidents in their initial approach to designing a national security process. Each hoped for strong, thorough cabinet government. The design of each of their systems had origins in a reaction to their predecessor's decision-making style and a true belief that with good advice they would make well-informed, quality decisions. Carter was widening a decision circle he felt had been too centralized under Nixon and Ford. Reagan was bringing what he thought would be ideological consistency and decisiveness from inauguration day to a process he felt was directionless during the Carter years. While Reagan was clear about his views of the USSR, his administration was divided. These disagreements became bureaucratic warfare for essentially two reasons. First, Reagan leadership style called for consensus.[63] He was reluctant to make decisions unless a clear majority of his major advisers had reached agreement. Though he had strong opinions on national security, he was not an expert, nor were members of the troika or even Clark. Without a strong and guiding hand to take charge, the need for consensus gave dissenters or spoilers the ability to grind policy to a halt.

Second, consensus within any administration can be achieved in only two ways: either all the senior players must agree on the issue, or the president (or someone acting on his behalf) must settle the issue, creating, in essence, a consensus of one. Since there was no natural consensus within the administration, it was up to the president to create one. Surprisingly, given Reagan's hardliner convictions, the president did not perform this task. Reagan had called the USSR an "evil empire" in arguing that the Soviet Union was the "focus of evil in the modern world."[64] He had been a member of the Committee on the Present Danger, a critic of both SALT I and II and the Nixon/Kissinger policies on detente. Yet within administrative decision making, Reagan failed to end the feuding. He did not take the hardliners' side, nor did he rule in favor of the pragmatists with any consistency. He simply allowed the fighting to continue. His leadership style left him reluctant to settle these differences.[65] In a worst-case scenario Iran-Contra developed from this failure to control the process as administration officials created their own independent policies and hid them from opponents of their ideas.[66]

The Bush administration provides a useful contrast to the Carter and Reagan administrations. Where the Carter administration decision-making processes shifted steadily though dramatically from the Vance-Brzezinski feud to centralization of decisions in the White House, the Bush administration developed, from its inception, a balance between a strong secretary of state and a strong but deferent ANSA. Where the Reagan administration was hamstrung by ideological feuds and personal power struggles among the senior decision makers, the Bush administration contained a senior core of decision makers who were ideologically similar (realists), and personal friends who had all worked with each other before. In this sense, all the major obstacles that the Carter and Reagan decision-making teams had to overcome were already settled by inauguration day of 1989 when the Bush team took office. The president and his senior staff were all experienced in government service at the federal level, with years of expertise in foreign affairs. They were also familiar with each other. If the president and his senior advisers within the Carter and Reagan administrations can be considered amateurs, the Bush administration national security team can be seen as professionals.

This general analysis of decision making in each administration presents a context for the case studies that follow. How the overall changes in decision making and the specific adaptations in the realm of arms control and national security fit together is addressed in the concluding chapter.

Chapter Four

THE CARTER ADMINISTRATION:
A LESSON IN LEARNING

IN A PRE-ELECTION INTERVIEW IN 1976 JIMMY CARTER ASSERTED that in his administration "the NSC staff would not again play the role of trying to run the other agencies from the White House." During his re-election campaign, in October of 1980, Carter stated plainly: "There have been presidents in the past, maybe not too distant past, that let their secretaries of state make foreign policy. I don't."[1] These two statements epitomize the strengths and weaknesses of the Carter decision style. Although it is crucial to have an involved president aware of his responsibilities in foreign affairs, an overinvolved president becomes his own greatest liability. Carter may have backed off from his desk officer role from the early days of his administration, but the case studies that follow illustrate that Carter still wanted hands-on control of both policy content and process. By mid-term, and even more so in the final year of his presidency, Carter turned to his ANSA, Zbigniew Brzezinski. Brzezinski was given nearly Kissingerian authority to make sure the bureaucracies satisfied his policy and political needs.

These changes in the process fit the evolution model well. The Carter case study is one in which institutional and political pressures pushed Carter to the logical conclusion drawn by the evolution model—severe narrowing of participation in some decisions, a reliance on informality, and deliberate bypassing of the interagency process. Unlike the Reagan and Bush cases, Carter's personal style and the pressures of decision making flowed in the same direction toward centralization of power in the National Security Council (NSC) and careful exclusion of officials and departments that might be impediments to presidential political strategy.

Evolution and change in the Carter administration are traced episodically through a focus on two cases of decision making for arms control and nuclear strategy, respectively the SALT II Deep Cuts proposal of March 1977, and the nuclear strategy embodied in Presidential Directive 59. The key elements of each case study are the political context (the international and domestic political environment surrounding the issue), the way in which the issue was placed into the standard interagency process, the organizational dynamics as they play out on the specific decision, and the presidential choices made during the process concerning the president's leadership, the president's political strategy, and his management strategy. The latter category ultimately focuses on a deliberate presidential decision to change the process.

For the SALT II decision, the system was initially designed to maximize the bureaucratic depth and breadth of decision-making participation through the use of the standard NSC process. It eventually was narrowed to a smaller core group of senior advisers, and greater reliance on presidential involvement as well as on Brzezinski and the NSC staff. Doctrinal revisions in nuclear strategy that had begun through the interagency process narrowed ultimately to the NSC staff and discussions between the president, ANSA Zbigniew Brzezinski, and Secretary of Defense Harold Brown. PD-59 was produced without the participation of Secretary of State Cyrus Vance, his successor Edmund Muskie, and the State Department in an ad hoc manner. In both cases either Carter, Brzezinski, or both felt that he had learned that the State Department would be an obstacle to designing policies based on the evolving direction of presidential priorities.

These case studies also clearly illustrate the relationship between learning, economy in decision making, and political dynamics. Identifying which advisers and organizations will be obstacles to policy and which will be most useful to the president is crucial to a swift and conclusive decision. By maximizing the input of those who will create the desired policies and minimizing the input of those who may act as brakes on the process, presidents can respond to the political imperatives of the moment. The key lesson of the Carter administration may be that although presidents learn a great deal on the job, the most important things they will learn are about their own advisers. The interagency process provides that forum for learning. Repeated decisions, whether routine or crisis, give the president a sense of who he can trust and who may cause problems. A pecking order may evolve because it serves the president's needs. The interagency process becomes an audition for parts the president will assign. The lead role is for the person the president may trust the most. In the Carter administration, Brzezinski won that part.

DECISION MAKING FOR SALT II: THE DEEP CUTS PROPOSAL

The Carter administration's decision-making process for its initial SALT proposal illustrates why presidents often choose to change aspects of their national security decision-making systems. The standard interagency process was perceived to be inadequate because of its failure to produce policy options that met presidential guidelines and the political dynamics of the moment. Carter's desire for a specific type of policy—one that led to deep cuts in U.S.-Soviet strategic arsenals —led the president to move beyond his own interagency process. He achieved this by getting more deeply involved in the decision process to guarantee a specific policy choice and by giving the NSC staff primary responsibility for developing the negotiating proposals to the exclusion of many officials from the departmental bureaucracies. The proposal of March 1977 represented both a new approach to U.S.-Soviet arms negotiations and a modification in the standard Carter decision process.

The International and Domestic Political Environment

The Carter administration inherited an institutionalized U.S. policy of arms control with the USSR. From the time that these negotiations were inaugurated in November 1969 during the Nixon administration, presidents were expected to participate in talks to limit the weaponry in the United States and Soviet nuclear arsenals with the goal of slowing down the arms race. The political and operational continuity for the Strategic Arms Limitation Talks (SALT) had solidified; the American public supported the policy, and there had been no interruptions in SALT since the Nixon administration. Even after the Anti-Ballistic Missile Treaty and the Interim Agreement on Offensive Arms (these have been collectively referred to as SALT I) had been signed in May of 1972, the negotiators barely took time out to catch their breath before they began work on SALT II. The Ford administration had signed the Vladivostok Accords in November of 1974. These accords were not binding in any way, but did represent a political understanding about what both sides had agreed upon up to that point. Following Vladivostok, the negotiations began to slow as disagreements both related and unrelated to SALT took their toll on the pace of U.S.-Soviet agreement.[2]

An approach based on deep cuts in U.S.-Soviet nuclear arsenals was favored by Senate critics of the Nixon-Ford-Kissinger policy of weapons limitations. This group was headed by Senator Henry Jackson (D-Wash.), chairman of the Subcommitteee on Arms Control and International Security of the Senate Foreign Relations Committee. His approval or disapproval of Carter's arms control policy would go a long way toward setting the odds on Senate passage of a SALT II Treaty. Jackson was not shy about pushing the administration in a specific direction.

For different reasons, Carter agreed with the criticisms of his predecessors and supported deep cuts in the U.S. and Soviet arsenals. Carter realized that if he was to achieve a major breakthrough in arms control he had to do it quickly. The pressure on his administration from the left, the conservative Democrats, and the right would only increase. Political pressures required him to go boldly, and swiftly.

As other presidents before him, Carter wanted to distance himself from his predecessors, but this was even more crucial for him. The previous presidencies had been fraught with the greatest political crises in the U.S. since the Great Depression. Although it was a great stride in creating a "more perfect union," the civil rights movement had unleashed powerful and poorly understood political forces. In addition, the loss in Viet Nam, the first oil shock, the Watergate crisis, and, finally, Ford's pardon of Nixon seemed to have ended the American Century and ushered in an era of political, economic, and social uncertainty. Ford had seen his presidency as "a time to heal."[3] Carter saw his presidency as a new start.

Of course, the SALT process begun by Nixon and Kissinger made a new start difficult. Carter stepped into the middle of ongoing negotiations in which the outline of a new agreement had already been established by the Vladivostok Accords. The November 1974 accords had specified the basis for SALT II. The U.S. and USSR were limited to 2,400 strategic nuclear delivery vehicles (ICBMs, SLBMs, and heavy bombers). A sublimit on ICBMs and SLBMs with multiple independently targeted reentry vehicles (MIRVs) was fixed at 1,320. The issues that held up a final agreement were the usual technical details of implementation and verification, but two other issues promised to be potential deal breakers. The first were air-launched cruise missiles (ALCMs). The problem was in how to count these new systems under the limits and sublimits of the Vladivostok Accords. The second issue was the Soviet Backfire bomber (Tupolev 26). The Soviets had just begun to deploy the system in its arsenal. The U.S. considered it to be a strategic heavy bomber capable for use in a nuclear strike on the U.S. The Soviets argued that it was a tactical bomber of medium range that should not be considered in U.S.-Soviet arms control.[4]

This is essentially where negotiations stood as the Carter administration was handed responsibility for U.S. arms control policy. Following Carter's nomination as the Democratic standard-bearer, he had sent Averill Harriman to Moscow with a reassuring message. Under a Carter administration there would be continuity; the Vladivostok Accords and the unsettled issues that remained would be the basis for the Carter-Soviet negotiations.[5] However, upon assuming office, Carter and his senior policy makers quickly abandoned this pledge and opted for a new approach.

The Standard Interagency Process

The standard structure for SALT was quite complex. The Special Coordination Committee (SCC) was given responsibility for SALT. Sometimes the "mini-SCC" served in this role. A SALT Working Group and ad hoc working groups provided the working-level staffing for the SCC decisions on SALT. These committees contained representatives from the State and Defense departments, the Arms Control and Disarmament Agency (ACDA), the Joint Chiefs of Staff (JCS), and the CIA. However, they were chaired by an NSC staff member.[6]

The SALT delegation in Geneva that actually negotiated with the USSR was headed by ACDA Director Paul Warnke. The delegation included representatives from the State and Defense departments and the JCS, but Warnke's dual role gave him considerable power. The immediate support group for the Geneva delegation that provided guidance on routine matters was the SALT Backstopping Committee under the direction of Spurgeon Keeny, Deputy Director of ACDA. But overall direction came from the SCC or Mini-SCC.[7]

At first glance, it seems that with the SCC assuming the role of directing policy on SALT, Brzezinski and the NSC staff might have taken charge of the policy. However, this was in the early stages of the administration. The structure of decision making reflected a genuine desire for a collegial decision-making process in which all opinions were considered. Overall policy was hashed out in the SCC. This represents the NSC's role in coordination as originally designed in the National Security Act of 1947. Warnke and ACDA's centrality in the chain of decision making represents its role in implementation. In all other ways, the structure for SALT was a classic interagency design.

The process for developing the initial U.S. position illustrates this. SALT policy was developed by Presidential Review Memorandum-2 (PRM-2). The NSC issued PRM-2 on 24 January. It asked for agency studies of SALT options. Once the PRM had been finished and included a full accounting of agency and interagency views, it would be given to the SCC for consideration. The key players in the PRM-2 process were both holdovers from the Ford administration. Roger Molander, a member of the NSC staff Defense Coordination Cluster, chaired the study, and William Hyland, of the USSR/East Europe Cluster, provided expertise on the USSR. Their roles were simple: they provided institutional memory. If the new administration attempted to reinvent the wheel in the middle of a long trip, these two could explain what had been tried and what had failed or succeeded in the past. Both, however, pushed for continuity. The other key players at this level were Leslie Gelb, Assistant Secretary of State for Political-Military Affairs, and Walter Slocombe, Principal Deputy Assistant Secretary of Defense for International Security Affairs and DOD SALT Task Force. Representatives from the State and Defense departments and the NSC staff worked together in a collegial and inclusive process. The results of PRM-2 were presented to the SCC on 3 February.[8]

Organizational Dynamics

The fruits of PRM-2 represented what is usually expected from the bureaucracy —inertia and incremental change. Three options were created. Slocombe fleshed out these options in interagency meetings with a chart that became known as the "Slocombe Triptych." Each option was a variation on Vladivostok with different options for addressing ALCMs, the Backfire bomber, and ground-launched cruise missiles (GLCMs).[9]

None of Carter's senior advisers were happy with the outcome of PRM-2. Brzezinski felt that the current direction of U.S.-Soviet negotiations—SALT I and Vladivostok—allowed the USSR to maintain superiority in some areas. The Soviet nuclear buildup that had accelerated from the mid-1960s, allowing the USSR to reach strategic parity, had continued. SALT could serve as more than simply a codification of both sides' strategic modernization plans. SALT could be a way to end the Soviet buildup.[10] Brown agreed with this assessment. While Brzezinski played the classic role of honest broker, Brown was the most forceful bureaucratic player when it came to discussions of strategic developments and SALT. His motivations for deeper cuts than those outlined in Vladivostok were shared by Brzezinski, Aaron, and Vice President Walter Mondale.

There essentially were two concerns: ICBM vulnerability and Soviet strategic thinking. The current SALT approach placed limits on the number of delivery vehicles that could be MIRVed, but it placed no limit on the number of MIRVs that could be loaded on each delivery vehicle. Many believed that this gave the USSR a distinct advantage in ICBM capability. Soviet ICBMs were larger than U.S. ICBMs and therefore could carry more warheads. In the overall strategic balance the U.S. and USSR may have had rough equality. In head-to-head comparisons of ICBMs, however, the USSR had a distinct advantage in overall delivery vehicles and an even larger advantage in the number of warheads that could be delivered by ICBMs. ICBMs were often considered first-strike weapons. Accurate and loaded with MIRVs, they might give the USSR the ability to launch a first strike that could destroy enough U.S. weapons and command and control facilities to render a U.S. second strike weak enough to produce only "acceptable" losses for the USSR. This vulnerability of U.S. ICBMs was Brown's major concern.[11]

This was related to the second issue. What was the basis for Soviet nuclear strategy? How did the USSR view deterrence? Within the administration it was assumed that the Soviet leadership believed in mutual deterrence, but there were doubts about the future in the eyes of Brown, Brzezinski, Aaron, and Mondale. Leadership changes would occur within the USSR. The next leadership might not be as certain that mutual deterrence was the best policy. If the USSR did gain a serious edge in deployable ICBM warheads, enough to place a U.S. retaliatory strike in doubt, would the next Soviet leadership still believe that a first strike would be foolish, even suicidal? In a sense, the question was whether U.S. ICBM vulnerability would lead to a change in Soviet doctrine.[12]

For these reasons, Mondale, Brown, Brzezinski, and Aaron all saw deep cuts as the best option for furthering U.S. interests within the SALT II negotiations. It was a way of slashing into the growing Soviet ICBM force, and solving the problem of U.S. ICBM vulnerability. This group also felt uncomfortable with the idea of completing the Ford-Kissinger negotiations. For strategic and political reasons they wanted something new, something bold. Vance and Warnke, however, were skeptical of the deep cuts idea. They felt that reductions in both the

U.S. and USSR arsenal were a more long-term goal. For now, the U.S. should focus on sealing the deal begun at Vladivostok and then move on to deep cuts for SALT III.[13]

The first SCC meeting considering SALT was held on 3 February 1977. Carter had opened the meeting, turned it over to Brzezinski, and then left. Brzezinski had suggested Carter use such a formality to ensure that everyone understood that Brzezinski was acting as the president's process manager, not as another principal adviser. Nothing was settled at the meeting, but the discussion centered on two possibilities: Vladivostok-based options and deeper reductions. The study of these options fell to the SALT Working Group, primarily Slocombe, Hyland, and Gelb. The advisory process at this point was the classic hierarchical interagency process. Working-level representatives of the State Department (Gelb), the DOD (Slocombe), and the NSC staff (Hyland) sweated the details in preparation for SCC meetings during which their efforts were hashed out at the senior level by Vance (State), Brown (Defense), and Brzezinski (NSC staff).[14]

Presidential Choice

Political Strategy

Carter's leadership style naturally led him to become deeply involved in the process. In particular, nuclear weaponry was an issue that Carter felt strongly about. This leadership style combined with Carter's political strategies for the issue pushed him toward perhaps more involvement than usual. Relations with the USSR were a high-profile subject. Concluding a SALT II agreement was the centerpiece of Carter's détente policies. In a 1975 autobiography, Carter mentioned an "ultimate goal" for arms control of "elimination of nuclear capability among all nations." He had mentioned nuclear disarmament in his inaugural address, and felt that SALT should not be negotiated in terms of arms "limitations," but rather arms reductions. Carter made it clear to everyone in the administration that these were not simply campaign slogans. The point here is not that Carter was thinking about any unilateral reductions. He was, however, predisposed to doing more than just incremental limitations to nuclear arsenals or management of the arms race. This was more than just a way to show the American people that electing Jimmy Carter was, in fact, a break with the past. Hyland called Carter's commitment to something more than just the business-as-usual approach to arms control an issue of "character" for Carter; simply signing an agreement based on the Ford-Kissinger work might have seemed to Carter "an admission of failure."[15]

During this period, a major influence on Carter's thinking was Senator Jackson. Jackson and Carter met on 4 February. Jackson made it clear that he was disappointed with the Vladivostok Accords, that the administration must look for deeper cuts in the Soviet arsenal. Jackson's argument was similar to Brown's. The current policy of limiting strategic delivery launchers only allowed the USSR to gain an advantage in deployable warheads. This made U.S. ICBMs vulnerable. Jackson outlined his argument in a twenty-three-page memo to Carter on 15 February (co-written by Jackson aide Richard Perle). Carter had asked for the memo following their discussion. He passed it out to his senior advisers and asked them to spread it around the bureaucracy. He also referred back to the memo from time to time during the SALT negotiations to make sure that he kept Jackson's perspective in mind.[16]

Management Strategy

At an SCC meeting on 10 March, little was accomplished that altered the decision process. The bureaucratic order of battle was simply reinforced. Brown and the JCS urged deep cuts, while Vance and Warnke argued for a continuation of the old approach based on Vladivostok. Ultimately, the issue was settled at a 19 March, secret Saturday morning meeting. Initially, this was scheduled as an SCC meeting, but to the surprise of some attendees, the president arrived and steered the discussion toward the idea of deep reductions. The meeting began with the usual debate over the three original options of PRM-2, modified as they were by this time, but Carter and Brown pushed the meeting toward a consensus. In the end, over the objections of Vance, it was Carter who wanted the bold proposal —deep cuts and an abandonment of the agreements made at Vladivostok.[17]

For the purposes of this study the content of the proposal is not crucial.[18] The real significance of this meeting is the way it changed the decision process. This meeting included the president, Mondale, Vance, Brown, General George Brown of the JCS, Director of Central Intelligence Admiral Stansfield Turner, and Brzezinski, without deputies or support staff. [19] Here, the principals essentially overruled the efforts of the bureaucracy and chose to go in a new direction. By unexpectedly coming to an SCC meeting, Carter had streamlined the NSC process and pushed the principals into making a final decision.

The results of this meeting, even its existence, were kept quiet within the administration. In background conversations with reporters, those involved in that decision claimed they closed ranks to prevent leaks of the new policy and to prevent the decision from sparking a large bureaucratic battle.[20] Following this meeting, officials who had been previously involved in the SALT decision process but were not present at the 19 March meeting could be divided into two categories: those who were told of the outcome of the meeting and were surprised at Carter's decisive entry into the process and those who were unaware of both the meeting and the change in policy it produced. Here was a case in which the interagency process was bypassed. Not only had the senior officials grabbed control of the policy, but they deliberately worked to keep the lower levels of the interagency process unaware of the decisions that had been made.

The secrecy was maintained through Vance's trip to Moscow in late March. Carter and Brezhnev had maintained a correspondence since before the election. Brezhnev had made it clear that he saw the Vladivostok Accords as the basis for SALT II. Carter had agreed, but had also hinted at the idea of deeper cuts in these letters and through the USSR Ambassador to the U.S., Anatoly Dobrinin. Though the Soviets had a clue which direction the U.S. would take, the vast majority of the Carter administration did not. Hyland was charged with producing a formal proposal under the supervision of Aaron. This meant that the proposal Vance brought to Moscow was created not by the interagency process or the negotiating team, but by the NSC staff. Hyland accompanied Vance to Moscow and was assigned the unenviable task of making sure the other members of the team—Gelb, Slocombe, and Rowny—did not find out the detailed contents of the proposal.[21] In an organizational sense, the NSC had the job of keeping the State Department, DOD, and the Joint Chiefs uninformed.

Vance actually had a fallback position to propose in case the USSR rejected the deep cuts proposal as expected. At the regularly scheduled NSC meeting on 22 March, Vance made his case that he should be allowed to offer a Vladivostok-based option. Carter gave Vance the green light for this, but reminded him to make it clear to the USSR that he supported the deep cuts option. This option became known as the "deferral" option.[22]

The deep cuts proposals were swiftly rejected by the USSR. The announcement on 30 March of the Soviet response did not score the Carter administration political points for trying something worthy. Instead, it was perceived as a poor way to kick off the new administration's Soviet policy. The Soviets held to the argument that they had made all along—SALT II should be based on the Vladivostok Accords. Reductions were possible in the future, but only after firm limits had been ironed out.[23]

Following the failure in March, U.S. policy and process on SALT significantly changed. The policy changes were obvious. If the U.S. wanted some type of agreement, it would have to start with Vladivostok as the baseline and move from there. In terms of process, the NSC staff took a greater role in the routine staffing of ideas from the Geneva negotiations and in directing those negotiations. Since the new policy was essentially the policy that Vance and Warnke had supported all along, their roles were elevated. The strongest proponents of the deep cuts ideas, the DOD and the JCS, saw their roles diminish. If the bureaucratic battle had been Brown versus Vance and Warnke, the USSR had settled the issue temporarily by refusing the deep cuts idea. Carter took on a larger role on a routine basis as was his tendency. This would remain the administration's standard policy and process through the SALT II negotiations as they dragged on for two more years until a treaty was produced in June of 1979.[24] In many ways, the new approach to SALT, both policy and process, was a slightly refracted image of the Nixon-Ford-Kissinger approach.

The pattern of decision making within the administration confirms the hypotheses of the evolution model. Participation in the decision was narrowed, informality took over the process, and in the end the interagency process was avoided for the sake of secrecy. Carter's intervention in the process was the catalyst for these changes. The key reason why the pattern of decision making changed here may be economy related to political pressures. Carter's hope for deep cuts was blocked by his own interagency process, which focused on Vladivostok-based options. He then seized the process and implemented the policy option he preferred on the timetable required for the next round of SALT. This case shows a clear confluence between the changes in the decision process and Carter's leadership tendencies, almost a pure version of the evolution model.

DECISIONS ON NUCLEAR STRATEGY: PRESIDENTIAL DIRECTIVE 59

Decision making on nuclear strategy in the Carter administration began early in 1977 and culminated with the signing and public announcement of Presidential Directive 59 (PD-59) in August of 1980. What had started out within the interagency process eventually was isolated within the NSC staff. As the prime mover of policy that would refine U.S. nuclear targeting policy, Brzezinski created a consensus on the need for a public statement of U.S. strategic developments. The creation of PD-59 illustrated Brzezinski's successful conversion of

Carter from opponent to advocate of limited nuclear war. The conversion is related to political pressures for Carter. Carter's reelection needs led to this new mind-set. The state department, which opposed the idea, was kept unaware of the policy change. Its expected opposition might have delayed the decision and jeopardized the delicate political timing of the reelection campaign.

The International and Domestic Political Environment

Since the development of atomic and nuclear weaponry, U.S. nuclear employment policy has undergone a number of revisions. By implementing its overall policy of flexible response, the Kennedy administration created the basic strategic framework that endured for the remainder of the cold war and beyond. Flexible response emphasized targeting USSR military assets in response to Soviet provocations in an effort to avoid an all-out nuclear retaliatory policy that would simply obliterate the USSR. Such a policy had been in place during the Eisenhower years. Eisenhower's New Look nuclear policy threatened the USSR with a "massive retaliation" if the Soviets took aggressive actions that provoked the U.S. The new targeting policy, counterforce, targeted Soviet military assets, both nuclear and conventional. It was a deterrent based on threatening what, in U.S. eyes, the Soviets valued most, their capability to fight a nuclear war. This new policy lent credibility to the U.S. nuclear threat by communicating to the Soviets that they could not gain anything from the use of nuclear weapons. The U.S. could match them at any level of violence. In theory, it gave the president the ability to fight a limited nuclear war, allowing the U.S. to respond in a controlled and politically meaningful way if deterrence failed. Ending a war short of complete destruction of both sides was now a goal. [25]

From the Kennedy administration forward strategic nuclear policy was continuously refined to develop policy and operational systems to meet the goals of fighting a limited nuclear war. Flexible response as applied to nuclear war became known as *warfighting*. Opponents of warfighting supported a policy of assured destruction or mutual assured destruction (MAD). Assured destruction rested on the notion that the best deterrent possible was the older reliance on the threat of massive retaliatory strikes in response to a Soviet nuclear strike. To these analysts flexible response had the effect of making nuclear war less dangerous, less of a cataclysm, by giving both sides the ability to limit the damage of a nuclear war. If nuclear war was less horrible, the argument stated, it was more likely. Any weakening of deterrence in this manner was a mistake. The strongest deterrent would be one in which nuclear war remained suicide for anyone who might start it. Assured destruction advocates fundamentally doubted the ability of the U.S. and USSR to wage a limited nuclear war. What might begin as limited strikes would end with massive destruction and the collapse of both societies. Warfighting, therefore, was an illusion that could lead policy makers, confident in their ability to fight a nuclear war, into inadvertently committing suicide.[26]

Although flexible response provided the basis for U.S. nuclear weapons policy, the vast majority of Americans assumed that assured destruction was official U.S. policy. Presidents, senators, representatives, and senior cabinet officials often spoke as if assured destruction was U.S. policy, and they often differentiated that policy from the Soviets' warfighting stance. Much of this misperception can be explained as the result of successive presidents' unwillingness to explicitly say that they had directed the U.S. military to prepare to fight a nuclear war. Presidents emphasized deterrence and left it up to their secretaries of defense to explain the warfighting aspects of the policy.[27]

In spite of this, refinement of flexible response continued. The Nixon administration, in 1970, began to review the Kennedy guidelines for nuclear war. Studies within the Department of Defense and NSC staff ultimately produced National Security Decision Memorandum 242 (NSDM-242), which provided guidance for the Pentagon's nuclear strategy in 1974 and was incorporated into SIOP-5 in January of 1976. The policy was dubbed limited nuclear options (LNOs) or the Schlesinger Doctrine after Secretary of Defense James Schlesinger. The policy reemphasized the counterforce nature of targeting, gave escalation control to the National Command Authority (NCA), and designated targets to be avoided during a nuclear strike.[28] This was merely the latest update of the U.S. policy of flexible response. It was this policy that was in place when the Carter administration assumed responsibility for the development of U.S. nuclear strategy.

The domestic politics of this issue were nearly nonexistent in 1977 when the policy process began. Only in 1980, when Carter faced a difficult reelection campaign against a hawkish Reagan-Bush team, did Carter's policy on nuclear weapons become a method for Carter to show his credentials as a cold warrior. This will be discussed below in the context of Carter's political strategy.

The Standard Interagency Process

Review of U.S. nuclear strategy began within the formal interagency process. PRM-10, entitled "Comprehensive Net Assessment and Military Strategy and Force Posture Review," was issued on 18 February 1977.[29] PRM-10 is a useful illustration of one of the dilemmas of the interagency process. Presidents want a full range of opinions from the bureaucracies, but which agency will be chosen to direct the study and write the report that eventually comes to the president? Initially, the SCC was given the task of staffing out PRM-10. The State and Defense departments argued against this and won. Each department felt it should be in charge; State emphasized its responsibility for developing foreign policy, while Defense reiterated its role in developing military policy.

The solution was to divide the study into two parts, one part under the PRC and one under the SCC. The SCC examined overall strategic aspects of U.S. national security that included a general threat assessment and an analysis of global military, technological, economic, and political trends. The other half of the study was undertaken within the auspices of the PRC; the lead agency was the Department of Defense. This study focused more specifically on military strategy and force structure, including nuclear weapons.[30]

The debates revealed deep disagreements over the nature of U.S. nuclear strategy and even the wisdom of having a discussion of targeting doctrine and force development needs. The results of the review reflect the deep divisions between the participants. The final report reflected the disagreements over doctrine and force posture. No consensus was reached. PRM-10 made no real recommendations for U.S. nuclear strategy; it simply revisited the issue from the ground up.[31]

Organizational Dynamics

The SCC considered the issue at meetings on 7 July and 24 August 1977.[32] The fact that this was discussed within the purview of the SCC is important. The initial argument over what department would be lead agency had been settled by splitting the study between the PRC and SCC. However, when the issue of military and nuclear strategy was considered at the principals level it was done within the SCC. In effect, the PRC was given responsibility for the staff work, while the ultimate power to make a recommendation to the president stayed within the hands of Brzezinski and the NSC staff.

At this level of decision making the individual views of the principals become important. A clear division existed between those who believed in assured destruction as the guiding principle of nuclear strategy and those who favored warfighting. Carter seemed to lean in the direction of assured destruction. He had high hopes for eventual nuclear disarmament, had questioned the JCS on the potentials of a finite deterrence force, and criticized advocates of limited nuclear war. Vance and Warnke represented the State Department position, which clearly favored an assured destruction posture. Brown's view is a bit harder to assess. It seems he initially leaned in the direction of assured destruction, but eventually became a believer in the necessity of a warfighting posture.[33]

Brzezinski and Brown were the keys to maintaining and refining the U.S. warfighting doctrine, and Brown was the prime mover in developing the Pentagon's policy for nuclear doctrine. However, it was Brzezinski who worked on changing Carter's views on nuclear weapons. Brzezinski was not in favor of pure assured destruction–based policy, nor was he accepting of ideas that were simply extensions of the Nixon-Schlesinger policy of Limited Nuclear Options. Brzezinski's dissatisfaction could be summed up by his analyses of two issues. As stated above, he was uncertain if the USSR believed in mutual deterrence. Their weapons might be designed for use in fighting wars when the leadership decided that war was the best method of achieving current political objectives.[34] If true, then the only real deterrent would be to convince the USSR that it cannot achieve its political objectives through the use of nuclear weapons. The threat of retaliation, as in assured destruction, would not be enough. The U.S. needed to continue to develop its capability to fight a nuclear war.

Brzezinski also became more convinced that the U.S. did not have the capability, especially in terms of Command, Control, Communications, and Intelligence (C3I), to actually fight a limited nuclear war, even one based on the current nuclear war plans. He had attempted to encourage Brown to take an interest in these issues as early as March of 1977. He requested from Brown several memoranda outlining U.S. policy on nuclear strategic issues: a succinct statement of nuclear war doctrine, a brief statement of procedures for conducting nuclear war beyond the initial stage, and a statement of U.S. political-military objectives in a limited nuclear war.[35] Clearly, Brzezinski was searching for allies. If Brown could be persuaded to see the wisdom of warfighting and the folly of assured destruction policies, then Brzezinski would have a chance to convince Carter of the same.

Presidential Directive 18 (PD-18), entitled "U.S. National Strategy," the follow-up to PRM-10, was issued on 24 August 1977. It reflected the division within the administration. U.S. nuclear strategy would remain based on the Schlesinger Doctrine, the Nixon-era NSDM-242, pending further review. The directive, written by the NSC staff, called for the Pentagon to review U.S. nuclear policy in six areas: nuclear targeting, the definition of strategic weapons, the Triad concept, counterforce needs, civil defense, and the "interrelationships with the allies at the level of strategic weaponry." Other portions of the directive asked the defense department to develop limited nuclear responses and to prepare for the maintenance of a strategic reserve force, which would be withheld in an initial nuclear exchange, for use if the nuclear war became a protracted conflict.[36]

These last points attest to Brzezinski's power to write presidential directives within the NSC staff that would be sent to the president without review by the other agencies. PD-18 respected the dispute within the administration, but the studies it requested were analyses of how to increase U.S. capabilities to fight a limited nuclear war. It even stated that one of the goals of U.S. nuclear doctrine should be to end a nuclear war on terms favorable to the U.S.[37] This went beyond the Schlesinger Doctrine, and certainly did not fit the notions of assured destruction that existed within the state department. Most importantly, Carter was allowing the bureaucracy to examine ways to fight nuclear war. He could have rejected such studies, and instead ordered the bureaucracy to examine ways of creating a finite deterrent force, a minimum force that could serve only as a second-strike retaliatory force. Carter's signature on PD-18 reveals Brzezinski's behind-the-scenes efforts to change Carter's thinking. His efforts continued.

The debate over nuclear strategy then moved out of the interagency process and into the DOD with a Nuclear Targeting Policy Review (NTPR). The NTPR considered two tracks: nuclear targeting and the strategic reserve force. The first part of the study was completed in December of 1978. The second part seems not to have been completed. Based on the assumption that the USSR was increasing its capability to fight a nuclear war, the NTPR developed a more detailed strategy for fighting a limited nuclear war. It considered issues such as greater targeting flexibility, options designed to meet specific political goals, withholding of a reserve nuclear force, targeting Soviet conventional forces, more survivable C3I, and the ability to fight a nuclear war for an extended time period. Reportedly, officials of the Pentagon and the NSC staff saw the study as a "revolution" in U.S. nuclear strategy.[38]

If this was a revolution, Brzezinski was the revolutionary. He had converted Brown to his cause, and Brown soon became the chief spokesman for the administration's refinement of warfighting. Supporters of assured destruction in the State and Defense departments were unhappy with the tone of the report. The JCS were unhappy with what they felt were new demands for ever more capability to fight a limited nuclear war that ignored the fact that the U.S. did not have the capability to meet even the old demands.[39] The opposition to these ideas accounts for the long delay between the completion of the NTPR (December 1978) and the creation of PD-59 in July of 1980.

Brzezinski had hoped to create a presidential directive codifying the results of the NTPR. Carter opposed the idea. Reportedly, Carter still had doubts about the wisdom of policies other than assured destruction. Even after the Pentagon had announced a change in U.S. nuclear strategy, revealing the "Countervailing Strategy" in Brown's annual reports to Congress of 1979 and 1980,[40] officials in the White House argued that they had not approved the policy. Brown was against moving forward on a presidential directive. Once he accepted the ideas within the NTPR, he felt revealing them in the annual reports was enough. He worried that an official policy statement from the White House would be too controversial and would add problems to the already significant difficulties of deploying the MX ICBM. Essentially, he understood that the political arena would treat White House pronouncements very differently than Pentagon statements. Vance was also against the PD. It would only interfere with the SALT negotiations, which remained his highest priority.[41]

Brzezinski was outnumbered in this decision-making environment. Reportedly, he felt that if he tried to push a PD at this point it would just result in an ugly bureaucratic war that would settle nothing, and, worse, would most likely leak to the public. By 1980, Brown had come significantly closer to Brzezinski's way of thinking. It was in May of 1979, according to Brzezinski, when Brown agreed that a presidential directive was necessary. Vance at this point was still in the loop concerning the issue. The general changes in U.S. nuclear strategy as embodied in the Countervailing Strategy were still topics of discussion at NSC meetings; Vance received copies of correspondence between Brzezinski and Brown on the issue.[42] His opposition to these ideas continued.

Presidential Choice and Political Strategy

Carter was the most important target of Brzezinski's efforts, efforts that did not succeed until the political demands of reelection led Carter to reassess his views. Since the early days of the administration Brzezinski had urged Carter to become familiar with U.S. nuclear war plans. Carter was given a detailed look at the SIOP before the inauguration and continued to study it from time to time. He was the first president to ride in the National Emergency Airborne Command Post (NEACP) that would theoretically allow the president to command U.S. nuclear forces from inside an airplane, miles above the U.S. in the middle of a nuclear war. The more Carter learned about U.S. war plans, the more dissatisfied he was. His engineer's mind sweated the technical details, particularly concerning command and control. He even asked Brzezinski to simulate the evacuation of the president from the White House to the NEACP, which would be waiting at Andrews Air Force Base.[43]

In 1978 the fruits of this effort began to appear in the form of a series of presidential directives, written by the NSC staff, signed by the president, and not scrutinized through the usual interagency process. They were not related to any specific PRM study. PD-41 of 1978, PD-53 of 15 November 1979, PD-57 of 3 March 1980, and PD-58 of 30 June 1980, all added to the U.S. ability to carry out its nuclear warfighting strategy.[44] These PDs can be seen as Brzezinski's way of getting the president acclimated to ideas that he was reluctant to accept. As a child is coaxed into learning to swim by first dipping a foot, then a leg, then standing up to his waist in the water before he dunks his head, these PDs slowly submerged the president into the sea of nuclear strategy.

The drafting of PD-59 illustrates the final shift in Carter's thinking and the complete evolution of the decision-making process. In early 1980, Brzezinski gave his military assistant Lt. General William Odom the green light to begin drafting a presidential directive on nuclear strategy.[45] The timing was political in nature. With Brown on board, and an election year underway, the internal and external political mix was right for the PD. Events such as the revolution in Iran, the seizure of hostages in November of 1979, and the Soviet invasion of Afghanistan all called for a tougher response from Carter. The president had withdrawn SALT II from Senate consideration on 3 January 1980, and had committed the U.S. to defending the sources of U.S. oil in the Persian Gulf from outside intervention with force if necessary. The state of the union enunciation of what became known as the Carter Doctrine illustrated Carter's new attitude. Carter had stated in an interview that the invasion of Afghanistan "has made a more dramatic change in my opinion of what the Soviets' ultimate goals are than anything they've done in the previous time I've been in office."[46] Carter's views of the USSR had been severely changed. With Brown's backing, Brzezinski would be able to take advantage of this development.

In mid-May, a draft PD was submitted to Carter for his signature. Carter signed PD-59 on 25 July 1980. It developed more extensive plans for the U.S. to fight limited nuclear war, including conflicts that might last for several months. While this was not a huge change from previous doctrines, the misperception over U.S. strategic policy led to immediate and heated controversy. Those who believed that U.S. nuclear policy had been based on assured destruction viewed it as a radical departure in U.S. nuclear strategy. The administration, however, portrayed it simply as the next step in refining a decades-old U.S. policy based on the ability to fight a nuclear war.[47]

The existence and content of PD-59 was leaked to the press on 5 August 1980. This fact clearly reveals the motivation behind Carter's approval of the PD. The Democratic Convention was to begin on Monday, August 11, six days after PD-59 became public. The press and country had a week to digest and debate the news. Both the swiftness with which the policy was made in 1980 and the leak of the information before the convention were guided by political pressures. Initially, Brown was to reveal PD-59 to the public in a speech at the Naval War College on August 20. Brown still gave the speech, but instead of introducing the policy, Brown defended it.[48]

Presidential Choice and Management Strategy

What is significant at this point is not what happened, but what did not happen. The State Department had not been involved in the drafting process, and this became quite a controversy when the existence and contents (in part) of PD-59 were detailed in the morning editions of the *New York Times* and *Washington Post* on 6 August 1980. Clearly, there was a deliberate leak of the information and the speculation is that Brzezinski was the one who provided the information.[49] Logic also suggests that this is what happened.

Edmund Muskie had replaced Cyrus Vance as secretary of state on 8 May. Vance had submitted his resignation following the hostage rescue mission in April. He had been against such a rescue mission from the beginning of the hostage crisis, and was prompted to resign by the fact that the decision to launch the mission had been taken when he was on vacation.[50] Deliberately avoiding the secretary of state if he might oppose a specific policy seemed to be a trend in the last year of the Carter administration. Muskie stated that he did not learn of the existence of PD-59 until the Muskie-Brown-Brzezinski (MBB) meeting of August 5, the same day that the information was leaked to the press.[51]

In the controversy that followed, details of the decision-making process were revealed.[52] All reports describe a process in which the State Department had been deliberately excluded from the decision-making process since approximately April of 1979. State Department records released at the time showed three interagency meetings in April and none following after this point. Other

State Department officials claim that their attempts to get involved in the decision process were blocked. Vance stated that he had discussed it with Brzezinski and Brown and understood the ideas behind the changes. However, these details support the notion that Brzezinski pulled the issue out of the interagency process and simply worked on changing the minds of Carter and Brown.

Once the draft of PD-59 had been given to Carter in May, Carter met with Brzezinski and Brown to discuss the draft. Between that point and Carter's approval of PD-59, five MBB meetings were held (11 June and 3, 17, 24, and 31 July). Nuclear strategy was not a topic of discussion. The written agendas for these MBB meetings did not include the subject of nuclear weapons strategy.[53] However, the agenda for the 5 August MBB meeting lists "Item 3 PD-59." The line on the agenda is handwritten, added to the agenda after it had been typed.[54] PD-59 was added to the agenda because Brown wanted to discuss it at the meeting. In a memo from Odom to Brzezinski, dated 5 August, Odom remarks that he had been told by Slocombe that Brown would address PD-59 at the MBB meeting. The memo provides evidence that Muskie was unaware of the existence of PD-59; Odom comments in the memo, "The sooner you let Muskie know the better."[55] 5 August became a deadline of sorts. The policy was leaked to newspapers that same day.

Carter's role in excluding Muskie is confirmed by the FFPB meeting of 25 July, the day PD-59 was signed. During this meeting, one week before PD-59 would become public, Muskie was not informed of the changes to come in nuclear strategy. Not only were Brzezinski and Brown ready to shut Muskie out of this decision process, but the president was a willing accomplice. Another telling indication of the exclusion of the State Department can be found in a comparison of the distribution lists for various presidential directives. Each presidential directive lists the officials who will receive a copy. The list for PD-18, the administration's first cut at dealing with nuclear doctrine issues, was distributed to the vice president, the secretaries of state and defense, the director of the Office of Management and Budget, the ANSA, the director of the Arms Control and Disarmament Agency, the chairman of the Joint Chiefs of Staff, and the director of Central Intelligence. PD-59, however, was distributed only to the vice president, secretary of defense, ANSA, and chairman of the Joint Chiefs of Staff.[56]

Carter had narrowed the decision-making process significantly. Brzezinski and Brown were the voices that mattered on this issue, voices who had given advice to Carter informally. Even the informal FFPB and VBB sessions were bypassed. They were not part of the formal NSC interagency system, but they were interagency in nature. The Carter process had evolved away from its original design.

Scholars of the policy process and experienced national security officials would judge the exclusion of the secretary of state as unfortunate, but not unusual. The VBB/MBB/FFPB were treated as too formal and too interagency in scope for discussions of nuclear strategy. Carter faced a dilemma. One of his senior advisers had rejected a policy that he was slowly coming to accept. He could have continued to try to change Vance's mind or to give Vance an ultimatum to accept the policy or resign. The former was deemed as unrealistic, and the latter might have led to premature leaks of the policy. He chose to exclude that adviser and his department from the deliberations.

Underneath both policy and process changes was Carter's need to illustrate his toughness during an election year as he faced the political pressures of the election campaign and an opponent who had consistently portrayed him as soft on the USSR. This illustrates the basic points of this study. Carter and Brzezinski had learned who would be the obstacles to a change in nuclear policy. The State Department believed in assured destruction and would put up a fight if the administration tried to reemphasize warfighting. In news reports administration officials referred to the differences of opinion on nuclear strategy within the administration as "profound."[57]

Those obstacles would reveal themselves in the form of extended bureaucratic conflict if the interagency process on nuclear strategy were allowed to continue. The feud between Vance and Brzezinski had already become standard copy for the nation's newspapers and newsmagazines at this point. Articles had already been written by mid-summer about a growing Muskie-Brzezinski feud.[58] It was the common storyline that explained the hesitancy, inconsistency, and change within Carter's national security policy. A major blowup over nuclear strategy would simply throw gasoline onto the fire. It would slow down the process, possibly preventing Carter from taking decisive action on the issue before the democratic convention. Given that conventions are for the party faithful who are usually more to the left for Democrats and more to the right for Republicans than the average voter, the convention might have pulled Carter to the left during an election year in which the nation was pulling to the right. PD-59 would help Carter position himself to the right of the Democratic Party on foreign policy, national security, and defense issues. Truly this seems to be a tactical move. Given that Carter, in his memoirs, criticizes those who believe in limited nuclear war, his signature on PD-59 seems to represent his immediate political needs during 1980, rather than a growing belief in the potential for fighting a limited nuclear war.[59] For the sake of economy, Carter could not afford a lengthy interagency debate that would slow down the process, so he bypassed the process.

CONCLUSIONS

The decision-making processes that led to the SALT II Deep Cuts proposal of March 1977 and that generated PD-59 illustrate narrowing, an increase in informality and ad hoc processes, and both streamlining and bypassing of the interagency system. Taken together these changes add up to the three concurrent structures. The formal interagency process of the NSC/SCC/PRC was never abandoned during the administration's time in office. However, it was supplemented with the informal VBB/FFPB. The March 1977 decisions occurred before this informal system was functioning; however, these committees became regular venues for discussions of SALT II thereafter. The two decisions provide evidence for the evolution of the confidence system. In 1977, Vance and Brzezinski were equals. The inclusion of the deferral option is the best example. By 1980, Carter had come to rely on Brzezinski as first among equals. Other advisers' roles suffered by comparison. Carter's leadership style allowed the confidence structure to carry significant weight here, even pushing aside the formal and informal processes in the case of PD-59. A deeply involved president comfortable with immersion in the policy details will be quick to see the rocky path to interagency consensus as a nuisance and hindrance to swift decisions. Carter's confidence allowed him to push the other structures aside, rely on Brzezinski almost exclusively, and make decisions that he believed were the correct ones. The parallels to Nixon and Kissinger are obvious. In both cases, presidents confident in their abilities to make the best decisions moved beyond their advisory machinery when it did not come to the same conclusions.

Ultimately, these case studies of the Carter administration emphasize the power of the president in national security. The decision-making process was designed to serve Carter's needs. When the process or people participating in that process no longer served those needs well, the roles were reduced or they were excluded from the process. The president's power to manage the process, the key element of the presidential management model, is manifest here. The standard interpretations of the Carter administration, as described in the previous chapter, focus on the changes in the administration's policies, or Carter's process of learning about the world. An analysis of the policy process adds irony to the story of the administration's national security policy. In both these case studies, Carter's policies and decision-making processes eventually resembled the policies and processes of the administration that came before him.[60] Carter had come to power heavily critical of Kissinger's role as the "Lone Ranger" of U.S. national security. By 1980, however, Brzezinski had assumed a similar role. He had the president's ear, complete access to the president, and the ability to shut the secretary of state out of the policy process. The evolution of Carter's process had brought him full circle. His initial instincts led him to design a system that could be the antithesis of the Nixon-Kissinger centralization. The institutional forces, described by the governmental politics and new institutionalism models, combined with his needs in office, as embodied in the principles of economy, learning, and political pressure, pushed him toward the Nixon-Kissinger design.

As stated earlier, Carter's thinking on policy went through a major evolution from 1977 to 1980. There was also an equally powerful evolution in Carter's thinking on the nature of decision making. This is related to the learning principle. Carter had entered office stating that he wished to make the best decisions possible, not decisions based on political considerations. These purely analytical decisions would be based on an interagency process capped by a cabinet of great minds who would analyze the problem and make the right decision. However, in both cases described above, the decision-making process began to change when it did not produce the policies that Carter or an important senior adviser or advisers favored. Here the interagency process can be seen as an audition. The best roles in the national security policy play are for advisers who earn the president's confidence and trust. Senior advisers share their ideas and analyses with the president as part of the day-to-day decision-making process within the NSC system. Eventually, the president gets to know them, their ideas, and their strengths and weaknesses well enough to know which advisers will be the most useful to him in specific situations or in general. He will base his modifications to the policy process on this new knowledge. Carter learned, given the new tensions between the U.S. and USSR and the tough campaign rhetoric of Ronald Reagan, that Brzezinski, not Vance, was his most useful adviser. Vance's power declined and Brzezinski evolved into a less muscular Kissinger.

Carter's leadership style was a key element of these changes. He was prepared to change his policy priorities and processes as he learned more about his responsibilities as president, the U.S. role in a changing world, and his political needs. He had stated that he would be his own secretary of state; he would make national security decisions. He would not be beholden to the bureaucracy and Washington's business as usual. He had run his campaign as an outsider and wanted the flexibility to govern as an outsider. When he made a decision on an issue, he expected the rest of the government to respond. He discovered that his own executive branch could be an obstacle to his policies; sometimes he needed to make an end run around his own national security machinery.

Ultimately, the development of Carter's policies on arms control and nuclear strategy provides a lesson about learning. Of the three principles that identify the causes of the evolution in decision making, learning seems to be the most important in Carter's case. First, Carter learned more about his political needs as president. He may have learned that it is impossible to take the politics out of government. He may be the chief executive of the U.S., but he does more than execute policy. He is also chief diplomat, party leader, administrative chief, legislative leader, commander-in-chief, popular leader, and a politician seeking to make his impact on the nation and win the next election. Carter learned that once the election is over, he cannot simply stop being a politician. He has political needs, and these needs often become the needs of the administration, or the needs of the "presidential branch" of government, the EOP and the White House Office (WHO).

Second, Carter learned which advisers and processes could best serve those political needs. It is useful to point out the distinctions between the needs of organizations or individual officials within the executive branch and the needs of the president. When Carter's presidential needs conflicted with the needs of different agencies or different officials, Carter found a method of tinkering with the decision-making process to factor out those influences or ideas. In order to do this Carter first needed to understand which advisers and agencies would further his agenda and which might act as spoilers and try to block it. He could then adjust the decision-making process to produce the desired policy outcome. In sum, Carter had specific policy needs at different times and modified the decision-making process to generate, as quickly and efficiently as possible, policies that served those needs. The most important modification is in the way Carter used his advisers. The interagency process had served one of its subtle roles— letting the president get to know his advisers. If the interagency process is seen as an audition, then Brzezinski won the part.

Chapter Five

THE REAGAN ADMINISTRATION: A TALE OF EXECUTIVE BRANCH GRIDLOCK

SECRETARY OF STATE GEORGE SHULTZ WAS ONCE QUOTED BY an aide about making arms control policy during the Reagan years as saying that he had "been around this city a lot in government but he'd never seen anything as intense and vicious as that." The feuds within the Reagan administration were legendary. Resolving bureaucratic warfare is ultimately the president's responsibility, but President Reagan was reluctant to make the difficult choices necessary to end the infighting. Robert McFarlane, then ANSA, tried to get the president to deal head-on with the issue. The struggle between Shultz and Secretary of Defense Caspar Weinberger crippled administration policy making at the time. McFarlane suggested that Reagan remove either one of these antagonists or accept his resignation; he simply could not mediate between them successfully. Reagan refused to accept any of these options, explaining that "they are both my friends. I don't want to fire either one of them. I know that means you're going to have to work harder."[1]

This example of the tale of Reagan administration decision-making for arms control is a microcosm for policy making on most issues. Deep fissures between senior officials precluded consensus, and the president was often unwilling to take action to create it. In the case of arms control, however, real efforts to end the bureaucratic bloodshed were made. Decision-making adjustments, particularly the rise in power of ANSA William Clark (1982–1983) as detailed in chapter three, illustrate the evolution model. Clark's rise to power, particularly in arms control, is similar to ANSA Zbigniew Brzezinski's ascendance in the Carter administration. However, Reagan's inability and unwillingness to address conflict or hurt the feelings of his friends allowed the White House troika to force Clark out of the ANSA position, demolishing the administration's confidence structure. Without that central figure the National Security Planning Group (NSPG) could not play its role as an informal collegial forum. The decision-making landscape became a battlefield once again; the eventual result was Iran/Contra.

The tale of arms control from 1981 to the fall of 1983 tells a story of what might have been if Reagan had been willing to continue to provide one official with the power to manage the process on his behalf. Details of decision making for arms control illustrate the evolution of the process during 1981–1983. The way in which decision making for arms control and nuclear strategy evolved in the Reagan administration is traced through three case studies: the initial U.S. Strategic Arms Reduction Talks (START) positions given as the Eureka proposals of May 1982, the Build-Down START proposal of October 1983, and the president's 23 March 1983 speech on the Strategic Defense Initiative.

In the case of arms control, a cabinet system based on inclusion of all relevant departments failed to reach consensus on the key issues. During 1982 and 1983, Reagan allowed Clark to take control of the process, centralizing power in his office and ultimately using informal contacts with Congress and complete bypassing of the interagency process to develop an arms control proposal that could satisfy congressional demands. For the decision on strategic defense, senior White House aides created an extremely narrow decision process in an attempt to isolate a policy innovation that represented a significant departure in U.S. nuclear doctrine. They were convinced that if the idea of shifting nuclear strategy to reliance on missile defense rather than on the deterrence of attack through retaliation was placed into the interagency process, it would be crushed by the hardliner-pragmatist feud.

The story of Reagan decision making on arms control highlights the problem of interagency gridlock and the role of domestic political pressures. Political pressures were the key factor in the development of arms control policy. Delay in the administration's strategic arms control proposals and the resulting congressional and public groundswell for a nuclear freeze led to the Eureka proposals of May of 1982. An inability to resolve differences within the administration and between the administration and Congress over strategic modernization and arms control, resulted in an ad hoc process of legislative-executive bargaining that deliberately ignored the intra-administration arguments. The bargaining achieved a compromise in October 1983; the administration accepted into its negotiating stance proposals on a Double Build-Down and a de-MIRVing process in strategic weaponry. Those who supported a shift to strategic defense had also learned about the ineffectiveness of the interagency process. For the sake of economy, and for the sake of protection, they brought the idea straight to the president where they knew it would enjoy a receptive audience, shielding the idea from most senior officials until immediately before the president's speech of 23 March 1983.

THE EUREKA PROPOSALS OF MAY 1982

The decision process that led to the Reagan administration's first START proposal provides a stark illustration of why presidents manipulate their decision-making processes from time to time. Interagency gridlock on arms control placed the administration under severe political pressure. Over a year had passed since the Reagan team assumed power, and it had yet to initiate talks on strategic arms control with the USSR. In the absence of presidential leadership, the American public and Congress developed their own plans for arms control in the form of a nuclear freeze. Reagan was faced with a dilemma. The political environment demanded some form of arms control, but the ideas in vogue at the time were antithetical to the administration's preferences. However, the standard interagency process seemed incapable of coming up with alternatives. The solution for the president was to allow the NSC staff to push the interagency process harder and to bypass that process completely when necessary. The Eureka proposals represent a compromise designed by the NSC staff outside of the interagency process.

International and Domestic Political Environment

It would be a vast understatement to suggest that the Reagan administration was never in a hurry to continue strategic arms control. Continuing the negotiations that had resulted in SALT I and II, the main targets for the Committee on the Present Danger's (CPD) attacks on detente and the Carter administration, was far down the list of Reagan administration priorities. Simply put, the administration's view of the U.S.-USSR strategic relationship was based first on an overall assessment of the worldwide balance of power. In its view, that balance of power had tilted decidedly in favor of the USSR during the 1970s. A third wave of Marxism was evident in the loss to Communism of nations such as Angola, Mozambique, Ethiopia, Viet Nam, Cambodia, Laos, and Nicaragua, and in Soviet direct intervention or assistance to Marxist groups in Afghanistan and El Salvador. The U.S. defeat in Viet Nam led to a lack of resolve on the part of both elites and the public in the U.S. when faced with the possibility of using force. This "Viet Nam Syndrome" prevented the U.S. from acting as a superpower, giving the USSR free reign to expand its influence throughout the world. In addition, the decline in U.S. defense spending during the 1970s in a "decade of neglect" had nearly amounted to unilateral disarmament. The CPD, which had essentially moved into the senior levels of the administration, had blasted SALT II from the early days of the Carter administration.[2] SALT II was dead and the administration was not inclined to resurrect it.

Overall, the administration had no desire to mend the tattered fabric of detente. The goal instead was to fight back against growing Soviet power by rolling back the Soviet territorial gains of the 1970s, learning to use force again as a superpower should, and rebuilding U.S. military power.

Two issues held priority over strategic arms control: the Intermediate Nuclear Force (INF) issue, and the strategic modernization program. The deployment of NATO's new missiles in Europe, Pershing IIs and GLCMs, was a response to the modernization of Soviet intermediate range missiles in the early 1970s, in particular the deployment of the mobile SS-20 with three MIRVed warheads. U.S. deployments were based on a two-track policy hammered out by the NATO nations in December of 1979. The first track was deployment. The second track was arms control. If the U.S. could convince the USSR to remove its SS-20s, the U.S. would forego deployment of its new-generation intermediate-range missiles. Eventually this was dubbed the Zero-Zero Option or Zero Option. The Reagan arms control team was busy developing these proposals and never really turned its attention to strategic arms control until after Reagan unveiled the Zero-Zero Option for European nuclear arms control in November of 1981.[3]

In addition, the Reagan administration felt that the USSR had achieved superiority in strategic weaponry during the U.S. "decade of neglect." The U.S. needed to rebuild its defenses before it entered into any arms control with the USSR. On one level, a positive outcome in any negotiation depended on the U.S. being able to negotiate from strength. On another level, it gave the U.S. the ability to forgo the negotiating table and simply compete with the USSR. The priority was placed not on security through arms control, but security through military buildup. This buildup initially called for 8% real growth in the U.S. defense budget and included both conventional and nuclear forces, in particular the deployment of two new strategic systems—the MX missile and the Trident D-5 missile.[4]

The argument that the USSR was winning the strategic arms race often focused specifically on ICBMs. In this context, a "window of vulnerability" had been created by the significant buildup of Soviet MIRVed ICBMs. Two views of this window of vulnerability existed. One is based on the warfighting school of deterrence, while the other has roots in the assured destruction school. At issue here was the question of what the U.S. required of its ICBM force. Neither side considered the triad in its full capacity; SLBMs and strategic bombers were usually ignored in these debates.

The hardliners within the administration, commensurate with their warfighting views of nuclear strategy, believed that the window of vulnerability was caused by the USSR's capability to place U.S. ICBMs at risk of a first strike and the inability of the U.S. to place Soviet ICBMs similarly at risk. The window was really a relative comparison of hard target kill capability. The U.S. was vulnerable because it could not threaten the USSR with a first strike that would knock out significant numbers of Soviet ICBMs. This left the U.S. vulnerable to coercion. It might be self-deterred from taking action against the USSR in recognition of its inferiority in ICBMs.[5] Importantly, the overall throw weight for USSR and U.S. ICBMs—the sum of the payloads of all ICBMs and the true reflection of the potential number of warheads and penetration aids each side could place atop its ICBMs—stood at 8.3 million pounds for the USSR and 2.4 million pounds for the U.S.[6] This was the key issue for the hardliners. The USSR had superiority because the size of its missiles allowed it to fractionate to a much larger degree than the U.S.; it had the capability to add more warheads to its ICBM force and therefore threaten U.S. ICBMs with destruction in a first strike. The core of the USSR ICBM force consisted of the SS-17 with four MIRVs, the SS-18 with ten MIRVs, and the SS-19 with six MIRVs. The mainstay of the U.S. force was the Minuteman III with three MIRVs. The administration sought to close this window of vulnerability by completing deployment of the MX missile, which carried ten MIRVs.

Those who believed in assured destruction, a group including most Democratic and many Republican members of Congress, as well as arms control interest groups and many scholars of strategic policy, saw the window of vulnerability as a function of the survivability of the U.S. ICBM force. The U.S. ability to ride out a Soviet first strike and still launch a retaliatory second strike with its ICBM force was the key to closing the window of vulnerability. In this sense, the issue was not the size of the U.S. ICBM force or its ability to place Soviet ICBMs at risk, but its basing mode. How certain was the U.S. that its silos would provide enough protection for the U.S. ICBMs? If uncertain, what new basing mode could be developed that would provide greater confidence that U.S. ICBMs would survive a Soviet first strike?[7]

Though there was disagreement on the problem, both sides agreed on the solution—the MX. The MX was all things to all people. It had the capability to redress the ICBM balance with its ten warheads per missile. This closed the window of vulnerability from the point of view of those who worried about placing the USSR ICBM force at risk. The Carter administration's decision to deploy the MX in a Multiple Protective Shelters (MPS) mode provided for the survivability of the MX, which closed the window of vulnerability in the eyes of those who were fearful over the lack of survivability of U.S. ICBMs.[8] Importantly, within the Reagan administration, both the pragmatists and the hardliners were warfighters and viewed the window of vulnerability either as a function of the ICBM balance or as a function of both the ICBM balance and the survivability of the basing mode.

Twisting in the winds of the new cold war was SALT II. The Soviets made it clear before the inauguration that they hoped to continue the SALT process and, if possible, exhume SALT II from its premature grave. The administration informed the Soviets of its view. SALT II was history, and any further progress on strategic arms control depended on Soviet actions in Poland, Afghanistan, and Cuba. Soviet requests by Ambassador Anatoly Dobrynin and General Secretary Leonid Brezhnev for an early summit were met with the same response. However, in a brief but typical battle between hardliners and pragmatists, the administration decided to adhere to the SALT II limits temporarily until a new arms control policy could be devised, since these limits did not impede the administration's existing strategic modernization plans. [9]

Given the Reagan administration's lack of enthusiasm for strategic arms control, its priority on strategic modernization rather than limitation, its focus on the European-based systems, and its hardliner-pragmatist disagreements, it was not surprising that after a year in office the administration still had not revived strategic arms control with the USSR. A lack of action on the administration's part led to the growth of the nuclear freeze movement. While administration officials slugged it out in the Arms Control IG, Congress and the American people were busy developing their own policies on arms control. Other players were now setting the agenda on arms control—calls for a freeze on the development, testing, and deployment of nuclear weapons.

That agenda has origins that go back to the late 1970s. At the 1978 UN Disarmament Session the American Friends Services Committee called for a nuclear weapons freeze. A resolution calling for such a freeze to be negotiated by the U.S. and USSR was introduced in the U.S. Senate by Senators George McGovern (D-S.D.) and Mark Hatfield (R-Ore.) in 1979. Action on the freeze remained contained at the grassroots level or in state legislatures until the winter of 1982, when the administration's delay allowed it to grow toward critical mass. In addition, some administration loose talk on nuclear war helped fuel the fire. On several occasions during the 1980 campaign and again after the administration was in office, Reagan, Bush, and a number of State Department and DOD officials commented on the feasibility of fighting and winning a nuclear war.[10]

As the administration was forced to spend too much time denying that it believed a nuclear war could be fought and won, resolutions to support a nuclear freeze were introduced in the House by Edward Markey (D-Mass.) on 10 February 1982, and in the Senate by Edward Kennedy (D-Mass.) and Hatfield. Though these were the main congressional bills, approximately twenty-five different resolutions on limiting strategic weapons, including the freeze, were in the congressional pipeline.[11] The political pressure on the administration peaked in the spring of 1982. It had to act to regain the arms control agenda or lose control of its policy to a Congress ready to surge ahead as the administration stumbled.

Standard Interagency Process

The basic structure for decision making on START reflected the overall process of administration decision making. An IG on arms control provided the basic working-level forum for policy making. Under the Arms Control IG were a number of subordinate Working Groups created and convened as needed. The IG itself was chaired by Assistant Secretary of State for Political-Military Affairs Richard Burt, and reported to the SIG-FP, chaired by Secretary of State Alexander Haig. However, the IG functioned as if Burt and Assistant Secretary of Defense for International Security Policy Richard Perle were co-chairs. Burt and Perle, respectively, were the State Department's and DOD's point men on arms control. Since strategic modernization had priority over arms control, Perle's role as the Office of the Secretary of Defense representative was elevated to an equal of Burt. In theory, the Arms Control IG would make recommendations to the SIG-FP, which would then make recommendations to the full NSC. In the winter of 1982 the Arms Control IG was divided into an INF IG and a START IG.

Organizational Dynamics

The division within the administration over arms control reflected the overall division between pragmatists and hardliners. The State Department represented the pragmatists: Haig, Undersecretary of State for Political Affairs Lawrence Eagleburger, and the department's working level soldier, Burt. They often had allies in the JCS. The hardliners, a more cohesive group, were led by the civilians in the Pentagon within the Office of the Secretary of Defense—Weinberger, Undersecretary of Defense for Policy Fred Ikle, and Weinberger's chief aide on arms control, Perle. They had allies within the State Department in the ACDA and in the White House—Counsellor to the President Edwin Meese, ANSA Richard Allen, and eventually his replacement William Clark. In the arguments over the years on arms control, the battle lines were essentially the same; hardliners squared off against pragmatists with the JCS often playing the role of the balancer in this power struggle.

Both sides, however, agreed on two issues.[12] First, SALT II must be replaced with arms control that prevented the USSR from achieving significant advantages. Second, the new negotiations should be based on real reductions in Soviet nuclear capability to end their ability to build up their forces while abiding by the SALT limits. The debate within the administration was over the proper method of attempting reductions, specifically what unit of measurement was to be used to gauge the strategic balance. In simple terms, reductions were to be made, but reductions in what?

Within the Arms Control IG two competing positions formed and solidified.[13] The hardliners wanted to use throw weight as the unit of measurement for arms control. In their view the only real measure of the strategic balance was a comparison between the numbers of warheads each side was capable of delivering based on the payload of their ICBM and SLBM forces. They focused their attention on proposals that asked the USSR to reduce its throw weight by as much as 60% and dismantle a large number of their SS-17, 18, and 19 ICBMs. The U.S. would be required to decrease its throw weight only slightly. The pragmatists were willing to settle on the number of warheads or launchers as the unit for measuring the strategic balance. Burt felt that the increasing accuracy of warheads rendered throw weight less relevant than it had been in the past. Fewer and lighter warheads could do the same damage in the early 1980s than larger quantities and heavier warheads could do in the past. Therefore the payload of a missile did not directly correspond with its destructive power. Limits on ICBM and SLBM launchers and warheads could still be an effective way of maintaining parity in the strategic balance. Such limits also had a higher probability of success since the USSR could see them as a continuation from the SALT process. SALT had used launchers as a unit of measurement and had begun to place limits on the number of launchers that could be MIRVed. This took the logical next step by focusing on the specific number of warheads. It would be more negotiable than a completely new unit of measurement. The USSR did not like surprises or sudden innovations in established procedures. The Carter failure in March of 1977 illustrated this point.

The hardliners were led by Perle and included ACDA Director Eugene Rostow, START negotiator Edward Rowny, and INF talks negotiator Paul Nitze. Perle held a unique position. In the past, the Pentagon's mini–State Department was contained within the Office of International Security Affairs (ISA). The Reagan defense team had reorganized that office and created a sister office of International Security Policy (ISP). ISP was given jurisdiction over theater and strategic arms control, U.S.-Soviet relations, NATO, nuclear weapons policy, and East-West technology trade. ISA was in charge of the rest of the world and all other issues. Both offices reported to Ikle, the Undersecretary for Policy.[14] Perle's ISP was essentially designed to focus U.S. defense policy on the Soviet threat, an excellent example of designing a policy process to prioritize a specific point of view.

Burt was the main bureaucratic battler for the pragmatists at this level. It became clear as these debates within the Arms Control IG continued that the hardliners saw delay in the resumption of U.S.-Soviet strategic arms control negotiations as a preferred alternative to arms control based on the old SALT measures of launchers and/or warheads. Perle was viewed by the pragmatists simply as an obstacle to arms control, though his real purpose was to be an obstacle to anything resembling the SALT approach. His view was simple: he would not compromise on his goal of seeking deep reductions in Soviet ballistic missile throw weight. If this called for bringing the policy process to a grinding halt, that was acceptable. Ultimately, he was prepared to render the Arms Control IG and later the START IG completely useless. He was prepared to be the ultimate spoiler. Kicking the issue up to the SIG-FP would give Weinberger or Ikle the opportunity to do the same. For the hardliners it was a simple matter of throw weight reductions or nothing.[15] The pragmatists understood that arms control was a domestic political imperative, while the hardliners seemed to want to take the domestic politics out of arms control.

Presidential Choice: Political and Management Strategy

While the administration battled itself, the nuclear freeze gained momentum in the Republican-controlled Senate, Democratic-controlled House, and in public opinion. A Reagan public relations offensive against the freeze failed to end the groundswell. In a prime-time news conference on 31 March 1982, Reagan pointed out that a freeze would lock in place the current strategic balance in which the USSR had superiority. Congressional allies of Reagan on arms control, Senators Henry Jackson (D-Wash.) and John Warner (R-Va.), introduced a resolution two days earlier calling for a freeze at equal and reduced levels.[16] The administration endorsed it publicly. It was essentially the Reagan arms control policy up to that point—unspecified but deep reductions on both sides to a level of equality.

Reagan's arguments against the freeze would be perceived as hollow rhetoric if the administration could not develop an alternative. The administration had begun to feel the pressure from Congress. By early 1982, the NSC staff was under new leadership, William Clark as ANSA and Robert McFarlane as his deputy. Clark's new management style, as detailed in chapter three, extended to arms control. In February of 1982 he set a deadline for an initial proposal on START and provided detailed instructions on what types of strategic requirements any proposal should meet. The proposal was scheduled to be discussed at an NSC meeting on 21 April. Later, in March, Clark set a deadline of 1 May for a final proposal on START that could be used as the opening U.S. position in talks with the USSR. The deadline was a politically mandated one. The National Conference of Catholic Bishops was scheduled to hold a special meeting in Chicago to consider a Pastoral Letter criticizing U.S. nuclear weapons policies on 3 and 4 May.[17] The administration was feeling the pressure from within and outside of Congress.

Interestingly, it was Clark, not Reagan, who pushed the process. The most plausible explanation for this seems to be Reagan's overall lackadaisical approach to decision making. It was not Reagan's style to ride herd on the process or even get deeply involved in the process. If the bureaucracies needed to be persuaded or badgered or forced into a decision, someone else would have to do the job. Clark's role as ANSA was to do just that. In this sense, the administration's decision-making process was designed to provide the president with advice, while placing the president above the fray.

With the pressure from the White House increasing, the two factions within the START IG intensified their rivalry. A 21 April START IG meeting and a 29 April SIG-FP meeting settled nothing. The hardliners pushed proposals based on throw weight reductions, while the pragmatists countered with launcher- and warhead-based cuts. The outcome rested with an all-day meeting in the situation room on 1 May that was intended to design a proposal for submission to the president at an NSC meeting on 3 May.[18]

The State Department and the OSD/ACDA coalition were never going to see eye to eye. The deciding factor was to be the JCS. They had yet to decide where they stood on these issues. Chairman General David Jones, Army Chief of Staff General Edward Meyer, Chief of Naval Operations Admiral Thomas Hayward, Air Force Chief of Staff General Lew Allen, and Commandant of the Marine Corps General Robert Barrow were all holdovers from the Carter administration. They had endorsed SALT II and were suspect in the eyes of some of the hardliners for that reason. From the JCS perspective, arms control needed to enhance U.S. national security requirements by fitting the U.S. nuclear war plans contained in the SIOP for the employment of nuclear weapons. The Reagan administration had already completed its nuclear weapons review by this time. NSDD-13, "Nuclear Weapons Employment Policy," had been completed in October of 1981, and the Defense Guidance for 1984–1988 that outlined strategic goals of nuclear strategy and procurement policy to fit that strategy had been completed early in 1982. Essentially the JCS were tasked with hitting a larger number of targets in the USSR over a longer period of time than ever before. The very notion of deep reductions in the U.S. nuclear arsenal troubled them. It might prevent them from carrying out their military strategy. The best possible world to the JCS was a strategic situation in which there were fewer targets and more warheads to cover those targets. This suggests fewer launchers on both sides, but a larger number of MIRVs.[19]

The hardliners' focus on throw weight moved in the opposite direction toward fewer warheads, but perhaps the same number of launchers. The logical extension of this would be complete de-MIRVing, in which the ratio of launchers to warheads approached 1:1. For this reason, the JCS sided with the State Department. The State Department adjusted its proposal to allow for only 850 ballistic missile launchers, the figure the JCS had desired.[20]

These were serious philosophical divisions with real and lasting implications for the future of U.S. nuclear strategy and forces. Often these types of disagreements are described as petty arguments among bureaucrats seeking power. In this case the divisions reflected an underlying disagreement about the definition of strategic stability and methods of moving toward such stability. It became clear that more meetings were not going to result in a proposal that satisfied anyone. The 1 May meeting produced instead what was ironically called the "consensus proposal." It was Burt's way of preventing the START IG from delivering two proposals to the NSC on 3 May. The consensus proposal envisioned a two-phase process. Phase I would move toward deep cuts through the traditional method—launcher and warhead limits based on the State Department/JCS agreement. Phase II would introduce direct throw weight limits that could be designed to satisfy the OSD/ACDA position. Still no real consensus was reached. The hardliners felt that the consensus proposal was simply a way to begin arms control using the old launcher/warhead units from SALT, then forget all about throw weight limits once the negotiations were underway. They felt this was simply a trick to develop a two-phase process that would be completed after Phase I.[21]

However, Deputy ANSA McFarlane, who had attended the 1 May session, liked the consensus proposal and explained it to the president at the morning briefing on 3 May. Reagan seemed to favor the idea. Phase I was similar to arms control approaches of the past, and would be easier for the U.S. people to understand than more complex throw weight calculations. Ultimately, at the NSC meeting later in the day, McFarlane began the discussion with the consensus proposal. The usual battle lines were drawn. Weinberger and Rostow led the attack on the proposal, while Haig and JCS Chair Jones defended it.[22] No decision was made at the meeting. Though Haig attempted an end run to influence the president by having Burt try to convince Baker to persuade the president, Baker made it clear that this was not necessary. The president was leaning in the direction of the consensus proposal.

The details of the proposal were developed by McFarlane without the participation of the members of the START IG. It was his job to draw up an NSDD based on the 3 May NSC meeting. Reagan would then accept the NSDD or have McFarlane redraft it. McFarlane acknowledged the depth of the disagreements and tried to create a proposal that would satisfy everyone. NSDD-33, "U.S. Approach to START Negotiations," was signed on 14 May 1982. A draft of the NSDD was used by Burt to write the initial draft of Reagan's 9 May speech at Eureka College. The text of the NSDD emphasized that the primary goal of the U.S. in the START negotiations was to reduce the "most destabilizing Soviet systems, ballistic missiles, and especially ICBMs." Though the pragmatists seemed to be the winners in the battle, since their approach to arms control was the first phase, McFarlane made sure that the goal of throw weight reduction favored by the hardliners would not be forgotten. The NSDD explicitly stated that the Phase I launcher and warhead limits must bring USSR throw weight down to 2.5 million kg. This number, however, was to be kept top secret. Only the most senior people would be allowed to know it. McFarlane was making sure that Phase I and Phase II would stay linked. NSDD-33 set a date of 18 May for the START IG to produce a detailed approach to achieving these goals. NSDD-36 of 25 May outlined further guidelines of the administration's START policy and assigned a date of 4 June for the START IG to settle several outstanding issues. On 9 May Reagan made the initial compromise of 3 May public in a speech at his alma mater Eureka College. The speech gave a general description of the two-phase approach, but provided few details. The substance of the U.S. proposal to be brought to Geneva was bargained out between 14 May and 25 June between the START IG, SIG-FP, and NSC staff until approved by the NSC.[23]

President Reagan's role in all of this can only be speculated upon. His hands-off management style and preference for delegation explains why he is rarely mentioned in descriptions of the decision-making process in the winter and spring of 1982. The most detailed description of the 21 April NSC meeting, for example, describes the debate and adds that Reagan seemed slightly bored and began to doodle a horse. In addition, McFarlane's NSDD was not changed by Reagan after it was written. Reportedly, McFarlane placed the 2.5 million kg limit on throw weight into the NSDD, not because he was instructed to do so by the president, but in response to Reagan's comment during the 3 May meeting that he agreed with a Weinberger point about the importance of the Soviet lead in throw weight. Reagan, at least in this instance, seemed to supplement delegation with neglect, leaving McFarlane to infer Reagan's preferences from his comments at the NSC meetings. No further meetings between McFarlane, Clark, and Reagan on how to summarize the debate at the 3 May meeting were reported, and the decision was not made at the meeting itself. McFarlane made the policy compromise, and the president added his signature to make it official.[24]

The Soviet responses to the U.S. proposal are secondary issues for this study.

The USSR in mid-May had endorsed a nuclear freeze. At the Geneva negotiations the Soviets were not very interested in dismantling most of their medium and heavy systems, especially while the U.S. deployed the MX and pushed cruise missile limits back to Phase II. As an opening move in the arms control game between the U.S. and USSR, the Eureka proposals served only to highlight the differences between the Soviet and American views.

What is crucial here is the fact that political pressures were created by the inability of the administration's interagency process to develop a proposal. This caused the new ANSA Clark to crack the whip on the sluggish interagency process. In this case, political pressure was the key to changes in the decision-making process, yet all three principles are evident. The pressures of domestic politics at the grassroots level and within Congress taught the administration a lesson. When policy needed to be produced swiftly, the decision-making process was adjusted—narrowing participation and bypassing the interagency process as necessary. A learning process was under way that continued to lead the more politically sensitive members of the administration to conclude that the national security apparatus of the administration (both personnel and process) was unable to keep up with the political expectations for arms control.

THE BUILD-DOWN PROPOSAL

This second episode of Reagan's arms control policy begins in December of 1982 with the defeat of funding for the MX Missile Closely Spaced Basing (CSB) scheme and ends with the formulation of a new set of START proposals in October 1983 based on the idea of a strategic build-down. The basic source of the evolution during this period was again the administration's inability to break the interagency deadlock. The compromise of 3 May 1982 was never accepted by either of the two factions in the START IG and their senior-level benefactors. Though the NSC staff had designed the compromise and Reagan had approved it, the rest of the administration's arms control advisers continued to squabble. Once negotiations with the USSR began, each decision on how to respond to Soviet initiatives or how to modify the initial U.S. proposal presented another opportunity to unravel McFarlane's compromise and reargue the basics of throw weight versus warhead/launcher limits.[25] Attempts to end these arguments by creating higher level committees to run START decision making failed. In the end, the Blue Ribbon Scowcroft Commission and its chair, Brent Scowcroft, served as a go-between for the administration and congressional leaders on arms control. The decision had bypassed the interagency process and narrowed to a small ad hoc interbranch decision group consisting of ANSA William Clark, his deputy Robert McFarlane, six members of Congress, and leaders of the Scowcroft Commission. Together they negotiated a new U.S. proposal for the Geneva talks with the USSR in defiance of the administration's interagency battles.

International and Domestic Political Environment

The international environment had not changed significantly since the administration entered office. The increase in U.S.-Soviet tensions dating back to the late-1970s crumbling of détente still defined the relationship. The Reagan administration's defense buildup and inability or refusal to take arms control seriously only added to the sense of a reinvigorated cold war. The domestic political environment was the real source of political pressure on the administration.

Congress was unhappy with the lack of progress on arms control and used its powers of the purse to make its unhappiness felt within the administration. The leverage was the MX missile. The Carter administration had seemingly settled the issue of the MX missile with its September 1979 decision to place the MX in a Multiple Protective Shelters (MPS) mode. Reagan as a candidate was against this decision and vowed to overturn it as president. Once assuming office, however, Reagan had difficulty finding a permanent basing mode for the missile. The Townes Commission, charged by Reagan in March 1981 to find a basing mode for the MX, simply opened up the debates that had been going on since 1973 over how to deploy the MX—in silos, on railroads, on trucks, underground, on small submarines, or on constant airborne alert. The administration's interim decision to place 100 MX missiles in super-hardened silos did not please Congress. The entire purpose of developing the MX, in the minds of many in Congress, was to provide a survivable retaliatory force. Silo basing only provided the USSR with more attractive targets for its own ICBMs. Congress began to turn the screws on the administration, using the authorization and appropriation deadlines of the congressional budget cycle to threaten MX funding unless the administration came up with an acceptable basing mode. The administration finally decided upon the closely spaced basing (CSB) system in which 100 missiles would be deployed in 100 silos less than 2,000 feet apart.[26]

The CSB was introduced to Congress on 22 November 1982, in time for consideration in the Fiscal Year 1983 Defense Appropriations Bill. Reagan, in a letter to members of the House, deliberately linked the deployment of the MX to the success of arms control with the Soviets. He reiterated his belief that the MX was the best bargaining leverage the U.S. had in pushing the USSR toward deep reductions. However, both the House and Senate separately voted to limit MX funding pending the resolution of the basing issue and, through different legislative maneuvers, rejected the CSB system. The result of the Conference Committee was a final bill that contained no money for procurement, a ban on flight-testing of the MX, and a fencing of research and development funds until Congress approved a basing mode.[27]

The Standard Interagency Process and Organizational Dynamics

Since this case study picks up soon after the Eureka case study, the standard interagency process and the organizational dynamics within the administration are the same. By this time, the standard interagency process within the START IG was so mired in gridlock that it was nearly irrelevant to the decision making. Its role, or lack thereof, is better explained by examining the president's management strategy for dealing with the problem. The organizational dynamics within the administration were also the same—hardliners in the DOD and ACDA pushed for throw weight reductions, while the State Department fought to preserve the precedents of using launcher and warhead limits as the method of accounting. The NSC staff, however, had taken on the role of broker between the groups. McFarlane's May 1982 compromise represents an attempt by Clark to use the NSC staff on the president's behalf. The executive departments could argue over their different preferences forever. The president needed to introduce an arms control policy that satisfied public opinion. Clark and McFarlane worked to achieve just that.

Presidential Choice: Political and Management Strategy

As described above, this case study is really an extension of the previous case study. The president's political strategy had not changed. He still saw the USSR as a growing threat to the U.S. and was not enamored of either détente or arms control. However, he also had to respond to Congress or see his strategic modernization plans fail. For Reagan's part, the only way to achieve his national security goals was to come up with some arms control policy that satisfied those in Congress who were willing to hold up MX development until START showed some real progress.

The president turned to a traditional way of dealing with executive branch gridlock—the Blue Ribbon Commission—that could protect the issue from bureaucratic and organizational competition by removing it from the executive branch. Inside this quasi-governmental cocoon, a compromise could be reached. Soon after the votes on the MX, Deputy ANSA McFarlane spoke to several Senators who were known as the leading congressional voices on defense issues. Senator Sam Nunn (D-Ga.), ranking Democrat on the Senate Armed Services Committee, and Senator William Cohen (R-Maine) both suggested that Congress had lost confidence in Secretary of Defense Weinberger. They hinted that any proposal brought to Capitol Hill by Weinberger might be rejected at this point regardless of its merits. Cohen and Senator John Tower (R-Tex.), Chair of the Senate Armed Services Committee, proposed a bipartisan commission to solve the problems of the MX and the lack of progress in START. McFarlane brought the idea to Clark, who quickly approved.[28]

The swiftness with which the administration agreed to take the decision out of the normal legislative-executive battleground as well as out of the interagency process is explained simply by the difficulty the administration had in producing decisions. Congress and the administration could not agree on a basing mode, and within the administration the interagency process on START was breaking down. McFarlane had already assumed the leadership of the START IG in hopes that if the NSC staff ran the committee, the fighting between State and Defense might be muted.[29] In the case of relations with Congress, the problem was not a partisan one. Even with Republican control of the Senate, the MX appeared to be in trouble. Cohen and Tower, supporters of the commission idea, and Charles Percy (R-Ill.), Chair of the Senate Foreign Relations Committee and critic of the MX and the administration's START proposals, were key leaders of a Republican-controlled Senate. The House, controlled by Democrats, promised to become an even more unfriendly place to the MX and to a slothlike arms control process.

The President's Commission on Strategic Forces, also known as the Scowcroft Commission after its Chairman General Brent Scowcroft, was officially instituted on 3 January 1983. The commission had a broad mandate—to examine the MX program, strategic modernization in general, and its impact on arms control and overall U.S. national security policy.[30] The commission brought together experts on defense from both parties, including former senior governmental officials and business executives. Scowcroft, a retired Air Force General who had been ANSA under Ford, directed the work of the commission with assistance from R. James Woolsey, who had held various defense and arms-control posts in several administrations and had been on the Townes Commission. Importantly, the Scowcroft Commission deliberately set out to create a political compromise, something that would satisfy Congress and the administration over the long haul. The issue of how to deal with the growing Soviet threat and its impact on the credibility and capability of the U.S. deterrent force had gone on for nearly a decade at this point. The commission hoped to generate a recommendation that might quiet the debate until the next technological developments threw the entire issue up in the air again. In creating the commission, those involved hoped to free the MX and START from the political infighting that had marked strategic modernization and arms control throughout the Carter and early Reagan years. The existence of the commission did not mean that Congress and the administration had ended their argument over these issues. Congress continued to hold the MX hostage, while the administration threatened a "reassessment" of its START position if Congress did not fund an MX basing mode.[31]

The commission began its work on 7 January and finished on 6 April, though the report was released to the public only on 11 April. The most productive work of the commission may have taken place during weekend meetings between Scowcroft, Woolsey, and Les Aspin of the House Armed Services Committee. Aspin represented the interests of congressional Democrats along with Nunn and Senator Henry Jackson (D-Wash.).[32] The contacts with Nunn, Jackson, and Aspin provided political feasibility checks for the commission. As the three noted defense experts of the Democratic party within Congress, their opinions carried substantial weight with other members as well as with the administration. The commission members were also in constant contact with the administration, mostly through McFarlane, who had worked under Scowcroft on the Ford NSC staff. This provided a negotiating channel between congressional leaders and the administration. These discussions also highlight the informality and ad hoc nature of the process at this point.

The compromise reached by the commission was threefold: silo deployment was recommended for the MX; development of a small, mobile, single warhead missile was the solution to the vulnerability problem; and the administration's arms control stance should be based on warheads, not launchers.[33] The compromise gave something to everyone. Those in the administration and Congress who saw the window of vulnerability as a function of the imbalance in U.S. and Soviet hard target kill capability received the MX and its ten warheads, either as bargaining chips to trade for Soviet heavy and medium missiles or as a way to catch up with Soviet capability. Those in the administration and Congress who saw the window of vulnerability as a problem stemming from the lack of survivable land-based forces received what became known as the Small ICBM (SICBM) or Midgetman, a small, single-warhead, mobile missile that would be a very difficult target for the Soviets. A decision to focus on warheads rather than launchers or throw weight might end the fighting within the interagency process. Strategic modernization and arms control would be merged to essentially build a new strategic relationship based on deMIRVing the ICBM forces of both sides for the sake of strategic stability. Implicitly, the MX became something of a strategic lure to entice the USSR to eliminate its medium and heavy ICBMs.

Whether this satisfied everyone within the administration and Congress can be debated. The real question was how the compromise would hold up. Its success depended on three decision-making arenas: the relationship between the House and Senate and between Republicans and Democrats in Congress; the relationship between the administration and Congress; and the relationship between the hardliners and pragmatists in the administration. The infighting within the administration was the greatest threat to the compromise.

Following the Scowcroft Commission compromise, Congress assumed a more prominent position in arms control policy. It presented a bipartisan front to the administration. Aspin, Norman Dicks (D-Wash.), and Al Gore (D-Tenn.) led the way on the MX and START within the House. They pressured the administration to move toward a deMIRVed stance based on the SICBM, but also worked to keep other members of the Democratic party from skewering the MX. In the Senate, Nunn, Cohen, and Percy led the bipartisan pressure on the administration. They also helped to keep the MX alive, but most importantly provided an alternative approach to arms control for the administration. It would have been unfair for Congress, but perhaps more welcome from the administration's viewpoint, if the Senate simply criticized the administration's approach to arms control but never offered a second option. These Senators instead provided an option on arms control called the "build-down."[34] Support for the build-down concept initially began in the Senate in 1982. It was a response to the inability of the administration to design an acceptable basing mode for the MX or an arms control proposal that had the potential to succeed in Geneva, by those in the Senate who saw the freeze as locking in Soviet superiority and/or U.S. vulnerability. They sought another new innovation in arms control besides the freeze.

A discussion of different versions of the build-down can become quite complex. However, the most basic version of it captures the heart of the concept. For each new warhead deployed in either nation's arsenal, two old warheads must be dismantled. Both sides could therefore modernize, but at the same time would reduce the number of warheads they possessed. This fit into the scheme of deMIRVing and also addressed the throw weight issue. Actual throw weight would not be reduced, but the number of warheads on the Soviets' medium and heavy missiles would decrease. In theory, this closed the window of vulnerability. The build-down option allowed Congress to measure the administration's commitment to what were in members' eyes serious proposals on arms control. These Senators essentially told the administration that it must include aspects of the build-down in its Geneva proposals or the MX would be in jeopardy.[35] Ultimately, Aspin, Gore, Dicks, Nunn, Percy, and Cohen formed an alliance that allowed for both houses of Congress and both sides of the aisle to bargain as one with the administration. They became known as the Gang of Six, even though a large number of other members of the Senate and House backed their efforts.

That bargain became explicit in late April and early May of 1983. Percy, Cohen, and Nunn wrote a letter to the president on 29 April, which was followed by a letter from Gore, Aspin, Dicks, and six others in the House on 2 May. Both letters were endorsed by bipartisan groups in both the House and Senate. Most importantly, the letters explicitly stated the bargain: if Congress did not feel that the administration was being serious on arms control, the MX was dead. Seriousness on arms control meant some form of the build-down. Such statements from Democrats might be ignored in the partisan environment of Washington; however, in this case Republicans Cohen, Percy, Senator Warren Rudman (R-N.H.), and Representative William Dickinson (R-Ala.), all supporters of the build-down, placed intense intraparty pressure on the administration. Republican efforts in the Senate were intended to tilt the intra-administration balance in favor of the pragmatists.[36]

The administration had to hold up its end of the bargain. This was not an easy task. The basic conflict between the hard-line throw-weight-or-nothing faction and the pragmatists' more flexible stance had not ended. In addition, Clark, McFarlane, and the NSC staff wanted to quash the build-down idea as quickly as possible. The president liked the build-down idea, however, and the START IG was instructed to consider it seriously.

Secretary of State George Shultz, the new leader of the pragmatists once Haig had resigned, was more sympathetic to the throw weight argument. An expert on international economics rather than political-military affairs, he essentially remained neutral in this debate. Shultz did attempt an organizational move to give the State Department more control over arms control policy. With White House approval, Shultz created a more senior-level committee that was designed to oversee the arms control efforts of the START IG. The committee was headed by Shultz's Deputy Kenneth Dam and became known as the Dam Group. However, the group never made much of an impact on policy. Dam did not see it as a real force in arms control policy making, simply a discussion forum.[37] The membership of this group overlapped with the START IG and SIG-FP, also often chaired by Dam, so its ability to do anything substantially different was undermined.

The interagency process was pushed aside again at this point. The legislation initiating the Scowcroft Commission gave the administration forty-five days to act on the Commission's recommendations, or else all funds for the MX appropriated but fenced could not be spent. Congress was scheduled to begin making decisions on MX financing on 12 May. On 9 May, the day before a scheduled NSC meeting, Clark, McFarlane, and representatives of the Meese/Baker/Deaver troika met with several of the representatives and senators who had written the letters of April and May. This was a final sounding out of Congress before the administration would revise its START proposals at the NSC meeting. The basic purpose of the NSC meeting was to produce letters for Congress detailing the new START proposals and the administration's end of the MX bargain. The letters endorsed the Scowcroft Commission recommendations and explained how the administration was adjusting its START stance to accept those recommendations. The entire START proposal was to be reviewed, with a specific focus on raising the 850 ballistic missile launcher limit. (The fewer ballistic missiles a nation has, the more incentive there is to MIRV. Allowing more launchers fits the Scowcroft idea of deMIRVing.) They stated the administration's acceptance of the SICBM idea, but made it clear that the administration's actions were contingent on funding of the MX by Congress.[38]

The letters worked. In the following weeks Congress approved funds for MX testing and engineering. Congress had used its leverage of appropriations to extract promises from the administration for changes in the START proposals. This pattern of consultations with Congress persisted into June when the next round of START negotiations with the USSR began. However, the build-down was still an afterthought in its proposals. A Reagan speech on 8 June and NSDD-98, "U.S. Approach to START Negotiations—VI," the official policy for this next negotiating round, included only a brief reference to the build-down, calling for further study of its merits.[39] The hardliners in the START-IG, SIG-FP, and NSC were able to keep the administration's proposal under their sway. In reality, very little had changed. The congressional build-down approach was given lip service at this point. Congressional leverage had also not changed. The administration still wanted the MX, and Congress could still use it as a bargaining chip to push the administration in the favored direction. The Scowcroft Commission, whose tenure had been extended to 1 January 1985, provided the mechanism for keeping the administration and Congress honest in this bargaining process.

The endgame of this executive-legislative bargaining came in September and October of 1983. Final votes on MX funding for fiscal year 1984 came in October, and the fifth round of START was scheduled to begin 6 October. The administration had to present its START proposal before Congress voted. This forced the administration to make a commitment to the build-down or face MX defeats. However, the factional disputes within the interagency process still threatened to unravel the entire deal. The solution within the administration was to make a change in the process as a prelude to making a change in the policy.

In July the administration created the Senior Arms Control Policy Group (SACPG, pronounced sack-pig). The group was chaired by Clark and included McFarlane, Dam, Jonathan Howe (new Director of the State Department Politico-Military Affairs Bureau), Burt (now the Assistant Secretary of State for European Affairs), Ikle, Perle, ACDA Director Kenneth Adelman (a hardliner), and representatives from the CIA and JCS. Its job was to end the bureaucratic and organizational infighting within the administration. The START IG still existed, but it was now taking orders from the SACPG. In addition, the SACPG was given authority to deal directly with the negotiators in Geneva.[40] In this way, decisions were made and then directly transmitted to chief negotiator Edward Rowny without the possibility of interpretations of these decisions by the various bureaucracies that might undercut the wishes of the SACPG or president.

The decision-making process had been narrowed; the interagency process had been streamlined. In response to the pressures of politics and economy the administration finally refused to continue hoping that the normal interagency process might produce a consensus. Instead the SACPG was designated as the body that would produce consensus. The key to that was the fact that it was Clark's group. The ANSA had assumed responsibility for the president's policy-making process when the bureaucracies simply refused to cooperate. Clark acted on the president's authority, an authority that allowed him to make decisions and negotiate with Congress.

Clark, however, was one of the hardliners. His motivation for maintaining the deal with Congress was not that he agreed with the build-down or deMIRV-ing, but that he wanted to make sure that Reagan was not politically battered by Congress and by the public for being an obstacle to arms control and better relations with the USSR. For this reason, Congress had to come up with some way to satisfy the throw weight gang. Perle still wielded a great deal of power to scuttle the Scowcroft consensus. In the summer of 1983, a plan that addressed throw weight through a build-down process was brought into the mix. Scowcroft and Woolsey held meetings with Perle, while Scowcroft subsequently held meetings with Nunn and Aspin as well as other members of Congress.[41]

Ultimately, retired Air Force General Glenn Kent was asked to develop a method to solve the problem. The trick was to devise a single measurement that compared destructive power of various systems, for example, bombers, ICBM/SLBM warheads, and cruise missiles. Using this measurement any type of nuclear weapon could be discussed in terms of its absolute destructive power and be fully comparable to every other system. The measure of potential destructive capacity was designated as standard weapons stations (SWS). Every nuclear weapon's destructive capacity was measured in terms of SWS, and negotiations between the U.S. and USSR could focus on reducing each side's overall destructive capacity by reducing each side's SWS. By the fall, Scowcroft, Woolsey, and the Gang of Six had accepted what became known as the "double build-down."[42] The double build-down would reduce U.S. and Soviet nuclear forces through deep reductions in ballistic missile warheads and standard weapons stations for all strategic forces. The remaining issue was getting the administration to accept this policy as part of the proposals for the upcoming fifth round of START.

In early September, Nunn, Cohen, and Percy wrote to the commission suggesting the double build-down approach. Acting as go-between, Scowcroft then passed the proposal on to the administration. The Gang of Six met with Clark on 21 September to explain the double build-down and to again remind the administration that the MX was in danger. The president had promised to examine the build-down in May but had yet to respond.[43]

At an NSC meeting on 29 September the administration accepted only half of the double build-down approach. It would propose a year-by-year schedule for ballistic missile warhead reductions, but not reductions based on the standard weapons stations unit of measurement. Clark met with the Gang of Six the next day and was informed that they were not satisfied. The proposal still treated ballistic missiles and bombers separately, completely ignoring the SWS approach.[44]

To settle this disagreement, and to reinforce congressional seriousness, Scowcroft met with Shultz, enlisting his help in convincing the president. Shultz was crucial in convincing Reagan to add the build-down to the U.S. proposals at START. Clark's role in getting Reagan to end the dispute was also critical. Importantly, though the meeting of the NSC on 29 September had essentially rejected the build-down, the decision was overruled by Reagan. On 3 October Clark met with the Gang of Six and Scowcroft and hammered out the deal. The build-down was to be added to the mix of proposals for START. Both Reagan and Bush dropped by the meeting to illustrate the seriousness of the administration. A memorandum of understanding between the administration and Congress was written that outlined what the administration intended to do to meet congressional demands.[45]

The current START proposals remained basically the same. A special working group to focus specifically on the build-down was to be added to the normal joint U.S.-Soviet working groups that formed the basis for the negotiations in Geneva. Perhaps most significantly, Woolsey was added to the START delegation as member-at-large, and as a member of the build-down working group. NSDD-106 of 4 October 1983, spelling out U.S. policy in START for the fifth round of negotiations, lists the details of the administration's build-down proposals. Interestingly, it does not include the word *throw weight,* but instead talks about the *destructive capacity* of ballistic missiles, the term used by those who designed the double build-down.[46] Congress, finally seeing the build-down introduced at the START negotiations, held up its end of the bargain and passed legislation in early November appropriating funds for procurement of the first twenty-one MX missiles.

Though a deal had been struck within the U.S., a deal with the USSR did not materialize. A lack of progress in the INF talks led to the beginning of U.S. deployment of its own new generation of Eurostrategic missiles as a response to the Soviet SS-20s. This caused the USSR delegation to walk out of the INF talks on 23 November 1983. After the rejection of the build-down proposals, the Soviet delegation at the START talks ended the fifth round on 8 December, refusing to set a date for the resumption of talks.[47] The deployment of the INF systems and the lack of progress in START came on the heels of an increase in U.S.-Soviet tensions. That fall, notable incidents included the shooting down of Korean Air Lines flight 007 in September, the invasion of Grenada in October, and the massive Able Archer 83 NATO exercise in Europe that alarmed the Soviets into thinking NATO was about to begin conventional and nuclear operations against the USSR.[48] The potential for arms control in the first term had effectively ended. A new forum for discussing strategic arms control did not begin until 1985.

This case study reveals a process that was adjusting itself to the political needs of the moment—the need to find some consensus among the important players. Narrowing, informal negotiating, and eventually bypassing the interagency process were the ways to achieve that consensus. The Reagan administration efforts on strategic arms control highlight the role of the political pressures of domestic politics. As in the case of the nuclear freeze and the Eureka proposals, the failure to reach an interagency consensus allowed Congress to essentially seize the arms control agenda. Congress developed the build-down innovation while the administration argued over throw weight–based, warhead-based, or launcher-based limitations. Reagan and Clark ultimately learned that the standard interagency process was simply incapable of producing a decision that might satisfy Congress. To save time and effort (economy principle), and to rescue the MX and the administration's political fortunes, Clark was given power to negotiate directly for Reagan and to ignore the decisions of the NSC. In each episode examined, domestic politics was the overriding motivation forcing the administration to break the deadlock in the interagency process.

It is unclear if any decision-making process could have brought consensus on arms control to this administration. Clearly the differences in opinions could not be smoothed over. One of the main reasons was that the hardliners did not want them to be smoothed over. If a lack of agreement within the administration prevented the U.S. from beginning negotiations with the Soviets, they essentially won the argument. In any case, they were willing to continue that battle until the U.S. strategic modernization plan was complete. For them, the stakes could not have been higher. The issue, after all, was nuclear weapons, and the hardliners felt the U.S. was walking toward unilateral disarmament and a possible Soviet first strike. This partially explains the fierceness of the bureaucratic and organizational infighting.

Perhaps a basic rule of political pressure is that if Congress wants decisions to be made, they must be made or at least appear to be made. The necessity of dealing with Congress was a learning experience as well. Interestingly, these lessons were learned the hard way by Carter and Reagan. Both men had been governors, and perhaps as governors they had functioned as the biggest fish in a small pond. Each may have believed after taking the oath of office that he had become the biggest fish in the biggest pond. They soon learned that relative to their old jobs, they had become smaller fish. Congress had the power to compete with the presidency, and even within the executive branch there were limitations to the president's ability to make his own assets work on his behalf.

DECISIONS ON STRATEGIC DEFENSE

The Reagan administration's decisions regarding strategic defense represented such radical departures from established national security doctrine that they were moved outside the interagency process almost from the inception of the idea. Strategic defense also was a pet project of the president and the product of the work of policy entrepreneurs both inside and outside the administration. Once having taken root in the administration, the president nurtured the policy along. Such high-level attention makes for a unique decision process. Here was a case in which the president was proposing a new direction in U.S. nuclear strategy that might fundamentally alter the U.S.-USSR strategic relationship and the nature of deterrence. However, the decision to launch what became known as the SDI was made in a very short period of time, without thorough interagency review, and with the participation of only a handful of aides.

International and Domestic Political Environment

In 1983, the administration, or more accurately, the president and several close aides, proposed a major departure from previous strategy on nuclear war. The story of the shift to a strategy that included a major emphasis on strategic defense provides an example of how a small group of people with a self-acknowledged controversial idea works to protect that idea from the volatility of interagency decision making. The tale has been told elsewhere in great detail; this analysis only intends to highlight the unusual nature of the decision.[49]

The idea of ballistic missile defense was certainly not new in the 1980s. The United States had been working on defenses against missiles since the German

V-1 was introduced in World War II. The debates over antiballistic missile systems (ABMs) in the 1960s were politically charged and intense. Ultimately, the development of the Sentinel and Safeguard ABM systems was stopped with the signing of the ABM Treaty in 1972 that effectively ended the debate by limiting U.S. and Soviet ABM systems and banning nationwide ballistic missile defense systems. Studies of ballistic missile defense continued within the DOD as part of ongoing research in defense technologies and systems.[50]

That did not prevent strategic analysts, in particular conservatives, from hoping that the U.S. might one day revive the idea of ballistic missile defense. They often noted that the USSR was taking its ability to continue research on ABM technologies and systems much more seriously than the U.S. Many of these people were members of the CPD and saw a clear connection between Soviet ICBM capability, the window of vulnerability, and ballistic missile defense. One method of closing the window of vulnerability was with ballistic missile defense. Edward Teller, a member of the CPD and noted physicist who had been one of the key designers of the hydrogen bomb, had been an active supporter of ballistic missile defense based on new technological developments. Daniel O. Graham, working out of the Heritage Foundation, a conservative think tank, had authored plans called "High Frontier" for ballistic missile defense based on current technologies. Senator Malcolm Wallop, Republican from Wyoming, was a proponent of ballistic missile defense in the late 1970s. Campaign officials felt it was too bold a change in U.S. policy for an election campaign.[51] The idea slipped into dormancy.

The Standard Interagency Process and Organizational Dynamics

The standard interagency process is irrelevant to this decision. SDI was never vetted through it until after Reagan's March speech. The abandonment of the interagency process here was a deliberate move intended to spare the idea from the nature of the administration's organizational dynamics. The hardliners and pragmatists had declared war on each other over the relatively simple matter of continuing decade-old arms negotiations with the USSR. A truly revolutionary departure from standard policy, such as a shift to ballistic missile defense in U.S. strategic policy, might cause the administration's already contentious policy process to implode.

The idea of reviving ballistic missile defense survived within the White House and in conservative nongovernmental circles with ties to the administration.

Within the White House, Meese, Allen, Anderson (now Director of the Office of Policy Development), and Science Adviser George Keyworth formed a small ad hoc informal group to discuss ballistic missile defense. The White House group kept in close contact with a subset of Reagan's kitchen cabinet dubbed the High Frontier Panel. The group, headed by businessman Karl Bendetsen, included fellow business executives Joseph Coors, William Wilson, Jacquelin Hume, as well as Teller and Graham. They hoped to use their friendship with the president combined with Teller's and Graham's ideas to eventually convince Reagan to launch an initiative on ballistic missile defense. Wallop was also included in these discussions. Keyworth acted as liaison between the panel and the White House.[52]

Both Anderson and Meese explicitly state in their memoirs that the purpose of this informal group was to avoid the DOD and normal interagency channels. Anderson identified three reasons why the small group had decided to keep the program under wraps: avoidance of the bureaucracy of the DoD; the possibility that it would be rejected by the bureaucracy because the idea had not originated there—the Not Invented Here syndrome; and the possibility it would be seen as a threat to funds allocated to other programs. Meese was clear about this: "The idea of strategic defense against nuclear missiles could hardly have surfaced if the president had relied on standard bureaucratic measures."[53]

Presidential Choice: Political and Management Strategy

These advisers nurtured the idea of ballistic missile defense, hoping for a day when they could get the president to endorse the idea. Philosophically, Reagan agreed with them. Like Carter before him, he hated nuclear weapons. He also disliked the entire concept of assured destruction. He seemed never to have accepted the paradox of nuclear strategy enshrined by the ABM Treaty—that mutual vulnerability, the ability for each side to bombard the other with nuclear warheads, was the safest and surest way to prevent a nuclear war. Teller briefed Reagan on ABMs during his term as California governor and Reagan had toured North American Aerospace Command (NORAD) in July 1979. He came away from that visit surprised that the U.S. had no defense against ballistic missiles and convinced that the U.S. must shift its nuclear strategy from a policy based on deterrence to a policy based on defense.[54] However, once elected, Reagan seems to have let the idea drop into policy limbo.

Interestingly, the management strategy for SDI was not the president's responsibility until 1983. Before this, the White House Group and High Frontier Panel guided the policy-making process. Reagan was briefed on strategic defense by the White House group and the High Frontier Panel on 14 September and 12 October 1981. The High Frontier Panel was asked to prepare a report on ballistic missile defense, which was presented to the president in a third meeting on 8 January 1982.[55] However, policy on this issue seemed to have run aground until late 1982. Perhaps this was a function of the unusual decision making at this point. The entire process was ad hoc, with two informal groupings, one within the administration and one outside the administration, in charge of the policy. The question of how these informal groupings could bring the idea into normal administration processes without losing control of the ideas was a difficult one to answer. In addition, the flurry of criticism that met other administration policies that seemed to imply that the administration was planning to fight and win a nuclear war—NSDD-13, the 1984–1988 Defense Guidance—provided an important lesson. Everything will leak and then will be interpreted in the most unflattering way possible. No ideas, let alone major shifts in policy, could withstand the scrutiny of the press and the rarified atmosphere of debates on nuclear strategy until they were ready. The ad hoc groups may have decided to put the issue on the back burner until the heat from these other controversies had subsided.

Another explanation for the lack of progress in 1982 is that Anderson left the government soon after the January meeting; the White House group stopped meeting at that point. The High Frontier Panel was becoming nervous about the administration's seriousness regarding strategic defense. Their report of January 1982 had recommended space-based systems using the cutting edge of technology to defend against missile attacks. They felt the issue had reached a point where the president might appoint a Blue Ribbon Presidential Commission to study the idea. Instead, under the direction of Keyworth, a panel of the White House Science Council (an advisory board to the president) had convened under Edward Frieman, vice president of Science Applications Incorporated, to study the issue. The report was due in December of 1982. To members of the High Frontier Panel, this was a disappointment.[56] They had made their pitch to the president, but their idea had not caught fire.

Without any additional effort by the kitchen cabinet, however, the idea did pick up momentum after Reagan's quarterly meeting with the Joint Chiefs on 22 December 1982. Reagan had questioned the Chiefs on the idea of ballistic missile defense, but the discussion did not go very far. However, after the meeting the attention on the issue continued. ANSA William Clark asked the JCS and McFarlane to study the idea in preparation for the next meeting with the president scheduled for February. He also asked his deputy, McFarlane, to do the same. Chief of Naval Operations James Watkins, a skeptic on assured destruction, met with Teller in January 1983 and commissioned further study by the Navy.[57] Discussions between Watkins and the NSC staff continued informally, while the JCS began to address the issue seriously in their internal meetings. Chairman General John Vessey and Air Force Chief of Staff General Charles Gabriel were interested in the idea, and the Chiefs agreed to present the notion of serious study on ballistic missile defense to the president at their meeting in February.

The 11 February meeting of the president, the JCS, Weinberger, Clark, and McFarlane shifted the policy process into fast forward, in ways that neither the JCS nor Clark and McFarlane had suspected. The JCS saw the necessity for a review of ballistic missile defense in the wake of technological developments since the ABM Treaty had been signed. McFarlane saw research into strategic defense as a bargaining chip to use against the Soviet Union.[58] Weinberger argued against it; Reagan, however, was extremely interested. He tossed the JCS numerous questions. He saw strategic defenses as a way to end the vulnerability of the American people to ballistic missile attack, effectively an end to assured destruction. Reagan made up his mind at the meeting; he became an active proponent of ballistic missile defense within the administration. As president, he got his way.

At this point, Reagan took hold of the policy process. The White House Group and the High Frontier had been able to get the idea floating around the administration. It finally hooked the president and took charge of the policy. Reagan wanted to go public with the idea right away. He was scheduled to give a nationally televised speech on national security on 23 March. McFarlane was asked to draft a new ending to the speech that proposed ballistic missile defenses. The regular speechwriters were told that an additional ending would be added to their draft. Reagan also wanted secrecy surrounding the speech. McFarlane and NSC staffers Admiral John Poindexter, Ray Pollack, and Dick Boverie wrote the speech. Other than that, only Clark, Meese, and Brent Scowcroft, Chairman of the President's Commission on Strategic Forces, were told of the president's plans.[59]

There was no interagency process at this point. The decision-making process here started narrow and remained that way. Secretary of State Shultz even had a discussion with Clark about strategic defenses, but was not informed of the upcoming speech. Undersecretary of State Lawrence Eagleburger found out about the speech from McFarlane on 21 March. Once having been informed, and having received a draft copy of the speech, Shultz began a two-day effort to change the tone of the speech in negotiations with Clark and McFarlane. He felt the speech was too sweeping in its rhetoric and implied that the U.S. was changing the foundation of its strategic doctrine. Weinberger, whose department would have the responsibility to oversee the development of ballistic missile defense, was kept in the dark. He knew that some decisions had been made on strategic defenses through his friendships with Clark and Meese, but he did not know that Reagan was going to introduce the issue to the public with a major speech until the morning of the speech. Weinberger was in Portugal at a meeting of the NATO Nuclear Planning Group. He requested permission to brief the NATO Defense Ministers on the upcoming speech, but could not get an answer from the White House staff. Weinberger implied in his memoirs that he was deliberately blocked by White House staffers who wanted to maximize the surprise effect of the speech. Ultimately, he spoke directly to the president and received permission, but did not have enough time to brief all the NATO allies. Ikle and Perle, the two officials of the DOD who would have to fit ballistic missile defense into U.S. nuclear and arms control policy, also found out about the speech the morning it was delivered.[60]

That night, 23 March 1983, President Reagan appeared on national television to announce a new initiative on ballistic missile defense. In criticizing assured destruction, Reagan asked rhetorically, "Wouldn't it be better to save lives than to avenge them?" and outlined his "vision of the future," which he claimed held "the promise of changing the course of human history." He challenged the scientific community of the U.S. "to give us the means of rendering these nuclear weapons impotent and obsolete."[61]

Reagan's speech revealed a great deal about his thinking on the issue. He had become enamored of the idea of strategic defense because he saw the issue on many levels. The moral level is clear from both the speech and Reagan's dislike for nuclear weapons. On the strategic level, functioning defenses could end the threat of the large Soviet missiles that were the focus of START. The fact that Scowcroft was told of the speech suggests that those in the administration working on the initiative realized that strategic defense was another alternative to breaking the START and MX deadlock of which the commission should be aware. Reagan also saw the issue in a political context. He was attempting to change the entire nature of the debate on nuclear weapons. The freeze movement, the criticism of Reagan's nuclear policy, the impasse over the MX and

START could all be neutralized politically by changing the issue from offense to defense. Though the SDI created its own wake of controversy, Reagan was successful in redirecting the discussion on nuclear weapons.[62]

The shift in policy had taken place without thorough review by the interagency process. Only after the president's speech did the policy process begin. NSDD-85, "Eliminating the Threat from Ballistic Missiles," of 25 March 1983, asked for a comprehensive review of ballistic missile defense. By June the initial process for examining the issue was underway. The main thrust of the policy process was based on ad hoc groups that reported to government officials.[63]

A basic premise of the evolution model is that decision making changes over time. By 1982–83 it had become clear that substantial disagreements over U.S. foreign and defense policy existed within the administration. Everyone in the upper levels of the administration, line officers and staff, understood that any issue might be an occasion for knock-down, drag-out fights between bureaucratic and organizational combatants. This learning about the process within the administration, about the disagreements between the two major factions, becomes crucial knowledge to anyone wishing to make a mark in the policy process. The idea of ballistic missile defense was therefore protected. Those in favor of ballistic missile defense wanted to control the speed of the decision-making process. They believed that allowing it to enter the interagency process was a certain way of letting it sink into interagency quicksand.

CONCLUSIONS

The decision-making process on START exhibits a narrowing of the process, an increase in ad hoc and informal processes, and a streamlining and occasional abandonment of the interagency process. When faced with political pressures to develop arms control proposals that satisfied Congress and the public, the administration narrowed participation, added informality to the process, and often bypassed the interagency system entirely. The policy process that led to the strategic defense speech, however, began narrowly, informally, and outside the interagency process. The changes in the decision-making process illustrate and explain the emergence of the three concurrent structures.

The origins and function of the informal and confidence structures were deeply affected by the president's management style. Though the formal SIG-IG process remained the backbone of administration decision making, Reagan's confidence in Clark allowed Clark to become Reagan's first-among-equals adviser. He put a deadline on the START-IG's deliberations and gave McFarlane the job of creating the compromise that became the Eureka proposals. He was the lead administration negotiator with Congress and the Scowcroft Commission over the Build-Down and the MX. Along with Meese, another close adviser to the president, Clark guided the strategic defense idea around the interagency minefield.

However, Reagan's detached style and his willingness to allow the hardliners and pragmatists to continue their rivalry allowed the formal interagency process to capture the informal structure and obliterate the confidence structure. As detailed in the previous chapter, Reagan's confidence structure fell victim to his inattentive leadership. As the confidence structure emerged with Clark in the lead role, his rivals moved against him. The troika tried to weaken him and Reagan did not come to his defense. A confidence structure that had allowed Reagan to forge policy out of his divided administration disappeared when Clark left the ANSA position. The informal structure should have been where the principals worked out their differences. Instead, hardliners and pragmatists fought within the NSPG, refusing to use it to resolve the controversy. Instead of a forum for consensus building, the NSPG informality was merged into the SIG-IG process. Reagan was left with only a fully formed formal structure, which was tied up in knots.

In short, the evolution of the decision unit proceeded during 1982 and 1983 in similar fashion to the way the Carter administration had. However, Reagan's leadership style—his desire for delegation and unwillingness to resolve conflict—led to a reversal in this evolution. Reagan allowed his White House troika to dismantle the system that had evolved and he failed to nurture the collegiality that could have made the NSPG an important informal forum. A new informal process did not begin until 1984 when Shultz, Robert McFarlane (Clark's replacement), and Reagan began having Wednesday and Friday meetings.[64]

The tale of Reagan administration decision making on arms control and nuclear strategy highlights the importance of domestic politics as an influence on the decision-making structure and the importance of presidential involvement in managing the decision-making process. Reagan's arms control policies provide clear evidence of the political impact of the passage of time. A president is on the clock once he is inaugurated. He has a limited amount of time to fill major policy voids by following the precedent of past administrations. In the case of arms control, whether the administration was for or against it, the American people expected negotiations between the U.S. and USSR on nuclear missiles.

The administration was pressed into coming up with the Eureka proposals and pressed again to add the build-down when the administration's initial proposals failed to generate any progress in Geneva. This could be blamed on the Soviets, which is precisely what the administration did. However, the perception among many in Congress that the administration's proposals were not fair, that they were simply designed to antagonize the Soviets while providing the facade of arms control, explains congressional action. The political timing of the budget cycle, which allowed Congress to push the administration to include the build-down in the mix at Geneva, is an anticipated pressure that the administration learned to accommodate. The MX was simply the tool Congress used to change administration policy.

Importantly, the administration learned that legislative-executive competition exists no matter what the partisan makeup of Congress might be. Usually, divided government—when one party controls the executive branch and another controls Congress—is seen as the cause of executive-legislative tension. The first term Reagan Congress was not such a case. At first glance, since Republicans controlled the Senate and Democrats controlled the House, it might be expected that the Senate would side with the administration and the House would provide the criticism. However, over arms control and the MX, while many Republicans supported the administration and most Democrats did not, enough Republicans were unhappy with administration policies to cause the government to operate in classical Madisonian fashion. The legislative branch fought the executive branch for control of policy.

This look at political pressures constitutes only part of the reason why the administration's decision-making process evolved. Pressure from Congress does not necessarily result in changes in the decision-making process within the administration. In the case of the Reagan administration it did because of the basic characteristics of the administration's structural and bureaucratic makeup. The highly decentralized cabinet structure, combined with a wide philosophical rift among administration officials and a president unwilling to settle those differences, made it impossible for the administration to respond to political pressures without modifying the decision process. The point should not be underestimated. The limitations on the president's ability to make the bureaucracy work for him are the oldest story in the study of presidential decision making. However, in this case, it seems that the president never realized that he needed to manage his decision-making machinery to get it to work for him. He had delegated this job to the troika. When Clark tried to manage foreign policy on the president's behalf, he met such resistance from the troika, that he decided to leave the ANSA post rather than fight the president's battles in surrogate. The president never stepped in to protect Clark or manage the process himself. His leadership style allowed the hardliner-pragmatist division to define the administration's tenure.

Strategic defense policy making was an exception. Reagan and his troika had learned a great deal about decision making. The move of Clark to the ANSA position and the upgrading of that position signals that they had come to understand the need for some centralization of leadership within the administration. The shielding of the strategic defense idea is a learned response to the realities of Reagan's interagency process. New ideas can get crushed. Reagan seemed to understand this as well. Once he became enamored with the idea, he gave the job of writing the speech and committing the administration to the NSC staff, not the bureaucracies. This deliberate bypass from beginning to end is a clear indication that the new administration had learned about decision making.

What is interesting here is the contrast between arms control and strategic defense decision making. Arms control decisions and changes in the process were made in response to congressional pressure, a reaction to political competition. The strategic defense policy was an innovation. The type of policy being made had a deep effect on the style of policy making. That relationship between policy and process will be explored more deeply in the concluding chapter. However, this notion appears to be the reverse of the usual focus. Generally, scholars examine the policy process to understand how it affects the policy produced within that process. Here are examples of how characteristics of the policy itself influence the decision process.

Chapter Six

THE BUSH ADMINISTRATION:
DECISION MAKING
AMONG FRIENDS

BRENT SCOWCROFT, ANSA IN THE FORD AND G. H. W. BUSH administrations and the model for how an ANSA can effectively manage the interagency process and be a presidential adviser, stated it simply: "I believe that good personnel can make even a poor organizational structure work, but that even a good structure cannot compensate for poor personnel." He spoke not only of the individuals in each important position, but also of their relationships. The joint memoirs of President Bush and Scowcroft provide a telling glimpse at those relationships as it describes, for two full pages, the annual award given by the administration to the cabinet official who falls asleep during important meetings, but recovers with style, pretending to never have nodded off.[1] The comradery, self-deprecation, and good-natured ribbing contained in these passages are a far cry from the bitterness and recriminations that usually lie just below the surface of many memoirs.

As detailed in chapter three, one of the keys to the success of the Bush administration's decision process was a natural collegiality among friends and colleagues who had worked together before. In spite of this, the decision-making process did narrow slightly for decision making on arms control, informality was added to the process, and the standard interagency process was streamlined from time to time. The changes were not as stark as in the Carter administration, nor were they made to overcome a paralyzing gridlock as in the Reagan administration. In this case, these changes were made to supplement the standard interagency process, not to replace it. The administration's response to the pressures for centralization and necessity for control was to carefully add informal processes that retained a basic interagency structure in an effort to compensate for the often slow pace of even the best designed formal system.

The evolution of Bush decision making on arms control includes accounts of three decision-making periods: from inauguration to the Malta Summit of December 1989; 1990 through the signing of START I in July of 1991; and the administration's proposals for a follow-up agreement, START II, contained in speeches given on 27 September 1991 and 28 January 1992.

The case studies illustrate how START decisions often streamlined the interagency process. However, whenever the process was streamlined, it never lost its interagency flavor. Either all relevant agencies were included or, if excluded from the process temporarily, they were allowed to reenter the process during the final debates in the policy process. An informal NSC staff–State Department committee performed the preplanning for the Malta Summit without DOD participation, but Secretary of Defense Dick Cheney was brought into the process to help decide what proposals, if any, would be made at the summit. The spring of 1991 saw the creation of a committee at the undersecretary level that backstopped the core group of decision makers; this "Ungroup" contained full interagency participation even though it was detached and often shielded from the standard formal system. The follow-up to START, contained in two Bush speeches of September 1991 and January 1992, had its origin in ideas that were developed in secrecy by Bush and Scowcroft. Others within the Gang of Eight were brought into the discussion after the main thrust of the policy had been set. Bush's personal style and his desire to maintain collegiality were the key elements here. No matter what changes would be made to the decision-making process, full participation of all the senior decision makers would never be sacrificed.

Importantly, these adaptations were seen by the senior decision makers to be typical and trusted methods of making decisions based on their vast experiences in government. One of the primary motivations for these changes was an effort to conserve the president's time and energy.[2]

Political pressures influenced decision making on START in several ways. Each was related to the need for economy in decision making. Administration delays in completing the treaty led to questions. Most notably, after the collapse of Communism in Eastern Europe in 1989, critics of the administration complained about the failure to reduce cold war arsenals as the cold war passed into history. Decision-making shortcuts were used not to exclude officials, but to concentrate the administration's energy on the task of ensuring that politically inspired deadlines would not lead to mediocre policy. These same factors help explain the narrowing, the ad hoc nature, and the interagency streamlining in the development of the speeches of September 1991 and January 1992. These speeches represent the domestic political necessities of moving forward on arms control in preparation for the presidential race of 1992. The international context played a key role as well. The coup of August 1991 in the Soviet Union had delegitimized the Communist Party and eventually led to the demise of the USSR itself. As the Soviet Union collapsed, Bush moved quickly to speed up the reduction of both sides' nuclear arsenals as a way to hedge against the potential reemergence of hard-line elements in Russia.

Learning was a factor in the evolution of the Bush administration in an interesting way. The senior members of the administration, all veterans of the Ford and/or Reagan administrations, had already learned many of the decision-making lessons that the Carter and Reagan teams had to learn on the job. Their initial decision-making structure and several other instances in which the administration made decisions in secrecy among only the core group of senior advisers are testaments to that. However, they also seemed to learn that further centralization is necessary at times—the spring of 1991 and the fall–winter of 1991–92. Most important in this case may be what they did not have to learn. They did not have to learn about each other.

FROM THE INAUGURATION TO THE MALTA SUMMIT

The Malta Summit of 2 and 3 December 1989, was the administration's first formal meeting with the leaders of the Soviet Union. In the midst of the sweeping change in Eastern Europe, the administration chose not to be a bystander. However, it was unsure how to gauge any changes in the U.S.–USSR relationship or the sincerity of the Soviet leadership. In this episode, the administration's decision process narrowed, creating informal groups, then ultimately moved against the current toward broader participation. The evolution of the process was temporary and designed to support, not replace, the formal system.

International and Domestic Political Environment

The U.S. deployment of intermediate range nuclear missiles in Europe in the fall of 1983 led the USSR to walk out of the INF talks in November of that year. It also ended the START negotiations for Reagan's first term. When the then-current round of negotiations ended on 8 December 1983, no date for resumption was set. In the fall of 1984 the U.S. proposed continued talks on arms control. The proposal led to discussions between Secretary of State George Shultz and Soviet Foreign Minister Andrei Gromyko in January of 1985, which produced agreement to begin negotiations again in March of 1985. These new negotiations were more comprehensive in nature. Dubbed the Nuclear and Space Arms Talks (NST), they were actually three sets of negotiations dealing with the issues of strategic weaponry (a continuation of START), intermediate nuclear force issues (again a continuation of previous negotiations), and space weapons including strategic defenses.

Mikhail Gorbachev's ascendance to leadership in the USSR and his initiation of policy reforms led to rapid progress on some of these issues. The INF treaty that eliminated all short- and intermediate-range ballistic missiles in Europe between the ranges of 500 and 5,500 kilometers was signed in December of 1987. The space weapons portion of the talks foundered on differing views of Reagan's Strategic Defense Initiative (SDI). The Soviets insisted that SDI was a violation of the Antiballistic Missile (ABM) Treaty of 1972 (part of SALT I). The Reagan administration countered that it was abiding by a "broad" interpretation of the ABM treaty, which allowed testing, development, and deployment of new technologies for strategic defense. The Soviet desire to end the SDI program contributed to Gorbachev's willingness to cut deeply into his own strategic arsenal. As a tradeoff for the elimination of SDI, the Soviet leadership began to seriously negotiate real and significant reductions in offensive strategic weaponry. By the time the Reagan administration prepared to leave office, the outline of a START treaty based on limits and sublimits that forced both sides to cut between 25% and 33% of their ballistic missile warheads had been settled.[3]

The Bush administration did not rush to conclude an agreement. First, the administration was skeptical of Gorbachev and felt that the Reagan team had been overly enthusiastic about the reforms in the USSR in general and arms control in particular. Commensurate with their realist assumptions, the administration recognized Soviet power as the key factor in its perception of the Soviet threat, no matter who was in charge of the nation; the Bush team still viewed the Soviet Union as the chief adversary to the U.S. When it came to nuclear weapons, the hallmark of the relationship was still deterrence. Bush and Scowcroft shared an uneasiness about deep cuts in strategic arsenals. For them the issue was the stability of the U.S. deterrent, not the need for reductions in both nations' arsenals.[4]

This is related to a second issue. Deep reductions might decrease the effectiveness of the U.S. deterrent, particularly if issues of strategic modernization were not ironed out first. ICBM modernization had not been settled. The issues that had been in play since the genesis of the MX program in the early 1970s still dogged U.S. defense planning in spite of the window-of-vulnerability debate, Carter and Reagan's searches for a basing mode, and the Scowcroft Commission. The Scowcroft Commission had settled on a temporary silo-based home for the MX and research and development on a small mobile single-warhead missile, dubbed the small ICBM (SICBM) or Midgetman. Plans to place the MX on a railroad-based mobile deployment were currently in the works. Congress had set a deadline of 15 February 1989 for a decision on spending $600 million for ICBM modernization.[5] The choice was between spending the money for development of the rail-MX system or a road-mobile SICBM. The question seemed obvious: How can the U.S. decide what strategic forces it can cut unless it decides what type of strategic forces it wants?

Scowcroft had been co-chair of a panel in 1988 that examined this very issue of ICBM modernization. He left the panel once he had been selected as ANSA; however, the majority of the panel's conclusions had already been decided. The resulting report, "Deterring through the Turn of the Century," was a joint project of the Johns Hopkins University Foreign Policy Institute and Georgetown's Center for Strategic and International Studies. The panel's report, released in early February, favored delaying the deployment of the rail-MX and concentrating first on deploying the B-2 bomber and the mobile SICBM. The recommendations were based on the potentially prohibitive cost of building all three and the rail-MX reliance on strategic warning for dispersal.[6]

The importance of this panel lies not in its recommendations, but its politics. Within this panel, the incoming ANSA had worked closely with the two key members of the democratic-controlled Congress on defense issues—Senate Armed Services Chair Sam Nunn and House Armed Services Chair Les Aspin. There was a clear understanding of the politics of ICBM modernization between Congress and the administration. Democrats leaned toward the SICBM; Republicans favored the rail-MX. START was still shadowed by this issue. Until the U.S. could settle internal administration disagreement on strategic modernization (see below) and legislative-executive battles over strategic modernization, the U.S. START position would be in flux. The fact that the draft START treaty included a mobile missile ban only made the issue more complex. Nearly all of the major players in the administration and Congress believed this proposal was a mistake.

Third, the administration's less than enthusiastic reading of Gorbachev's reforms included the Reagan draft treaty. Many aspects of the treaty beyond the issue of mobile missiles were seen to be incomplete or unwise. More needed to be done on the treaty; it simply was not ready for signing. The issue of verification was a particular area of concern. This was even more true within the U.S. Senate. The Senate, particularly the Republican members, had given the INF Treaty a rough ride.[7] This was a strong reminder to the administration that any START Treaty must be written to pass muster as if it were 1969 or 1979, even though it was 1989 and the Communist bloc was crumbling. As long as the USSR possessed enough nuclear weapons to destroy the United States, arms control agreements would be judged on how they contributed to strengthening deterrence and ensuring strategic stability.

The Standard Interagency Process

Bush's policy on START during most of 1989 can best be described as one of delay. The target date set by the Reagan administration for the eleventh round of START was mid-February 1989. The Bush administration, however, made it clear very early that it was freezing all negotiations with the USSR pending the outcome of its numerous strategic reviews. The next round for START was eventually set for 19 June 1989. During the five months of preparation the Bush team worked on its approach to the negotiations and established its procedures for making decisions on arms control. The National Security Review on arms control, NSR-14, was undertaken by the Arms Control Policy Coordinating Committee and chaired by Arnold Kanter, the NSC staff's senior director for defense policy and arms control. Ideas under review included a ban on SS-18 test flights, new counting rules for ALCMs, withdrawal of the mobile missile ban in the draft treaty, or modifications to the ban that would allow single-warhead missiles (the SICBM) but not mobile MIRVed missiles (the MX). The fact that NSR-14 was headed by an NSC staffer says a great deal about how the division of labor on arms control was structured within the administration. Scowcroft had, by far, the greatest expertise within the administration on arms control. Baker had never held a position in which arms control was a central responsibility, and Cheney, though secretary of defense, was limited to his experiences as a congressman. Bush states in his memoirs that one of the reasons for choosing Scowcroft was to get an expert on defense policy and arms control, issues about which Bush had less training.[8]

This did not mean that the NSC controlled arms control policy. NSR-14 was an interagency review. The key contributor from the State Department was Under Secretary of State for International Security Affairs Reginald Bartholomew. Bartholomew's position was part of a State Department reorganization that placed responsibility for weapons proliferation and strategic arms negotiations under the authority of this new undersecretary. Bartholomew, though not part of Baker's inner circle, became the State Department's interagency point man on arms control for the formal interagency process. The new State Department management style, in which the assistant secretaries reported to the undersecretaries and not to the secretary of state, also gave Bartholomew more responsibility in the formal process, leaving Baker and his advisers more freedom to make decisions informally. The other key lower-level player in this review was Richard Burt, the U.S. negotiator for START.[9]

U.S. policy to open the START negotiations was hammered out in a series of NSC meetings in June. NSR-14 provided the backdrop for possible proposals. More importantly, Congress loomed as a silent, but powerful player in these deliberations. For congressional Republicans the issue was the verifiability of the treaty. For congressional Democrats a decision on ICBM modernization was the key. NSC meetings on 6, 14, and 15 June provided the forum for coming up with a "Bushified" START proposal.[10] Ultimately, the decisions produced by these meetings were nondecisions. Nothing was actually settled. No consensus had been reached within the administration on any of the key issues, except perhaps that movement on START could wait until Soviet intentions were clearer.

Organizational Dynamics

One of the possible outcomes of the strategic review process was that the administration would back away from some of Reagan's START positions. In general, most of the senior decision makers felt that the Reagan administration enthusiasm for the changes in the USSR had led it to make too many concessions on START for the sake of achieving an agreement. A brief look at the administration's views of Gorbachev and the changes in the USSR will illustrate this point and the minor divisions that existed among the senior decision makers. By 1988 Reagan policy toward the USSR had turned completely around from where it had started in 1981. Reagan came to office seeing the USSR as the evil empire and left office proclaiming a partnership with Gorbachev. The incoming Bush administration was more skeptical. As realists and pragmatists, Bush and his senior advisers were more cautious about the changes in the USSR and whether the Russian bear could become a teddy bear so quickly. They felt the cold war was not yet over, but it could be ending. Bush and Scowcroft felt that the harsh rhetoric of the early Reagan years and the enthusiasm with which Reagan embraced Gorbachev in 1988 were both exaggerations. Cheney was more skeptical than Bush and Scowcroft, even saying in April of 1989 that Gorbachev's attempts to reform the USSR would fail. Gates also shared the belief that the Reagan administration was overly optimistic following the signing of the Intermediate Nuclear Force (INF) Treaty in December 1987 and that the jury was still out on whether Gorbachev's reforms were real. In 1989, Powell in an optimistic assessment argued that by 1994 the USSR would have 40% cuts in defense spending and 50% cuts in manpower, the Warsaw pact would be gone, and Germany would be reunified. Baker was the least skeptical of all the senior advisers, but even he saw in Gorbachev's reforms an effort to divide NATO. The collapse of the detente of the 1970s was a seminal event for all of them. Veterans of the Ford administration were particularly sensitive to this, but all of the administration's decision makers had watched the 1970s begin with hope for real change in the U.S.-USSR relationship and end with a new and potentially more dangerous cold war. They were committed to making sure this did not happen again.[11]

All of the principals agreed that Gorbachev was better than the alternative, that there still might be reversals in Soviet policy, and that the U.S. needed to test Gorbachev to see how far he was willing to go for the sake of improving U.S.-USSR relations.[12] To put it simply, Gorbachev needed to prove his seriousness to the members of the Bush team. Some needed more convincing than others. Eventually, Gorbachev convinced them all. As the administration's tenure wore on, the skepticism and suspicion faded. The USSR pulled out of Afghanistan; Eastern Europe was freed; the situation in Central America was stabilized; conventional and nuclear arms control made remarkable headway. Ultimately, the U.S. and USSR became allies in the conflict with Saddam Hussein's Iraq.

The natural caution inherent in the pragmatic views of each member of the

Bush team meant that the overall approach to the USSR was a "wait-and-see" policy. However, as the administration began developing its policy on various issues from Soviet support of the Contras to START, there was plenty of room for debate on the nature of the changes in the USSR. These disagreements never became the knock-down-drag-out warfare evident in the Reagan administration. They were not about fundamental perspectives on international relations or the basic views of the USSR. These were different analytical perspectives within the realist paradigm on national security. The differences between the officials were smaller than those in the Reagan administration, and the friendships between these men prevented the small arguments from escalating into major decision-making rivalries.

There were specific differences related to arms control that became key factors in the administration's deliberations. Scowcroft was allied with congressional Democrats in his support for the SICBM. Within the Pentagon, both Cheney and Strategic Air Command Chief General John Chain favored the MX over the SICBM, in either mobile or nonmobile variants.[13] For Cheney and the Joint Chiefs the issue was the U.S. ability to carry out the SIOP and deter the USSR with significantly fewer ICBMs. Scowcroft hoped to settle the modernization issue before the resumption of START.[14]

Presidential Choice and Political Strategy

Bush had political reasons to delay the signing of the START treaty. He did not want his arms control legacy to be his signature adorning the bottom of a Reagan treaty. As in the case of overall national security, Bush did not want his administration to be a third Reagan term. Bush wanted new bold initiatives in an effort to make the START treaty a Bush treaty.[15] Though Bush had been Reagan's vice president, the need to highlight significant differences with a presidential predecessor was a factor in Bush's decision making.

The Bush team decided to fend off congressional pressure as it waited for some intra-administration consensus on arms control. Talks on conventional weapons were given priority over strategic weaponry. The issue of SDI was still one being fought primarily within the Pentagon. The concrete decisions that came out of the June NSC meetings reflected the administration's attention to congressional concerns. Bush had made a decision in April to deploy both the rail-MX and SICBM. This satisfied both Scowcroft and Cheney as well as Democrats and Republicans in Congress. The responsibility for modernization and the U.S. START position was then placed in Congress's hands as the START talks got underway in June. In meetings with senior leaders in Congress, including Nunn, Aspin, and Al Gore (D-Tenn.), Bush and his senior advisers explained that they would rescind the ban on mobile missiles in the current draft treaty if Congress would fund both the rail-MX and the SICBM.[16] These negotiations with Congress took precedence over the negotiations with the USSR at this point.

In a bone for congressional Republicans and perhaps a clever way of delaying any real progress in START, the administration announced as part of its initial negotiating position a verification initiative. The initiative called for refocusing START on verification of potential treaty provisions before those provisions were actually negotiated. The logic for this is simple. The U.S. and USSR should not agree to limit their systems in ways that cannot be verified. For this reason, the Bush initiative called for the two sides to set up working groups in Geneva to discuss verification methods and proceed from there to actual dry runs of verification techniques.[17] Once the limits of verification technologies and confidence-building measures were understood, then the two sides would have a better understanding of what types of reductions in strategic systems could be confidently verified.

The actual proposals presented to the USSR at the June round of START bypassed all the major issues that had been left over from the Reagan years, and all the issues that were pending consensus within the administration and between the administration and Congress. The proposals dealt with verification and several peripheral issues.[18] For the purposes of this research, the details are not crucial. What is important is the fact that these decisions were made through an interagency NSR process that led to NSC meetings. This differed greatly from the decisions in the fall concerning the Malta Summit.

Presidential Choice and Management Strategy

Bush's leadership style set the tone for his administration's method of managing decisions. Baker, in particular, seems to have shared Bush's belief in personal diplomacy. Though Baker had gone to Moscow in May of 1989 to talk directly with Soviet Foreign Minister Eduard Shevardnadze and Gorbachev, the real top-level discussions on START did not begin until September of 1989. Bush had sent Gorbachev a letter on 20 June outlining some new ideas on START. Shevardnadze traveled to Washington on 21 September with Gorbachev's response. The START negotiations truly got under way during Shevardnadze's trip. Baker planned for Shevardnadze to accompany him to his home in Jackson Hole, Wyoming, on 22 and 23 September. The publicity that dogged them led Baker to convince Shevardnadze that they should travel together on Baker's plane and hold private talks during which they could get to know each other. On the flight from Washington to Wyoming, accompanied by only a few key aides, Baker and Shevardnadze formed a partnership that served as a strong foundation for U.S.-Soviet relations. Baker was convinced during this trip that the changes in the USSR were real, that Shevardnadze and Gorbachev were sincere, and that the U.S. should do all it could to help move along Soviet reform, reform that was in the U.S. interest. Shevardnadze confided in Baker on the deep difficulties in restructuring the USSR, the obstacles to better relations with the U.S., and his views on why these reforms were necessary. Ultimately, what was established here can be seen as an institutionalized back channel through which Baker and Shevardnadze communicated directly as a matter of standard procedure and met face to face on many occasions, always with the understanding that their growing trust could push the relationship between the two nations along.[19]

Shevardnadze's trip to Washington and Wyoming gave START a much-needed push. Sensing that the Bush administration was less interested in START than they were, Gorbachev and Shevardnadze made significant concessions on SDI, the Krasnoyarsk radar, and SLCMs to move the process along. The U.S. responded with a proposal to lift the mobile missile ban pending congressional action on ICBM modernization. A target date for a summit where a START treaty would be signed was set for May or June of 1990. Agreements on trial runs for verification measures and notifications of strategic exercises were signed.[20]

All three of these concessions gave impetus for the Bush administration to end its delay on START. The Soviets were making unilateral concessions and giving more evidence to allay the suspicions of officials within the administration. Even when Shevardnadze's requests for reciprocal U.S. proposals were refused, the Soviets did not withdraw their initial offerings. These concessions may have turned the tide on another administration debate. From the early months of the administration, Bush had favored a get-acquainted summit with Gorbachev. If forming personal relationships with foreign leaders was important, this might be the most important relationship to nurture. Scowcroft had been reluctant to schedule a summit without some concrete accomplishment to set as the centerpiece of the meeting. Bush had decided on 13 July, after visits to Hungary and Poland, that he wanted to set a date for a no-agreement summit, just a meeting during which he and Gorbachev could get to know each other better.[21]

Secret negotiations began on where and when to hold the summit. Only a handful of officials knew of these negotiations that were conducted mostly by Bush and Baker. Those in the know at the senior level also included Quayle, Scowcroft, Gates, Chief of Staff John Sununu, and Press Secretary Marlin Fitzwater. In each case, the principals may have told some of their senior aides. Importantly, Cheney and DCI William Webster were kept out of the loop for most of the summer and fall.[22] The reasons for their exclusion are unclear, though one guess might be that their input was not needed in preparation for the summit until policy decisions were ready to be made. Bush may have been acting more in his old role as CIA director, limiting participation and knowledge of events to only those who needed to know. The summit was set to take place on U.S. and USSR naval ships off the coast of Malta on 2 and 3 December. The scheduling of a summit was not made public until October 31. The entire secret process and surprise announcement fits Bush's desire to confound the "experts" who said he was too cautious and too reactive. It also illustrates the deep centralization that the administration favored at times and its deep resentment of leaks.

A small group made up of NSC staffers and members of Baker's inner circle performed the staff work for Malta. From the NSC staff Senior Director for Europe and Soviet Affairs Robert Blackwill and Director for Soviet and East European Affairs Condoleezza Rice teamed up with the State Department's Counselor Robert Zoellick and Director of the Policy Planning Council Dennis Ross (hereafter referred to as the BRZR group). One of the sources of potential ideas was Bartholomew. He was placed in charge of developing new ideas for the State Department and submitting them to Ross who then presented them to Baker.

Decision making for the summit diverged from the standard interagency NSC process. Informal streamlining of the interagency process within a subset of the Gang of Eight and their staff (BRZR group) was the pattern for this decision. The reasons for closing the circle to these groups relates to political pressures and economy. Bush did not want press coverage of the debates within the administration. The more public the summit became the more pressure there would be to reach some agreements at the summit, and the Bush team was adamant that this be an informal getting-to-know-you meeting. Secondly, if there were to be any proposals made at the summit, they would need to be staffed-out quickly. Therefore the formal interagency process was streamlined in favor of these more narrow groupings.

The proposal that caught Baker and Scowcroft's eyes was one proposed by both Burt and Bartholomew for a ban on mobile MIRVed ICBMs, essentially a trade of the MX for the Soviet SS-24 (a rail-based ICBM with ten warheads). When Baker proposed the idea to Bush, Bush suggested an even bolder approach —a complete ban on MIRVed ICBMs. Baker and Scowcroft also supported the proposal, though Cheney, an MX proponent, did not. For Baker and Scowcroft, this was just the type of bold initiative that could make the administration's mark on the START process. In addition, Scowcroft believed it added to stability, eliminating what had been the greatest concern to the U.S. since the mid-1970s— Soviet quantitative superiority in medium and heavy MIRVed ICBMs. Scowcroft had already discussed the problem of MIRVed ICBMs with General Sergei Akhromeyev, Gorbachev's chief military adviser. Akhromeyev also saw the vulnerability problems created by MIRVed ICBMs.[23]

To Cheney, a ban on MIRVed ICBMs reversed the Pentagon's preferred modernization plans by calling for the end of the MX program, dismantling of the Minuteman III, and a modernization program that could only include the SICBM. The MIRVed ICBM ban was discussed at a meeting of the Gang of Eight while Cheney was on a trip outside of Washington. He was unhappy to find out when he returned that the idea had gained some headway. From a bureaucratic standpoint, he had been excluded from the early negotiations on the Malta Summit, and ideas that ran counter to his positions were generating momentum in his absence. However, the ultimate decision on whether to bring the MIRVed ICBM ban to Malta was made at a Breakfast Group meeting of Baker, Cheney, and Scowcroft.[24] Cheney's argument won the day. He feared that proposing a termination to the MX program that was already in danger within Congress might kill it altogether, whether the Soviets agreed to the MIRVed ICBM ban or not. The MX could die while the Soviet medium and heavy MIRVed missiles might survive. Even if the MIRVed ICBM ban was successfully negotiated, he argued, doing so without clear signals from Congress that the SICBM would be funded undercut U.S. modernization plans. Within the Breakfast Group, the three most senior decision makers decided to recommend to Bush that the MIRVed ICBM ban be held back. It was not introduced at the Malta Summit. The quick decision and the lack of infighting are in stark contrast to the Carter and Reagan administrations. Here, consensus mattered; preventing administration infighting mattered. Maintaining a smooth decision-making process was a priority over making specific decisions. Political pressures for a swift conclusion of START were resisted.

Nothing concerning START was settled in Malta. Bush and Gorbachev's get-acquainted meeting may have smoothed the way for further negotiations, but the two sides agreed once again that START should be signed at a June 1990 summit. Baker's and Shevardnadze's attempts to write a joint communiqué failed since there was nothing to announce, save that both sides would continue the negotiating process.[25]

The secrecy surrounding the existence of the summit and the search for arms control proposals that might accompany it illustrate a narrowing of the process. The BRZR group staffed out the options for Baker and Scowcroft, while a Breakfast Group meeting finally decided the issue on arms control—there would be no major proposals to the USSR yet. More centralized and nimble groups were favored over the full interagency process and even the Gang of Eight. At times very few people knew whether a summit was even in the offing, let alone what the U.S. and USSR might accomplish there. However, to the administration, generating the final recommendations to Bush within the Breakfast Group was a way of maintaining the interagency nature of the decision process. In the end, none of the key senior advisers was excluded.

The decision not to make any major moves on arms control seems to confound the political pressures. If the Reagan administration was near completion of a START treaty in the summer of 1988, surely the Bush team should be ready to sign on the dotted line by early 1990. Though indications are that Bush wanted Malta to be a get-acquainted summit, it also relieved some of the political pressure. The administration was prepared to weather the anticipated political criticism it would earn for its delay. In addition, the simple sight of Bush and Gorbachev meeting seemed to indicate progress in the U.S.-USSR relationship whether anything was accomplished or not. The necessity of the summit and Bush's secretive approach reveals the impact of the need for economy. Secrecy allowed Bush to make decisions on his own timetable, outside of the political pressures calling for a swifter meeting and a more substantial outcome to that meeting. Narrowing the decision making to the BRZR and the breakfast groups pushed the interagency process out of the way, allowing Bush to make decisions at his pace. Bush chose this method because his previous service in government had taught him the lesson that most presidents only learn on the job—a smaller, closely knit decision-making unit is more controllable, more adaptable, and more likely to produce the types of decisions the president favors.

CONCLUDING START: 1990 TO JULY 1991

Decisions on START I, from January of 1990 to 31 July 1991, when the treaty was signed, illustrate a merger of the negotiating and decision making that one might expect in the final stages of a negotiating process. The decision process within the administration was modified to accommodate the growing need to complete the treaty. The regular interagency process in Washington was streamlined into the Ungroup—a high-level interagency group created to backstop the START negotiations. The Ungroup was kept secret from most of the bureaucracy to allow it to isolate itself from the regular NSC process and the subordinate levels of the cabinet departments to which members of the Ungroup belonged. The Ungroup, in turn, soon supplanted the regular Geneva negotiations, providing a backstopping function for the negotiations between senior officials of the USSR and the administration.

International and Domestic Political Environment/
Standard Interagency Process

Because nothing concerning START was settled at Malta, the central issue remained the same: Should the administration accept the draft treaty it inherited from the Reagan-era negotiations, or should it try to "Bushify" the treaty in some fashion? This remained the administration's dilemma throughout 1990 and into 1991 when the START treaty was signed. The international and domestic political environment remained the same as it had been leading up to Malta. However, those political pressures seemed to intensify in a subtle way. As the Bush administration's term in office lengthened and a START Treaty was still not concluded, pressure from those in Congress and the public who supported arms control increased. Adding to this was the inevitable sense that since the cold war was ending and Eastern Europe was free, the START negotiations should become easier.

The standard interagency process was already streamlined significantly by this time, and the Gang of Eight came to dominate decision making more and more. Ultimately, members of the Gang of Eight even began negotiating directly with Soviet leaders. The senior members of the administration had become familiar enough with the details of arms control and strategic modernization (if they had not been from previous governmental service) that they did not need continuous reviews by the lower echelons of the bureaucracies.

Organizational Dynamics

START was addressed at an NSC meeting on 4 January 1990, and in Gang of Eight meetings later in January and February. The reluctance of Congress to make budgetary commitments to ICBM modernization worried Scowcroft. While the draft START Treaty included a ban on mobile missiles, the Soviets had already begun to develop the SS-24 and SS-25. They were analogous to the rail-MX and road-mobile SICBM, respectively. If Congress could not find a way to deploy new systems, perhaps the U.S. could cut into Soviet modernization through these START provisions. Scowcroft still favored what he saw as a more stable future— a movement to single warhead missiles through a ban on mobile MIRVed ICBMs. Cheney wanted to move slowly on arms control and swiftly on modernization. He favored working with the Reagan draft. He felt that a ban on mobile MIRVs and silo deployment of the MX would leave the U.S. back in the use-them-or-lose-them quandary that had led to the search for mobile basings in the first place. The stationary MX would become an attractive target for the Soviet war planner and place both nations in a situation where the incentive was to launch first. Baker and Powell agreed that the Reagan draft should form the basis for an agreement at this point, though for a different reason. They felt that the momentum built by signing a treaty early in the administration would speed up the political momentum of the relationship. Cheney won this point, and the U.S. negotiating position stayed relatively unchanged. Bush, however, in a letter to Gorbachev on 21 March, told the Soviet president that the U.S. was considering a ban on MIRVed ICBMs. This was still a matter of personal diplomacy, a diplomatic heads up, if you will. Neither a ban on MIRVed ICBMs nor mobile MIRVed ICBMs was formally proposed by the U.S.[26]

With a summit scheduled for June in Washington, D.C., the institutionalized back channel between Baker and Shevardnadze became the real forum for negotiations. Issues concerning ALCMs, SLCMs, and telemetry encryption were partially resolved during high-level meetings between them. By early March, the debate over Scowcroft's ideas on MIRVs had been settled in Scowcroft's favor. A secret proposal was given to Shevardnadze by Baker during a meeting in Windhoek, Namibia. The proposal and its contents were known by only a handful of members of the administration. They called for a two-phased approach to further ICBM arms control in START. In the first phase all mobile MIRVed ICBMs would be banned. The second phase would ban all MIRVed ICBMs. Shevardnadze was thankful that Baker broached the issue secretly to him rather than publicly or through the Geneva negotiations; however, he was not sanguine about the potential for agreement on this. The Soviets rejected the U.S. proposal and quickly responded with a proposal banning MIRVs on SLBMs as well. The U.S. rejected this counterproposal.[27]

Civilian hardliners within the USSR, allied with the Soviet General Staff, were placing pressure on Gorbachev to slow down what they saw as repeated Soviet concessions to the West. To protect himself politically from those who felt his domestic and foreign policy reforms were going too far, Gorbachev began to back away from some of the agreements on ALCMs and SLCMs achieved in February. A pattern was repeated through April and May in which Baker and Shevardnadze agreed on critical issues only to have the Soviet hardliners on the negotiation team in Geneva unravel the deal by adding new conditions to the proposed agreement. START was stalled. Though the Baker-Shevardnadze channel solved several issues during a four-day meeting in mid-May in Moscow, no agreement could be reached in time for the Washington Summit of 31 May through 3 June 1990.[28]

A summit to finish off START was set for February of 1991, but several obstacles made this impossible. Some of them were the typical minutia of arms control.[29] Others related to Soviet hardliners pushing Gorbachev to take tougher negotiating stands. More importantly, international developments diverted the attention of U.S. and Soviet decision makers. START simply was not as important as it had been. An immediate issue related to the U.S.-Soviet relationship was the Soviet crackdown in Lithuania. However, the two largest issues were the pending reunification of Germany and the Iraqi invasion of Kuwait. High-level attention to START really did not pick up again until after the Persian Gulf War ended.

Negotiations continued, however, in the two-level process that had become the norm for these negotiations. The Geneva negotiators plugged away at the details, while Baker and his new partner, Soviet Foreign Minister Alexander Bessmertnykh, worked on the larger issues. By mid-spring three issues remained in play that were holding up the signing of START.[30] The first was the issue of telemetry encryption. Questions remained over what types of data during what types of missile tests could or could not be encrypted. This was primarily an issue held up by the differences in the U.S. and Soviet positions.

The second issue was one in which Scowcroft and Cheney were the main protagonists. Again, however, this was a matter of disagreement over a strategic issue between colleagues, not an acrimonious conflict between rival advisers. In question was the procedure for moving to single-warhead ICBMs and SLBMs. Two ways existed to decrease the number of warheads on U.S. and USSR missile systems. Both sides could destroy their MIRVed missiles and build new single-warhead systems. This was prohibitively expensive, especially for the USSR. Downloading—removing warheads from a missile already in service and deploying it with fewer warheads than it was capable of carrying—was the other alternative. The problem was that these missiles had been tested with larger numbers of warheads than they would be deployed with after START, and those warheads would not be destroyed. In theory, either side could place those warheads back on the missiles in time of crisis. The potential for this type of breakout was the issue. The dilemma for the U.S. was how to structure a downloading process that decreased the incentive and capability for the Soviets to plan for such breakout. Scowcroft, in line with his preference for an evolution of both sides' forces toward single-warhead missiles, wanted both sides to move toward new single-warhead missiles. Cheney and the JCS preferred downloading. The internal battle within the U.S. was temporarily settled with a tentative proposal to allow both sides to download one type of missile. The Soviets, however, wanted to be allowed to download three types of missiles. This unraveled the consensus on downloading within the administration. The overall question of how many warheads would be allowed to be removed was also in play.[31]

The third issue was the definition of a new type of missile within the treaty. The U.S. wanted to require new types of ICBMs and SLBMs to differ from old types in throw weight by 30%. In this way, if the Soviets wanted to build new missiles, they would also need to build new silos for those missiles rather than build a new system with the potential capability to carry more warheads and place it in an existing silo. This raised the costs of new types of ICBM and SLBMs. The Soviets wanted new types of ICBMs and SLBMs to be those that differed in throw weight by 15%. In theory, then, their new types could be placed in existing silos, decreasing the costs of deploying new types of missiles. Specifically in question was the potential for MIRVing of the single-warhead, road-mobile SS-25. The U.S. believed it was possible that modifications to the SS-25 would allow it to carry two warheads, but still be launchable from existing mobile platforms.[32]

Presidential Choice: Political and Management Strategies

Bush's political strategy had not changed. He still favored something new, a bold approach that would make the treaty his treaty and answer the critics who claimed that he was too cautious. However, his management strategy based on consensus within the Gang of Eight outweighed his desire for a completion of START.

Bush pushed decision making and negotiating on START to the senior level, into the Gang of Eight. As a management strategy, this allowed the divisions within the administration to become the key variables in delaying the signing of the treaty. Bush was not going to sign any treaty until each of the senior players was satisfied. He wanted a consensus and was satisfied to wait until the Soviet position met those requirements. This position is an aspect of formalism; Bush was not going to exclude dissenting officials from the process as a method of moving the policy process forward. Consequently, the internal organizational dynamics within the administration were as important to the success of START as were the U.S.-Soviet talks. This is a typical situation in administations, as the Carter and Reagan case studies suggest. However, the difference here is the very direct participation of the Gang of Eight and the special Ungroup designed to back it up.

The endgame for START began in June. Already the U.S. had begun to re-shape aspects of its START decision making to bring more high-level attention to issues of arms control once the Persian Gulf War had ended. Earlier in the spring Bush established the Ungroup to coordinate the administration's policies and responses to Soviet initiatives. In a sense, it was an arms control brain trust designed to speed up the administration's decision process. The Ungroup met in the White House Situation Room, and nothing concerning the deliberations or even the existence of the Ungroup was placed in writing. There was to be no paper trail for this group; its existence was designed to be a secret. It was headed by Senior Director for Defense Policy and Arms Control Arnold Kanter of the NSC staff and, importantly, included full representation of all the relevant agencies.[33] Though initially charged with resolving the problem of the status of Soviet naval infantry units under the Conventional Forces in Europe (CFE) Treaty, it turned its attention to START in mid-June once this issue had been settled.

The motivation for forming the Ungroup is related to political pressures and economy. The Persian Gulf War had ended; the CFE treaty had been signed; START stood out prominently as unfinished business. It was originally scheduled to be signed in June of 1990, then February of 1991. The pressure to sign an agreement that had been in the works since 1981 was mounting. The Ungroup provided a way to speed up the process, a shorthand for the interagency process. As Bartholomew began negotiating with the USSR, the Ungroup merged the decision-making and negotiation processes, again to save time. For the Bush administration, this was an aspect of what the senior officials had learned during government service. Bumping up the process to a higher level, limiting the number of participants, and operating with back channels as standard operating procedure was the most efficient way of getting something resolved. The creation of the Ungroup represents a narrowing of the decision-making process, a streamlining of the regular interagency process and, given the secrecy of the group, a measure of improvisation.

The Gang of Eight gathered together for two days in early June to discuss START. Bush, Baker, Cheney, Scowcroft, and Powell met to come up with ways to move the negotiations forward. The debate reflected some of the initial arguments concerning START. Baker was the most optimistic, while Scowcroft's doubts about the downloading issue persisted. Baker was preparing to meet with Bessmertnykh in Geneva on the seventh. Bartholomew was also waiting for negotiating instructions before he flew on to Geneva. Baker brought a letter for Gorbachev outlining some methods of breaking the deadlock on the three outstanding issues. By the end of June, Bartholomew and members of the Ungroup was negotiating directly with a Soviet team led by Bessmertnykh's deputy Alexi Obukhov. Bush explicitly told Gorbachev that while in Geneva Bartholomew had authority to make deals on behalf of the administration.[34]

The administration was hoping to schedule a summit for the end of July. To this end, Bush wrote to Gorbachev on 5 July asking him to send Bessmertnykh to Washington for negotiations, but only if he had authority to make concrete deals that could end the deadlock.[35] During these negotiations, from 11 through 14 July, the negotiating and decision-making process merged even further. While Baker and Bessmertnykh worked with each other, the Ungroup attempted to resolve the downloading issue. Baker and Bessmertnykh agreed on 13 July that the only possible solution would be to allow three downloadable missiles, but place a specific numerical cap on the number of warheads that could be downloaded and, in theory, uploaded in a crisis. Essentially, this is a specific verifiable limit-to-breakout potential.

In a reversal of the expected pattern, Baker and Bessmertnykh had agreed on treaty provisions, but the decision within the administration had not yet been made. In a conference call, Baker pitched the deal he had made with Bessmert-nykh to Bush, Cheney, Scowcroft, and Powell. It was clear that Bush's emphasis on consensus meant that Scowcroft, a skeptic on the issue of downloading, had been given license to quash the deal. Powell, Cheney, and Baker convinced Scowcroft that this deal would be satisfactory. With Scowcroft finally relenting, Bush gave Baker the green light to put the downloading compromise into treaty language.[36]

The telemetry issue had also been settled during the Washington meetings in favor of the U.S. position of banning encryption and other interference in the transmission of data from flight tests. The only outstanding issue after the mid-July meetings was the definition of a new type of missile. Bush and Gorbachev met on 17 July in London at the summit of the Group of Seven industrial nations to resolve the final issue. Both leaders wanted it settled before they actually met, so they could simply accept an agreement already in place and set a date for a summit in Moscow. The deal was finalized that morning in London. Bessmertnykh, Chief of the Soviet General Staff Mikhail Moiseyev, and Soviet Defense Minister Dmitri Yazov agreed on a proposal, which was then debated by Bush, Baker, and Scowcroft. The Soviets offered a compromise in which a new type of missile differed in throw weight from an old type by 21%, and other new type definitions were added to address other concerns. Once the U.S. team in London was satisfied with the Soviet offer, the Ungroup, on call in Washington, went over the treaty language. Kanter and Bartholomew informed Scowcroft and Baker that the treaty language was satisfactory and, with minutes to spare, Bush and Gorbachev set the date for a summit. Nine years after negotiations began, the START treaty was signed on 31 July 1991, at the Bush-Gorbachev summit in Moscow.[37]

The successful negotiation of START had reflected a slight shift in administration decision-making style. The Gang of Eight, operating in an abbreviated form in most instances, consisting of only Bush, Baker, Cheney, Scowcroft, and Powell, was backstopped by the Ungroup. This truncated version of the Gang of Eight was standing in for the full NSC, while the Ungroup substituted for the regular interagency process. The narrowing of the process helped the administration maintain secrecy concerning its decisions. Both the Gang of Eight and the Ungroup were more informal and streamlined stand-ins for the more formal structures that existed within the administration. Their use depended primarily on the need to focus the decision-making resources of the administration on the problem and to maintain secrecy. In an aspect of formalism within the informal process, full horizontal interagency participation was evident in both groups. However, decision making was concentrated at the upper levels.

The key motivations were political pressures and economy. Almost all the arguments (or excuses) for delaying a START treaty had vanished. Refusal to conclude a strategic arms treaty in 1991 seemed to run contrary to Bush's own vision of his "new world order." For political reasons a treaty was necessary, and the administration's goal was to conclude a treaty quickly. This meant swift decision making, and the Bush administration had one typical method for advancing the pace of decision making—moving to small, ad hoc groups of decision makers. Dominance of the Gang of Eight and the Ungroup is a reflection of this. These small groups allowed the best minds to consider issues without delay. The Bush administration had learned that this was the key to getting things done.

THE GENESIS OF START II

The speeches of 27 September 1991 and 29 January 1992 that led to the START II treaty illustrate a familiar pattern. The genesis of the first speech can be traced to informal discussions between Bush and Scowcroft on the back porch of Bush's home in Kennebunkport, Maine. The eventual content of the speech delivered in September reflected a widening of the participation in the decision as the rest of the Gang of Eight was brought into the loop. Secrecy was crucial, however, and knowledge of the new proposals was limited to a handful of people outside the Gang of Eight. The State of the Union speech was developed within the Gang of Eight, and its contents were closely guarded. The main issue was the size of the cuts in strategic arsenals the U.S. would propose. Scowcroft and Cheney were the main protagonists here, with Cheney holding the line on cuts at about 5,000 warheads. In this instance, the decision-making process began at the most senior level and stayed there.

International and Domestic Political Environment

The failed August 1991 coup against Gorbachev that ultimately led to the dissolution of the Communist Party of the Soviet Union, the collapse of the USSR itself, and the birth of fifteen post-Soviet nations was also the impetus for Bush's next decision on arms control. What was soon called START II was the last round of U.S.-Soviet negotiations on strategic weapons and the first round of U.S. nego-

tiations with the successor states to the USSR who possessed nuclear weapons
—Russia, Ukraine, Belarus, and Kazakhstan.

With history accelerating at a rapid pace, the Bush administration had to
sprint to keep up. The coup had delegitimized the Communist Party of the USSR
so deeply that it was soon banned. Most of the republics that had made up the
Soviet Union had declared independence. It seemed that the USSR was shatter-
ing and Russia would be its successor state; the Soviet nuclear assets might be
divided among four states. Importantly, Gorbachev, who had become the administration's partner in so many endeavors—from the Gulf War to START—would
soon be the president of a nation that no longer existed. In August and September some of these developments were speculative, but the signs were clear that
nothing would ever be the same again. The cold war had ended, but the changes
did not stop there. The world was becoming less dangerous for the U.S., but perhaps more complex. If the administration hoped to bring at least some strategic
stability to the post-coup Soviet Union (eventually the post–Soviet Union states),
it had to put proposals in play for a post-START strategic relationship before more
changes radically altered the Soviet Union. It was crucial to gain some basic understanding of START II while Gorbachev still had the power to commit the
USSR to agreements and while the hardliners in the USSR were on the defensive. In addition, 1992 was an election year. Signing START II sometime in 1992
might help Bush's reelection chances. Political pressures demanded swift decisions. Bush turned to the methods that experience had taught him were the best
—a small group of his friends making decisions in secret.

Standard Interagency Process and Organizational Dynamics

The rapidity with which the administration wished to move on a new proposal
for arms control and the experience the senior officials had gained during the
START negotiations made full interagency reviews unnecessary at this point.
Decisions began and ended at the senior level. Though the organizational dynamics within the Bush administration were always collegial in nature, in this
case, any little disagreement that did exist was muted by the president. Bush's desire to move quickly toward START II was made known to all the senior players.
The president was the moving force behind this initiative, and all of his senior
advisers understood their roles clearly. They were to help the president fulfill his
goals. Any opposition that may have existed quickly faded.

Presidential Choice: Political and Management Strategies

In the days immediately following the failed coup of 20–23 August, Bush and Scowcroft began to discuss a follow-up to START. On the back porch of Bush's Walker's Point home in Kennebunkport, Maine, while vacationing, Bush and Scowcroft decided to move quickly to take advantage of the hardliners' weaknesses and to act before more changes occurred within the USSR. Bush made it clear to everyone involved that he wanted something bold. A strategic window of opportunity had opened. Bush could also use a new initiative as a way to put to rest the popular perception that he was too cautious.

Bush used a familiar style of high-level decision making shrouded in secrecy. The difference in this case was the pace of the decision. To take advantage of and keep up with the changes in the USSR, Bush pushed the process hard. Cheney and U.S. Ambassador to the USSR Robert Strauss came to Kennebunkport for consultations on the issue on 27 August. Cheney was asked by Scowcroft to develop some bold proposals with the aid of the JCS. Essentially, Bush and Scowcroft were asking Cheney to brush aside the usual administration caution (not to mention his personal cautious nature). Bush and Scowcroft had some additional brainstorming sessions on 28 August at breakfast and on Bush's speedboat off the coast of Maine.[38] During the first week of September, Bush, Cheney, and Scowcroft met again to discuss the issue. The issue was presented to the full Gang of Eight (Bush, Baker, Cheney, Scowcroft, Powell, Gates, Sununu, and Quayle) on 5 September.

Knowledge of these discussions was limited to the Gang of Eight and some of their senior aides. The task of developing these proposals was given to Cheney and Powell, even though Cheney was against moving swiftly toward any post-START negotiations. The fact that Cheney's Pentagon had been the most pessimistic about arms control since the inception of the administration provided a built-in check on doing something too creative. Bush, Scowcroft, and Baker had already made up their minds to go further than ever before. It is possible that Bush's instinctive caution caused him to create an institutionalized brake on his own policies. In addition, the depth of the cuts already made in START was significant enough that Bush's requests to the Pentagon had an ulterior motive. He was searching for the Pentagon's real sense of how low the U.S. arsenal could be cut without endangering deterrence. Pushing the Pentagon on this issue might get Bush past its usual position that cuts in strategic arsenals were inadvisable. It also could be the case that Bush was using an old bureaucratic method of converting the dissenters. Presidents often assign policy development or policy implementation to those who disagree with the policy. It is a way to force them to join the consensus, or at least act as if they have. In this case, Cheney was forced to join Powell on 9 and 17 September in presenting the new initiatives to the Gang of Eight. Scowcroft, Cheney, and Powell also met to debate the issue between these dates.[39] Since it was clear that Bush wanted something very imaginative, Cheney, however reluctantly, had to serve his president.

The formal presentation on 17 September included a number of proposals: eliminating short-range nuclear weapons, eliminating nuclear weapons on surface ships, ending the policy of keeping a certain percentage of the U.S. bomber force in the air on alert, and banning MIRVed ICBMs. The decision was made on that date to go ahead with the proposal. Bush, Scowcroft, and Cheney worked on the draft together.[40] Bush wanted total secrecy on the contents of and even existence of a follow-on to START. Once again, Bush delighted in surprising his critics. He would be bold and innovative, rather than cautious and pragmatic.

On the night of 27 September, after only minimal leaks that something major was in the works, Bush gave an Oval Office address containing new arms control proposals. The address called for far-reaching actions on strategic weapons, notably cancellation of the rail MX program (its funding had been defeated in the Senate the day before) and the mobile version of the SICBM, as well as a proposal for negotiations on deMIRVing both sides' ICBM forces.[41] The address had the desired effect. The speech was seen as a signal that the end of the cold war had finally come to the U.S.-Soviet strategic relationship. Negotiations on START II had begun.

Gorbachev responded on October 5 with his own set of proposals, including the destruction of tactical nuclear weapons on surface ships, taking strategic bombers off alert, cuts in fissile material, and deeper reductions in both sides' strategic arsenals. Negotiations on a follow-on to START began that same day in Moscow. Bartholomew, of the Ungroup, was the lead negotiator for the U.S. By mid-December the debate on a follow-up to Bush's September speech and responses to Gorbachev's October proposals was taking place. Within the Department of State and DOD the senior levels of decision makers were discussing potential options for continued arms cuts. One of the alternatives in play was a 50% cut in strategic nuclear warheads to a total of under 5,000. Cheney and Scowcroft had sparred over Gorbachev's proposed cuts in fissionable material, with Cheney winning the argument and blocking the U.S. from negotiating on this point. However, when it came to the issue of further cuts in strategic arsenals the decision making was rather swift and painless. On the weekend of 18 and 19 January, Bush, Baker, Cheney, and Scowcroft agreed on the basic framework of new proposals on strategic arms that would be included in the State of the Union (SOTU) speech. Again, the proposal reflected the influence of Scowcroft, calling for complete deMIRVing and elimination of mobile systems from both sides' arsenals. The SICBM would be eliminated as well. The ideas that had been left out of the Malta Summit in 1989 finally made it to the negotiating table. The speech, given on 28 January 1992, called for complete deMIRVing for both sides, cancellation of the SICBM, and reductions in strategic weaponry down to 4,700 warheads each.[42]

For the purposes of this study the details of the negotiation on START II are not important. The treaty was signed in Moscow by Bush and Russian President Boris Yeltsin on 3 January 1993. It took a year of negotiations to produce the treaty. The problem of four nations—Russia, Ukraine, Belarus, and Kazakhstan—inheriting the Soviet Union's nuclear arsenal was added to the expected complications over the exact details of treaty provisions and verification procedures. Ultimately, the elimination of MIRVed ICBMs (which completely dismantled the Soviet SS-18 force) and the reduction of both sides' arsenals to between 3,000 and 3,500 warheads were the core of the treaty.[43]

A temporary, but significant narrowing was apparent here as Bush and Scowcroft, the president and his personal national security policy adviser, decided to launch a major arms control initiative. Even after the decision was made, the discussion of the decision remained mostly within the Gang of Eight. Secrecy and speed were the motivations. Bush wanted swift decisions and he wanted his new proposals to be a surprise. The way in which musings by Bush and Scowcroft became a major initiative in arms control is an example of informality and improvisation. The same motivations of secrecy and speed kept the decision process to the informal Gang of Eight. Only they were trusted by Bush to give him both expert advice and the discretion of silence. The formal interagency process was relegated to the background for these same reasons. All decisions were made by the Gang of Eight and held within that tight circle. Since this policy initiative concerned the content of a speech, it was easy for Bush to simply debate the ideas and write the speech outside the interagency process.[44]

The swiftness with which the USSR fell apart from August to December 1991 created tremendous unanticipated political pressures on the Bush administration. These were not pressures of crisis, but pressures of opportunity. Bush needed to respond quickly for both strategic and political reasons. He turned to the method that he felt had served him best in the past—small-group decision making. His years of government service had taught him that this was the best method to conserve time and effort while still making well-designed policy.

CONCLUSIONS

The analysis of Bush's decision making on arms control illustrates an evolution of the decision-making process that was deeply influenced by his leadership style. Unlike the Carter administration, in which the pressures on the administration were taken to their logical conclusions (an ANSA-dominated process), or the Reagan administration, in which a similar evolution occurred but was then reversed, the Bush administration illustrates a careful and controlled evolution. Narrowing participation, creating informal structures, and streamlining the interagency process developed as adjuncts to the formal process, adaptations added to the process for use as necessary. The BRZR group, the Ungroup, and even the Bush-Scowcroft brainstorming sessions were never allowed to push aside the formal process, nor was the informal collegiality of the Gang of Eight and Breakfast Group.

These changes lead to the emergence of the three concurrent structures. The formal NSC process was always the backbone of the administration's decision process, but the informal structure (Gang of Eight or Breakfast Group) dominated the process. Bush's confidence structure centered on his relationship with Baker and Scowcroft; however, all the relationships within the informal structure were so strong that Baker and Scowcroft were truly first among equals rather than rivals to everyone else. They worked to make sure that none of the senior officials was excluded from any final decisions. The Malta Summit is the best example of this. Baker and Scowcroft's staffs worked on arms control proposals to the exclusion of Cheney's staff. When it came to a final decision, however, Cheney was still able to veto the proposals for a mobile missile ban.

President Bush's leadership style was the key to this. He demanded inclusion of all the senior players and ultimately would not move until he had consensus among them. Bush and his senior advisers understood the pressures that they faced. However, they refused to follow the path toward deep centralization that Carter had, and they were unhampered by philosophical divisions. They adapted to the pressures in a deliberate and careful way, adding informal and confidence style structures as supplements, not replacements or rivals to their formal structures. This allowed the collegiality of the Gang of Eight to become the dominant feature of the decision process, formalism within the informal process. It also explains why the Bush administration does not provide a tale of bureaucratic rivalry as in the Carter administration or vicious competition as in the Reagan administration.

Bush administration decision making for arms control and in general brings attention to three points about decision making: the important role of Congress, even if it is simply a background feature of the political context of the decision; the relationship between formal and informal decision-making processes; and the unique nature of the Bush administration as Bush placed his kitchen cabinet into the Cabinet.

As already mentioned, political pressure was a factor in each case, whether as a prod to stimulate administration decision making (Malta and START I) or as a catalyst for policy (START II). The three case studies reveal an interesting political dynamic. Bush first swam against the tide, then drifted with it, and, finally, anticipated the changes in political currents. He moved from a policy of cautious response to one of bold activity, revealing a vast difference between the Bush of October 1989 who hesitated to become involved in the Panamanian coup, and the Bush of 1992 who sent troops to Somalia with little public notice or government preparation. This change could also be a function of the rapid international developments between 1989 and 1991. For the Bush administration, the changes in the USSR in 1989 were still suspect. Gorbachev was certainly a new type of Soviet leader, but his sincerity and his future were in doubt. By 1991, the revolutions in Eastern Europe and the U.S.-USSR alliance in the Gulf War had established a new era. The change in style could also be a function of a president gaining confidence in office as he learns about the job and the policy challenges he faces.

The one constant during these years was the political pressure from Congress. The word "constant" is used here with a caveat. The attention Congress pays to international affairs can be sporadic. However, cautious presidents and cabinet officers understand that making policy can be like navigating a minefield. There will be times when a sleepy, inattentive Congress explodes in criticism, both partisan and intra-party. In this sense, even if Congress is a silent partner on certain issues, an administration must be wary of provoking a noisy reaction. For Bush, Congress was more of a consistent buzzing always audible in the background than a roaring tiger ready to swallow the administration's strategic plans. Unlike the Reagan administration, the Bush administration seems to have considered the reaction of Congress as a factor in deciding its policies. While the Reagan administration fought Congress over strategic modernization and START, the Bush administration always seemed to be preparing to avoid that fight by considering how Congress might react to its policies. The result for Reagan was a tumultuous relationship with Congress over arms control. For Bush, the relationship was much more amicable.

An additional influence was the fact that the Senate would eventually have to ratify START. Verification was the key issue, and the Senate debate on the INF Treaty illustrated that even in a new environment in which the U.S. and USSR were becoming better friends, the strategic nuclear relationship lagged behind.[45] Both sides still aimed their missiles at each other and based their deterrence policies on their capability to destroy each other. Within the Senate, particularly on the Republican side, the START treaty would be judged on its merits; it would not glide through on the wings of U.S.-Soviet rapprochement. In the midst of the mid-July 1991 negotiations with the Soviets in Washington that settled the telemetry and downloading issues, the ranking Republican on the Senate Foreign Relations Committee, Jesse Helms, reportedly advised Secretary of State Baker that if the administration did conclude a treaty, it had better be perfect because the Soviets were "cheats, liars, and scoundrels."[46] The world was changing, but the administration still had to remember that for many the "evil empire" was still evil.

In a sense, there are two aspects of anticipated political pressures at play here. The overall climate or strategic aspect of political pressure reflected competing challenges facing the administration. The consistent call for cuts in the defense budget and the need to make sure that START could meet the rigorous arms control requirements of the cold war pushed the administration in two directions. The administration eventually solved this dilemma by proposing an end to MIRVed ICBMs. This eliminated the need for ICBM modernization and mobile systems by dismantling the Soviet missile systems that had presented the threat to the U.S. ICBM force back in the 1970s. The specific or tactical aspects of political pressure can refer to the more immediate and perhaps less lasting constraints on the administration. Deadlines for congressional budget decisions can create these types of pressures. For the Bush administration, the expectation of a successful conclusion to the START negotiations after the Gulf War was such a pressure. By the spring of 1991, it had been almost three years since the Reagan administration had claimed it could see the light at the end of the tunnel.

The fall of 1991 was rife with unanticipated political pressure. The turmoil in the USSR opened a slim window of opportunity. The administration saw a fleeting chance to push arms control even further while the hardliners in Moscow were on the defensive and while the Soviet Union still existed. Political pressures either create a problem or become a motivation toward action. Restructuring decision-making processes may provide a solution or a method of initiating action.

The administration viewed both the Gang of Eight and the Breakfast Group as standard and formal committees.[47] For analytical purposes, the distinction between formal and informal is important. The Gang of Eight and the Breakfast Group existed because they provided decision-making advantages over the NSC and the NSC/PC—principally the freedom of officials to speak their minds, an insulation from pressures of departmental subordinates, and protection against leaks. Though the senior decision makers saw them as an aspect of the formal process, they did, in fact, differ from the standard NSC committees or there would have been no need to create them. Since these groups were not built into the decision structure from the beginning or detailed in the National Security Directives that established the administration's formal process, their use is an important modification in the initial design. Their formal aspect, and perhaps the reason they functioned so well, was their makeup—they included full horizontal participation of all the relevant agencies. They were not created to exclude any agency or official. On the contrary, they were created to make it easier to achieve diversity and inclusiveness that really mattered at the senior levels.

The decision-making processes of the Bush administration suggest that there is a deep relationship between the formal and informal structures in any administration. If nonprincipals are included in the informal process, it will lose one of its characteristics—the frankness and secrecy that can be nurtured within the Gang of Eight. In addition, without a fully functioning formal process, the informal process may take on so many responsibilities that it also loses another of its other main attributes—speed of decision.[48]

The blend of formal and informal decision making served the administration well on arms control. It allowed Bush to control the pace with which decisions were made. When Bush wanted to delay decisions, as in 1989, he placed the issue within the formal process. The issues were reviewed in NSR-14 and thereafter within the NSC. By 1991, the policy was clearly within the informal side of the decision process—the Gang of Eight and the Ungroup. Decision making was speeded up as needed. When economy was necessary, Bush modified the decision process to accommodate.

The evolution toward a more narrow, informal/ad hoc process that streamlined the interagency process began very early on. However, in the case of arms control this evolution was nonlinear. Decision making for the Malta Summit was, in some respects, more narrow, informal/ad hoc, and semi-independent of the interagency process than the decision making for START in 1990 and 1991. However, the speeches of September 1991 and January 1992 are examples of greater evolution in the process than the other cases. The rate of evolution of the process seems to be influenced by the context of the decision being made. Decisions on the Malta Summit were a reaction to strategic events and political pressures. The START II speeches were an opportunistic decision that sought to take advantage of an opening window for policy change before it closed. START I decisions were taken in the context of an ongoing bilateral negotiation. More exploration of this idea is included in chapter seven.

The most unique aspect of the Bush administration concerns the personnel. The senior national security decision makers all had high-level government experience, all possessed a similar world view, and all were friends. Bush, in some ways, selected the members of his kitchen cabinet for positions in his institutionalized cabinet. The merging of his friends and his senior advisers was in stark contrast to previous administrations. Where national security was concerned Carter had been an amateur, and his advisers, while experienced, disagreed on several major issues and were not friends of the president or each other. In the Reagan administration, the ideological disputes were legendary, the friendships, if any, were shaky, and those with experience were often replaced by those without it. In the Bush administration, the decision-making lessons that a president and his senior officials normally learn on the job had already been learned. For this reason, the Bush administration had less distance to travel toward the end stage that the evolutionary model hypothesizes and moved in that direction more quickly and smoothly than other administrations. They had traveled that road before and had learned how to avoid the potholes. They knew how to shape and reshape decision making to serve their policy needs. The Gang of Eight developed quickly, as did the Breakfast Group. They were freer in their use of secrecy. They saw the benefits of making decisions within that small and closed circle. Possibly, most importantly, Bush knew what to expect from all of his key advisers on foreign affairs. There were no real mysteries about how each one thought, or questions about how well they would get along. The interagency process often serves as a series of auditions through which senior officials can impress the president and, as a result, earn inclusion in the inner circle. Bush never needed to hold these auditions.[49] Casting had been completed before the inauguration. Bush's long experience in government had merged his personal and professional circle of friends.

The question of rivalry between these friends was still a factor. Even the best of friends could wind up disagreeing over issues or find their friendship strained given the weight of the political pressures on the president and his senior advisers. Bush, however, worked to overlay his personal pecking order with the institutional hierarchy. For example, Baker, the closest friend of all Bush's advisers, was chosen to be secretary of state, the most important and public of the national security posts. Scowcroft, another trusted friend, but not on a par with Baker, was given the post of ANSA. Importantly, this institutionalized the dominance of the secretary of state over the ANSA, and prevented the kind of feuding that was evident in the Nixon, Carter, and Reagan years. Baker and Bush had become friends, then later colleagues. Scowcroft and Bush were colleagues first, then friends. That made a world of difference in administration decision making. Journalistic accounts have suggested that the Bush-Baker relationship had been strained by their disagreements over U.S. policy during the Gulf War and that Bush became closer to Scowcroft by early 1991.[50] Whether this is true or not, it was not reflected in the roles played by Baker and Scowcroft. Baker was still the diplomatic face of U.S. national security and maintained access to Bush. If the assumption of a rift between Bush and Baker is accepted, then perhaps if Baker and Bush had not been such close friends, their Gulf War differences might have spelled the end of Baker's effectiveness. There is little evidence of that. The friendships and ideological harmony that marked the Gang of Eight allowed them to survive as a cohesive unit throughout important disagreements.

The problem of the small group becoming isolated from the rest of the executive branch or succumbing to groupthink is beyond the scope of this study. Since this book focuses on the changes in the structure of decision-making style and the quality of the decision making in terms of the relationships between the senior officials, attention to the process/outcome issue is not addressed. However, the failure to recognize the threat from Iraq in 1990 or, on the domestic side, the recession in 1991 and 1992 may be evidence of too much insularity within the senior decision-making level. It could be argued that if collegiality becomes an end in itself, serious debate may end. Pressure to conform, to not rock the boat, could stifle dissent. The case studies above do not illustrate that phenomenon. In decision making for START I, dissent by Cheney (Malta Summit) and Scowcroft (end stage of START I) delayed policy consensus. In each case, the advisers were confident enough in themselves to challenge the entire group, and Bush was concerned enough about consensus to delay action until a policy consensus could be achieved. In some ways, this is a smooth middle ground between groupthink and gridlock-style paralysis. All the decision makers believed consensus could be achieved around some policy and they would work to find that policy, but not act until it was found.[51]

Chapter Seven

CONCLUSIONS

THE ULTIMATE PURPOSE OF THE STUDY OF NATIONAL SECURITY
decision making is to uncover ways in which presidents can avoid the problems
such as those encountered by Carter and Reagan, while steering their decision
processes toward the types of structures that helped Bush avoid those problems.
Previous experience in government cannot be the only prerequisite to solid administrative processes. Incoming presidents need to learn from the successes and
failures of previous presidents. This chapter examines the theoretical and policy
implications of the evolution model of national security decision making. The
utility of the evolution model to provide a clearer picture of the developments
within a decision-making system over time can lead to a better understanding
of the decision needs of presidents as well as the pressures every national security team should expect.

A discussion of the characteristics and principles of the evolution model and
the three concurrent structures focuses on what is similar and what is different
about the evolution of decision making in each administration studied here.
Given that each administration began with a similar interagency model of decision making and operated within a similar political environment, a useful con-

trol is established. The interagency starting point is the same; political pressures push the administrations to make the same adaptations. How did the leadership style of each president shape the evolution of the process?

The second part of this chapter considers the policy implications of the model. First, the lessons of the Carter, Reagan, and Bush case studies support the notion that decision making functions best when the informal structure is used to hold all three concurrent structures together. It should not eclipse or be captured by the formal structure; it should not be rendered irrelevant by the confidence structure. All three structures play significant roles, serving different roles for the administration. Second, the question of whether a "best" national security decision-making system can be created yields an answer of yes and no. Presidents can design a generic model of their decision-making needs in terms of structures and processes, but they cannot know which advisers will fill those generic roles until after the administration has made numerous decisions over an extended period of time. The exception may be a situation in which most of the senior decision makers have worked together previously while holding similar positions. They have already made decisions with each other in the rarified environment of advising the president. This was the case for the Bush administration. Third, it becomes clear that presidents use different types of policy processes for different types of decisions. Three types of decisions evident in the case studies are addressed here: innovative, reactive, and opportunistic.

THE EVOLUTION MODEL REVISITED

The main hypotheses of the evolution model are summarized below:

1. Changes in the international and domestic political environment, organizational dynamics, and presidential choices can lead to changes in the structure of decision making.

2. These changes in the structure of decision making are made deliberately by the president when he feels that the initial structures cannot give him the control over process and policy that he desires.

3. These changes are based upon three principles of decision making—economy, learning, and political pressure. These principles describe forces acting upon an administration that push all administrations toward similar decision structures.

4. These changes have a similar pattern in all administrations because of the similar pressures. Administrations will begin to do the following: narrow the range

of participation in decisions, add more informality and ad hoc processes, and increasingly bypass or streamline the standard interagency process.

5. These changes generally lead to the use of three identifiable concurrent structures: the formal interagency process designed at the inception of the administration tenure, an informal process in which the president and his senior advisers will meet without staff, and a confidence structure in which the president comes to rely on one or two advisers more than all the rest.

6. These changes are nonlinear. They represent general tendencies. The idiosyncratic leadership style of individual presidents will define how much of this evolution takes place, whether presidents give in to the pressures to make changes, ignore those pressures, or learn from them.

7. Differences in the origin, use or operation, and relationships between the three concurrent structures are due to the leadership style of the president.

The case studies confirm the hypotheses. The international and domestic political environments, the organizational dynamics within the executive branch, and presidential choices concerning leadership style, management style, and political strategy had important effects on the decision process in each administration; changes in these influences caused changes in the decision process (hypothesis 1). These changes were made deliberately by each president (hypothesis 2). Each administration reacted initially to the pressures of decision making (principles of evolution) in a similar way (hypotheses 3 and 4). Each developed informal structures and each had a confidence structure (hypothesis 5). The leadership style of each president, however, was the crucial element that determined how these pressures would ultimately lead administration decision making (hypotheses 6 and 7).

The overall pattern of change or the characteristics of the evolution model are similar in some ways for each administration, yet unique to each president in other ways. Carter's inclination for deep involvement led him to follow the pressures toward their more extreme destination—centralization of the process, frequent abandonment of the interagency process, and a reliance on one official at times to the exclusion of others. Reagan followed a similar path until late 1983, when his instinct for delegation, his detachment, and his unwillingness to make decisions that alienated his closest advisers allowed his White House troika to gut the system that had developed. Bush made adjustments to his decision-making process as needed with great care, balancing informality, formality, and relationships. Having established the model in its general form, a more systematic look at the answers to the initial structure-focused comparison questions through a cross administration analysis can yield generalizations about decision making in any administration.

Overall Pattern of Change: Narrowing

The narrowing of participation in the decision process in each of the case studies was related to the president's need for control over the decision—its content and pace—and the president's growing knowledge of his decision-making needs, the usefulness of various officials, the costs associated with the standard interagency process, and the utility of that process. Ultimately the decision making evolved to the point where the president was relying on a smaller number of individuals for advice.

On certain issues—high-priority issues or items that particularly interest the president—presidents come to feel the need for more control over the decision-making process and narrow participation in many decisions in an effort to maintain that control. Control refers to the president's or a senior official's desire to manage the pace of the decision, define the content of the policy, and/or exclude participants from the decision process. Protection of the idea from opponents or premature leakage is a crucial element of control over a policy. All three presidents narrowed the participation in decision making to protect a policy from opponents (SALT II, PD-59, strategic defense, and the START II speeches). Reagan and Bush also narrowed the participation to control the pace of deliberations during their decision making on START I. Each case was one in which the standard process was seen as too unwieldy or too slow, or simply unable to produce policy in a timely manner.

Presidents narrow the participation in the process, excluding officials, departments, or levels in the hierarchical process, as a manner of choosing specific officials or departments over others. The issue is trust and confidence. Narrowing is evidence that a president has decided which officials can get things done faithfully and swiftly. As time passes within an administration, a president seems to learn that if he wants something done right, he must do it himself or choose specific reliable officials to do it for him. Presidents may begin to rely on one or two individuals who can make things happen. Carter and Reagan both made major adjustments in the policy process to achieve this. Reagan eventually reversed those changes. Bush only made minor and usually temporary modifications to his policy process.

Overall Pattern of Change: Increasing Informality and Ad Hoc Processes

In the cases studied within this book the increased use of informal and ad hoc processes is related again to the expanding need, in the president's eyes, for control over the decision-making process, in terms of the pace of the decision process, the content of policy, and the range of participation. These changes are shortcut adaptations to the standard process. After repeated decisions and increased familiarity with both the issues and the politics within the administration, within the nation, and in the international arena, decision makers feel more confident about the decisions they make. They have learned a great deal about politics, processes, and people. More confidence leads to less of a need to subject ideas and policies to the in-depth and sometimes exhaustive analysis of the bureaucracies. Instead, a shortened version of the standard process will provide "enough" analysis given the time frame involved or the need for secrecy. The pressure of politics may necessitate decision making on a schedule that will be difficult to meet without the use of informal or ad hoc processes.

Informal processes are usually interagency. Though the above ideas can also lead to bypassing the interagency process, the reasons are different. Informal processes are typically additions to the interagency process, designed to carry out a specific task. Informal and ad hoc processes should be seen as attempts to find ways of getting things done, a shot of adrenaline to the interagency process meant to focus interagency resources on a specific problem.

What most of these case studies have in common is a specific policy direction. The president or another senior official had in mind a specific policy outcome and wanted to find a way to subject the idea to solid policy review without beginning an administration-wide debate on the subject. Carter wanted deep cuts for SALT II; Brzezinski wanted a new nuclear doctrine; the negotiators in the fall of 1983 wanted some build-down style proposal in the mix for START; several groups of people inside and outside the Reagan administration wanted to see an initiative ballistic missile defense; Bush and Scowcroft hoped to move quickly on START II in the fall of 1991.

The Bush administration is unique in that its standard operating procedures for decision making were heavily reliant on informal processes. Bush developed ad hoc decision groups for policy analysis not simply in cases where the president wanted to develop a specific policy, but as a general method of making decisions. Politics and the potential for leaks seemed to be the key for Bush. He wanted strict control over when and how these policies would be presented to the public.

Overall Pattern of Change: Bypassing or Streamlining the Interagency Process

When a president deliberately bypasses the interagency process, he does so to remove certain officials or organizations from participation in a specific decision. These officials or departments normally would be part of the formal interagency process. The president and/or other officials know this and move the decision out of the interagency process to prevent spoilers from blocking decisions, to preclude any knock-down, drag-out fights, or to guarantee that opponents of a policy do not have the opportunity to leak information to the public that may jeopardize the success of the policy. The interagency process was designed for inclusion and diversity. When that design morphs from inclusion and diversity to rigid coalitions, departmental rivalries, or personal feuds, it becomes less useful to a president. Carter and Reagan learned these ideas after a time in office. They learned which people or agencies might act as spoilers; they learned what the bureaucratic order of battle might be on any given issue; they learned which advisers agreed with them and would therefore provide the most faithful implementation plans. However, the knowledge that each president gained concerning who stood where on any issue, a knowledge only gained through repeated decisions, is the key.

Bypassing the interagency process is an example of a president putting this knowledge to use. In the Carter administration, Vance and the State Department were excluded over key issues. Reagan's bypassing of the interagency process in the case of the Build-Down and strategic defense was not aimed at excluding any single official or organization. Instead, it was the interagency process itself that was avoided. Streamlining is a different dynamic. Exclusion is not the purpose of the adaptation; conserving time and energy is. Carter streamlined his process by turning the 19 March SCC meeting into an NSC meeting. Bush's decision modifications were all cases of streamlining. The administration had no glaring rivalries or inflexible coalitions or diehard spoilers in its mix. There was no reason to exclude anyone.

Initial Decision-Making Structure

Of the eight episodes examined over three administrations, only two—strategic defense and START II—did not begin with a vetting of the policy through the standard interagency process. Strategic defense began with ad hoc groups outside the government (the High Frontier panel) and in the White House. The genesis of the START II speeches was a series of informal discussions between President Bush and ANSA Brent Scowcroft at Bush's home in Kennebunkport, Maine. All other decisions were first subjected to the standard interagency review as designed by the initial configuration of the administration's National Security Council (NSC) process. Strategic defense and START II were innovative policies, significant departures from existing policy that depended more on presidential inspiration than bureaucratic perspiration. For this reason the ideas were developed in small, somewhat secretive groups and announced publicly before they were place into the interagency maelstrom. Further discussion of this idea can be found below.

Roles and Relationships

In each case, there was a prime mover of policy, either the president or the ANSA. In the cases of SALT II, strategic defense, the Malta Summit, and START II the president, alone or in tandem with a favorite advisor, was the prime mover. In the case of PD-59 and both the Reagan and Bush START I policies, a senior adviser was the prime mover: Brzezinski, ANSA William Clark, and Secretary of State James Baker, respectively. The president's role as prime mover seems simple to explain. The president has decided to push a certain policy and acts to create an administration consensus or as in the case of strategic defense, presents the administration with an offer it cannot refuse. When a senior official is the prime mover the situation is more complex. These officials are either acting as policy entrepreneurs (Brzezinski in PD-59) or carrying out their official roles on behalf of the president (Clark and Baker in START).

The prime mover's ascendance may be a key reason why an administration's overall structure evolves. The role of prime mover is both protector and catalyst for an idea or a policy. If the study of national security decision making tells us anything, it suggests that there will always be competing interests within an administration. Consensus on anything but the broadest outlines may be difficult.

No compromise is immune to bureaucratic forces that could unravel it. Presidents understand this and design methods of creating consensus, or at least revealing policy differences. A president or a manager of the process will try to make sure that policy does emerge from the interagency battle. The prime mover does not necessarily manage the entire process. He or she manages one specific issue area or policy idea. This differs slightly from the general notion of a policy entrepreneur who tries to "sell" an idea to colleagues, although a policy entrepreneur can be a prime mover. The prime mover may simply be managing the decision making on a specific issue, rather than pushing a pet project. The prime mover may be making sure that some decision is made, rather than seeking to forge a specific policy outcome.

The creation of new structures or the inclusion of additional decision makers seems related to two factors. A first element is gridlock within the administration. As in the Reagan case, gridlock in the standard process leads to attempts to break the impasse with new committees (Dam Group of SACPG). Second, simple statutory reality plays a role. The ultimate goal of an administration's arms control policies is a formal treaty that must be approved by the U.S. Senate. Therefore, the Senate can have a large impact even early in the process as the negotiations are under way. A wise president should seek Senate counsel as a way to ensure that the direction of treaty negotiations stays within politically feasible parameters as well as to soothe important egos whose votes may decide whether a treaty lives or dies. Senator Henry Jackson's role in SALT II and the Scowcroft Commission/Gang of Six's role in START I are examples of this political reality that is defined by the constitution's shared treaty power. These factors are related. If the executive branch is paralyzed, Congress may be willing to step in and provide a solution as in the Reagan case (Scowcroft Commission and the Build-Down).

The Bush administration's BRZR group and the Ungroup were adjuncts to the process, not replacements. They were created to allow the process to run more smoothly. For circumstances that required more focused attention than the senior officials could give, but not full interagency review, new structures were added as shortcuts to policy consensus. Again, strategic defense decisions appear to be a unique case. The High Frontier Panel and the White House Group were examples of additional decision makers and new structures created in defiance of the administration's normal processes and policies.

Any evolution in the coalition structure or the organizational dynamics of the administration is intimately interrelated with the president's relationships with each adviser. First, a president makes decisions about who should fill out his initial cabinet. Subsequently, a president makes a number of choices based on his assessments of the wisdom of his original choices. Essentially, he must continually ask himself whether his choices were good ones: are the advisers within the administration serving their purpose? If advisers are found wanting, a president must decide what to do about it. Should the adviser be forced to change his ways; should the adviser be pushed out of the inner circle; should the adviser be fired?

No evolution in the coalition structure occurred in either the Reagan or Bush cases, but for different reasons. Bush made his first decisions so well, in his judgment, that he never had to deal with the second question. The friendships within the Bush administration, the ideological harmony, and the experience each brought into the administration created an environment that remained collegial for the duration of the administration's tenure. Reagan made his initial choices so poorly, in his view and in the view of the troika, that he removed ANSA Richard Allen, Secretary of State Alexander Haig, and Clark in the first three years. The Reagan national security team existed on two tectonic plates (hardliners vs. pragmatists) that consistently smashed against each other. The administration often appears to be a continuing series of major earthquakes that always resulted in casualties—in terms of both personnel and then Iran-Contra.[1] Only the Carter administration underwent an evolution in the coalition structure, from a collegial body to one in which Secretary of State Cyrus Vance and Brzezinski became major policy antagonists, a battle Vance lost.

Only in the Carter case study was there real evolution in the relationships between the president and his senior advisers. The case studies suggest that the evolution of a president's relationship with his advisers depends on the maturity of the president's views on foreign affairs. If the president's own ideas on foreign affairs are well developed, his relationships with his senior advisers will change little. If the president's own views of foreign affairs are less certain, the maturation process of his thinking will shape the relationships with his advisers. His relationship with the advisers whose beliefs he comes to share will evolve into a stronger one. Carter's story contrasts sharply with the other presidents' cases. Reagan and Bush had well-developed views on foreign affairs. Reagan was an ideological anticommunist, committed and forceful. By nature, he sided with the hardliners. Bush was a realist to the core and maintained that view as the basis for U.S.-Soviet/Russian relations even as the cold war structure of the international system collapsed. He chose a group of realists for his senior advisers, and their relationships remained collegial. Baker, the president's dearest friend, was a slight first among equals. Carter's notions of U.S. national security were in flux. He entered office as a man who leaned toward idealism, who saw the world in the context of complex interdependence, and who hoped to move the emphasis of U.S. policy from containment to North-South relations and human rights. As he left office he laid the foundation for Reagan's renewed cold war: aid to anticommunist rebels in Afghanistan and Nicaragua, the resumption of aid to the military government in El Salvador, the withdrawal of SALT II from Senate consideration, an increase in the defense budget, and a commitment to protect from Soviet interference, with military force if necessary, the U.S. oil supply in the Middle East. Whether this evolution in thinking was a result of the changes in his relationships with Vance and Brzezinski, or the evolution in his relationships was a result of the changes in his thinking, is a difficult question to answer. However, the relationship between Carter's thinking on foreign affairs and his relationships with his senior advisers is clear. Vance's ideas were closer to those that Carter held when he entered office; Brzezinski's views were more along the lines of Carter's policy choices in 1979 and 1980.

Process

All of the case studies illustrate a decision process that depended upon informal processes. These informal procedures varied in style. President Carter seemed to be the key player in his administration's transition from formal to informal in SALT II and PD-59. The Reagan informalities were of two types: those that helped break the administration stalemate (Clark and McFarlane's negotiations with Congress) and those that bypassed the interagency process completely (strategic defense). Within the Bush administration the BRZR group, the Breakfast Group (Malta Summit), and the Gang of Eight (START I and II) were all created to ease the process of creating a consensus within the administration. They were all adjuncts to the formal process, not replacements. In all cases, except for strategic defense, the informal processes developed as methods to move the administration toward policy consensus. The president and/or his senior advisers had decided that the interagency process had not created a timely or sufficiently strong consensus. The informal processes were added on to the formal processes to move the policy along.

Changes in the hierarchical level at which decisions are made should be expected. The standard interagency process is a series of hierarchically connected committees. Policy analysis moves its way up the pyramid of interagency committees as a matter of standard procedure. Changes in hierarchy, then, may not be a sign of changes in the decision-making process, but simply a sign of the standard interagency process at work. For this reason, it is necessary to differentiate between normal changes in the hierarchical level of decision making and situations where the policy is seized by the upper-level officials at unusual points in the decision-making process.

Interestingly, in all the case studies considered here, issues were moved up the hierarchical chain in part to speed up the decision-making process. Carter's appearance at the 19 March 1977 meeting of the SCC can be seen as a normal hierarchical change. Eventually, the SCC was to present its ideas to the NSC. Carter only sped up the process. Within the Bush administration the BRZR group and the Ungroup illustrate the same dynamic. The issue was bumped up the hierarchical chain because the lower levels had not produced a sufficient recommendation in the necessary amount of time. Administration gridlock was an additional factor during Reagan's START and strategic defense decisions. For START, the Dam Group and the SACPG were upper-level committees created because the lower-level committees were paralyzed in disagreement. Reagan's kitchen cabinet and White House staff and then Reagan himself started the policy process at higher levels than usual specifically to avoid the potential for gridlock. Bush decision making on START II began at a high level for the sake of secrecy and speed.

In each case study, changes in horizontal participation were a by-product of other changes in the decision-making structure, particularly the ascendance of a prime mover in the policy process. Those officials or departments that were perceived as potential enemies of a policy were shut out of the process for the sake of meeting a political timetable or protecting an idea. In each administration departments or officials were excluded as a function of the prime mover's assessment of the organizational dynamics within the administration. The Carter administration's growing State-NSC staff rivalry led Carter and Brzezinski to choose to exclude the State Department partially (March 1977) and completely (PD-59) from the deliberations. In both cases, the State Department's opposition to the policies emanating from the White House led to an end run around it. Reagan's hardliner-pragmatist feud led the NSC staff to push aside the interagency process and create its own compromise when it became clear that full horizontal participation in arms control decisions would only lead to more delay. In the case of strategic defense, there was almost complete exclusion of anyone from any department who was not seen as an enthusiastic supporter of the idea. Within the collegial amity of the Bush administration, notably, complete horizontal participation in the decision process was the norm for decisions. Even in the case when the DOD was temporarily shut out of preparations for the Malta Summit, Secretary of Defense Dick Cheney was eventually pulled into the process as an equal partner, with the power to quash the ideas that had been developed while his department was excluded. This reflects the lack of real divisions within the Bush administration.

Political Factors

Political factors played a role in each decision-making case in both expected and unexpected ways. The political need to do something different from the previous president was present in all cases. The partisan affiliation of the predecessor made no difference. Carter felt the need to move beyond the Republican Ford administration's Vladivostok accords. Reagan rejected SALT II, judging it as another example of Democrat Carter's weak response to Soviet aggression. Bush shied away from finishing Reagan's START treaty, even though it was negotiated while he was vice president.

The role of Congress is crucial. First, in all of the case studies, even if Congress did not directly involve itself in decision making, it loomed as a shadow over administration decisions. The partisan makeup of the executive and legislative branches seemed to make no difference. Differences between the factions within the parties were more significant. As Burns and Bond and Fleisher have written, there really seems to be a four-party system. There is a Republican base and a Democratic base and then two minority factions in each party that have a tendency to lean away from the liberal base of the Democratic Party and the conservative base of the Republican Party. These conservative Democrats and liberal Republicans are "cross pressured" factions that often form coalitions with the other side of the aisle, leaving presidents to face bipartisan coalitions who oppose their policies. As the case studies illustrate, this was true during the Carter, Reagan, and Bush administrations on arms control policy, although recent research on Congress suggests that the cross-pressured factions are diminishing as the Congress becomes more polarized.[2]

Democrat Carter had as much trouble with a Democratic-controlled Congress as Republican Bush had with a Democratic-run Congress. Carter felt great pressure from Senator Jackson and the more conservative wing of the Democratic Party. Reagan had bipartisan challenges from Congress. With a Democratic-controlled House of Representatives and a Republican-controlled Senate, Reagan found himself pressured by Democrats and moderate Republicans. The Reagan administration was challenged by a group of liberal Republicans in Congress who allied themselves with groups of Democrats (the Gang of Six and the Scowcroft Commission). Bush also found the same alliance of moderate Republicans and Democrats pushing him toward a completion of the START treaty. As a moderate, this pressure was less of a problem for him. He never abandoned START; he simply delayed it. Ultimately, he was in agreement with the prevailing coalition in Congress.

The second point that stands out is the logic and consistency of the political struggle over arms control during the Carter, Reagan, and Bush administrations. This issue itself could be a separate book, so it will be discussed here in brief. A disagreement existed about the best way to develop the U.S. deterrent. It encompassed both arms control and strategic modernization. The strategic logic was reflected in the political battle both inside each administration and between Congress and the Carter, Reagan, and Bush administrations. It can best be described as part of the window of vulnerability debate. The details are contained in the case study chapters. Essentially, those on one side believed that as long as the United States had survivable land-based nuclear forces U.S. deterrence remained strong. They defined the window of vulnerability as the potential ability of the USSR to launch a first strike so devastating as to preclude a U.S. retaliatory response by its land-based forces. These people supported an arms control process based on the Nixon precedents of SALT I and saw U.S. strategic modernization in the context of survivability of U.S. ICBMs. They could make do with launcher limits (though warhead limits would be better) and could support the small ICBM. On the other side were those who saw the window of vulnerability as a function of the hard target kill capability of each nation. The key issue, therefore, was not the survivability of U.S. forces, but the ability of U.S. forces to threaten Soviet ICBMs. Arms control must be designed to reduce the Soviet medium and heavy ICBM arsenal. Strategic modernization must include the MX, the only medium ICBM the United States had in the pipeline.

This debate threaded its way through each administration. During the Carter period, Vance and Paul Warnke of ACDA were concerned with survivability and satisfied with the Vladivostok accords' launcher-based limits. Senator Jackson and Brzezinski focused more on deep cuts to destroy the perceived Soviet ICBM advantage and wanted launcher limits that would place some limitations on warheads as well. In the Reagan administration, the debate was more obvious. The State Department faced off against the DOD and ACDA. The former was satisfied with launcher limits, the latter nearly obsessed with eliminating the SS-18 or conceding nothing in the realm of arms control. The State Department eventually found allies in Congress—the Gang of Six—and in the Scowcroft Commission. The DOD/ACDA group found fewer allies in Congress, but enough to keep the MX alive, even after the Scowcroft Commission had given life to the SICBM, a missile that fit the concerns of those who saw survivability as the key. It was small enough to be survivable, but to the chagrin of the hardliners in the administration it was a light ICBM, not a major threat to the Soviet ICBM force. Within the Bush administration the competition between these sides was muted by the end of the cold war and the fact that START was already nearly finished. The Soviets had already conceded so much that eliminating the Soviet ICBM advantage was not a real factor anymore—the SS-18 fleet was to be cut in half. However, the debate between the MX and the SICBM continued. The Pentagon (led by Cheney) supported the MX, viewing its ten warheads as the key to maintaining the U.S. deterrent. Others in the administration, led by Scowcroft and most legislators in Congress, were satisfied with the SICBM, which would be survivable but not as threatening. Ultimately, the entire debate became irrelevant when the USSR collapsed. Bush eliminated both mobile missile programs.

Strategic defense was Reagan's attempt to solve this political impasse over arms control and strategic modernization. Ballistic missile defense could be all things to all people—a remedy for the problem of survivability and a way to negate the Soviet heavy and medium missile threat. Since the political debate seemed stuck in gridlock, Reagan tried to change the nature of debate in a way that might satisfy everyone. This did not work, but it was a politically motivated initiative.

The logic of this debate was consistent and never resolved itself internally, whether the debate was within Congress, between Congress and the administration, or within the administration. There never was a consensus on the proper way to deal with the threat. Plans to build both the SICBM and MX represent a decision based on giving everyone something, not a consensus. Resolution of these debates and the pressures they placed on the administration came from the passing of a historical era. The Soviet Union faded into history before this dilemma was resolved.

The above discussion really concerns premises underlying the executive-legislative relationships and leads to a third point. The key question is this: when does congressional pressure affect the decision-making processes of the administration? In each case, it was the inability of the administration to reach timely decisions and/or any decision that paid even lip service to congressional preferences that allowed Congress to make its presence a decisive one. The nuclear freeze resolutions during the Reagan years and the use of the MX as leverage over the arms-control policies of both Reagan and Bush were such cases. Congress decided to become more deeply involved in setting the agenda when it felt that the president would not or could not.

The case of PD-59 illustrates a different dynamic based on the electoral cycle. PD-59 satisfied Carter's political need to look tougher and more assertive in the face of Reagan's charges that he was too soft on the USSR. He needed this tougher image during his reelection campaign. PD-59 was a campaign ploy for Carter, a strategic necessity for Brzezinski. Their interests coincided in the summer of 1980, and PD-59 was signed. When reelection looms, presidents seem ready to abandon their normal policy-making process in favor of one that will satisfy political needs. Carter gave Brzezinski near-Kissingerian powers over decision making. Bush asked Baker to step down from the most prominent diplomatic post on the planet to become chief of staff and de facto campaign manager. The electoral needs of the president-candidate outweighed the needs of the president-diplomat.

The Principles of Decision Making

The three principles of decision making described by the evolution model suggest that the institutional and political pressures that presidents face combined with their own decision-making needs create a similar dynamic within each administration (see chapter two). In short, the pressures of the decision-making environment become the same for each administration. This is why each president represented in this book initially or at least occasionally moved to reshape his decision processes in a similar manner. The initial decision-making process was the same for each—the standard interagency process. The interagency process is in some ways like a door that opens decision making to all the dynamics explained by the governmental politics model of national security decision making—political infighting, rivalries, personal and organizational ambitions, narrow interests, and standard operating procedure–based policy options, to name a few. The design of the U.S. government also gives Congress a shared role in policy making. The new institutionalism model describes its influence over the process. It is an understatement to point out that these realities are not always seen regarded by the president as helpful. As a result, the president adjusts or manipulates the decision process to gain more control over the pace of the decision, the content of the policy, the range of participants, and the timing of the public release of the policy. This is the basic premise of the presidential management model. Presidents create decision-making processes that suit them best.

Rockman's point that decision-making systems are designed to "compensate for the deficiencies and complement the strengths of the leader" is well taken.[3] It helps to explain initial decision-making design. However, this book adds a point about the way decision-making systems are modified over time. A president redesigns his decision-making system to compensate for the deficiencies of that system and the shortcomings of his advisers in his own eyes or in the eyes of a trusted senior adviser. The principles described in chapter two detail, in general, the decision-making dynamics that lead to these changes. A comparison of how these principles influenced the specific decision modifications in the case studies yields more insight into these principles.

The Economy Principle

The economy principle deals with the conservation of both time and effort. The manipulation of the decision process is like a governor on an engine. It enables the engine to move the vehicle faster or slower or to reduce the amount of energy needed to continue operating the engine at a certain speed (a decision-making overdrive if you will). It is the need to conserve time and energy that led Carter, Reagan, and Bush to narrow the range of participation, create informal and ad hoc processes, and bypass the interagency process. These adaptations are shortcuts to a decision, a decision-making shorthand that can produce a decision outside of the full process.

Carter allowed the State Department to be bypassed during the decisions on PD-59 to prevent a fight that Carter would have to take time and effort to referee. The Reagan administration also sped up its decision processes to regain control of the arms control agenda from nuclear freeze advocates and to prevent a fight with Congress over the Build Down and the MX. Bush designed two speeds and two levels of effort into his decision-making process almost from the beginning. The fact that he and his group of advisers were so experienced allowed them to do so. The Gang of Eight was a faster choice for decision making than the NSC process (even one that was considerably streamlined compared to those of Reagan and Carter) and required less effort from the principals. Administrations, however, must avoid treating every decision as if it were a crisis decision. The entire decision-making process cannot stop on a dime and veer from one decision to the next. This is the danger of relying on shortcuts too often, which will be addressed below.

The Principle of Political Pressure

The initial hypothesis about political pressures stated in the introductory chapter of this book suggested that administrations face anticipated and unanticipated political pressures. The crucial point is that the pattern of these political pressures pushes the administration to narrow the range of participants in the decision, move to ad hoc and informal processes, and bypass or streamline the interagency process. Four types of political pressures helped cause changes in the decision-making structures of the Carter, Reagan, and Bush administrations: the pressure to distinguish the new administration from its predecessor; the pressure to meet expectations set by the precedents of previous administrations; the pressure from Congress; and electoral pressure as reelection becomes the overriding goal of the administration. These pressures seem to form a regularized pattern for any administration.

DISTINGUISHING THE NEW ADMINISTRATION

All three administrations reacted to this pressure or placed this pressure upon themselves. Carter needed his initial SALT II proposal to go beyond the Ford administration's Vladivostok Accords, and the concept had to be developed quickly. Reagan and Bush also wanted to differentiate themselves from their predecessors, but the pressure was toward inaction. Carter had negotiated SALT II, and Reagan wanted to turn away from SALT-style arms limitations. Bush, similarly, wanted to move away from Reagan's progress on START and used NSR-14 as a way to slow momentum toward an agreement.

MEETING EXPECTATIONS

Once the SALT I agreements had been signed during the Nixon presidency, the American public expected further progress in arms control. Negotiations with the USSR became one of the ever-expanding standard responsibilities of a president, issues the president is expected to deal with. Carter was somewhat inoculated from this pressure; he set out from the beginning to make a SALT II agreement a priority. Reagan and Bush faced serious political pressure to act in arms control. This is a key issue because the longer the public has to wait for that newspaper headline proclaiming a breakthrough on arms control, the more pressure is brought on the administration.

CONGRESSIONAL PRESSURE

These expectations are intimately tied up in the congressional role in policy making. The first aspect of this is agenda setting. When the Reagan administration delayed strategic arms control for over a year, it ratcheted up the political pressure on itself. By the spring of 1982 the freeze movement was proceeding quickly. The public and the Congress had set their own agenda for strategic arms control in the absence of any Reagan agenda. In terms of political pressures, the Reagan administration had failed to act quickly enough. The result was increased pressure on the administration, which in turn resulted in an evolution of the decision-making process—the NSC staff's more central role. Similarly, when the Bush administration failed to reach agreement with the USSR on START by the spring of 1991, political pressures again pushed the administration to move ahead quickly by creating the Ungroup.

The second element of this is linkage. If leaders in Congress feel that the administration has delayed too long or is moving in the wrong direction, those leaders can use their statutory power to hold hostage programs that the administration holds dear. The Gang of Six's linkage of the MX missile to START gave them the political leverage to enter the process, ultimately forcing the Build-Down proposals into the mix at Geneva. The leverage came through the statutory authorization and appropriations process. The administration manipulated the decision process in several ways to deal with this pressure: the Dam Group, the SACPG, the Scowcroft Commission, and Clark's increasingly prominent role. Similarly, Congress used the MX and SICBM in 1989 to push the Bush administration toward restarting START.

ELECTORAL PRESSURE

Elections are influential as well. They are the ultimate political pressure. The pressure here is toward action that will make a political point. Both Carter and Bush are useful illustrations of this aspect of political pressure. By the time of Reagan's reelection campaign, U.S.-Soviet relations were so strained that arms control negotiations had ended. Carter's timed release of PD-59 during the Democratic Convention when the eyes of the nation would be focused on him and Bush's swift movement on START II in September of 1991 and at the State of the Union speech in January 1992 have important similarities. In both cases, the president made the decision while relying on a select group of assistants. Carter relied on Brzezinski and Brown. Bush relied on Scowcroft and to a lesser extent Cheney and Powell. Both presidents made these decisions with a measure of secrecy in the process. Control of the decision and the timing of its release to the public was a paramount concern. The political pressure here led both administrations to treat these policies more as campaign announcements than as part of an ongoing policy process.

Unanticipated political pressures seem to cause the same evolutionary patterns in decision-making structure. Reagan's use of Clark and McFarlane to kick the interagency process into gear during the spring of 1982 was a response to the unanticipated success of the freeze movement. The Bush administration's somewhat extreme narrowing, informality, and bypassing of the interagency process after the August coup in the USSR is also an example of a response to an unanticipated pressure. In some sense, these responses to unanticipated political pressures may resemble the structural changes in decision style caused by crisis decisions.

The Learning Principle

The notion of learning considered here refers to learning about both process and personnel. Presidents and their senior advisers learn about the decision-making processes they instituted during the transition period of the administration. Presidents learn about their senior advisers. Senior advisers learn about each other and they learn about their president. The decision-making process evolves because the president and key senior advisers feel they have learned something about the process as it already exists, or about their decision-making needs, or about the people who participate in the process.

In the case of learning about the decision-making process, all three case studies provide useful illustrations. Reagan or Clark, it is unclear which, learned that when decisions needed to be made, sometimes the interagency process had to be pressured (Eureka proposals) or simply bypassed (Build-Down). Reagan and the troika also learned that the decentralized national security policy process based on competing SIGs without a strong ANSA resulted in a fractured process. There is a reason why every president since Eisenhower (and Eisenhower himself had the idea) has centralized the national security decision process and come to rely on a strong ANSA. Both Carter and Reagan learned that national security policy made in the White House was better than national security policy made elsewhere. (Whether that is true or not is another issue, but it can be inferred from the centralization in both administrations that Carter and Reagan came to believe this.) Bush is an unusual case. He and his advisers were so experienced in national security that they seemed to need to learn less. Even so, the Gang of Eight was created as an alternative to the NSC, and the Breakfast Group was created as a supplement to the NSC/PC. The Bush team developed an NSC process based on all their experience-born wisdom, then bypassed it as needed.

In terms of decision-making needs, Carter's decisions on PD-59 are the most instructive. Carter learned that for the sake of the 1980 campaign he needed policies that would make him appear tougher on the USSR. He also learned that Brzezinski could provide him with those policies. This is true in a general national security sense as well; Brzezinski's harder, realism-inspired analysis of the world made more sense to Carter following the seizure of hostages in Iran and the Soviet invasion of Afghanistan than Vance's notions of complex inter-dependence and idealism. Bush also learned, though he needed less convincing, that when it came to policy initiatives inspired by international events and/or electoral concerns—his speeches of September 1991 and January 1992—reliance on only a small handful of senior officials is the best way to meet those decision-making needs.

The Carter case also provides an example of the president learning about his advisers and those advisers learning about each other and the president. The oft-repeated analysis that Carter came to rely on Brzezinski more than on Vance is a statement about learning. Carter learned that Vance was less useful to him than Brzezinski. Brzezinski learned that Vance was an obstacle to his hope that Carter would become more of a realist than an idealist, and specific to nuclear strategy, Brzezinski's hope for a presidential directive on warfighting. Brzezinski also learned how to time his proposals to the president for maximum effect. He did not push the president on the issue of nuclear doctrine until late 1979 when various crises seemed to support his policy preferences.

In this sense, the interagency process performs the function of an audition. Through repeated decisions and repeated interactions, the president comes to learn which advisers he can rely upon and which advisers are less useful to him. It is a matter of trust and confidence. This is not a new idea. Kennedy and Johnson Secretary of State Dean Rusk's quote on the issue still speaks volumes:

"The real organization of government at higher echelons is not what you find in textbooks or organization charts. It is how confidence flows down from the president."[4] Nixon's ANSA and Secretary of State Henry Kissinger put it a different way: "Presidents listen to advisers whose views they think they need, not to those who insist on a hearing because of the organization chart."[5] The question is one of building trust between the president and an adviser or an adviser gaining the confidence of the president. It is a matter of the president learning to whom he should listen.[6] Possibly the best statement of this is President Kennedy's comment that "I must make the appointments now; a year hence I will know who I really want to appoint."[7]

The Carter, Reagan, and Bush administrations could not provide a better contrast. Carter learned to trust Brzezinski. Reagan learned to rely on Clark for a time, but the fact that he allowed the White House troika to pressure Clark out suggests that he never learned how important a single-process manager and national security alter ego could be to him. Bush came into office with a select group of people he already trusted and came to rely on them rather than the rest of his national security machinery for increasingly more advice. He learned that his preferred method of making decisions was within the Gang of Eight rather than his NSC.

Presidents are extremely busy individuals. They do not and cannot devote all their energies to national security. Therefore, when they desire more control over the process, they need to know which of their advisers can provide that control. When a president enters office, his senior national security advisers are chosen from a number of places. They may be loyalists to the president, politicians of significant stature, or experts in their chosen field. Presidents hope they have chosen the right mix of advisers. Carter chose three experts in Vance at state, Brown at defense, and Brzezinski as ANSA. Reagan chose two experts—Alexander Haig then George Shultz at state—and three loyalists —Richard Allen, then Clark as ANSA, and Caspar Weinberger at defense. (Weinberger can be considered a loyalist since he had no experience in defense policy, but significant experience with Reagan.) At first glance, it seems that Bush chose one of each: loyalist Baker at state, politician Cheney at defense, and expert Scowcroft as ANSA. However, Baker was also an expert in Washington politics. Cheney and Scowcroft were also extremely close to Bush. Loyalist is not the right word. Colleague is more appropriate. Bush was a member of a group of old hands at Washington politics and national security; he just happened to be the one of the group who was elected president. Unfortunately for most presidents, they cannot enter office as part of a group of close friends who also happen to be national security experts. They choose advisers, then set the process in motion and learn whom they can trust. Rusk's point about how confidence "flows" down from the president provides a useful metaphor. If confidence flows, to where does it flow? It flows wherever the president thinks it should flow. That direction is something a president must learn.

The Three Structures of National Security Decision Making

As discussed in chapter two and the case studies, over time, three concurrent structures develop within any presidential administration: a formal interagency structure, an informal structure, and a confidence structure (see Figure 7.1).[8] The ultimate use of and relationships between the three structures is dependent on the president's leadership style. Though political and institutional pressures push the president in one direction, his natural leadership style may rechannel the direction of change.

The first structure is created at the start of an administration's tenure in office. The informal structure is narrower in participation than the interagency process. It contains more informality and more ad hoc processes. It bypasses the inter-

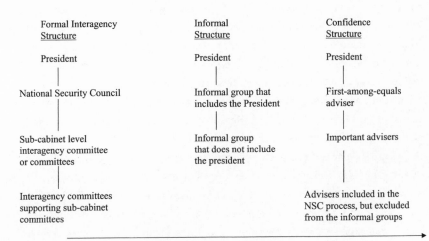

Formal Interagency Structure	Informal Structure	Confidence Structure
President	President	President
National Security Council	Informal group that includes the President	First-among-equals adviser
Sub-cabinet level interagency committee or committees	Informal group that does not include the president	Important advisers
Interagency committees supporting sub-cabinet committees		Advisers included in the NSC process, but excluded from the informal groups

Increasing narrowness of participation
Increasing use of informal and ad-hoc decision processes
Increasing instances of bypassing/streamlining of the interagency process

FIGURE 7.1. The Concurrent National Security Decision Making Structures

agency process in significant ways. The confidence structure is narrower still, even more informal and ad hoc, and almost defiantly outside the formal interagency system. The three structures as they operate within administrations complement each other. They are related in complex ways. They can be supplements to each other—concurrent structures working together. They can be rivals to each other—concurrent structures that compete for power over various decisions. They can be indifferent to each other—operating as if the other structures do not exist. Figures 7.2, 7.3, and 7.4 illustrate the three structures as they existed within the Carter, Reagan, and Bush administrations, respectively.

The initial design of the standard interagency NSC process is the formal structure described in chapter three. The second concurrent structure—the informal process—develops as an adjunct to the formal structure. As described in chapter three, the informal structure is created because the president and his senior advisers feel the NSC is too large, too slow, too leaky, or too impersonal a forum for serious consideration of crucial policy issues. Carter's VBB and FFPB, Reagan's NSPG, and Bush's Gang of Eight and Breakfast Group are these informal structures.

Past presidents had their own informal structures. For FDR the informal structure ruled over the formal cabinet system that made national security de-

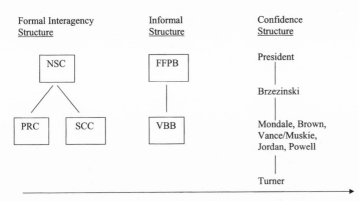

Key: NSC -- National Security Council   PRC -- Policy Review Committee
     SCC -- Special Coordinating Committee   FFPB -- Friday Foreign Policy Breakfast Group
     VBB -- Vance, Brzezinski, Brown lunches

FIGURE 7.2. The Carter Administration: Three Concurrent National Security Decision Making Structures

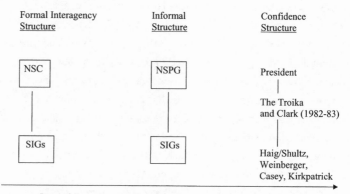

FIGURE 7.3. The Reagan Administration: Three Concurrent National Security
Decision Making Structures

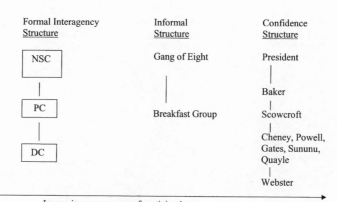

FIGURE 7.4. The Bush Administration: Three Concurrent National Security
Decision Making Structures

cisions before the National Security Act of 1947. The force of FDR's personality and his relationships with his cabinet and subcabinet officials formed the backbone of this informal structure. Truman tried a similar method of governing, though he did not pit his aides against each other. His formal structure, whether the cabinet or the NSC was used as an advisory body, was not a place to make decisions. Decisions were made informally through Truman consulting with specific selected advisers as needed. Eisenhower also had an informal structure that supplemented the formal structure. His penchant for ending NSC meetings when he had made up his mind, then selecting a few aides to come into the Oval Office where the final decision would be made, is an informal adjunct to the formal interagency system. Kennedy's informal structure was dominant. His collegial form of decision making made the formal structure less relevant. By watching a committee meeting, an observer would not necessarily know if the meeting was formal or informal. The informal structure was dominant because decisions were not left for NSC or cabinet meetings; they were more often made wherever, whenever, and with whomever the president was with as he made up his mind. Johnson's Tuesday Lunch Group was an informal decision-making body analogous to the processes in the Carter and Bush administrations. Outside of the large and unwieldy NSC, issues could be debated among the principals without interruption from less important players and without any unintentional leaks. Nixon and Ford had less informality in the sense of a second informal layer of committees or discussion groups. However, the power that the NSC staff enjoyed within the Nixon administration and the power that Kissinger's staff at the State Department had in the Ford administration can be seen as the makings of an informal structure.

The third concurrent structure can be called a confidence structure. It is based on the notion discussed above that the president learns to trust some advisers more than others. Every president seems to find one person who can be first among equals: Wilson had Colonel House, FDR had Harry Hopkins, Truman relied on Acheson, Eisenhower delegated to Dulles, and John Kennedy used his brother Robert as a surrogate. Johnson never seemed to find his most trusted adviser, a first-among-equals, but his situation is unique. He came to power after Kennedy's assassination and inherited Kennedy's cabinet. Ultimately, he leaned more and more toward his own chosen ANSA, Walt Rostow. Nixon and Ford, of course, had Kissinger as their main national security adviser. The president will implicitly or explicitly arrange his advisers in a hierarchy, from a first-among-equals adviser who has a unique relationship with the president, down to other important advisers often included in the informal structure, down to those advisers who may be NSC participants but not part of the informal structure.

Carter came to rely on Brzezinski, but the decision to use Brzezinski as a powerful ANSA came late in Carter's term. Carter's initial confidence structure could be described as an equal reliance on Vance and Brzezinski. Their philosophical and policy disagreements made that untenable. The Iranian hostage crisis and the invasion of Afghanistan gave Brzezinski the ability to edge Vance further away from Carter. Ultimately, Vance recognized that he had slipped to second-tier status and resigned. Brown was an important adviser, but never a challenger for the first-among-equals position. CIA Director Stansfield Turner was an example of someone included in the NSC system, but left out of the informal structure.[9]

Reagan's confidence structure (a reliance on Clark) began to develop, then was dismantled. This may stem from Reagan's on-again, off-again participation in the decision process. Reliance on a first-among-equals adviser implies that the president is often making decisions on his own, backed up by the wisdom of a trusted individual. It could also be a situation in which the president has delegated some decisions to that trusted adviser, as was the case with Truman and Acheson, Eisenhower and Dulles, and Nixon and Kissinger. Reagan, however, seemed to delegate most decisions to a number of advisers. In domestic policy, the troika of Meese, Chief of Staff James Baker, and Deputy Chief of Staff Michael Deaver were clearly Reagan's first-among-equals advisers. This power extended into the area of national security. The attempts by Haig, Shultz, and Clark to lead the foreign policy team were thwarted by the troika or because Reagan refused to choose any adviser as a first among equals. If a confidence structure existed, it began and ended with the troika, whose role in national security was ill defined. In a sense, they refused to allow any official to be given the tools to lead in foreign policy, but they would not perform the job themselves. The result was a national security policy process that began and ended in disarray.

Bush, in contrast, had a well-developed confidence structure from inauguration day. Baker was clearly the most important adviser. Scowcroft was a near equal, but deferred to Baker because of Baker's position as secretary of state and intimate relationship with Bush. Other advisers, even within the Gang of Eight, never came to rival either of these officials. DCI William Webster was someone who was included in NSC meetings, but not the Gang of Eight. (This is not merely a function of the fact that the DCI is considered a policy adviser, not a policy maker in most administrations. Bush included JCS Chair Colin Powell, a similar type of adviser, in the Gang of Eight.) The confidence structure was in place, even before the informal structure evolved. This is unusual, but it is revealing. A well-established confidence structure in the Bush administration helped ensure a smooth decision-making process. The uncertainty during the Carter administration and the lack of any consistent confidence structure in the Reagan administration helped to lead their national security policy processes toward breakdown. Interestingly, Reagan and Bush seem to be exceptions in the opposite direction. Bush had a cadre of trusted advisers; Reagan had none.

The origin, use, and relationship between these three structures depended on the leadership style of each president. Carter had created a collegial decision-making process, hoping to use the NSC and its subcommittees (the SCC and PRC) as places where the senior decision makers could openly and equally discuss their opinions. His plan to be his own secretary of state in some ways ran counter to that collegiality. If Carter was going to be the ultimate decider and one deeply involved in the minutiae of policy making, then collegiality might fall prey to the knowledge that NSC, SCC, and PRC meetings were advisory at best and possibly an irrelevant formality. Each aide might simply wait for the best opportunity to present his position to Carter in a private meeting. Carter might make the decisions alone or with one or two trusted aides. The creation of the VBB and FFPB committees further reduced the relevance of the formal process. When the senior players met informally to iron out consensus, then the NSC system became simply a tool to enforce that consensus on the rest of the bureaucracy. Carter's confidence in himself and his decision to act as his own chief of staff, intelligence analyst, and policy analyst led to the growing dominance of the confidence structure. With such a reliance on his own efforts, Carter would not want to wait for extensive staffing arrangements; full debate over various policies might become tedious for him. Instead, the use of one adviser as an alter ego and all-purpose foreign policy bureaucracy made more sense. Carter could sit in a room with one adviser and staff out his policies. Brzezinski gained Carter's trust and evolved from a staff manager to a near Kissingerian adviser/implementer/spokesman. Carter's confidence structure therefore came to overshadow and even eclipse the other structures. PD-59 is an example of this, but the more famous example was the decision to launch the hostage rescue mission. Vance ultimately resigned over this. He had been excluded from the confidence structure and subsequently felt irrelevant. Allowing the confidence structure to overwhelm the other structures can alienate advisers who are lower on the confidence ladder. The result could be process breakdown.

Reagan's lack of attention to his own decision-making process left the formal process dominant. While the principles of evolution discussed above suggest that presidents will move to centralize decision making, they also state clearly that this centralization is deliberate. Without a conscious decision to centralize and in an environment of intra-administration ideological conflict, the tendency is toward decentralization at best and chaos at worst. Reagan's process began an evolution toward an informal confidence structure just as Carter's and Bush's had. However, his unwillingness to directly become involved in managing the process or provide someone with the mandate to manage ultimately allowed the philosophical divisions of the formal structure to prevent the other structures from maturing. Without settling those differences or personally creating methods to reach consensus, Reagan allowed gridlock to continue. Iran Contra was the eventual result of a process so mired in disagreement that NSC staffers felt the need to privatize aspects of policy in order to pursue their goals.[10]

The Bush national security structures operated in a much more balanced way than the others. This is why the administration's decision process functioned so well. The key ingredient was Bush's leadership style. He understood the necessity of teamwork at the senior level, much like Kennedy, but he also had enough experience in government to know that the formal interagency process was important as well. His tenure at CIA gave him a unique perspective for an incoming president. He had led an agency of professionals, not political appointees, whose work was designed to be based on expertise. He and his senior advisers also knew that decision making at the cabinet level and between the president and his senior advisers was more a function of good relationships than good analysis. For these reasons, Bush's informal structure was the most powerful. It might be seen as a rival to the basic interagency system in the sense that increasingly more decisions were made within the Gang of Eight. However, the critical role of the NSC/DC and its chair Deputy ANSA Robert Gates, the only backbencher in the Gang of Eight, ensured that the Gang of Eight and Breakfast Group never allowed the formal structure to break down or work at cross-purposes to the informal structure. The formal and informal structures were always connected, working together and toward the same goals. Bush also made sure that the confidence structure did not become more important than the informal structure. This would lead to perhaps more rivalry than a collegial body such as the Gang of Eight could handle. Bush's Gang of Eight members all knew that deference to Baker was a basic premise of working within the administration. Arguments could be made; challenges to Baker's ideas were expected and desired by Bush, but challenges to Baker's role were not welcome. Of course, among friends this was easier to work out than among a group of strangers.

THEORETICAL AND POLICY IMPLICATIONS

Necessity of All Three Structures

The case studies of the Carter, Reagan, and Bush administrations suggest that the formal, informal, and confidence structures are all necessary for a smoothly functioning national security decision-making process. In addition, if any one of the structures is to take priority, it should be the informal structure.

The formal standard interagency process of the NSC system must continue to operate even if it is bypassed or ignored occasionally, even frequently. The formal system put in place by the Bush administration and used by the Clinton and George W. Bush administrations seems to be the best design for this formal system. The formal structure cannot be eliminated because it is where the day-to-day workings of the national security bureaucracies are channeled into the NSC process and into the awareness of the senior policy makers. Information, analyses, and alternative perspectives must be able to reach the senior decision makers in some form. The interagency process is the backbone of presidential decision making, a superstructure that connects the president's brain trust to the eyes and ears, arms and legs of the departments and agencies. To control the executive branch for the sake of implementation and to stay on top of world developments, that backbone cannot be eliminated or separated from the top decision makers. Using a multilayered NSC process to filter these ideas is a necessity, but the senior policy makers must take into account the perspectives of the bureaucracies. These are the resident experts on key issues and they are also the people who will implement policy. Their points of view are important to analytical inputs and policy outputs.

The informal structure is an adjunct to the formal structure. It does not replace the formal structure, but acts as a supplementary process that helps smooth the rough edges of the formal process. It is a method that allows the principal decision makers to work together without staff to build trust, teamwork, and collegiality, and to analyze national security issues from the broader perspective that their roles as heads of executive departments often preclude. As in the Carter and Bush administrations, the informal structure should include a committee consisting of the president and his hand-picked key advisers and a second committee that includes those advisers without the president and vice president. The meetings should be in informal settings—breakfast or lunch —and should not include staff. The committee should always meet in anticipation of an NSC meeting to give the principals a chance to essentially steer policy in the preferred direction. The focus that can be achieved in these groups cannot be developed in any other way than to simply place these officials in such a more discrete and informal setting.

The president does not need to see the building of consensus or the revelation of differences among the principal advisers. He certainly does need to know about this, but he does not need to see it develop. One of the key aspects of the principals' meetings is to conserve the president's time by ironing out any differences that can be settled before the issue is presented to the president. How much to protect the president from interagency infighting is something the advisers must learn. It is partly a function of the president providing adequate guidance about his process and policy preferences, and partly a matter of the president's senior advisers playing to his strengths and protecting him from his own weaknesses. The Carter case study provides a useful example of this. Carter's advisers learned to limit the amount of paperwork that made it to the Oval Office.

In addition, the president and his advisers need a forum for building collegiality and for in-depth discussion of foreign policy issues. The president needs to see and probe his principal advisers' consensus or lack thereof in a somewhat insulated environment. The president needs to learn about his advisers and he needs to learn to trust them. These informal settings create the environment in which the president can get the unvarnished advice and freewheeling discussion among advisers that he needs. The consensus or differences of opinion that develop in these informal groupings should be used to structure the formal NSC proceedings. The president's most important advisers should have the ability to steer the NSC process. If the president did not feel they were the most qualified people to advise him on defense and foreign affairs, he would not have chosen them for their jobs.

This does not mean that the formal process should be downplayed to irrelevancy. It should still function as if the informal process did not exist. The president needs input from both the formal and informal processes to make quality decisions. This is one reason why the Deputy ANSA should be included in the informal process. As the hands-on manager of the formal processes of the administration, the Deputy ANSA can provide a direct link between the formal process and the informal process. He can keep the president and his principal advisers informed about how the formal process is developing policy issues before reviews and policy options reach the NSC/PC.

The confidence structure is not truly something for which an administration can prepare. As stated above, the confidence structure is an implied structure. It is not something that can be shaped into a committee or process. It is a matter of relationships. As a president enters office, his advisers are chosen on the basis of theoretical assumptions. A president has a theory on the best way to make presidential decisions and an assumption about how each of his advisers will fit into this decision system. It is all theory because no president comes to office having been president before. Only after making decisions within the formal interagency and informal processes will a president discover how well his theories and assumptions have held up. Only after the administration struggles through routine and nonroutine decisions will he see how the relationships among his senior advisers and between himself and his senior advisers have evolved. Essentially, the president must learn who will be his most trusted adviser. Only then will the confidence structure develop. Some advisers will be more important to the president than others. A hierarchy of confidence will be established. All advice to the president is not equal. It is judged and weighted by the president based on how much confidence he has in a given adviser. This becomes an implicit confidence structure, though it can become explicit if the president spends more time or communicates more with some advisers than others or frequently adjourns NSC meetings by selecting a smaller subset of his advisers to participate in after-NSC decision forums.

The confidence structure usually develops quietly, unless a key official makes a large enough blunder to lose the confidence of the president in one bold stroke.[11] Two issues present themselves. First, as the confidence structure develops, it is crucial that the formal interagency system and the informal structures continue to function as if the confidence structure does not exist. The president needs all three structures to make high-quality decisions. The ANSA and his Deputy must ensure that the confidence structure does not overrun the other structures to the point that the administration's foreign policy making begins to resemble the Nixon-Kissinger policy process of the latter Nixon years in which the President and one adviser ran foreign policy nearly on their own in many respects. Second, the principal advisers must be given confidence that a special relationship between just one adviser and the president does not preclude the rest of them from having an impact on foreign policy making. If all the advisers understand that a confidence structure will develop, they may see foreign policy making as a competitive process. This could help the president in the sense that each adviser will seek to give the president the best possible advice as a method of maintaining the president's confidence. It could also backfire if advisers see the development of a confidence structure as an excuse for end runs and bureaucratic games. Again, the key becomes the continued functioning of the formal and informal structures. All the advisers should maintain their participation in the policy process through one, two, or all three structures. The confidence structure simply represents the unavoidable reality that some participants' advice will eventually mean more to the president than others.

As implied in the above analysis, the informal structure is the key to balancing the relationships between all three structures. If the formal structure dominates, there may be no method for the administration to iron out a consensus among the senior players. Formal meetings of the NSC and its subcommittees could remain battlegrounds between differing philosophies of foreign affairs or simply arenas for egos and ambitions to clash. Such was the case in the Reagan administration. If the confidence structure dominates, advisers who feel they are being shut out of the process and do not have an informal forum in which to gain intimate access to the president may leak to the press, try to act as spoilers, or resign in protest. This was the ultimate tale of the Carter administration. Only a strong and well-managed informal process can combine the formal and confidence structures into a smoothly operating decision process in which all departments and all senior advisers have their channels to the president.

The best organizational design cannot function if the personnel are not up to the task, however. In the same sense, the best personnel cannot function if the president is not up to the task. The president must take his own national security policy process seriously. He must enforce the roles of each official and the procedural designs of his system. He must remain the final arbiter of policy and process. In particular, the president must have an official who will manage the process on his behalf. As in most cases, his eyes and ears will be the ANSA. The ANSA and the deputy ANSA must be seen to be managing their parts of the process on the authority of the president. The roles of individual advisers and the committee relationships are not aspects of the national security process that a president can simply set in motion and then take for granted. They must be enforced. Occasionally, this means trips to the woodshed for those who break the rules, or the firing of officials who continually ignore the president's hopes for the policy-making process.

Of course, every president has his own leadership style, level of interest in foreign policy, view of the need for administration consensus, and comfort level with bureaucratic conflict. The three-tiered structure described here allows presidents to lean toward formality and informality as a general rule or as necessity and judgment of the moment dictate. Whatever the balance a president desires, he must use his ANSA or another official to monitor the decision-making process and adjust it depending upon his needs. However, he must support that official's efforts and enforce them or he will lose control of his own process. He cannot afford to do this, nor can he afford to manage it directly.

Skipping the Process of Evolution: Can a Mature Process Be Installed on Inauguration Day?

The previous analysis establishes a basic premise. As presidents enter office, they create a process for national security decision making. This process is based on a standard interagency model. Pressures on this process and the people operating within it cause the president and/or his senior advisers to modify that process. These pressures are explained as the principles of economy, political pressure, and learning. The changes in that process, its evolution, come in the form of a distinct pattern of narrowing, an increase in informal and ad hoc decision structures, and a bypassing or streamlining of the interagency process. This pattern of evolution exists within all administrations. Since this specific pattern of evolution is identifiable and the three concurrent structures can be described, is it possible to skip the evolutionary process and install the final version of this decision-making process on inauguration day? The answer is yes and no.

The yes answer comes from a look at the way the Carter, Reagan, and Bush administrations functioned. Since the three structures that evolve over the four years in office can be identified, it seems logical that a president could put all three of these structures in place at the beginning of his administration. The Bush administration seems to have done this. Bush had both a formal interagency process and a confidence structure on inauguration day. It is not a huge leap of faith to believe that he could have had his Gang of Eight up and running if he desired such a forum at that point. He did move to small-group decision making after only a few months. He might have felt that his Gang of Eight was his confidence structure. The Eisenhower and Nixon administrations could be seen as coming to power with a well-defined, though not necessarily implicit, version of all three structures. Eisenhower had a formal process, an informal post-cabinet, post-NSC decision process, and his relationship with Dulles. Nixon's NSC system was formal; his informal structure was the NSC staff's role in coordinating, even controlling, the process; and his relationship with Kissinger was unchallenged within the administration. Eisenhower made decisions in the years before a strong ANSA had become the norm, but he ultimately mused about creating an ANSA-like official in order to centralize policy in the White House. The Nixon and Bush decision processes evolved very quickly. Bush developed a collegial centralization. Nixon's centralization was of a more malevolent nature in its rapid exclusion of other officials and its brutal bureaucratic politics.

All three of these presidents had two things in common that make them a sharp contrast to Carter and Reagan. Eisenhower, Nixon, and Bush all had vast experience in cabinet-level decision making and unusual expertise in national security for a president. Carter and Reagan took their oaths of office and entered an unfamiliar world. They had never held any jobs in Washington politics, nor did they have any experience in foreign affairs. They had to learn not only how Washington and the world worked, but how to make decisions and whom in their own cabinet they could trust.

This is why the answer to the question is yes and no. Some presidents, unusual cases, may come to office with the knowledge of how they will make decisions and with, implicitly, this three-tiered structure. This does not mean they have nothing to learn; it means they need to learn less and they will learn more quickly. Other presidents do not yet know one or both of the following. They may not realize that the interagency process will be a necessary but often frustrating method of making decisions (hence the need for an informal process). They may also not know whom in their cabinet they can trust (no confidence structure yet exists). The basic point is that even if presidents do feel that they need to design three types of structures in order to make the best decisions, even if they understand that the interagency process will frustrate them and lead them to make changes in their decision structure, they will probably not know which advisers will fit into which roles in the process. It is a matter of understanding the proper roles, but not knowing who will play those roles. A better illustration might be to see the president as a baseball manager. He knows he needs certain types of hitters in his batting order—a leadoff hitter who gets on base, a number three spot hitter who hits for average, and fourth and fifth spot hitters who hit for power. However, he does not know which players will provide him with which types of hitting until after a few games are played. This is another reason why administration decision making evolves. Presidents need to audition their advisers, to understand their personalities, their ideas and methods of operating, and their relationships with each other. This takes time and repeated decision opportunities. Only then can they begin to produce a system that best serves their interests.[12]

Two points should be added here. First, all presidents seem to think of themselves as special cases. They come to office to place their indelible and inimitable stamp on the presidency and the nation. They may believe that their inauguration marks the beginning of a new era—a New Deal or a New Frontier or a New Federalism or a New Covenant. These are not merely the rhetorical flourishes of a campaign. They signify the ambitions of men with powerful egos surrounded by cadres of loyalists dedicated to building up and satisfying those egos. Who else would believe that the nation and even the world needs him desperately? For this reason, new presidents may believe that they have nothing to learn from past presidents or that the lesson is one of negation—what has been learned is how not to be president. In this sense, presidents, as noted in the case studies, may simply design systems that are different, even the opposite, of previous presidents. Scholars and wise men can tell the president that the stove is hot, but he will have to be burned at least once before he believes that the heat will affect even him. Presidents may experiment with decision adaptations. Gallucci's notion that a president is a "policy taster" can be amended to suggest that a president is also a "process taster"—playing around with his decision structure to see what works best.[13] Ultimately, however, it seems that a president's experimentation will lead him in the direction suggested by the evolution model.

Second, scholars who study national security or voters who care about national security more than domestic policy are in a distinct minority. The American president will most likely be a domestic policy expert, chosen for his domestic agenda. Consequently a president needs to learn a great deal about the policy process, but that learning will be hampered by a lack of knowledge about national security. This places the president at a disadvantage. In Washington, knowledge is power, and the less a president knows about national security, the more difficulty he will have trying to control the process of decision making. Both these points suggest that in most cases a lot of learning will take place over a four-year period.

Fitting Process to the Policy

The issues raised in this book suggest a new look at the relationship between process and policy. Typically, scholars want to know whether different styles of policy process will produce different policies.[14] The case studies in this book illustrate that policies with differing characteristics required each president to use different styles of policy process. As noted in chapter two, Chandler's dictum "structure follows strategy" holds true for these cases. The national security decision-making structure was modified with the specific intention of giving it the ability to develop a specific policy preferred by the president and/or to prevent the interagency process from precluding such an ability. These are examples of top-down decision making. The routine decision making of the interagency process can be seen as bottom-up decision making. In the standard interagency process the senior levels of the administration may ask very broad and general questions, such as What are the best ways of achieving U.S. national security goals through arms control? The NSC committees and departmental bureaucracies are tasked with answering the questions through the standard interagency process described above. However, in the cases studied here, the presidents and their advisers already had answers—specific policies they favored. In this sense, what they wanted from the interagency process were refinements of the policy idea and specific implementation plans, analyses that made all the political and strategic implications clear, and perhaps, arguments that would legitimize the policy. Essentially, a president says, "Here is what I want to do. You are the experts. Show me how to do it." Such a task is significantly different than what is asked of the interagency process in the routine conception of bottom-up decision making.

The adaptations themselves can be categorized as innovative, reactive, or opportunistic. Innovative policies are instances when a president is instituting a policy change on his own initiative. A president wants to change the course of an established policy and believes that the national security bureaucracies, wedded to the ongoing policy, may be obstacles to the new policy. Carter's March 1977 Deep Cuts proposal and Reagan's strategic defense idea are examples of this. Each president sought to move a policy in a new direction and adjusted the decision process to achieve these goals. The decisions made by both Reagan and Bush over START I (Eureka and Build-Down proposals, the Malta Summit and 1991 decisions) were reactive policies. The Reagan and Bush administrations were influenced by a domestic political environment that demanded initiation and completion of arms control negotiations, respectively. As each administration's arms control policies were considered to be inadequate, policy change and decision-making change were implemented as a reaction to shifts in the politics of arms control. Carter's PD-59 and Bush's START II speeches can be classified as opportunistic. They seem to be both innovative and reactive. The combination of motivations and the added factor of time pressure felt by the administration make the case significantly different from innovation and reaction. Both were exploiting a window of opportunity—domestic in Carter's case and international in Bush's. The Carter policy had been developing within Pentagon and NSC staff for several years, but did not get presidential approval until an electoral connection could be made. Carter could use PD-59 to counter Reagan's charges of softness toward the USSR. The Bush speech of September 1991 was a swift attempt to take advantage of the collapse of the Communist Party of the USSR and the continuing collapse of the Soviet Union itself.

Two important aspects of the policy-process relationship should be highlighted: policy making in an uncertain threat environment and the timing of policy. First, if different policies necessitate different processes, then policy making for a world in which there is one large and deadly threat (the USSR) should be different from policy making for a world in which the threats are more numerous but less dangerous (the post–cold war world). The U.S. design for national security policy making evolved in an era when the threat was stable and intensely focused on the single overarching threat of the spread of Soviet power. Centralization of the decision-making process makes sense in a world in which there is a central threat. It makes even more sense given the U.S. perceptions of a single unified strategy for Soviet domination of the globe that was often our judgment of our rival's character (whether that judgment was accurate is another issue). However, a more decentralized, more flexible process may be more appropriate for an era in which new and unique threats emerge swiftly.

After September 11, terrorism in all its forms and weapons of mass destruction have emerged as the new threats of the twenty-first century. These are unpredictable, complex, and truly global threats whose nature precludes a narrow focus such as that during the cold war. All issues during the cold war were seen through the lens of the cold war competition. Whatever strategic lens is used to explain terrorism (religion, Arab nationalism, criminality), combating terrorism requires a wider range of expertise (area studies, law enforcement, intelligence, diplomacy) and a proactive policy of prevention. It is an entirely different approach to national security than the cold war tandem of deterrence and defense of key strategic areas. In particular, much greater participation by experts in what formerly had been obscure regions may be a requirement. For example, during the Bush administration decisions on Somalia in 1992, experts on the USSR, Europe, and strategic arms control made decisions regarding U.S. policy in Africa.[15] Somehow getting the FBI and CIA to work together is also crucial. This issue needs further study from a theoretical and a policy point of view.[16]

The case studies also illustrate a relationship between the process and the timing of the policy. In spite of the name of the discipline political science, practitioners might argue that politics is more art than science. Presidents have a feel for policy, and that sensitivity is partly a function of the timing of an issue. Often presidents must act quickly before a perceived opportunity disappears. Kingdon calls these limited opportunities "policy windows."[17] These policy windows are instances when contentious issues are settled, dormant agendas spring to life, or new ideas swiftly mature. But these new or renewed policies must be generated from a process. The cases illustrate a presidential judgment that the policy needs of the moment could not be satisfied by the standard interagency process. None of the presidents abandoned their interagency systems, nor made deep changes in their NSC committee structures and processes. Certain policy needs require new decision styles. This notion reinforces the economy principle—presidents need policy machinery that can make decisions at different speeds and with varying levels of effort.

A normative question concerning the nature of the changes in the national security process remains at issue: Is modifying the standard interagency process or adapting the routine decision structure a wise way to make decisions, or can this lead to poorly staffed and insufficiently developed policies? The answer is beyond the scope of this book, but it is a key question for further research. A preliminary answer is two-fold. First, further research on whether changes in the standard decision-making procedures represent a potential danger to high-quality decisions might consider the following. The full interagency process was designed for inclusivity of executive departments, diversity of opinion, and coordination of policy. It is the style of decision a president sees as best before he is pressured and burdened by the realities of life inside the Oval Office. Changing the method of decision on the run as a response to immediate political needs at first sounds like a recipe for making poor decisions, perhaps by excluding diverse opinions or poorly coordinating implementation. For example, the Iran-Contra case in the Reagan years is an example of a change in decision-making practices that led to policy disaster. However, President Nixon's opening to China is an example of a change in policy making that led to significant and far-reaching strategic developments. One key difference between the two is that the Iran-Contra initiatives were never vetted through the interagency process once the initial political need for a breakthrough ended. The opening to China was made through a change in the decision-making process, but was moved back into the standard processes once the policy initiative had become reality.

Second, whether or not making ad hoc changes to the interagency process in mid-administration is advisable is irrelevant in some respects. These types of changes are inevitable. The nature of presidential decision making is that presidents make decisions in whatever manner they desire, regardless of how they intended to make decisions when they first entered office.

Further Study

The central premises of this book open up the study of national security decision making to many new avenues. Seeing decision making as a dynamic process that changes over time allows for a much deeper and broader perspective on policy making. First, the most obvious practical implication of this research is the notion that changes in the international environment will cause changes in the decision-making process. Over a decade since the collapse of the Soviet Union it is obvious, even clichéd, to point out that the international system has been fundamentally altered. However, the emergence of a new international environment calls not only for a reassessment of U.S. national security policies, but a reexamination of the decision-making processes that generate these policies. Simply put, senior policy makers are now operating in a more uncertain and dynamic environment. Threats are more inconsistent; regional power balances are more fluid; domestic political consensus on U.S. national interests abroad is more difficult to sustain. During the cold war the Soviet threat was a stable one that could ultimately prove fatal. Unexpected situations or new threats were the exception, not the rule. Today, the situation is reversed. The threats are less deadly, but more unpredictable. For this reason, scholars of decision making must turn their attention to the particular problems of policy making in situations characterized by frequent change. A less stable international political environment may call for a more adaptable and flexible policy-making process. Recognition that decision making already undergoes serious changes is a first step toward this goal.

When studying national security decision making, the international system needs to have a special place. The definition of U.S. national interests and the security threats to the U.S. are influences on every aspect of decision making. When it comes to national security and foreign policy, the study of U.S. decision making and the current study of international relations meet head-on. The dominant neorealist paradigm of international relations essentially factors foreign and national security policy decision making out of the field of international politics.[18] It is based on the notion of the structure of international systems as the independent variable. Neorealism argues that nation-state behavior is a response to the international system based upon rational choice; all nations are simply utility maximizers, and formal models can be used to map out their behavior.[19] Henehan has examined this idea in the context of the congressional role in foreign policy, viewing changes in the international system as the cause of changes in congressional procedure and policy.[20]

Obviously, the analysis in this book rejects the notion that the international environment is the only cause of change in the decision-making process. There needs to be some way to rejoin the subfield of international politics with the study of decision making that goes beyond rational choice models to recapture the richness and complexity of decision making. A possible method of doing this is to relax the strictures of rational choice decisions, but accept the premise that changes in the international system are the impetus for foreign and national security policy changes. However, if scholars of international relations accept that nonsystem-level factors can be legitimate independent variables, future research could include more attention to the ways in which domestic politics, organizational dynamics, and presidential choice affect the international system. Many scholars have already done this. For example, Katzenstein highlights the role of cultural factors, norms, and institutions; Wendt focuses on the role of ideas; Snyder, Christensen, and Zakaria talk about domestic political factors.[21] However, these scholars are then often considered to be outside the neorealist mainstream. Sadly, scholars are still trying to find one single cause of social and political phenomena rather than accepting that there may be more than one independent variable.

A second, related research agenda would focus on the difficulties of creating foreign policy in the absence of a clear threat and examine the definitions of U.S. national interest in two ways: the level of consensus within an administration and the level of consensus between an administration and Congress and the public. The study of national security decision making during periods of high or low consensus would help identify whether there is a relationship between the extent of consensus within government and society and the stability of decision making within an administration. Lack of consensus may make more of a differ-ence with some issues than others.

A third issue relates to organizational dynamics. This book has focused on de-cisions made through the interagency process. An earlier version of it included examinations of decision making for Reagan's National Security Decision Direc-tive 13 (NSDD-13) and Bush's reviews of the Single Integrated Operating Plan 7 (SIOP-7). These studies revealed no evolution of the decision-making structure. The pressures explained by the principles of the evolution model were not pres-ent; no evolution of the process took place. In both these cases, the decisions were contained within the DOD and were not subject to the trials of the inter-agency process. Whether this means that the decision-making processes within a single agency do not evolve is a question that is beyond the scope of this study. To get at the heart of this issue would take several case studies of decisions made within a single department. Several different departments would also need to be studied, comparisons of decisions made within the DOD and decisions made within the State Department, for example. The answer to this question is most likely "no." Decisions made within single agencies are not immune from the evolution process. Agencies such as the State Department and DOD are com-posed of different bureaus that have different interests on a given policy. Each bureau will fight for its interest within the department, just as the department will fight for its overall interest within the administration. Intraservice rivalries between the military services are legendary. Tales of friction between different functional and regional bureaus within the State Department are also a charac-teristic of memoirs and analyses of State Department decision making. If diffi-culty creating a consensus among different factions within a department exists, the pressures on the executive of that department to modify the process should be present. Some evolution of the process may be evident upon detailed study.[22]

Fourth, this study has focused on a single-issue area and one of crucial im-portance to U.S. national security—arms control and strategic doctrine. Does decision making evolve in a similar manner and for similar reasons for other issues? Are less important issues, such as policy on commercial negotiations, also subject to these decision-making dynamics? Does decision making for more regional issues develop in the same way, or does the fact that there is a lead bu-reau for a specific region within the State Department mute the changes? Issues with more economic content add entirely different characters to the interagency process, such as the Departments of Commerce and Treasury as well as the U.S. trade representative. How might that change the nature of the process? These questions can be answered through other case studies that begin with the assumptions of this study: decision making changes over time.

Finally, a longer longitudinal study that encompasses second terms can examine the evolution within each administration in the context of the overall evolution of national security decision making since 1947. It would also take into account the difference between second and first terms: personnel changes and the mix between newcomers and veterans, second term priorities such as the president's legacy and possible deep presidential involvement in a specific national security issue, and the impact of presidential scandals. The latter issue is intriguing. Since Eisenhower, no president has served two terms without a major scandal (Watergate, Iran-Contra, Whitewater/Lewinsky). The relationship between these scandals and the evolution of the decision-making process is an area that needs study.

Chapter One

1. Stephen Ambrose, *Eisenhower: The President*, vol. 2 (New York: Simon and Schuster, 1984), 444; and Townsend Hoopes, *The Devil and John Foster Dulles* (Boston: Little, Brown, 1973), 135–36, 138–40.

2. The new structures for homeland security are detailed in Bush (G. W.) Administration, *Executive Order Establishing Office of Homeland Security*, 8 October 2001. Available at http://www.whitehouse.gov/news/releases/2001/10/print/20011008-2.html. Accessed 14 February 2002; and Bush (G. W.) Administration, *Homeland Security Presidential Directive-1, Organization and Operation of the Homeland Security Council*, 29 October 2001. Available at http://www.fas.org/irp/offdocs/nspd/hspd-1.htm. Accessed 26 March 2002. Ridge explains his view in Alison Mitchell, "Disputes Erupt on Ridge's Need for His Job," *The New York Times*, 4 November 2002, B7.

3. Charles E. Walcott and Karen M. Hult, *Governing the White House* (Lawrence: University Press of Kansas, 1995).

4. The author is indebted to Paul Hammond for the use of the economy terminology.

5. A brief list of the second-term influences could include the impact of sweeping personnel changes, shifts in priorities away from electoral considerations and toward the building of a lasting presidential legacy (and often a commensurate prioritizing of some specific foreign policy issue), and complete process breakdowns due to scandals related or unrelated to foreign policy (Watergate, Iran-Contra, Whitewater/Lewinsky).

6. Alexander George, "Case Studies and Theory Development: The Method of Structured, Focused Comparison," in *Diplomacy: New Approaches in History, Theory, and Policy*, ed. Paul Gordon Lauren (New York: Free Press, 1979), 43–68; and Alexander L. George and Timothy J. McKeown, "Case Studies and Theories of Organizational Decision Making," in *Advances in Information Processing in Organizations*, vol. 2, ed. Robert F. Coulam and Richard A. Smith (Greenwich: JAI Press, 1985), 29–30.

7. George and McKeown, "Case Studies and Theories of Organizational Decision Making," 34–41.

Chapter Two

1. On cognitive models see *The Structure of Decision*, ed. Robert Axelrod (Princeton: Princeton University Press, 1976); Irving Janis and Leon Mann, *Decision Making* (New York: Free Press, 1977); *Judgment Under Uncertainty*, ed. Daniel Kahneman, Paul Slovic, and Amos Tversky (Cambridge: Cambridge University Press, 1982); Miriam Steiner, "The Search for Order in a Disorderly World: Worldviews and Prescriptive Decision Paradigms," *International Organization* 37, no. 3 (summer 1983): 373–414; and Joseph Lepgold and Alan C. Lam-

born, "Locating Bridges: Connecting Research Agendas on Cognition and Strategic Choice," *International Studies Review* 3, no. 3 (fall 2001): 3–29. Small group dynamics are treated in Irving Janis, *Groupthink*, 2d ed. (Boston: Houghton Mifflin, 1982); Charles F. Hermann, Janice Gross Stein, Bengt Sundelius, and Stephen G. Walker, "Resolve, Accept, or Avoid: Effects of Group Conflict on Foreign Policy Decision," *International Studies Review* 3, no. 2 (summer 2001): 133–68; and Paul Kowert, *Groupthink or Deadlock* (Albany: State University of New York Press, 2002). The operational code idea is illustrated in Nathan Leites, *A Study of Bolshevism* (Glencoe, IL: Free Press, 1953); and Alexander George, "The Operational Code: A Neglected Approach to the Study of Political Leaders and Decision Making," *International Studies Quarterly* 13, no. 2 (June 1969): 190–222. A review of crisis decision making literature is found in Ole R. Holsti, "Crisis Decision Making," in *Behavior, Society, and Nuclear War*, ed. Philip E. Tetlock et al. (New York: Oxford University Press, 1989), 25–37; and Patrick J. Haney, *Organizing for Foreign Policy Crises* (Ann Arbor: University of Michigan Press, 1997). The classic account of character is detailed in James David Barber, *The Presidential Character*, 4th ed. (Englewood Cliffs: Prentice-Hall, 1992); and Alexander George, "Assessing Presidential Character," *World Politics* 26, no. 2 (January 1974): 234–82.

2. Richard Fenno, *The President's Cabinet* (Cambridge: Harvard University Press, 1959), 4. See Philip Selznick, *Leadership in Administration* (Evanston: Row, Peterson, 1957), 91–99. Herbert Simon, *The New Science of Management Decision* (New York: Harper and Row, 1960), 1.

3. These system-level theories often consider the decision-making process within the U.S. executive branch to be irrelevant to the outcome of national security policy. Policy is a reaction to international systemic factors; therefore the way that policy is generated is of no interest to those examining the international system as an independent variable. See Kenneth Waltz, *Theory of International Politics* (New York: Random House, 1979); *Neorealism and Its Critics*, ed. Robert Keohane (New York: Columbia University Press, 1986); *Neorealism and Neoliberalism*, ed. David Baldwin (New York: Columbia University Press, 1993). A rejoinder to this is contained in Joe Hagan, "Does Decision Making Matter? Systemic Assumptions vs. Historical Reality in International Relations Theory," *International Studies Review* 3, no. 2 (summer 2001): 5–46.

4. The best explanations and criticisms of this model can be found in Charles Lindblom, "The Science of Muddling Through," *Public Administration Review* 19, no. 2 (spring 1959): 79–88; and Graham Allison and Philip Zelikow, *Essence of Decision*, 2d ed. (New York: Addison Wesley Longman, 1999), 13–75.

5. See Herbert Simon, *Administrative Behavior*, 2d ed. (New York: MacMillan, 1961); James March and Herbert Simon, *Organizations* (New York: John Wiley and Sons, 1958), particularly Chapters 2 and 6; Lindblom, "The Science of Muddling Through"; David Braybrooke and Charles Lindblom, *A Strategy of Decision* (New York: Free Press, 1963); and James G. March and Johan P. Olsen, *Ambiguity and Choice in Organizations* (Bergen: Norway, Universitetsforlaget, 1976). Scholars began to apply these ideas to foreign and defense policy decision making in the late 1950s and early 1960s. See Roger Hilsman, "The Foreign Policy Consensus: An Interim Research Report, *Journal of Conflict Resolution* 3, no. 4 (December 1959): 361–382; and Richard Neustadt, *Presidential Power and the Modern Presidents* (New York: Free Press, 1990). The first edition of this was published in 1960.

6. Graham Allison, "Conceptual Models and the Cuban Missile Crisis," *American Political Science Review*, 63, no. 3 (September 1969): 698–718; Morton H. Halperin, "The Decision to Deploy the ABM: Bureaucratic and Domestic Politics in the Johnson Administration," *World*

Politics 25, no. 1 (October 1972): 62–65; Graham Allison and Morton Halperin, "Bureaucratic Politics: A Paradigm and Some Policy Implications," *World Politics* 24 (supplement, 1972): 50–53; and Morton Halperin, *Bureaucratic Politics and Foreign Policy* (Washington, DC: Brookings Institution Press, 1974). See also Robert Art, "Bureaucratic Politics and American Foreign Policy: A Critique," *Policy Sciences* 4, no. 4 (December 1973): 467–90.

7. Art, "Bureaucratic Politics and American Foreign Policy," 472.

8. Paul Hammond, *Organizing for Defense* (Princeton: Princeton University Press, 1961); Warner Schilling, Paul Hammond, and Glenn Snyder, *Strategy, Politics, and Defense Budgets* (New York: Columbia University Press, 1962); Roberta Wohlstetter, *Pearl Harbor: Warning and Decision* (Stanford: Stanford University Press, 1962); Morton Halperin and David Halperin, "The Key West Key," *Foreign Policy* 52 (winter 1983/84): 114–28; U.S. Senate Committee on Armed Services, *Defense Organization: The Need for Change*, 99th Cong., 1st sess., 1985, staff report.

9. Hoyt and Garrison have categorized different manipulation strategies that advisers often employ. See Paul D. Hoyt, "The Political Manipulation of Group Composition: Engineering the Decision Context," *Political Psychology* 18, no. 4 (1997): 771–90; Paul D. Hoyt and Jean A. Garrison, "Political Manipulation Within the Small Group: Foreign Policy Advisers in the Carter Administration," in *Beyond Groupthink*, ed. Paul 't Hart, Eric K. Stern, and Bengt Sundelius (Ann Arbor: University of Michigan Press, 1997), 249–74; and Jean A. Garrison, *Games Advisers Play* (College Station: Texas A&M University Press, 1999).

10. See Morton Halperin and Arnold Kanter, "The Bureaucratic Perspective," in *Readings in American Foreign Policy*, ed. Morton Halperin and Arnold Kanter (Boston: Little, Brown, 1973), 9–10; Allison, *Essence of Decision*, 166–67; David Welch, "The Organizational Process Model and the Bureaucratic Politics Paradigm," *International Security* 17, no. 2 (fall 1992): 120–22; and Edward Rhodes, "Do Bureaucratic Politics Matter? Some Disconfirming Findings from the U.S. Navy," *World Politics* 47, no. 1 (October 1994): 1–41.

11. The continuity over the years in descriptions from scholarly, journalistic, and practitioner accounts is striking. See Keith C. Clark and Laurence J. Legere, *The President and the Management of National Security* (New York: Praeger, 1969); I. M. Destler, *Presidents, Bureaucrats, and Foreign Policy* (Princeton: Princeton University Press, 1972); I. M. Destler, Leslie Gelb, and Anthony Lake, *Our Own Worst Enemy* (New York: Simon and Schuster, 1984); Hedrick Smith, *The Power Game* (New York: Ballantine, 1988); John Prados, *Keeper of the Keys* (New York: Morrow, 1991); and Robert M. Gates, *From the Shadows* (New York, Touchstone, 1996).

12. Neustadt, *Presidential Power and the Modern Presidents*, 35.

13. Francis E. Rourke, *Bureaucracy and Foreign Policy* (Baltimore: Johns Hopkins University Press, 1972), vii; Stephen Krasner, "Are Bureaucracies Important? (Or Allison Wonderland)," *Foreign Policy* 7 (summer 1972): 168. See also Art, "Bureaucratic Politics and American Foreign Policy"; Desmond Ball, "The Blind Men and the Elephant: A Critique of Bureaucratic Politics Theory," *Australian Outlook* 28, no. 1 (April 1974): 71–92; Amos Pearlmutter, "The Presidential Political Center and Foreign Policy," *World Politics* 27, no. 1 (October 1974): 87–106.

14. Roger Hilsman, *The Politics of Policy Making in Defense and Foreign Affairs* (New York: Harper and Row, 1971), 18–21; George Reedy, *The Twilight of the Presidency* (New York: New American Library, 1970), 88–99; Fred Greenstein, *The Presidential Difference* (New York: The Free Press, 2000), 3.

15. Edward S. Corwin, *The President: Office and Powers*, 4th ed. (New York: New York Uni-

versity Press, 1957), 69–118; and Clinton Rossiter, *The American Presidency*, revised edition (New York: Harcourt, Brace and World, Inc., 1960), 19–22. On the fourth branch of government and its dilemmas, see James MacGregor Burns, *Presidential Government* (Boston: Houghton Mifflin, 1966); John Hart, *The Presidential Branch*, 2d ed. (Chatham, NJ: Chatham House, 1995); and Mathew J. Dickinson, *Bitter Harvest* (Cambridge: Cambridge University Press, 1997). The issue of the second American republic is detailed in Theodore Lowi, *The Personal Presidency* (Ithaca: Cornell University Press, 1985). A criticism of Lowi's ideas is contained in David Nichols, *The Myth of the Modern Presidency* (University Park: The Pennsylvania State University Press, 1994).

16. Alexander L. George, *Presidential Decision Making in Foreign Policy* (Boulder: Westview Press, 1980), 146; and Bruce Buchanan, "Constrained Diversity: The Organizational Demands of the Presidency," in *The Managerial Presidency*, ed. James P. Pfiffner (Pacific Grove: Brooks/Cole Publishing, 1991), 78–79.

17. H. R. Haldeman, "The Nixon White House and the Presidency," in *The Nixon Presidency*, ed. Kenneth W. Thompson (Lanham: University Press of America, and Charlottesville: Miller Center, 1987), 74.

18. *Report of the President's Special Review Board* (hereafter *The Tower Commission Report*), (New York: Bantam Books, Times Books, 1987), 13.

19. Quoted in Dom Bonafede, "Carter Staff Is Getting Itchy to Move to Washington," *National Journal* 8, no. 44 (1976): 1543–44.

20. Richard T. Johnson, *Managing the White House* (New York: Harper and Row, 1974); George, *Presidential Decision Making in Foreign Policy*; and Robert J. Thompson, "Contrasting Models of White House Staff Organization: The Eisenhower, Ford, and Carter Experiences," *Congress and the Presidency* 19, no. 2 (autumn 1992): 113–36.

21. Roger Porter, *Presidential Decision Making: The Economic Policy Board* (Cambridge, MA: Cambridge University Press, 1980). Colin Campbell, *Managing the Presidency* (Pittsburgh: University of Pittsburgh Press, 1986). Margaret G. Hermann and Thomas Preston, "Presidents, Advisers, and Foreign Policy: The Effects of Leadership Style on Executive Arrangements," *Political Psychology* 15, no. 1 (1994): 75–96. Thomas Preston, *The President and His Inner Circle* (New York: Columbia University Press, 2001). See also, Thomas Preston, "'Follow the Leader,': The Impact of U.S. Presidential Style upon Advisory Group Dynamics, Structure, and Decision," in *Beyond Groupthink*, ed. 't Hart, Stern, and Sundelius, 191–248. On the notion of a "custodian-manager" of the decision-making process see Alexander George, "The Case For Multiple Advocacy in Making Foreign Policy," *American Political Science Review* 66, no. 3 (September 1972): 751–85; I. M. Destler, "Comment: Multiple Advocacy: Some 'Limits and Costs,'" *American Political Science Review* 66, no. 3 (September 1972): 786–95; David K. Hall, "The 'Custodian-Manager' of the Policy Making Process," *Commission on the Organization of the Government for the Conduct of Foreign Policy (Murphy Commission)* 2, Appendix D, Chapter 12 (June 1975): 100–118; and Meena Bose, *Shaping and Signaling Presidential Policy: The National Security Decision Making of Eisenhower and Kennedy* (College Station: Texas A & M Press, 1998).

22. George, *Presidential Decision Making in Foreign Policy*, 147–48. Hermann and Preston, "Presidents, Advisers, and Foreign Policy," 81.

23. Johnson, *Managing the White House*, 137–38. See the descriptions of the Carter and Clinton decision-making processes in Alexander L. George and Eric Stern, "Presidential

Management Styles and Models," in *Presidential Personality and Performance*, ed. Alexander L. George and Juliette L. George (Boulder: Westview Press, 1998), 214–22 and 241–61.

24. Terry M. Moe, "The Politics of Bureaucratic Structure," in *Can the Government Govern*, ed. John E. Chubb and Paul E. Peterson (Washington, DC: Brookings Institution Press, 1989), 267–329. Terry M. Moe, "The Politics of Structural Choice: Toward a Theory of Public Bureaucracy," in *Organization Theory: From Chester Barnard to the Present and Beyond*, ed. Oliver Williamson (New York: Oxford University Press, 1995), 132–38. Graham Allison and Peter Szanton, *Remaking Foreign Policy* (New York: Basic Books, 1975), 20–23.

25. Moe, "The Politics of Structural Choice, 117–19; and Amy B. Zegart, *Flawed by Design* (Stanford: Stanford University Press, 1999), 14–15.

26. Terry M. Moe and Scott A. Wilson, "Presidents and the Politics of Structure," *Law and Contemporary Problems* 57, no. 2 (spring 1994): 1–44; and Terry M. Moe, "The Presidency and the Bureaucracy: The Presidential Advantage," in *The Presidency and the Political System*, 5th edition, ed. Michael Nelson (Washington, DC: Congressional Quarterly Press, 1998), 439. Joel D. Aberbach and Bert A. Rockman, "Mandates or Mandarins? Control and Discretion in the Modern Administrative State," in *The Managerial Presidency*, ed. Pfiffner, 159–62.

27. Zegart, *Flawed By Design*, 21–28. Aaron Wildavsky, *The Beleaguered Presidency* (New Brunswick, NJ: Transaction Books, 1991), 29–56. See also Richard Fleisher and Jon R. Bond, "Are There Two Presidencies? Yes, But Only for Republicans," *Journal of Politics* 50, no. 3 (August 1988): 747–67; *The Two Presidencies Revisited*, ed. Steven Shull (Chicago: Nelson-Hall Publishers, 1991); and Richard Fleisher et al., "The Demise of the Two Presidencies," *American Politics Quarterly* 28, no. 1 (January 2000): 3–25.

28. Hugh Heclo, "The Changing Presidential Office," in *The Managerial Presidency*, ed. Pfiffner, 34–39; and Thomas J. Weko, *The Politicizing Presidency* (Lawrence: University Press of Kansas, 1995), 109.

29. Zegart, *Flawed by Design*, 42–44.

30. Ibid., 76–108. This issue will be covered in more detail in a discussion of the NSC in the next chapter.

31. Ibid., 76–108.

32. This is the point made by John Burke, *The Institutional Presidency* (Baltimore: Johns Hopkins University Press, 1992).

33. Jerel Rosati, "Developing a Systematic Decision-Making Framework: Bureaucratic Politics in Perspective," *World Politics* 3, no. 2 (January 1981): 234–53; and Rourke, *Bureaucracy and Foreign Policy*, 63–65. Thomas Preston and Paul 't Hart, "Understanding and Evaluating Bureaucratic Politics: The Nexus between Political Leaders and Advisory Systems," *Political Psychology* 20, no. 1 (1999): 49–98.

34. William Gore, *Administrative Decision Making* (New York: John Wiley and Sons, 1964), 38.

35. See "Whither the Study of Governmental Politics: A Symposium," *Mershon International Studies Review* 42, Supplement 2, ed. Eric Stern and Bertjon Verbeek (November 1998): 205–56. The exception to this in the study of presidential management is Hermann and Preston, "Presidents, Advisers, and Foreign Policy," 75–96.

36. "Whither the Study of Governmental Politics," ed. Stern and Verbeek, 208.

37. Allison, *Essence of Decision*; and Allison and Zelikow, *Essence of Decision*, 2d ed.

38. Several studies of crisis decision making focus specifically on the administrative

adaptations necessary to deal with foreign policy crises. Charles Hermann, ed., *International Crises* (New York: Free Press, 1972); and Ole Holsti, "Theories of Crisis Decision Making," in *Diplomacy*, ed. Paul Gordon Lauren (New York: Free Press, 1979), 99–136.

39. See Preston, *The President and His Inner Circle*.

40. See Johnson, *Managing the White House*.

41. See Wilfrid Kohl, "The Nixon-Kissinger Foreign Policy System and U.S.-European Relations: Patterns of Policy Making," *World Politics* 28, no. 1 (October 1975): 1–6, 40–43; and Rosati, "Developing a Systematic Decision Making Framework: Bureaucratic Politics in Perspective," 247–49. Bert Rockman, "America's Departments of State: Irregular and Regular Syndromes of Policy Making," *American Political Science Review* 75, no. 4 (December 1981): 911–27.

42. Daniel E. Ponder, *Good Advice: Information and Policy Making in the White House* (College Station: Texas A & M Press, 2000); Zegart, *Flawed by Design*.

43. Charles E. Walcott and Karen M. Hult, *Governing the White House* (Lawrence: University Press of Kansas, 1995), 16–19.

44. James D. Thompson, *Organizations in Action* (New York: McGraw-Hill, 1967).

45. On structural contingency theory see Joan Woodward, *Management and Technology* (London: Her Majesty's Stationery Office, 1958); Tom Burns and G. M. Stalker, *The Management of Innovation* (London: Tavistock Publications, 1961); and Paul Lawrence and Jay Lorsch, *Organizations and Environment* (Cambridge: Harvard University Press, 1967).

46. Halperin and Kanter in *Readings in American Foreign Policy*, ed. Halperin and Kanter, 3; Rosati, "Developing a Systematic Decision-Making Framework: Bureaucratic Politics in Perspective," 248; Rourke, *Bureaucracy and Foreign Policy*, 65; and Zegart, *Flawed by Design*. See also Linda P. Brady, "The Situation and Foreign Policy," in *Why Nations Act*, ed. Stephen Salmore and Charles Hermann, (Beverly Hills: Sage Publications, 1978), 173–190. John Burke and Fred Greenstein, *How Presidents Test Reality* (New York: Russell Sage Foundation, 1989), 9; and Art, "Bureaucratic Politics and American Foreign Policy: A Critique," 480.

47. Walcott and Hult, *Governing the White House*, 16–19.

48. On this point see Burke and Greenstein, *How Presidents Test Reality*, 21, 275–279; Arthur Cyr, "The National Security Assistant: Helmsman, Captain, or First Mate," *Atlantic Community Quarterly* 20, no. 1 (spring 1982): 81; and Ponder, *Good Advice*, 9.

49. Alfred Chandler, *Strategy and Structure* (Cambridge: MIT Press, 1962), 11–14. John Child, "Organizational Structure, Environment, and Performance: The Role of Strategic Choice," *Sociology* 6, no. 1 (January 1972): 1–22. *Strategic Choice and International Relations*, ed. David Lake and Robert Powell (Princeton: Princeton University Press, 1999).

50. Kohl, "The Nixon-Kissinger Foreign Policy System and U.S.-European Relations"; Porter, *Presidential Decision Making*, 247; Thompson, "Contrasting Models of White House Staff Organization," 113; Walcott and Hult, *Governing the White House*, 14–16; and Burke and Greenstein, *How Presidents Test Reality*, 275.

51. Stephen Hess, *Organizing the Presidency* (Washington, DC: Brookings Institution Press, 1988).

52. March and Simon, *Organizations*, 140–41. See also Herbert A. Simon, "A Behavioral Model of Rational Choice," *Quarterly Journal of Economics* 69, no. 1 (February 1955): 99–118.

53. Neustadt, *Presidential Power and the Modern Presidents*, 169. Paul Charles Light, *The President's Agenda* (Baltimore: The Johns Hopkins University Press, 1982), 40–45.

54. See Lloyd Etheredge, *Can the Government Learn?* (New York: Pergamon Press, 1985);

George Breslauer and Philip Tetlock, eds., *Learning in U.S. and Soviet Foreign Policy* (Boulder: CO: Westview Press, 1991); Jack S. Levy, "Learning and Foreign Policy: Sweeping a Conceptual Minefield," *International Organization* 48, no. 2 (spring 1994): 279–312.

55. Henry Kissinger, *White House Years* (Boston: Little, Brown, 1979), 27.

56. James J. Best, "Presidential Learning: A Comparative Study of the Interactions of Carter and Reagan," *Congress and the Presidency* 15, no. 1 (spring 1988): 25–26; and Harold Seidman, *Politics, Position, and Power* (New York: Oxford University Press, 1986), 83.

57. See Best, "Presidential Learning," 25. Bert Rockman, "The Style and Organization of the Reagan Presidency," in *The Reagan Legacy*, ed. Charles O. Jones (Chatham, NJ: Chatham House Publishers, 1988), 19–20. I. M. Destler, "National Security Advice to Presidents: Some Lessons from Thirty Years," *World Politics* 29, no. 2 (January 1977): 174.

Chapter Three

1. I. M. Destler, *President's Bureaucrats and Foreign Policy*; I. M. Destler, "National Security Advice to U.S. Presidents," 143–76; I. M. Destler, "A Job That Doesn't Work," *Foreign Policy* 38 (spring 1980): 80–88; Peter Szanton, "Two Jobs, Not One," *Foreign Policy* 38 (spring 1980): 89–91; Philip Odeen, "Organizing for National Security," *International Security* 5, no. 1 (summer 1980): 111–29; Bert Rockman, "America's Departments of State: Irregular and Regular Syndromes of Policy Making," *American Political Science Review* 75, no. 4 (December 1981): 911–27.

2. Interview with Robert C. McFarlane, *The National Security Council Project: Oral History Roundtables: The Role of the National Security Adviser*, moderators Ivo H. Daalder and I. M. Destler (College Park, MD and Washington, DC: Center for International and Security Studies at Maryland, School of Public Affairs, University of Maryland and Brookings Institution, 1999), 39; Interview with Colin L. Powell, *The National Security Council Project: Oral History Roundtables: The Role of the National Security Adviser*, moderators Ivo H. Daalder and I. M. Destler (College Park, MD and Washington, DC: Center for International and Security Studies at Maryland, School of Public Affairs, University of Maryland and Brookings Institution, 1999), 52. Available at http://www.brookings.edu/dybdocroot/fp/projects/nsc/transcripts/19991025.htm. Accessed 20 March 2002.

3. Paul Y. Hammond, *Organizing for Defense*.

4. Stephen Hess, *Organizing the Presidency*; Joel D. Aberbach and Bert A. Rockman, "Mandates of Mandarins? Control and Discretion in the Modern Administrative State," 158–79; and John Hart, *The Presidential Branch*, 2d ed. (Chatham, NJ: Chatham House, 1995).

5. Phillip G. Henderson, *Managing the Presidency: The Eisenhower Legacy from Kennedy to Reagan* (Boulder: Westview Press, 1988).

6. For the evolution of the NSC staff see David K. Hall, "The 'Custodian-Manager' of the Policy Making Process," *Commission on the Organization of the Government for the Conduct of Foreign Policy (Murphy Commission)* vol. 2, appendix D, chapter 12 (June 1975): 100–118; Mark M. Lowenthal, "The National Security Council: Organizational History," in U.S. Senate Committee on Foreign Relations. *The National Security Adviser: Role and Accountability: Hearing before the Committee on Foreign Relations*, 96th Cong., 2d sess., 17 April 1980, 52–105; Zbigniew Brzezinski, "The NSC's Midlife Crisis," *Foreign Policy* 69 (winter 1987/88): 80–99; and Christopher Shoemaker, "The National Security Council Staff: Structure and Functions," Association of the U.S. Army Land Warfare Paper No. 3, December 1989.

7. *Report of the President's Special Review Board (hereafter known as Tower Commission Report)* (New York: Bantam Books, Times Books, 1987), 13.

8. This is not always true. A president may see some of these as useful tools on occasion. For example, burying a policy within endless interagency review is one way to show that the policy is being considered while preventing it from ever reaching the point of decision. Submitting difficult problems to interagency committees or asking these committees to undertake prodigious projects is also a method of keeping the bureaucracies busy while select teams of presidential advisers (usually NSC staffers) make the real decisions.

9. Victor A. Auger, "The National Security Council System After the Cold War," in *U.S. Foreign Policy After the Cold War*, ed. Randall B. Ripley and James M. Lindsay (Pittsburgh: University of Pittsburgh Press, 1997), 42–73.

10. See Alexander L. George, *Presidential Decision Making in Foreign Policy*; Miriam Steiner, "The Search for Order in a Disorderly World;" and James David Barber, *The Presidential Character.*

11. Jimmy Carter, *Keeping Faith* (New York: Bantam Books, 1982), 52, 59; "Foreign Policy by Committee: Can It Really Work," *U.S. News and World Report*, 21 February 1977, 27; Dom Bonafede, "Brzezinski—Stepping Out of His Backstage Role," *National Journal* 9, no. 42 (15 October 1977): 1596; Jimmy Carter, "Contemporary National and International Issues: Interview with Jimmy Carter," in *The Carter Presidency*, ed. Kenneth Thompson, 6–7. Quotation from Zbigniew Brzezinski, *Power and Principle* (New York: Farrar, Straus, Giroux, 1983), 8.

12. James Fallows, "The Passionless Presidency," *The Atlantic Monthly* 243, no. 5 (May 1979): 35; James Fallows, "Zbig without Cy," *The New Republic* 182, no. 19 (10 May 1980): 18; Carter, *Keeping Faith*, 57. The best explanation of this notion comes from Charles O. Jones, *The Trusteeship Presidency: Jimmy Carter and the United States Congress* (Baton Rouge: Louisiana State University Press, 1988).

13. Interview with Cyrus Vance, "Carter's Foreign Policy: The Source of the Problem," in *The Carter Presidency*, ed. Kenneth Thompson, 139–43. Author's interview with Zbigniew Brzezinski, 6 June 2001; and author's interview with David Aaron, 11 July 2001.

14. Author's interview with David Aaron, 11 July 2001.

15. Quoted from, respectively, Sara Fritz and Robert Kittle, "The Power Brokers around the President," *U.S. News and World Report* 90, no. 5 (9 February 1981): 19; and interview with Erwin Hargrove, "Reagan Understands How to Be President," *U.S. News and World Report* 90, no. 16 (27 April 1981): 23; Michael Deaver, *Behind the Scenes* (New York: William Morrow and Co., 1987), 11; and Edwin Meese, *With Reagan* (Washington, DC: Regnery Gateway, 1992), 22. On Reagan's delegation see Dilys M. Hill and Phil Williams, "The Reagan Presidency: Style and Substance," in *The Reagan Presidency*, ed. Dilys M. Hill, Raymond Moore, and Phil Williams (London: MacMillan, 1990), 4; *Report of the President's Special Review Board* (hereafter *Tower Commission Report*) (New York: Times Books and Random House, 1987), 80; and David Gergen, *Eyewitness to Power* (New York: Simon and Schuster, 2000). The most complete account of the Reagan style can be found in Martin Anderson, *Revolution* (Stanford, CA: Hoover Institution Press, 1990), 283–95.

16. Larry Speakes, *Speaking Out* (New York: Avon Books, 1989), 85; Edward L. Rowny, *It Takes One to Tango* (Washington, DC: Brassey's, 1992), 134; George Shultz, *Turmoil and Triumph* (New York: Charles Scribner's Sons, 1993), 1133.

17. Bob Schieffer and Gary Paul Gates, *The Acting President* (New York: Dutton, 1991); and Lou Cannon, *President Reagan: The Role of a Lifetime* (New York: Touchstone, 1991). On

Reagan's willingness to be fooled by his advisers see Robert MacFarlane, *Special Trust* (New York: Cadell and Davies, 1994), 174; and Shultz, *Turmoil and Triumph*, 1133

18. Quotation from Bert Rockman, "The Style and Organization of the Reagan Presidency," in *The Reagan Legacy*, ed. Charles O. Jones (Chatham, NJ: Chatham House Publishers, 1988), 8. See also Michael Beschloss and Allen Weinstein, "The Best National Security System: An Interview with Zbigniew Brzezinski," *Washington Quarterly* 5, no. 1 (winter 1982): 77.

19. On his cautious nature see Edward L. Rowny, *It Takes One to Tango*, 221; William Schneider, "For Bush, a Prudent Foreign Policy," *National Journal* 21, no. 20 (20 May 1989): 1278; Gillian Peele, "The Constrained Presidency of George Bush," *Current History* 91, no. 564 (April 1992): 151; and Michael Mandelbaum, "The Bush Foreign Policy," *Foreign Affairs* 70, no. 1 (America and the World issue): 5–22. Bush pragmatism is explored in Charles-Phillipe David, "Who Was the Real George Bush? Foreign Policy Decision Making Under the Bush Administration," *Diplomacy and Statecraft* 7, no. 1 (March 1996): 197; and Charles Kegley, "The Bush Administration and the Future of American Foreign Policy: Pragmatism or Procrastination," *Presidential Studies Quarterly* 19, no. 4 (fall 1989): 717. Bush's incrementalism is addressed in Donald M. Snow and Eugene Brown, *Beyond the Water's Edge* (New York: St. Martins, 1997), 120–21. Bush is described as a reactive decision maker in Daniel P. Franklin and Robert Shephard, "Is Prudence a Policy? George Bush and the World," in *Leadership and the Bush Presidency*, ed. Ryan Barrilleaux and Mary E. Stuckey (Westport: Praeger, 1992), 165–76; Terry L. Deibel, "Bush Foreign Policy: Mastery and Inaction," *Foreign Policy* 84 (fall 1991): 3, 8–9; Colin Campbell, "The White House and the Presidency under the 'Let's Deal' President," in *The Bush Presidency: First Appraisals*, ed. Colin Campbell and Bert Rockman (Chatham, NJ: Chatham House, 1991), 185–91; and Bert Rockman, "The Leadership Style of George Bush," in *The Bush Presidency*, ed. Campbell and Rockman, 15, 21, 25–26. On Bush's realism see Rockman, "The Leadership Style of George Bush," in *The Bush Presidency*, ed. Campbell and Rockman, 17; and Franklin and Shephard, "Is Prudence a Policy?" in *Leadership and the Bush Presidency*, ed. Barrilleaux and Stuckey, 165–76. On his tendency toward the status quo see William Schneider, "The In-Box President," *The Atlantic* 265, no. 1 (January 1990): 34–37; Michael Duffy and Dan Goodgame, *Marching in Place* (New York: Simon and Schuster, 1992), 11–12; David Mervin, *George Bush and the Guardian Presidency* (New York: St. Martin's, 1996), 28–37.

20. The principal decision makers were so concerned that Bush should have a wide range of opinions that they allowed analyses from within their departments with which they disagreed to reach Bush. On the pros and cons of access to President Bush and the ability for dissenting views to reach the president see Robert Hutchings, *American Diplomacy and the End of the Cold War* (Baltimore: The Johns Hopkins University Press, and Washington, DC: The Woodrow Wilson Center Press, 1997), 24; George Bush and Brent Scowcroft, *A World Transformed*, (New York: Alfred A. Knopf, 1998), 32; Charles Kolb, *White House Daze* (New York: Free Press, 1994), 345; and Colin Powell, *My American Journey* (New York: Random House, 1995), 439–40.

21. On Bush's role see Bush and Scowcroft, *A World Transformed*, 17–18; Peele, "The Constrained Presidency of George Bush," 153; Dan Goodgame, "Rude Awakening," *Time*, 20 March 1989, 22–23; Elaine Sciolino, "Bush Selections Signal Focus on Foreign Policy," *The New York Times*, 17 January 1989, A1; and William Safire, "Bush's Cabinet: Who's Up, Who's Down," *New York Times Magazine*, 25 March 1990, 30–33.

22. This structure was outlined in Carter Administration, *Presidential Directive/NSC-2*

(PD-2) The National Security Council System, 20 January 1977. Details on the operation of this structure can be found in Dom Bonafede, "Brzezinski—Stepping Out of His Backstage Role," 1598–1601; Lawrence Korb, "National Security Organization and Process in the Carter Administration," in *Defense Policy and the Presidency: Carter's First Years*, ed. Sarkesian (Boulder: Westview Press, 1979), 115–119; Jerel Rosati, *The Carter Administration's Quest for Global Community* (Columbia: University of South Carolina Press, 1987), 182; Cyrus Vance, *Hard Choices* (New York: Simon and Schuster, 1983), 36; and Zbigniew Brzezinski, *Power and Principle*, 59–60.

23. The best descriptions of the Cabinet Council system are: Dick Kirschten, "Reagan's Cabinet Councils May Have Less Influence Than Meets the Eye," *National Journal* 13, no. 28 (11 July 1981): 1242–1247; Dick Kirschten, "Decision Making in the White House: How Well Does It Serve the President," *National Journal* 14, no. 14 (3 April 1982): 584–589; and Edwin Meese III, "The Institutional Presidency: The View From the White House," *Presidential Studies Quarterly* 13, no. 2 (spring 1983): 191–197.

24. Hedrick Smith, "Haig Is Given Broad Policy Power, But Less Than He Initially Thought," *The New York Times* (27 February 1981): 1; Tad Szulc, "The Vicar Vanquished," *Foreign Policy* 43 (summer 1981): 184–185. Reagan Administration, National Security Decision Directive-2, "National Security Council Structure," as printed in *National Security Directives of the Reagan and Bush Administrations*, ed. Christopher Simpson (Boulder: Westview Press, 1995), 20–28; and Roy Melbourne, "The Odyssey of the NSC," *Strategic Review* 11, no. 3 (summer 1983): 51–64.

25. Bush Administration, NSD-1, "Reorganization of the National Security Council," as printed in *National Security Directives of the Reagan and Bush Administrations*, 892–93 and 903–5; Bernard Weinraub, "Bush Backs Plans to Enhance Role of Security Staff," *The New York Times*, 2 February 1989, A1; Leslie Gelb, "Who Makes Foreign Policy," *The New York Times*, 3 February 1989, A30; David Hoffman, "President Scales Back National Security Council," *The Washington Post*, 3 February 1989, A8; John Prados, *Keeper of the Keys* (New York: William Morrow, 1991), 548; Snow and Brown, *Beyond the Water's Edge*, 198–201; Hutchings, *American Diplomacy and the End of the Cold War*, 22–23; Bush and Scowcroft, *A World Transformed*, p. 35. A list of NSC/PCCs can be found in "NSD-10, List of Additional Policy Coordinating Committees," as printed in *National Security Directives of the Reagan and Bush Administrations*, ed. Simpson, 892–93 and 903–6.

26. For Carter see Bonafede, "Brzezinski—Stepping Out of His Backstage Role," 1601; Vance, *Hard Choices*, 36–37; Alexander Moens, *Foreign Policy Under Carter* (Boulder: Westview Press, 1998), 38; For Reagan see Reagan Administration, National Security Decision Directive 1, "National Security Council Directives," as printed in *National Security Directives of the Reagan and Bush Administrations*, ed. Simpson, 19; Dick Kirschten, "Clark Emerges as a Tough Manager, Not a Rival to the Secretary of State," 1244–48; Steven Weisman, "Clark Is Staking Out His Turf as Security Adviser," *The New York Times*, 19 January 1982, A22.; Robert Kittle, "New Force in Reagan's Foreign Policy," *U.S. News and World Report* 92, no. 14 (12 April 1982), 30; For Bush see Hutchings, *American Diplomacy and the End of the Cold War*, 24.

27. Vance, *Hard Choices*, 37–38. On the departmental competition see Bonafede, "Brzezinski—Stepping Out of His Backstage Role," 1601; and Elizabeth Drew, "A Reporter at Large: Brzezinski," *The New Yorker* 54, no. 11 (1 May 1978): 101.

28. Sara Fritz, "The 9–5 Presidency," *U.S. News and World Report* 90, no. 11 (23 March

1981): 28; Kirschten, "Reagan's Cabinet Councils May Have Less Influence Than Meets the Eye," 1243; and Schieffer and Gates, *The Acting President,* 93–94. Reagan reportedly came to only 20% of the meetings. Anderson, *Revolution,* 225.

29. Robert Toth, "Casey Security Post Raises Concern on CIA's U.S. Role," *The Los Angeles Times,* 23 April 1981, 1; and Melbourne, "The Odyssey of the NSC," 61. On the number of SIGs and IGs see Reagan Administration, National Security Decision Directive 276, "National Security Interagency Process," 6 June 1987, as printed in *National Security Decision Directives of the Reagan and Bush Administration,* ed. Simpson, 808; and Prados, *Keeper of the Keys,* 463.

30. Steven Weisman, "President's Men Jockey for Access to Oval Office," *The New York Times,* 8 February 1981, sec. 2; and H. Smith, "Haig Is Given Broad Policy Power," 1; Lou Cannon and Lee Lescaze, "Rocky Start in Handling Foreign Policy," *The Washington Post,* 25 May 1981, 1; and I. M. Destler, "The Evolution of Reagan Foreign Policy," in *The Reagan Presidency,* ed. Fred Greenstein (Baltimore: Johns Hopkins University Press, 1983), 119; and Dick Kirschten, "His NSC Days May Be Numbered, but Allen Is Known for Bouncing Back," *National Journal* 13, no. 48 (28 November 1981): 2114. On Meese's role see Alexander Haig, *Caveat* (New York: MacMillan, 1984), 76; Howell Raines, "White House Triumvirate Exercising Wide Power," *The New York Times,* 13 February 1981, 1; Destler, "The Evolution of Reagan Foreign Policy," 122; and Speakes, *Speaking Out,* 86.

31. Anderson, *Revolution,* 310–13.

32. Robert M. Gates, *From the Shadows* (New York: Touchstone, 1996), 458–59. Veterans of the administration all agreed that success of the NSC/DC was due largely to Gates's ability to make it work, a triumph of personality, rather than organizational design. See *The National Security Council Project: Oral History Roundtables: The Bush Administration National Security Council,* moderators Ivo H. Daalder and I. M. Destler (College Park, MD, and Washington, DC: Center for International and Security Studies at Maryland, School of Public Affairs, University of Maryland and Brookings Institution, 2000), 9, 11, and 37. http://www.brookings.edu/dybdocroot/fp/projects/nsc/transcripts/20000325.htm. Accessed 20 March 2002.

33. On this friendship see Bush and Scowcroft, *A World Transformed,* 18; James A. Baker, *The Politics of Diplomacy* (New York: G. P. Putnam's Sons, 1995), 19–21, 335; John Newhouse, "The Tactician," *The New Yorker* 66, no. 12 (7 May 1990): 58, 60–82; John R. Bolton, "The Making of Foreign Policy in the Bush Administration," in *The Bush Presidency,* ed. Kenneth W. Thompson, 109; and Maureen Dowd and Thomas L. Friedman, "The Fabulous Bush and Baker Boys," *New York Times Magazine,* 6 May 1990, 35, 58.

34. Quoted in Bush and Scowcroft, *A World Transformed,* 18. On the Bush-Scowcroft relationship in the Ford administration see Mervin, *George Bush and the Guardianship Presidency,* 160. Bush often joked that in the Ford administration Scowcroft was his boss. See Michael Beschloss and Strobe Talbott, *At the Highest Levels* (Boston: Little, Brown, 1993), 12. On the Baker-Scowcroft relationship see Beschloss and Talbott, *At the Highest Levels,* 20. During the 1976 Carter-Ford debates, after Ford had stated that Poland was not under Soviet domination, Baker, as campaign manager, and Scowcroft, as ANSA, were the ones who faced the feeding frenzy of reporters and political criticism. Bush and Scowcroft, *A World Transformed,* 19–20.

35. Quotes about Scowcroft are taken from, respectively, Baker, *The Politics of Diplomacy,* 25; Cheney quoted in R. W. Apple, "A Mover and Shaker Behind Bush Foreign Policy,"

The New York Times, 6 February 1989, A3; and Gates, *From the Shadows*, 457–58. On Scowcroft's view of his role see Christopher Madison, "No Sharp Elbows," *National Journal* 22, no. 21 (26 May 1990): 1277–81; David Lauter, "Scowcroft: The Man in the Shadows," *The Los Angeles Times*, 14 October 1990, A1; Jim Hoagland, "The Value of Brent Scowcroft," *The Washington Post*, 10 December 1991, A21. The tensions are described in *The National Security Council Project: Oral History Roundtables: The Bush Administration National Security Council*, moderators Ivo H. Daalder and I. M. Destler (College Park, MD, and Washington, DC: Center for International and Security Studies at Maryland, School of Public Affairs, University of Maryland and Brookings Institution, 2000), 14–15. http://www.brookings.edu/dybdocroot/fp/projects/nsc/transcripts/19990429.htm. Accessed 20 March 2002.

36. Author's interview with David Newsom, 6 July 2001. On FDR's decision making see Matthew J. Dickinson, *Bitter Harvest* (Cambridge: Cambridge University Press, 1997).

37. A good general treatment of the Vance-Brzezinski clash is Jean A. Garrison, *Games Advisers Play: Foreign Policy in the Nixon and Carter Administrations* (College Station: Texas A&M Press, 1999). On Vance's efforts to maintain his status within the administration see Dick Kirschten, "Beyond the Vance-Brzezinski Clash Lurks an NSC under Fire," *National Journal* 12, no. 20 (17 May 1980): 814; Hodding Carter, "How Jimmy Carter's Foreign Policy Bit the Dust," *Washington Post*, 5 January 1981, A17; Vance, *Hard Choices*, 38–39; and Interview with Cyrus Vance, "The Carter Years: The Source of the Problem," in *The Carter Presidency*, ed. Thompson, 141. Brzezinski's rise is detailed in Vance, *Hard Choices*, 35; Gaddis Smith, *Morality, Reason, and Power* (New York: Hill and Wang, 1986); Moens, *Foreign Policy under Carter*, particularly 21–24, 51–54; Bonafede, "Brzezinski—Stepping Out of His Backstage Role," 1596; Richard Burt, "Zbig Makes It Big," *New York Times Magazine*, 30 July 1978, 8–28; and Carter, *Keeping Faith*, 56. According to one senior state department official, one way Brzezinski enlarged his role was through the SCC's crisis management function. Once a crisis occurred in an area of the world, the SCC would take jurisdiction over the issue permanently. Author's interview with David Newsom, 6 July 2001.

38. G. Smith, *Morality, Reason, and Power*, 34–49; and John Dumbrell, *The Carter Presidency* (Manchester: Manchester University Press, 1993), 110–14. The press had a major role in exacerbating this competition by focusing on the rivalry in their reporting. See Marilyn Berger, "Vance and Brzezinski: Peaceful Coexistence or Guerilla Warfare," *New York Times Magazine*, 13 February 1977, 19–41; Robert Kaiser, "Brzezinski, Vance Are Watched for Hint of Policy Struggle," *The Washington Post*, 28 March 1977, A2; Anthony Lake, "Carter's Foreign Policy: Success Abroad; Failure at Home: Interview with Anthony Lake," interview by Kenneth Thompson, *The Carter Presidency*, ed. Thompson, 149–50.

39. The best illustration of the change in the administration's views of the world, a reflection of the evolution of Carter's view of the world, can be found in Rosati, *The Carter Administration and the Quest for Global Community*. See also Cyrus Vance, *Hard Choices*, 350; Brzezinski quoted in Zbigniew Brzezinski, *Power and Principle*, 189; Carter quoted in Arthur Schlesinger, "The Great Carter Mystery," *The New Republic* 182, no. 15 (12 April 1980): 19.

40. Following Vance's resignation Brzezinski sent Carter a memo suggesting that Vance and the state department were the sources of the administration's problems. He also stated that although he and Muskie would not have any of those problems, the State Department was still filled with Vance's appointees who did not have sufficient loyalty to the White House. See Zbigniew Brzezinski, "Memorandum for the President, Subject: Unity and the

New Foreign Policy Team," Box 23, Subject Files Four-Year Goals (4/77) through Meetings —Muskie/Brown/Brzezinski: 7/80—9/80, Folder: meetings—Muskie/Brown/Brzezinski: 5/80–6/80. Reportedly, Muskie and Brzezinski moved from friendship to rivalry. Leslie Belb, "Muskie and Brzezinski: The Struggle over Foreign Policy," *The New York Times Magazine*, 20 July 1980, 26–27, 32, 34–35, 38–40.

41. Meese, *With Reagan*, 101.

42. See Dick Kirschten, "Inner Circle Speaks With Many Voices, But Maybe That's How Reagan Wants It," *National Journal*, 15, no. 22 (28 May 1983): 1100–1103; Lawrence I. Barnett, *Gambling with History* (Garden City, NY: Doubleday and Co., 1983), 224–25; Cannon, *President Reagan*, 305–6; Raymond Garthoff, *The Great Transition* (Washington, DC: Brookings Institution Press, 1994), 45; Destler, "The Evolution of Reagan Foreign Policy," in *The Reagan Presidency*, ed. Greenstein, 122; Kirschten, "Reagan's Cabinet Councils May Have Less Influence Than Meets the Eye," 1243–46.

43. In particular, Meese's decision to allow Reagan to sleep for hours after a military skirmish with Libya in August and open feuding between Allen and Haig became key motivations for change. On the Libyan incident see Schieffer and Gates, *The Acting President*, 112–13; and Cannon, *President Reagan*, 191. On the arguments between Haig and Allen and Haig and the troika see Cannon, *President Reagan*, 191. Bernard Gwertzman, "Haig Charges a Reagan Aide Is Undermining Him," *The New York Times*, 4 November 1981, 1. Haig, *Caveat*, 17, 86; and Cannon, *President Reagan*, 195. On Allen's removal see Hedrick Smith, "Allen's Operation Examined by Meese," *The New York Times*, 4 December 1981, 25; John Goshko and Martin Schram, "Allen's Job Expected to Go to Clark," *The Washington Post*, 1 January 1982, A1; and Schieffer and Gates, *The Acting President*, 128–29. A small financial scandal in which Allen was accused of accepting money from a Japanese magazine in exchange for an interview with the First Lady helped ease Allen's removal, even though he was cleared of wrongdoing by investigators. On this see Schieffer and Gates, *The Acting President*, 128–29.

44. Hedrick Smith, "Reagan Picks a Mediator," *The New York Times*, 5 January 1982, A1; Speakes, *Speaking Out*, 128; Schieffer and Gates, *The Acting President*, 131; Kirschten, "Clark Emerges as a Tough Manager," 1244–47; and Destler, "The Evolution of Reagan Foreign Policy," in *The Reagan Presidency*, ed. Greenstein, 125. See Reagan Administration, NSDD 1, "National Security Council Directives," and NSDD-2, "National Security Council Structure," as printed in *National Security Directives of the Reagan and Bush Administrations*, ed. Simpson, 19–28. Clark had worked with Weinberger, Meese, Deaver, and Nancy Reagan from their days in California, with Casey from his work with Reagan's campaign, and with Haig from their year together at the State Department.

45. Haig had policy disagreements with the hardliners—Weinberger, Casey, Allen, and Meese in particular—over the Israeli invasion of Lebanon, the Soviet natural gas pipeline to Europe, the lifting of the embargo on grain sales to the USSR, and the sale of AWACS to Saudi Arabia, to name just a few. The troika had lost faith in Haig after his performance during Reagan's recovery from an assassination attempt. His announcement to the world that "I am in control here" rendered him a political liability. See Szulc, "The Vicar Vanquished," 177–78; Kevin Mulcahy, "The Secretary of State and the National Security Adviser: Foreign Policy Making in the Carter and Reagan Administrations," *Presidential Studies Quarterly* 16, no. 2 (summer 1986): 287–94; Cannon, *President Reagan*, 200–201; Speakes, *Speaking*

Out, 96; and Anderson, *Revolution*, 314–16. Shultz had been Nixon's secretary of labor, then director of the Office of Management and Budget. Weinberger was his deputy at OMB, then became director when Shultz became secretary of the treasury. At Bechtel Shultz was president and Weinberger was general counsel. On Clark's power in foreign policy and Shultz's reaction see Jack Nelson, "White House Staff: Baker Steps Ahead," *The Los Angeles Times*, 27 June 1983, 1; John Goshko and Michael Getler, "Shultz No Longer Seen as a Driving Force in Policy," *The Washington Post*, 15 August 1983, A1; Shultz, *Turmoil and Triumph*, 269; and Schieffer and Gates, *The Acting President*, 159. On the scheming to choose a successor to Clark see Deaver, *Behind the Scenes*, 129–30; Bob Woodward, *Veil* (New York: Pocket Books, 1987), 317–18; Schieffer and Gates, *The Acting President*, 161–62; MacFarlane, *Special Trust*, 259–60.

46. The memoirs of the members of the administration contain numerous descriptions of the disagreements between the major players over almost every issue. Some of the best nonparticipant descriptions can be found in Kirschten, "His NSC Days May Be Numbered, But Allen Is Known for Bouncing Back," 2114–17; Philip Taubman, "The Shultz-Weinberger Feud," *The New York Times Magazine*, 14 April 1983, 50, 91, 94–95, 98, 108; Mulcahy, "The Secretary of State and the National Security Adviser," 280–99; Hedrick Smith, *The Power Game* (New York: Ballantine Books, 1988), 558–86; and Schieffer and Gates, *The Acting President*, 121–29. A veteran of both the Carter and Reagan administrations, Robert Gates contends that the intra-administration warfare in the Reagan administration was worse. See Robert Gates, *From the Shadows* (New York: Touchstone, 1996), 285.

47. Bush diplomatic style is detailed in Gerald Seib, "Bush Shapes His Policy by Often Telephoning World Leaders," *The Wall Street Journal*, 30 November 1989, 1; James P. Pfiffner, "Establishing the Bush Presidency," *Public Administration Review* 50, no. 1 (January/February 1990): 70; and Burt Solomon, "Bush's Passion for Friendship Abets His Diplomatic Policy," *National Journal* 22, no. 49 (8 December 1990): 2986–87. The importance of friendships to decision making is illustrated in David Gergen, "Bush's Very Own Ford Foundation," *The Washington Post*, 2 April 1989, C2; Robert Shogan, *The Riddle of Power* (New York: E. P. Dutton, 1991), 268–73; Baker, *The Politics of Diplomacy*, 18; Gates, *From the Shadows*, 459; and Bush and Scowcroft, *A World Transformed*, 25. Rockman refers to this as a Bush belief that "internal harmony" was a prerequisite to good decisions. Rockman, "The Leadership Style of George Bush," in *The Bush Presidency*, ed. Campbell and Rockman, 21. The unusual phenomenon of powerful Washington decision makers becoming better friends as a result of their governmental experience is confirmed by author's interview with James Baker, 10 July 2001; and author's interview with Brent Scowcroft, 16 July 2001.

48. Carter states that he initiated the FFPB, and Brzezinski created the VBB lunches. Carter, *Keeping Faith*, 54; and Brzezinski, *Power and Principle*, 70.

49. On these lunches and their origin see Vance, *Hard Choices*, 39; Brzezinski, *Power and Principle*, 70; Kaiser, "Brzezinski, Vance Are Watched for Hint of Policy Struggle"; and Gerry Argyris Andrianopoulos, *Kissinger and Brzezinski* (New York: St. Martins Press, 1991), 143. Brzezinski's view of the VBB was detailed during the author's interview with Zbigniew Brzezinski, 11 June 2001.

50. Carter's hopes for the FFPB are detailed in Brzezinski, *Power and Principle*, 68. In later years others would be added from time: Jody Powell, Carter's press secretary; and special assistants Hedley Donavan and Lloyd Cutler. Brzezinski did take notes at the meeting, however. They would be reviewed by the Departments of State and Defense, then placed

in Carter's files. Interview with Jimmy Carter, "Contemporary National and International Issues," in *The Carter Presidency*, ed. Thompson, 7. Carter's sense that the FFPB would make implementation easier is found in Erwin Hargrove, *Jimmy Carter as President* (Baton Rouge: Louisiana University Press, 1988), 26. The change in the nature of the FFPB meetings was explained during the author's interview with Zbigniew Brzezinski, 11 June 2001. However, in the absence of formal minutes, often the only record of these meetings were notes taken by each principal attending. Each department was given a different version of the consensus formed at the meetings. Lower-level officials then would negotiate the meaning of the consensus. Author's interview with David Newsom, 6 July 2001.

51. General descriptions of the NSPG and its role can be found in Martin Schram, "Reagan Ends Daily Briefings with National Security Aide," *The Washington Post*, 12 July 1981, A1; Melbourne, "The Odyssey of the NSC," 61; *Tower Commission Report*, 14; John Endicott, "The National Security Council: Formalized Coordination and Policy Planning," in *National Security Policy*, ed. Robert Pfaltzgraff and Uri Ra'anan (Hamden, CT: Archon Books, 1984), 194; and Kirschten, "His NSC Days May Be Numbered, but Allen Is Known for Bouncing Back," 2115. Concerning working groups, see, for example, National Security Decision Directive 56, "Private INF Exchange," 15 September 1982, as printed in *National Security Directives of the Reagan and Bush Administrations*, ed. Simpson, 199.

52. *Tower Commission Report*, 14; and Schram, "Reagan Ends Daily Briefing with National Security Aide," A1.

53. See Cynthia J. Arnson, *Crossroads*, 2d ed. (University Park: The Pennsylvania State University Press, 1993); Chester Crocker, *High Noon in Southern Africa* (New York: W. W. Norton, 1992); Theodore Draper, *A Very Thin Line* (New York: Simon and Schuster, 1991); Constantine Menges, *Inside the National Security Council* (New York: Simon and Schuster, 1988); Shultz, *Turmoil and Triumph*; James M. Scott, *Deciding to Intervene* (Durham: Duke University Press, 1996); and Caspar Weinberger, *Fighting for Peace* (New York: Warner Books, 1991).

54. On these meetings see *The National Security Council Project: Oral History Roundtables: The Role of the National Security Adviser*, moderators Ivo H. Daalder and I. M. Destler (College Park, MD, and Washington, DC: Center for International and Security Studies at Maryland, School of Public Affairs, University of Maryland and Brookings Institution, 1999), 42–43. http://www.brookings.edu/dybdocroot/fp/projects/nsc/transcripts/19991025.htm, accessed 20 March 2002; and *The National Security Council Project: Oral History Roundtables: Arms Control Policy and the National Security Council*, moderators Ivo H. Daalder and I. M. Destler (College Park, MD and Washington, DC: Center for International and Security Studies at Maryland, School of Public Affairs, University of Maryland and Brookings Institution, 2000) 40. Available at http://www.brookings.edu/dybdocroot/fp/projects/nsc/transcripts/20000325.htm, accessed 20 March 2002.

55. The timing of the origin of the Gang of Eight was described to the author during the author's interview with Brent Scowcroft, 16 July 2001. The origins of the breakfast were detailed to the author during an interview with James Baker, 10 July 2001. Each of the major players in the small group of senior advisers had their own cluster of advisers they relied upon, their own brain trust surrounding them. See Gates, *From the Shadows*, 454; and Leslie Gelb, "Mr. Bush's Three Trios," *The New York Times*, 14 August 1991, A19; Baker, *Politics of Diplomacy*, 32–33; Newhouse, "The Tactician," 74–76; Beschloss and Talbott, *At the Highest Levels*, 26–27; Thomas L. Friedman, "Baker Brings an Inner Circle of Outsiders to

the State Department," *The New York Times*, 27 March 1989, A1; Elaine Sciolino, "Guardian of Baker's Door at State: A Quick Study Who Rose Rapidly," *The New York Times*, 23 February 1990, A12.

56. Bush and Scowcroft's views come from, respectively, author's interview with Brent Scowcroft, 16 July 2001; and Bush and Scowcroft, *A World Transformed*, 41. On the administration's inclusion rule see Gates, *From the Shadows*, 454; Rowny, *It Takes One to Tango*, 216. Baker's and Gates's frustration with the bureaucracies is recounted in Gates, *From the Shadows*, 454; Baker, *The Politics of Diplomacy*, 30–31. Scowcroft's assessment of the Bush NSC is detailed in Bush and Scowcroft, *A World Transformed*, 41.

57. Author's interview with Brent Scowcroft, 16 July 2001.

58. Ibid.

59. Bush and Scowcroft, *A World Transformed*, 42.

60. On the weekly breakfasts see Baker, *The Politics of Diplomacy*, 25; Bolton, "The Making of Foreign Policy in the Bush Administration," in *The Bush Presidency*, ed. Thompson, 110; and Hutchings, *American Diplomacy and the End of the Cold War*, 25.

61. Author's interview with Zbigniew Brzezinski, 6 June 2001; and author's interview with David Aaron, 11 July 2001.

62. Davis, Vincent, " The President and the National Security Apparatus," in *Defense Policy and the Presidency: Carter's First Years*, ed. Sam Sarkesian, 53–110; Raymond Garthoff, *Detente and Confrontation* (Washington, DC: Brookings Institution Press, 1985), 563; Rosati, *The Carter Administration's Quest for Global Community*; Donald Spencer, *The Carter Implosion* (New York: Praeger, 1988).

63. Smith, *The Power Game*, 567; and Shultz, *Turmoil and Triumph*, 166.

64. Quoted from Ronald Reagan, "Remarks at the Annual Convention of the National Association of Evangelicals in Orlando, Florida, March 8, 1983," U.S. President, *Public Papers of the Presidents of the United States* (Washington, DC: Office of the *Federal Register*, National Archives and Records Service, 1984), Ronald Reagan, 1983. On the Reagan administration's assumptions about the nature of the international arena see Charles W. Kegley and Eugene R. Wittkopf, "The Reagan Administration's World View," *Orbis* 26, no. 1 (spring 1982): 223–44. On Reagan's role or lack of a role in the administration feud, see Szulc, "The Vicar Vanquished," 174–75; Taubman, "The Shultz-Weinberger Feud," 50; Cannon, *President Reagan*, 56; and Shultz, *Turmoil and Triumph*, 1133.

65. Author's interview with James Baker, 11 July 2001.

66. Theodore Draper, *A Very Thin Line* (New York: Simon and Schuster, 1991).

Chapter Four

1. Respectively, quotations from Jimmy Carter, "Making Foreign and Defense Policy: Openness, Coherence, and Efficiency," *National Journal* 8, no. 43 (23 October 1976): 1528; and Zbigniew Brzezinski, *Power and Principle*, 513.

2. On SALT before the Carter administration see John Newhouse, *Cold Dawn: The Story of SALT* (New York: Holt, Rinehart, and Winston, 1973); *The SALT Handbook*, ed. Roger Labrie (Washington, DC: The American Enterprise Institute, 1979); Thomas Wolfe, *The SALT Experience* (Cambridge, MA: Ballinger, 1979); and Raymond Garthoff, *Detente and Confrontation* (Washington, DC: Brookings Institution Press, 1985), 127–98.

3. Gerald Ford, *A Time to Heal* (New York: Harper and Row, 1979).

4. See Garthoff, *Detente and Confrontation*, 442–53.

5. Strobe Talbott, *Endgame* (New York: Harper and Row, 1980), 39.

6. A general overview of this process can be found in Rose Gottemoeller, *Evolution of U.S. Organizational Setup for Dealing with SALT* (Santa Monica: The Rand Corporation, November 1978), 20–24.

7. Talbott, *Endgame*, 91.

8. The process of PRM-2 is detailed in Brzezinski, *Power and Principle*, 51; Garthoff, *Detente and Confrontation*, 801; and Alexander Moens, *Foreign Policy under Carter* (Boulder: Westview Press, 1990), 66. On the roles of Hyland and Molander see Brzezinski, *Power and Principle*, 571–72 and Talbott, *Endgame*, 44–45.

9. Talbott, *Endgame*, 46–47.

10. Brzezinski, *Power and Principle*, 146.

11. The debate within the administration is detailed in Talbott, *Endgame*, 50. See also David Holloway, *The Soviet Union and the Arms Race* (New Haven: Yale University Press, 1983), 152; John Prados, *The Soviet Estimate* (Princeton: Princeton University Press, 1986), 204–5; and Tom Gervasi, *The Myth of Soviet Military Supremacy* (New York: Harper and Row, 1986), 86–87. Brown's concerns are discussed in Garthoff, *Detente and Confrontation*, 804.

12. Talbott, *Endgame*, 52; and Cyrus Vance, *Hard Choices* (New York: Simon and Schuster, 1983), 51–52.

13. On the views of the two groups see, respectively, Talbott, *Endgame*, 50; Vance, *Hard Choices*, 47–49 and Moens, *Foreign Policy under Carter*, 71.

14. Brzezinski, *Power and Principle*, 157; Moens, *Foreign Policy under Carter*, 67; and Talbott, *Endgame*, 54.

15. Quoted in, respectively, Jimmy Carter, *Why Not the Best?* (Nashville, TN: Broadman Press, 1975), 153; and Jimmy Carter, *Keeping Faith* (New York: Bantam Books, 1982), 215–16. Carter's views on arms control are described in Moens, *Foreign Policy under Carter*, 66. Hyland quoted from William Hyland, *Mortal Rivals* (New York: Random House, 1987), 208. See also an early description by Secretary of Defense Harold Brown of the administration's priorities in arms control in David Binder, "Brown Sees Chance of Strategic Accord with Soviet in 1977," *The New York Times*, 25 January 1977, A6.

16. Reportedly, Carter and Jackson set up an informal channel that allowed Jackson to be informed of developments within the administration and the negotiations in Geneva. Talbott, *Endgame*, 52–54; Richard Perle, "Arms Control," in *Staying the Course: Henry M. Jackson and National Security*, ed. Dorothy Fosdick (Seattle: University of Washington Press, 1987), 89–100; Dan Caldwell, *The Dynamics of Domestic Politics and Arms Control* (Columbia: University of South Carolina Press, 1991), 40; and Richard L. Madden, "Jackson Aide Stirs Criticism in Arms Debate," *The New York Times*, 4 December 1977, 19.

17. Talbott, *Endgame*, 54–59; Moens, *Foreign Policy under Carter*, 68; Robert G. Kaiser and Murrey Marder, "In Pursuit of a SALT II Agreement," *The Washington Post*, 11 April 1977, A1; Brzezinski, *Power and Principle*, 159–60; and Garthoff, *Detente and Confrontation*, 158–60.

18. It reduced the limits on strategic nuclear delivery vehicles to 2,000 or 1,800 from the Vladivostok number of 2,400. MIRVed systems would fall from the old number of 1,320 to 1,200 to 1,100. A further sublimit of 550 on MIRVed ICBMs was added, as was a sublimit of 150 on heavy ICBMs. The Backfire bomber disagreement would be deferred and a ban on cruise missiles with ranges over 2,500 km would be negotiated. Vance, *Hard Choices*, 52.

19. Talbott, *Endgame*, 58; and Brzezinski, *Power and Principle*, 159.

20. Kaiser and Marder, "In Pursuit of a SALT II Agreement," A1; and Talbott, *Endgame*, 59.

21. Kaiser and Marder, "In Pursuit of a SALT II Agreement," A1; Talbott, *Endgame*, 59–60, 63–64; and Hyland, *Mortal Rivals*, 211–12.

22. These were Vladivostok limits on ICBMs, SLBMs, and Bombers and MIRVed ballistic missiles and a deferral of the cruise missile and Backfire bomber issues. Talbott, *Endgame*, 62; and Vance, *Hard Choices*, 52. Interestingly, it seems nearly all of Carter's senior advisers believed the USSR would reject the deep cuts proposal. See Brzezinski, *Power and Principle*, 160–61; and Garthoff, *Detente and Confrontation*, 807–8.

23. Garthoff, *Detente and Confrontation*, 807–8.

24. See *Treaty between the United States of America and the Union of Soviet Socialist Republics on the Limitation of Strategic Offensive Arms* (Washington, DC: U.S. Government Printing Office, 18 June 1979).

25. For an overview of the development on U.S. nuclear strategy see Lawrence Freedman, *The Evolution of Nuclear Strategy* (New York: St. Martins, 1983). Eisenhower administration nuclear policy is detailed in Saki Dockrell, *Eisenhower's New Look National Security Policy, 1953–1961* (New York: St. Martin's, 1996); and Robert R. Bowie and Richard H. Immerman, *Waging Peace: How Eisenhower Shaped an Enduring Cold War Legacy* (New York: Oxford University Press, 1998). Strategic developments in the Kennedy administration are detailed in William Kaufmann, *The McNamara Strategy* (New York: Harper and Row, 1964); Desmond Ball, *Politics and Force Levels: The Strategic Missile Programs of the Kennedy Administration* (Berkeley: University of California Press, 1980); and Scott Sagan, "SIOP–62: The Nuclear War Plan Briefing to President Kennedy," *International Security* 12, no. 1 (summer 1987): 22–52.

26. One of the best criticisms of the warfighting stance, by an assured destruction advocate, is Robert Jervis, *The Illogic of American Nuclear Strategy* (Ithaca: Cornell University Press, 1984). The idea has its roots in the early years after the development of atomic weaponry. Many believed that assured destruction was not simply a matter of policy, but a technical reality of the nuclear age. The destruction inherent in nuclear weapons was simply so great that using them was not an option. See Bernard Brodie, "The Weapon," in *The Absolute Weapon*, ed. Bernard Brodie (New York: Harcourt, Brace, 1946), 21–110.

27. On this point see Eric Mlyn, *The State, Society, and Limited Nuclear War* (Albany: SUNY Press, 1995), particularly 5–12.

28. Lynn E. Davis, *Limited Nuclear Options: Deterrence and the New American Doctrine*, Adelphi Papers 121 (London: International Institute of Strategic Studies, 1976); 68; Desmond Ball, "Counterforce Targeting: How New? How Viable?" in *American Defense Policy*, eds. John Reichart and Steven Sturm (Baltimore: The Johns Hopkins University Press, 1984), 228; Desmond Ball, *Targeting for Strategic Deterrence*, Adelphi Papers 185 (London: International Institute for Strategic Studies, 1983), 19; and Terry Terriff, *The Nixon Administration and the Making of U.S. Nuclear Strategy* (Ithaca: Cornell University Press, 1995).

29. Carter Administration, *Presidential Review Memorandum/NSC-10*, "*Comprehensive Net Assessment and Military Force Posture Review,*" 18 February 1977 (Washington, DC: National Security Archive). See also Desmond Ball, "The Development of the SIOP, 1960–1983," in *Strategic Nuclear Targeting*, ed. Desmond Ball and Jeffrey Richelson (Ithaca: Cornell University Press, 1986), 75; and Mlyn, *The State, Society, and Limited Nuclear War*, 115.

30. Samuel Huntington, of the NSC National Security Planning cluster, led the SCC's Comprehensive Net Assessment Group. Lynn Davis, Deputy Assistant Secretary of Defense for International Security Affairs, chaired the PRC part of the study. See Carter Adminis-

tration, *"PRM-10, Comprehensive Net Assessment and Military Force Posture Review,"* 18 February 1977; and Lawrence Korb, "National Security Organization and Process in the Carter Administration," in *Defense Policy and the Presidency: Carter's First Years,* ed. Sam Sarkesian, (Boulder: Westview Press, 1979), 120, 124–25.

31. See Thomas Powers, "Choosing a Strategy for World War III," *Atlantic Monthly* 250, no. 5 (November 1982): 82–110; and Janne Nolan, *Guardians of the Arsenal* (New York: Basic Books, 1989), 131–33. See Carter Administration, *PRM/NSC-10, "Military Strategy and Force Posture Review: Final Report,"* June 1977, particularly III-12–III-23 (Washington, DC: National Security Archive); Richard Burt, "U.S. Doubts Ability to Defend Europe in Conventional War," *The New York Times,* 6 January 1978, A1. The number of options reported can be found in, respectively, Powers, "Choosing a Strategy for World War III," 86, and Nolan, *Guardians of the Arsenal,* 132–33.

32. Ball, "The Development of the SIOP, 1960–1983," in *Strategic Nuclear Targeting,* ed. Ball and Richelson, 75–76.

33. Brzezinski, *Power and Principle,* 177 and 457–58; Carter, *Keeping Faith,* 214; Vance, *Hard Choices,* 416; Mlyn, *The State, Society, and Nuclear War,* 119–20; and Richard Burt, "Pentagon Told to Review Strategy for a Nuclear War against Soviet," *The New York Times,* 16 December 1977, A5. Vance's memoirs explicitly call for a nuclear posture that ends "speculation about the possibilities of fighting a so-called limited nuclear war—speculation that only increases the risks of conflict." See Vance, *Hard Choices,* 416. Brown's initial views are contained in Senate Committee on Armed Services, *Nominations of Harold Brown and Charles W. Duncan,* November 1977, 9. His eventual views are detailed below.

34. Nolan, *Guardians of the Arsenal,* 133; and Brzezinski, *Power and Principle,* 455.

35. Richard Burt, "The New Strategy for Nuclear War: How It Evolved," *The New York Times,* 13 August 1980, A3; Powers, "Choosing a Strategy for World War III," 95; and Brzezinski, *Power and Principle,* 456–57.

36. Carter Administration, *Presidential Directive/NSC-18, "US National Strategy,"* 24 August 1977 (Washington, DC: National Security Archive); George Wilson, "New Carter Directive Could Mean Rising, Not Falling, Defense Budgets," *The Washington Post,* 27 August 1977, A6; Desmond Ball, "Counterforce Targeting: How New? How Viable?" *Arms Control Today* 11, no. 2 (February 1981): 2; and Jeffrey Richelson, "PD-59, NSDD-13, and the Reagan Strategic Modernization Plan," *Journal of Strategic Studies* 6, no. 2 (June 1983): 128–29. Quotation found in Ball, *Developments in U.S. Strategic Nuclear Policy under the Carter Administration,* 10.

37. Ball, "The Development of the SIOP, 1960–1983," in *Strategic Nuclear Targeting,* ed. Ball and Richelson, 76.

38. Nolan, *Guardians of the Arsenal,* 135; Mlyn, *The State, Society, and Nuclear War,* 116–17; and Powers, "Choosing a Strategy for World War III," 87. The Pentagon's judgment of the new strategy is contained in Powers, "Choosing a Strategy for World War III," 96; Nolan, *Guardians of the Arsenal,* 133–34; and Burt, "Pentagon Told to Review Strategy for a Nuclear War against Soviets," A5.

39. Powers, "Choosing a Strategy for World War III," 96; Ball, "The Development of the SIOP, 1960–1983," in *Strategic Nuclear Targeting,* ed. Ball and Richelson, 72; Mlyn, *The State, Society, and Limited Nuclear War,* 116.

40. Brown's 1979 and 1980 annual reports to Congress began outlining the countervailing strategy. See Harold Brown, *Report of Secretary of Defense Harold Brown to Congress on the FY 1980 Budget, FY 1981 Authorization Request, and FY 1981–1984 Defense Programs* (25 January

1979), 76; and Harold Brown, *Report of the Secretary of Defense Harold Brown to the Congress on the FY 1981 Budget, FY 1982 Authorization Request, and FY 1981–1985 Defense Programs* (29 January 1980), 65–67.

41. Walter Pincus, "Decision Making Is Narrowing on A-Force Strategy," *The Washington Post*, 11 February 1979, A1; and John Edwards, *Superweapon: The Making of the MX* (New York: W. W. Norton, 1982), 174.

42. Brzeinski's view is reported in Powers, "Choosing a Strategy for World War III," 104. Brown's support for a PD is discussed in Brzezinski, *Power and Principle*, 458. Vance is listed as a recipient of the Brzezinski-Brown memos. See Zbigniew Brzezinski, "Memorandum for the Secretary of Defense," 1 May 1979, cc to Cyrus Vance, Subject File, Box 20, Alpha Channel (Miscellaneous) 4/78–4/79 through 11/80–12/80, Folder: Alpha Channel (Misc) 5/79–8/79 (Atlanta: Carter Presidential Library).

43. Powers, "Choosing a Strategy for World War III," 95; Peter Pringle and William Arkin, *SIOP* (New York: W. W. Norton, 1983), 216; and Hyland, *Mortal Rivals*, 209. Both Powers and Hyland describe Brzezinski's near disastrous dry run of the presidential evacuation plans. As a military helicopter tried to land on the White House lawn to rendezvous with Brzezinski, the secret service almost shot it down.

44. PD-41 authorized contingency plans for the evacuation of major cities during a nuclear emergency. See Samuel Huntington, "The Renewal of Strategy," in *The Strategic Imperative*, ed. Samuel Huntington (Cambridge: Ballinger, 1982), 39. PD-53 outlined the national security needs of the nation's communications facilities and required U.S. nuclear forces to remain under the command and control of the civilian leadership and to retain the ability to launch retaliatory nuclear strikes during and after an enemy nuclear attack. See Carter Administration, PD/NSC-53, "National Security Telecommunications Policy," 15 November 1979. It is also discussed in U.S. Congress, Senate, Committee on the Armed Services, *DOD Authorizations for Appropriations for FY 1982*, part 7, February–March 1981, 4210; Tad Szulc, "The New Brinkmanship," *The New Republic*, 8 November 1980, 21; and Joseph Albright, "The Message Gap in Our Crisis Network," *The Washington Post*, 19 October 1982, C4. PD-57, "Mobilization Planning," detailed the administration's assumptions about the duration of a nuclear war; such a war would be a prolonged conflict. Ball, *Targeting for Strategic Deterrence*, 35. PD-58, "Continuity of Government," described contingencies for the survival of U.S. leadership, such as rapid evacuation from Washington, DC, of the top military and civilian leaders, construction of hardened shelters for these leaders and their communications systems, and the upgrade of early warning systems. Ball, *Targeting for Strategic Deterrence*, 35, and Szulc, "The New Brinksmanship," 21.

45. Brzezinski, *Power and Principle*, 458. Powers contends that it was Odom who convinced Brzezinski to begin the process at that point. See Powers, "Choosing a Strategy for World War III," 104.

46. He continued, stating that, "My opinion of the Russians has changed most drastically in the last week than even in the previous two and a half years before that." The interview is reprinted in "Transcript of President's Interview with Frank Reynolds on Soviet Reply," *The New York Times*, 1 January 1980, 1.

47. PD-59 provided the guidance for a new Nuclear Weapons Employment Policy (NUWEP) that was called NUWEP-2 or NUWEP-80, codified in October. This in turn was operationalized as SIOP-5. Burt, "The New Strategy for Nuclear War: How It Evolved,"

A3; Powers, "Choosing a Strategy for World War III," 104; Mlyn, *The State, Society, and Limited Nuclear War*, 116; and Brzezinski, *Power and Principle*, 458. For details of the strategy see Ball, *Targeting for Strategic Deterrence*; Richelson, "PD-59, NSDD-13, and the Reagan Strategic Modernization Plan"; Walter Slocombe, "The Countervailing Strategy," *International Security* 5, no. 4 (spring 1981): 18–27; Harold Brown, "The Flexibility of Our Plans," *Vital Speeches of the Day* 46, no. 24 (1 October 1980): 741–44; *Report of the Secretary of Defense Harold Brown to the Congress on the FY 1982 Budget, FY 1983 Authorization Request, and FY 1982–1986 Defense Programs* (19 January 1981): 38–45; and Senate Committee on Foreign Relations, *Hearing before the Committee on Foreign Relations United States Senate on Presidential Directive 59*, 6th Cong., 2d Sess., 16 September 1980.

48. See Brown, "The Flexibility of Our Plans," 741–44.

49. Richard Burt, "Carter Said to Back Plan for Limiting Nuclear War," *The New York Times*, 6 August 1980, 1; and Michael Getler, "Carter Directive Modifies Strategy for a Nuclear War," *The Washington Post*, 6 August 1980, A10. Details of the strategy had actually leaked earlier in July, but were not met with the same reaction. See William Beecher, "U.S. Drafts New N-War Strategy vs. Soviets," *The Boston Globe*, 27 July 1980, 1. On the possibility of a deliberate leak see "PD-59: Why?" *Los Angeles Times*, 15 August 1980, sec. 2, p. 10.

50. Vance, *Hard Choices*, 398–413; Brzezinski, *Power and Principle*, 470–501; Carter, *Keeping Faith*, 433–514; and Gaddis Smith, *Morality, Reason, and Power*, 180–206.

51. See Don Oberdorfer, "Pentagon Says State Was Informed of Shift in A-War Strategy," *The Washington Post*, 11 August 1980, A5; and Don Oberdorfer, "State Denies Being Informed in Final Phase of A-War Strategy," *The Washington Post*, 12 August 1980, A2.

52. Burt, "The New Strategy for Nuclear War: How It Evolved," A3; George Wilson, "U.S. Shift in Nuclear Strategy Evokes Some Shudders," *The Washington Post*, 13 August 1980, A4; and Don Oberdorfer, "Muskie Indicates Omission of State Won't Be Repeated," *The Washington Post*, 14 August 1980, A2.

53. See Box 23, Subject Files Four-Year Goals (4/77) through Meetings—Muskie/Brown/Brzezinski: 7/80–9/80, Folder: Meetings—Muskie/Brown/Brzezinski: 5/80–6/80, and Folder: Meetings—Muski/Brown/Brzezinski: 7/80–9/80 (Atlanta: Carter Presidential Library).

54. See "M-B-B Agenda, 5 August 1980," Box 23, Subject Files Four-Year Goals (4/77) through Meetings—Muskie/Brown/Brzezinski: 7/80–9/80, Folder: Meetings—Muskie/Brown/Brzezinski: 7/80–9/80 (Atlanta: Carter Presidential Library).

55. William Odom, "Memorandum for Zbigniew Brzezinski, M-B-B Luncheon Item: Targeting," 5 August 1980, Box 23, Subject Files Four-Year Goals (4/77) through Meetings—Muskie/Brown/Brzezinski: 7/80–9/80, Folder: Meetings—Muskie/Brown/Brzezinski: 7/80–9/80 (Atlanta: Carter Presidential Library).

56. Carter Administration, PD/NSC-18, "U.S. National Strategy," 24 August 1977; and Carter Administration, PD/NSC-59, "Nuclear Weapon Employment Policy," 25 July 1980 (Washington, DC: National Security Archive).

57. See Michael Getler, "Changes in U.S. Nuclear Strategy," *The Washington Post*, 14 August 1980, A3; and George Wilson, "Change in Nuclear Target Policy Not a Radical One, Brown Says," *The Washington Post*, 21 August 1980, A1. On the Reagan campaign's criticism of Carter see Jack Germond and Jules Witcover, *Blue Smoke and Mirrors* (New York: Viking Press, 1981), 251, 266.

58. Leslie Gelb, "Muskie and Brzezinski: The Struggle over Foreign Policy," *New York Times Magazine*, 20 July 1980, 26–40.

59. Carter, *Keeping Faith*, 214.

60. In terms of the policies themselves, the failure of the deep cuts proposal led Carter back to Vladivostok, while PD-59 is an extension of the No-Cities doctrine and Limited Nuclear Option Schlesinger Doctrine.

Chapter Five

1. Shultz quoted in Hedrick Smith, *The Power Game* (New York: Ballantine Books, 1988), 576. McFarlane relates this story in Robert McFarlane, *Special Trust* (New York: Cadell and Davies, 1994), 286–87.

2. The Reagan administration's view of U.S. challenges is described in Stephen Rosenfeld, "The Guns of July," *Foreign Affairs* 64, no. 4 (spring 1986): 698–714; Charles W. Kegley and Eugene R. Wittkopf, "The Reagan Administration's World View," *Orbis* 26, no. 1 (spring 1982): 224–44; Colin S. Gray and Jeffrey G. Barlow, "Inexcusable Restraint: The Decline of American Military Power in the 1970s," *International Security* 10, no. 2 (fall 1985): 27–69; and Robert W. Komer, "What 'Decade of Neglect,'" *International Security* 10, no. 2 (fall 1985): 70–83. On the role of the CPD in debates on U.S. foreign policy see Jerry W. Sanders, *Peddlers of Crisis* (Boston: South End Press, 1983); and Simon Dalby, *Creating the Second Cold War* (London: Pinter Publishers, 1990). A collection of the CPD's papers can be found in Charles Tyroler, II, *Alerting America: The Papers of the Committee on the Present Danger* (Washington, DC: Pergamon-Brassey's, 1984).

3. See Thomas Risse-Kappen, *The Zero Option: INF, West Germany, and Arms Control* (Boulder: Westview Press, 1988); and Strobe Talbott, *Deadly Gambits* (New York: Alfred A. Knopf, 1984), 21–206.

4. Reagan explains this negotiate-through-strength thesis in his memoirs; see Ronald Reagan, *An American Life* (New York: Simon and Schuster, 1990), 13–14. A detailed account of the administration's views on arms control and the Soviet buildup is in Keith Shimko, *Images and Arms Control* (Ann Arbor: University of Michigan Press, 1991), 63–81, 101–20, and particularly, 124–33. On the Reagan defense buildup see Barry Posen and Stephen Van Evera, "Defense Policy and the Reagan Administration," *International Security* 8, no. 1 (summer 1983): 3–45; Jeffrey Record, "Jousting with Unreality," *International Security* 8, no. 3 (winter 1983/84): 3–18; and Lawrence J. Korb and Linda P. Brady, "Rearming America: The Reagan Administration Defense Program," *International Security* 9, no. 3 (winter 1984/85): 3–18.

5. Secretary of Defense Caspar Weinberger, in his annual report to Congress in 1983, referred to the U.S. inability to place Soviet ICBMs at risk as the de facto creation of an ICBM "sanctuary," using the analogy of a wildlife sanctuary where the inhabitants of an area are off-limits to outside threats. See Caspar Weinberger, *Report of the Secretary of Defense Caspar W. Weinberger to the Congress on the FY 1984 Budget, FY 1985 Authorization Request, and FY 1984–88 Defense Programs*, 1 February 1983, 53. The notion of inferiority was based on simple "bean counting" of U.S. and Soviet ICBM characteristics. According to the administration, as of May 1982 when the Eureka proposal was made public, the USSR had 1,400 ICBMs to the U.S. total of 1,052. In terms of warheads the imbalance was greater, 5,500 for the USSR to 2,150 for the U.S.

6. Michael Gordon, "In the Great Nuclear Strategy Debate, the Issue Is Where Do We Stand," *National Journal* 14, no. 20 (15 May 1982): 858.

7. On the window of vulnerability see Committee on the Present Danger, "Is America Becoming Number 2? Current Trends in the US-Soviet Military Balance," 5 October 1978, as reprinted in Tyroler, *Alerting America*, 39–93; Michael Johnson, "Debunking the Window of Vulnerability," *Technology Review* 85, no. 1 (January 1982): 59–65 and 70; Albert Carnesale and Charles Glaser, "ICBM Vulnerability: The Cures Are Worse Than the Disease," *International Security* 7, no. 1 (summer 1982): 71–93; David Morrison, "ICBM Vulnerability," *Bulletin of the Atomic Scientists* 40, no. 9 (September 1984): 22–29.

8. The MPS is a rail mobile system in which a transporter would carry a missile, within a launch canister, between 23 shelters arranged in an oval. Two hundred of these ovals, each with 23 shelters, and one missile shifting between shelters within its own oval were to be deployed in Nevada and Utah on military reservations. This would have added 2,000 survivable warheads to the U.S. ICBM force. On this system see Stephen Meyer, "Verification and the ICBM Shell Game," *International Security* 4, no. 2 (fall 1979): 40–68; Herbert Scoville, *MX: Prescription for Disaster* (Cambridge: MIT Press, 1981), 18–31; and Office of Technology Assessment, *MX Missile Basing* (Washington, DC: Government Printing Office, 1981). On the Carter decision see John Edwards, *Superweapon: The Making of the MX* (New York: W. W. Norton, 1982); and Desmond Ball, "The Carter Administration's Decision on MX Basing," in *American Defense Policy*, 5th ed., ed. John Reichart and Steven Sturm (Baltimore: Johns Hopkins University Press, 1982), 234–41.

9. Lawrence I. Barnett, *Gambling With History* (New York: Doubleday and Co., 1983), 86–87; Raymond Garthoff, *The Great Transition* (Washington, DC: Brookings Institution Press, 1994), 46–47; Smith, *The Power Game*, 569, 577; and Talbott, *Deadly Gambits*, 222–26.

10. On the freeze see Douglas C. Waller, *Congress and the Nuclear Freeze* (Amherst: University of Massachusetts Press, 1987), 33; and Edward Feighan, "The Freeze in Congress," in *The Nuclear Freeze Debate: Arms Control Issues for the 1980s*, ed. Paul M. Cole and William J. Taylor, Jr. (Boulder: Westview Press, 1983) 30–31. On the freeze and its origins see also David S. Meyer, *A Winter of Discontent* (New York: Praeger, 1990); and *Coalitions and Political Movements*, ed. Thomas R. Rochan and David S. Meyer (Boulder: Lynne Rienner Publishers, 1997). The freeze movement in the U.S. is analogous to the growth of the peace movement in several nations in Europe that protested the deployment of the Pershing II and GLCM systems. On these controversial statements see Bernard Gwertzman, "Reagan Clarifies His Statements on Nuclear War, *The New York Times*, 22 October 1981; Robert Scheer, "Reagan Acts to Counter Possible Soviet Attack," *The Los Angeles Times*, 15 January 1982, 1; Robert Scheer, "U.S. Could Survive War in Administration's View," *The Los Angeles Times*, 16 January 1982, 1; and Robert Scheer, *With Enough Shovels* (New York: Random House, 1982).

11. See Feighan, "The Freeze in Congress," in *The Nuclear Freeze Debate*, ed. Cole and Taylor, 32; Waller, *Congress and the Freeze*, 53–54; and Judith Miller, "Arms Pact Revival Is Being Promoted," *The New York Times*, 4 May 1982, A9.

12. Talbott, *Deadly Gambits*, 234.

13. Talbott, *Deadly Gambits*, 235–48; and Michael Gordon, "Administration Debates Arms Cuts with Congress as Well as the Soviets," *National Journal* 15, no. 32 (6 August 1983): 1624. It is estimated that nearly thirty different proposals were debated within the Arms Control IG; Leslie Gelb, "U.S. Forging a New Concept for Curbing Strategic Arms," *The New York*

Times, 2 May 1982, 1. The hardliners saw the Soviet throw weight advantage as a way for the USSR to add more and more MIRVs to their missiles as a matter of policy or as an option in the middle of a crisis. They therefore wanted to limit the overall throw weight of both sides to prevent the Soviets from adding warheads. Launcher or warhead limits of the type favored by the pragmatists would still leave the USSR with the capability to add warheads to its fleet of large missiles if it desired, even if these missile were not normally deployed with the additional warheads. Haig's and Burt's views are detailed in, respectively, Alexander Haig, *Caveat* (New York: MacMillian Publishing Co., 1984), 222–23; and Talbott, *Deadly Gambits*, 237.

14. Senate Committee on Foreign Relations, *International Security Policy: Hearing before the Committee on Foreign Relations*, 97th Cong., 1st sess., 27 July 1981, 12.

15. Weinberger's views are described in Caspar Weinberger, "Reagan and International Arms Agreements: Interview with Caspar Weinberger," in *Foreign Policy in the Reagan Administration*, ed. Kenneth W. Thompson (Lanham: University Press of America, 1993), 52–53. Perle's role is detailed in Talbott, *Deadly Gambits*, 16–17; and Jay Winik, *On the Brink* (New York: Simon and Schuster, 1996), 123.

16. Judith Miller, "Arms Pact Revival Is Being Promoted," A9; and Pat Towell, "Reagan Cites Soviet Power; Embraces Nuclear Reduction and Says Talks May Begin Soon," *Congressional Quarterly* 40, no. 14 (3 April 1982): 725–26; The Jackson-Warner freeze is detailed in Waller, *Congress and the Nuclear Freeze*, 92.

17. The strategic requirements included fit with current strategic modernization plans, equality, stability (in terms of reducing U.S. vulnerability), reductions, comprehensibility (in terms of ease of understanding for the public), concerns of NATO allies, verifiability, and sustainability (of the proposal in the face of Soviet reluctance to accept any real reductions). Talbott, *Deadly Gambits*, 246–48. On the Bishop's Conference see Judith A. Dwyer, "The Role of American Churches in the Nuclear Weapons Debate," in *The Nuclear Freeze Debate*, ed. Cole and Taylor, 77–92.

18. Talbott, *Deadly Gambits*, 239–51.

19. The hardliners' view of the JCS is discussed in Talbott, *Deadly Gambits*, 253. On the details of the Defense Guidance see Caspar Weinberger, *Report of the Secretary of Defense Caspar W. Weinberger to the Congress on the FY 1983 Budget, the FY 1984 Authorization Request, and the FY 1983–1987 Defense Programs*, 8 February 1982, I-17–I-18; Richard Halloran, "Pentagon Draws Up First Strategy for Fighting a Long Nuclear War," *The New York Times*, 30 May 1982, 1; Richard Halloran, "Weinberger Confirms New Strategy on Atom War," *The New York Times*, 4 June 1982, A10; Robert Scheer, "Pentagon Plan Aims at Winning Nuclear War," *The Los Angeles Times*, 15 August 1982, A1; and Michael Getler, "Administration Nuclear War Policy Stance Still Murky," *The Washington Post*, 10 November 1982, A24.

20. On the various viewpoints of all the senior players in this debate see Talbott, *Deadly Gambits*, 256–62. The JCS had actually submitted a proposal that limited ballistic missiles to 850 and ballistic missile warheads to 5,000 to 6,000 on April 19. Not all the JCS had agreed to it by that point. Perle used this as an excuse not to include this proposal in the NSC discussion on April 21. This surely could not have endeared Perle to the JCS. See Talbott, *Deadly Gambits*, 261.

21. Talbott, *Deadly Gambits*, 263–64.

22. Talbott, *Deadly Gambits*, 265–66. Reports at the time indicated that when Reagan made the general decision on May 6, the key factor had been the alliance between Haig and

Jones. Leslie Gelb, "U.S. Called Ready to Propose Limits on Nuclear Arms," *The New York Times*, 8 May 1982, 1.

23. A heavily edited version of NSDD-33, "U.S. Approach to START Negotiations," appears in *National Security Directives of the Reagan and Bush Administrations*, ed. Simpson, 118–20. Passages in the NSDD that outline the details have been deleted from the published copies. The 2.5 million kg limit is based on journalistic sources. See Talbott, *Deadly Gambits*, 268–69. Reagan Administration, NSDD-36, "U.S. Approach to START Negotiations—II," 25 May 1982, as printed in *National Security Directives of the Reagan and Bush Administrations*, ed. Simpson, 125–27. Reagan's speech is reprinted in Ronald Reagan, "Address at Commencement Exercises at Eureka College in Illinois," 9 May 1982, in U.S. President, *Public Papers of the Presidents of the United States* (Washington, DC: Office of the *Federal Register*, National Archives and Records Service, 1983), Ronald Reagan, 1982, vol. 1, 585. The proposal is outlined in Talbott, *Deadly Gambits*, 270–71.

24. On Reagan's role in the April and May meetings see Talbott, *Deadly Gambits*, 250 and 269, respectively. Further NSDDs on START were produced in the same manner: following NSC meetings, an NSDD was drawn up by McFarlane that outlined the issues that had been settled and assigned further tasks to the START IG along with deadlines for completing those tasks.

25. The standard operating procedures for negotiations had the Geneva delegation contacting the START Backstopping Committee when it had questions or needed clarifications. The Backstopping Committee was another interagency committee that served the START IG. The same philosophical and strategic gridlock that gripped the START IG existed here as well. John H. McNeill, "U.S.-USSR Nuclear Arms Negotiations: The Process and the Lawyer," *American Journal of International Law* 79, no. 1 (January 1985): 61. The Geneva delegation was an interagency body itself, led by Rowny of ACDA, but composed of representatives from the State and Defense Departments and the JCS.

26. On Reagan's efforts to find the MX a permanent home see Edwards, *Superweapon*; Lauren H. Holland and Robert A. Hoover, *The MX Decision* (Boulder: Westview Press, 1985); R. James Woolsey, "The Politics of Vulnerability, 1980–1983" in *The Nuclear Controversy*, ed. William P. Bundy (New York: Meridian Books, 1985), 211–26. The CSB depended upon a fratricide effect. In theory, after the first detonations of incoming Soviet ICBMs further incoming warheads would be destroyed by the blast effects of the initial detonations. The initial detonations by themselves would not be enough to penetrate the super-hardened silos. In this way the MX would be able to ride out a Soviet barrage attack.

27. The House voted to allow research and development, testing and engineering, but not procurement. The Senate provided procurement funds, but fenced them until a basing mode could be chosen. See Holland and Hoover, *The MX Decision*, 227–28. One of the key events in December was the announcement on December 8 by General John Vessey, Chairman of the Joint Chiefs, that there was no unity among the chiefs in support of the MX-CSB. The Air Force approved, but the Army, Navy, and Marines did not. See also George Shultz, *Turmoil and Triumph* (New York: Charles Scribner's Sons, 1993), 248–49.

28. Lou Cannon, *President Reagan: The Role of a Lifetime* (New York: Touchstone Books, 1991), 324; and Robert McFarlane, *Special Trust*, 224.

29. McFarlane, *Special Trust*, 196.

30. Reagan Administration, NSDD-73, "The Peacekeeper Program Assessment," 3 Janu-

ary 1983, as printed in *National Security Directives of the Reagan and Bush Administration*, ed. Simpson, 250–51.

31. The administration's threat was issued through a letter to Jack Kemp (R-N.Y.) on 4 January 1983, the day after the commission was officially charged. Michael Getler, "Reagan Links Arms Cut Stand to MX Approval by Congress," *The Washington Post*, 7 January 1983, 1. The purpose of the commission is stated by Woolsey, "The Politics of Vulnerability, 1980–1983," in *The Nuclear Controversy*, ed. Bundy, 219. For profiles of the commission members see Talbott, *Deadly Gambits*, 303.

32. Talbott, *Deadly Gambits*, 304; and Margaret Hornblower and George Wilson, "Recommendations on MX Basing 'Has a Chance' for Hill Approval," *The Washington Post*, 12 April 1983, 1.

33. *Report of the President's Commission on Strategic Forces* (Washington, DC: Government Printing Office, April 1983). The Scowcroft Commission saw the future as one in which strategic stability would be based upon small, mobile, single-warhead systems. These would be unattractive targets with great survivability. On these ideas and the SICBM see *The President's Commission on Strategic Forces*, 22–25; Jonathan Rich, "Midgetman: Superhero or Problem Child," *Arms Control Today* 14, no. 4 (May 1984): 1, 6–9; William Arkin, "Going with Small ICBMs," *Bulletin of the Atomic Scientists* 40, no. 5 (May 1984): 7–8; Barry Schneider, Colin Gray, and Keith B. Payne, eds., *Missiles for the Nineties* (Boulder: Westview Press, 1984); and Paul Walker and John Wentworth, "Midgetman: Missile in Search of a Mission," *Bulletin of the Atomic Scientists* 42, no. 9 (November 1986): 20–26.

34. See Michael Gordon, "The Aspin Paradox—A 'Liberal' Who Helped Keep the MX Alive," *National Journal* 16, no. 27 (7 July 1984): 1296–99.

35. Michael Gordon, "Administration Debates Arms Cuts with Congress as Well as the Soviets," *National Journal* 15, no. 32 (6 August 1983): 1624. The basic notion of the build-down is detailed in Alton Frye, "Strategic Build-Down: A Context for Restraint," in *The Nuclear Controversy*, ed. Bundy, 155–80.

36. Michael Getler, "Bipartisan Letters to President Link MX Vote, Arms Control," *The Washington Post*, 3 May 1983, A8; Lou Cannon, "President Considering Revised Arms Proposal," *The Washington Post*, 11 May 1983, A1; and Lou Cannon and George Wilson, "Reagan Reassures Congress, Is Rewarded with MX Vote," *The Washington Post*, 12 May 1983, A1. Percy told the *Washington Post*: "I have no doubt that there are certain people around [the president], in the NSC and DOD, who will do anything to prevent arms control. These are the guys I am out to get." George C. Wilson, "House Panel Gives Twist to MX Plan," *The Washington Post*, 17 March 1983, A12.

37. On Shultz's and Dam's role, respectively, see Shultz, *Turmoil and Triumph*, 247–48, and Talbott, *Deadly Gambits*, 154–55. On the interagency struggles at this point see Michael Getler, "State, Pentagon at Odds on Altering Arms Control Stance," *The Washington Post*, 30 May 1983, A1; Gordon, "The Aspin Paradox—A 'Liberal' Who Helped Keep the MX Alive," 1624–29; and Talbott, *Deadly Gambits*, 306–10.

38. Steven Roberts, "Basing of MX Could Have Long-Term Effect on Foreign and Military Policy," *The New York Times*, 26 April 1983, B7; and Hedrick Smith, "Reagan Calls Meeting on Arms Talks," *The New York Times*, 10 May 1983, A3. "Text of Reagan's Letter on Arms Control Policy," *The New York Times*, 12 May 1983, B9; "Excerpts from Letter to 3 Senators," *The Washington Post*, 13 May 1983, A18; and Steven Roberts, "President Pledges to Shift Approach on Arms Control," *The New York Times*, 12 May 1983, 1.

39. Appropriations Committee votes were followed up by full House and Senate approval on 25 May. Roberts, "President Pledges to Shift Approach to Arms Control"; Steven V. Roberts, "MX Plan Clears Another Hurdle by a 17–11 Vote," *The New York Times*, 13 May 1983, 1; and Holland and Hoover, *The MX Decision*, 238–40. Administration-congressional negotiations are detailed in Hedrick Smith, "U.S. Plans to Shift Arms Bid to Soviets in Geneva Parlay," *The New York Times*, 2 June 1983, 1; Hedrick Smith, "Reagan Reviewing 2 Options for Strategic Weapons Talks," *The New York Times*, 7 June 1983, A16; Leslie Gelb, Aides Say Reagan Will Modify Plan on Strategic Arms," *The New York Times*, 8 June 1983, 1; and George Skelton, "Reagan Finishes Work on 'Flexible' Position for Strategic Arms Talks," *The Los Angeles Times*, 8 June 1983, 14. Administration policy is outlined in Ronald Reagan, "Remarks Announcing Changes in the United States Position at the Strategic Arms Reduction Talks," 8 June 1983, Ronald Reagan, Book I, 831–33; and Reagan Administration, NSDD-98, "U.S. Approach to START Negotiations—VI," as printed in Simpson, *National Security Directives of the Reagan and Bush Administrations*, 309–11.

40. "Reagan Is Tightening Grip on Arms Control," *The New York Times*, 20 July 1983, A3; Associated Press, "President Creates Task Force as Link to Arms Negotiators," *The Washington Post*, 20 July 1983, A15; and "Key U.S. Demands Dropped in Talks on Arms Control," *The New York Times*, 6 August 1983, 1.

41. Talbott, *Deadly Gambits*, 333–34.

42. The concept is best explained in Frye, "Strategic Build-Down: A Context for Restraint," in *The Nuclear Controversy*, ed. Bundy, 173; Glenn A. Kent and Edward L. Warner, "Key Aspects of a Compulsory Double–Build-Down Approach," Rand Corporation, 14 September 1983, mimeo; and Glenn A. Kent with Randall DeValk and Edward L. Warner, *A New Approach to Arms Control* (Santa Monica: The Rand Corporation, June 1984). The congressional acceptance of the double build-down is detailed in Talbott, *Deadly Gambits*, 337; Woolsey, "The Politics of Vulnerability, 1980–1983," in *The Nuclear Controversy*, ed. Bundy, 222–23; Michael Getler, "Panel Urged to Suggest New Arms Stance," *The Washington Post*, 30 August 1983, A5; and Charles Mohr, "Reagan Panel Receptive to Aspin's Arms Proposal," *The New York Times*, 2 September 1983, A12.

43. Woolsey, "The Politics of Vulnerability, 1980–1983," in *The Nuclear Controversy*, ed. Bundy, 223; and Walter Pincus, "START Plans Being Studied by President, *The Washington Post*, 22 September 1983, A15.

44. Talbott, *Deadly Gambits*, 338–39.

45. Associated Press, "Reagan Is Said to Overrule Arms Advisers," *The Washington Post*, 7 October 1983, A20; Bernard Gwertzman, "Reagan Approves New Arms Offer for Geneva Talks," *The New York Times*, 4 October 1983, 1; and Pat Towell, "START Talks Resume with New U.S. Offers," *Congressional Quarterly* 41, no. 40 (8 October 1983): 2099–100. On Shultz's role see Talbott, *Deadly Gambits*, 339.

46. Towell, "START Talks Resume with New U.S. Offers," 2099–100; and Reagan Administration, NSDD-106, "U.S. Approach to START Negotiations—VII," 4 October 1983, as printed in *National Security Decision Directives of the Reagan and Bush Administrations*, ed. Simpson, 335–38.

47. The Soviets saw the build-down as a proposal tendered for domestic political reasons only. They never believed the administration took it seriously. Talbott, *Deadly Gambits*, 340–41.

48. For a discussion of these events and their affect on U.S.-Soviet relations, see Garthoff, *The Great Transition*, 85–141.

49. Donald R. Baucom, *The Origins of SDI, 1944–1983* (Lawrence: University Press of Kansas, 1992), 141–94; Cannon, *President Reagan*, 319–32; Martin Anderson, *Revolution* (Stanford: Hoover Institution Press, 1990), 72–93; Janne Nolan, *Guardians of the Arsenal* (New York: Basic Books, 1989), 140–69; and Frances Fitzgerald, *Way Out There in the Blue* (New York: Simon and Schuster, 2000).

50. Jonathan Stein, *From H-Bomb to Star Wars* (Lexington: Lexington Books, 1984), 51–56; and Baucom, *The Origins of SDI, 1944–1983*, 114–22. The ABM Treaty allowed the U.S. to deploy only 200 interceptor missiles, 100 each at sites guarding an ICBM field and the national command authority. The 1974 protocol to the ABM Treaty further limited this to 100 ABMs at one site, either an ICBM field or the national command authority. The U.S. chose to use Malmstrom Air Force Base in Grand Forks, North Dakota, as a test site for ABMs.

51. See Committee on the Present Danger, "Is America Becoming Number 2?" in Tyroler, *Alerting America*, 55–56; Stein, *From H-Bomb to Star Wars*, 54–55; Caspar Weinberger, *Fighting for Peace* (New York: Warner Books, 1991), 299; and Baucom, *The Origins of SDI, 1944–1983*, 114–46. On the campaign's view of missile defense see Anderson, *Revolution*, 83; Richard Halloran, *To Arm a Nation* (New York: MacMillan, 1986), 308; and Cannon, *President Reagan*, 320.

52. Nolan, *Guardians of the Arsenal*, 159 and 162; Anderson, *Revolution*, 91–92; and Baucom, *The Origins of SDI, 1944–1983*, 146–55.

53. Anderson, *Revolution*, 93; and Edwin Meese, *With Reagan* (Washington, DC: Regnery Gateway, 1992), 192.

54. In his memoirs, Reagan called deterrence through vulnerability "madness." When thinking about assured destruction, Reagan often talked about Armageddon, the war described in the New Testament that destroys the world. See Reagan, *An American Life*, 13–14, and 257; and Cannon, *President Reagan*, 288–91, and 320; and Shultz, *Turmoil and Triumph*, 246. Reagan's meeting with Teller is discussed in Cannon, *President Reagan*, 319. The story of Reagan's trip to NORAD is recounted in Anderson, *Revolution*, 80–83.

55. Anderson, *Revolution*, 93–95; and Meese, *With Reagan*, 193.

56. Cannon, *President Reagan*, 323; and Baucom, *The Origins of SDI, 1944–1983*, 166–68.

57. Anderson, *Revolution*, 97; Baucom, *The Origins of SDI, 1944–1983*, 188; and Nolan, *Guardians of the Arsenal*, 328. In particular, following the defeat of the latest scheme for MX basing, Watkins argued that ballistic missile defense might be the best way to end MX vulnerability. He also emphasized his moral problems with leaving the American people open to nuclear attack. Cannon, *President Reagan*, 327–28; McFarlane, *Special Trust*, 226; Baucom, *The Origins of SDI, 1944–1983*, 190; and Nolan, *Guardians of the Arsenal*, 164.

58. Nolan, *Guardians of the Arsenal*, 164–65; Cannon, *President Reagan*, 329; and McFarlane, *Special Trust*, 234. On this meeting see Weinberger, *Fighting for Peace*, 304; and Cannon, *President Reagan*, 328–29.

59. McFarlane, *Special Trust*, 230–32; and Cannon, *President Reagan*, 331.

60. Weinberger, *Fighting for Peace*, 305–6; and Shultz, *Turmoil and Triumph*, 254. Shultz's views are discussed in Shultz, *Turmoil and Triumph*, 249–55.

61. Ronald Reagan, "Address to the Nation on Defense and National Security, 23 March 1983," in U.S. President, *Public Papers of the Presidents of the United States* (Washington, DC: Office of the *Federal Register*, National Archives and Records Service, 1984), Ronald Reagan, 1983, 442–43.

62. On the political, strategic, and technical debates that followed see Office of Tech-

nology Assessment, *Ballistic Missile Defense* (Washington, DC: Government Printing Office, 1984); Stein, *From H-Bomb to Star Wars*; Ashton Carter and David Schwartz, eds., *Ballistic Missile Defense* (Washington, DC: Brookings Institution Press, 1984); "Weapons in Space Vol. 1: Concepts and Technologies," *Daedalus* 114, no. 2 (spring 1985); "Weapons in Space Vol. 2: Implications for Security," *Daedalus* 114, no. 3 (summer 1985); and Antonia Handler Chayes and Paul Doty, eds., *Defending Deterrence* (Washington, DC: Pergamon-Brassey's, 1989).

63. A policy study group under Ikle's authority was charged with studying the "impact of defensive technology on deterrence and arms control." Its government component was chaired by Franklin Miller, and its nongovernmental team was chaired by Fred Hoffman. A second group under the authority of Undersecretary of Defense for Research and Engineering Richard DeLauer was chaired by James Fletcher, and, as its name suggests (Defensive Technologies Study Team), worked on the technological and engineering side of the issue. See Reagan Administration, NSDD-85, "Eliminating the Threat from Ballistic Missiles," 25 March 1981, as printed in *National Security Directives of the Reagan and Bush Administrations*, ed. Simpson, 287; and Gerold Yonas, "The Strategic Defense Initiative," in *Daedalus* 114, no. 2 (spring 1985): 76–77.

64. On these meetings see *The National Security Council Project: Oral History Roundtables: The Role of the National Security Adviser*, moderators Ivo H. Daalder and I. M. Destler (College Park, MD, and Washington, DC: Center for International and Security Studies at Maryland, School of Public Affairs, University of Maryland and Brookings Institution, 1999), 42–43. http://www.brookings.edu/dybdocroot/fp/projects/nsc/transcripts/19991025.htm. Accessed 20 March 2002; and *The National Security Council Project: Oral History Roundtables: Arms Control Policy and the National Security Council*, moderators Ivo H. Daalder and I. M. Destler (College Park, MD, and Washington, DC: Center for International and Security Studies at Maryland, School of Public Affairs, University of Maryland and Brookings Institution, 2000) 40. http://www.brookings.edu/dybdocroot/fp/projects/nsc/transcripts/20000325.htm. Accessed 20 March 2002.

Chapter Six

1. See, respectively, Bush and Scowcroft, *A World Transformed,* 25 and 33–35.

2. James Baker, interview by author, 10 July 2001, and Brent Scowcroft, interview by author, 16 July 2001.

3. Bomber, SLBM, and ICBM warheads were capped at 6,000 for each side. ICBM and SLBM warheads were limited to 4,900. A total of 1,600 bombers, SLBMs, and ICBMs were allowed. Heavy ICBMs, a category that included only the Soviet SS-18, were held to 1,540 missiles. This cut the SS-18 fleet in half. Outstanding issues included limitations on SLCMs, counting rules for limitations on ALCMs, and mobile missile systems (tentatively banned in the draft treaty). The issue of strategic defense presented the real obstacle to agreement. The Soviets were not ready to cut offensive weaponry if the U.S. planned on taking its SDI program from the drawing board to deployment. SDI ended all possibilities for a START agreement under Reagan. On these issues of Reagan's START negotiations see George Shultz, *Turmoil and Triumph*; Kenneth Adelman, *The Great Universal Embrace* (New York: Simon and Schuster, 1989); Max M. Kampelman, *Entering New Worlds* (New York: Harper Collins, 1991); Garthoff, *The Great Transition*, 191–372; Strobe Talbott, "Why START Stopped,"

Foreign Affairs 67, no. 1 (fall 1988): 49–69; Max Kampelman, "START: Completing the Task," *Washington Quarterly* 12, no. 3 (summer 1989): 5–16; Michelle A. Flournoy, "START Ends Temporarily as Reagan Team Puts Last Touches on Negotiating Position," *Arms Control Today* 18, no. 10 (December 1988): 28. On the Reagan administration's broad interpretation of the ABM Treaty see Raymond L. Garthoff, *Policy versus the Law: The Reinterpretation of the ABM Treaty* (Washington, DC: Brookings Institution Press, 1987).

4. Michael Beschloss and Strobe Talbott, *At the Highest Levels*, 114–15; and Bush and Scowcroft, *A World Transformed*, 45–46.

5. R. Jeffrey Smith, "Bush Will Miss Deadline on Land-Based Missile Pick," *The Washington Post*, 15 February 1989, A17.

6. Neil Munro, "Report: Defer MX, Field Midgetman and B-2 Bomber," *Defense News* 4, no. 6 (6 February 1989): 1; Michael Gordon, "U.S. Is Considering a Tactical Shift on Strategic Arms," *The New York Times*, 16 April 1989, 1; and R. Jeffrey Smith, "Panel Urges Delay on MX Rail Plan," *The Washington Post*, 4 February 1989, A12.

7. See U.S. Senate Committee on Armed Services, *NATO Defense and the INF Threat*, parts 1–5, 1988; and U.S. Senate Committee on Foreign Relations, *INF Treaty*, parts 1–6, 1988.

8. Bush and Scowcroft, *A World Transformed*, 19. On the ideas under review in NSR-14 , see "Review of United States Arms Control Policies," 3 April 1989, George H. W. Bush Presidential Library. Available at http://bushlibrary.tamu.edu, accessed 17 July 2001; and Gordon, "U.S. Is Considering a Tactical Shift on Strategic Arms," 1.

9. Edward Rowny, *It Takes One to Tango* (Washington, DC: Brassey's, 1992), 214–15; and Michael Gordon, "State Department Weighs Plan for Arms Control Focus," *The New York Times*, 9 February 1989, A13. Burt had several ideas including an SS-18 ban, an SS-18 flight test ban, and a ban on mobile MIRVed ICBMs. Gordon, "State Department Weighs Plan for Arms Control Focus," A13; and Beschloss and Talbott, *At the Highest Levels*, 116.

10. On these meetings see Michael Gordon, "Bush Rejects Pressure to Soften Antimissile Policy," *The New York Times*, 9 June 1989, A3; Robert C. Toth, "Bush Exploring Bold Cuts in Long Range Arms," *The Los Angeles Times*, 9 June 1989, 1; Michael Gordon, "Pentagon Offers Plans to Help Smooth Arms Talks," *The New York Times*, 16 June 1989, A6; and Michael Gordon, "U.S. Places Priority on Cuts in Troops, Not Missiles," *The New York Times*, 19 June 1989, A11.

11. The views of the senior administration officials on these issues can be found in Bob Woodward, *The Commanders* (New York: Simon and Schuster, 1991), 50–51; Don Oberdorfer, *From the Cold War to a New Era*, updated edition (Baltimore: Johns Hopkins University Press, 1998), 329; and Bush and Scowcroft, *A World Transformed*, 11–12; James A. Baker, *The Politics of Diplomacy* (New York: G. P. Putam's and Sons, 1995), 70; Colin Powell, *My American Journey* (New York: Random House, 1995), 436–437, 439; Robert M. Gates, *From the Shadows*, 474; and Raymond Garthoff, *The Great Transition* (Washington, DC: Brookings Institution Press, 1994), 375. Scowcroft contends that the U.S. mistake in the 1970s was in believing that a strategic change had occurred when in reality the Soviets were openly making a tactical shift in its competition with the U.S. The U.S. let down its guard and the results were costly in Ethiopia, Afghanistan, Angola, and Central America to name a few; Bush and Scowcroft, *A World Transformed*, 12–13. See also David Gergen, "Bush's Very Own Ford Foundation," *The Washington Post*, 2 April 1989, C2.

12. Vice President Dan Quayle was the only official who saw Gorbachev as simply an-

other in a long line of Stalinist Soviet leaders. Beschloss and Talbott, *At the Highest Levels*, 11–13; Garthoff, *The Great Transition*, 37–39; Marlin Fitzwater, *Call the Briefing* (New York: Times Books, 1995), 250–251; Baker, *The Politics of Diplomacy*, 70; Gates, *From the Shadows*, 474; and Bush and Scowcroft, *A World Transformed*, 13–15.

13. See Jack Beatty, "Reagan's Gift," *The Atlantic* 263, no. 2 (February 1989): 59; David Hoffman, "Gorbachev Seen as Trying to Buy Time for Reform," *The Washington Post*, 23 January 1989, A9. Smith, "Bush Will Miss Deadline on Land-Based Missile Pick," A17; and Gergen, "Bush's Very Own Ford Foundation," C2.

14. Gates, *From the Shadows*, 460; Beschloss and Talbott, *At the Highest Levels*, 116; and Don Oberdorfer and Robert McCartney, "Baker Voices Concern over START Pact," *The Washington Post*, 13 February 1989, 1. This division was a much milder version of the Reagan-era hardliner-pragmatist battle. SICBM supporters favored its survivability and its reduced attractiveness as a target due to its single warhead. MX proponents focused on its ability to redress the hard target kill imbalance on ICBMs.

15. Toth, "Bush Exploring Bold Cuts in Long Range Arms," 1.

16. In a phased modernization process, the fifty MX missiles already in silos were to be redeployed on railroad cars on military bases in the western U.S. as phase I. The rail-MX initial operating capability (IOC) was set for 1992. Following this, the SICBM was to be deployed in its mobile basing. Between 250 and 500 missiles were to be deployed during phase II with an IOC of 1,997. On administration views of the MX see John D. Morocco, "Cheney Endorses MX Rail Garrison, Calls for Few Cuts in USAF Budget," *Aviation Week and Space Technology*, 24 April 1989, 22. The administration's MX-SICBM plan and agreements with Congress are detailed in Thomas E. Halverson, "First Bush Defense Budget Reveals Program Cuts, Strategic Decisions," *Arms Control Today* 19, no. 4 (May 1989): 21, 27; Michael Gordon, "Bush Makes Proposal to Congress to Gain Funds for Mobile Missiles," *The New York Times*, 21 June 1989, A2; and Robert C. Toth, "Bush Appears to Win Significant Support for Missile Plan," *The Los Angeles Times*, 21 June 1989, 14.

17. See R. Jeffrey Smith, "U.S. to Seek Inspections to Ensure Strategic Arms Pact Is Verifiable," *The Washington Post*, 17 June 1989, A15; and R. Jeffrey Smith, "U.S. to Propose Monitoring Arms Plants Prior to Treaty," *The Washington Post*, 20 June 1989, 1.

18. These included notification of strategic exercises including missiles and bombers, a ban on the testing and deployment of depressed trajectory missiles, permanent on-site inspection of mobile missile production facilities, several verification experiments (tagging of mobile ICBMs, and verifying the number of warheads on a missile), a ban on telemetry encryption, and further data exchanges. James P. Rubin, "As START Resumes, Bush Pushes Early Verification," *Arms Control Today* 19, no. 6 (August 1989): 24–25.

19. On the importance of the Jackson Hole talks see Baker, *The Politics of Diplomacy*, 145–152. Baker and Shevardnadze two met six times in 1989, and 19 times in 1990 before Shevardnadze's resignation on 20 December 1990. Garthoff, *The Great Transition*, 382.

20. First, the Soviets ended their insistence that any START agreement be accompanied by an elimination of the SDI program. Second, Shevardnadze admitted that the Krasnoyarsk radar was a violation of the ABM Treaty and signaled that it was to be dismantled. Third, Shevardnadze agreed that SLCMs should not be included in the limits already set in the draft treaty. They could be dealt with in a separate protocol. Garthoff, *The Great Transition*, 384–85; Beschloss and Talbott, *At the Highest Levels*, 117–19; and "Joint Statement on

Arms Control," "Agreement on Verification and Stability Measures," and Agreement on Notification of Strategic Exercises," as printed in *Arms Control Today* 19, no. 8 (October 1989): 22, 24, 25, respectively.

21. Oberdorfer, *From the Cold War to a New Era*, 367; Bush and Scowcroft, *A World Transformed*, 46; and Beschloss and Talbott, *At the Highest Levels*, 127.

22. Garthoff, *The Great Transition*, 404; and Beschloss and Talbott, *At the Highest Levels*, 126–27.

23. Oberdorfer, *From the Cold War to a New Era*, 376; Garthoff, *The Great Transition*, 404–5; and Beschloss and Talbott, *At the Highest Levels*, 144–45.

24. Beschloss and Talbott, *At the Highest Levels*, 146.

25. Rowny, *It Takes One to Tango*, 236; Fitzwater, *Call the Briefing*, 269; Beschloss and Talbott, *At the Highest Levels*, 152–71; and Oberdorfer, *From the Cold War to a New Era*, 374–82.

26. Bush and Scowcroft, *A World Transformed*, 208; R. Jeffrey Smith, "Scowcroft Seeking Ban on Some Mobile Missiles," *The Washington Post*, 15 January 1990, 1; and Michael Gordon, "Bush Faces Decision on Arms Talks," *The New York Times*, 14 February 1990, A11; Bush and Scowcroft, *A World Transformed*, 219; and R. Jeffrey Smith, "Bush Rules Out Push to Junk Mobile Missiles," *The Washington Post*, 29 March 1990, A22.

27. In discussions in Moscow between Baker and Shevardnadze as well as Akhromeyev, issues concerning SLCM and ALCM counting rules and telemetry encryption were settled. On these exchanges see Matthew Bunn and Lee Feinstein, "Baker and Shevardnadze Clear START Road Blocks," *Arms Control Today* 20, no. 2 (March 1990): 21–22, 26; Garthoff, *The Great Transition*, 422–423; Beschloss and Talbott, *At the Highest Levels*, 183; Michael Gordon, "U.S. and Soviets Differ over a Ban on Multiple Warhead Missiles," *The New York Times*, 8 April 1990, 1; and Baker, *The Politics of Diplomacy*, 236.

28. Internal Soviet politics slowed the pace of successful negotiations by Baker and Shevardnadze. For details see Oberdorfer, *From the Cold War to a New Era*, 407–10; Michael Gordon, "U.S. Invites Ideas from the Soviets on Strategic Cuts," *The New York Times*, 12 February 1990, 1; and Garthoff, *The Great Transition*, 423. On the mid-May deal made by Baker and Shevardnadze on SLCM limits and specific ALCM counting rules see Dunbar Lockwood, "Bush-Gorbachev Concur: START to Be Finished by Year's End," *Arms Control Today* 20, no. 5 (June 1990): 28–29.

29. Negotiations were slowed by issues such as the reuse of warheads, the transfer of nuclear technology, U.S. sale of SLBMs to the United Kingdom, SDI research, the status of the Backfire (Tu-26) bomber, limits on SS-18 flight tests, and assorted verification problems. R. Jeffrey Smith, "Strategic Arms Talks at a Virtual Halt," *The Washington Post*, 5 August 1990, A8; Lockwood, "Bush-Gorbachev Concur: START to be Finished by Year's End," 28–29; and Dunbar Lockwood, "START Talks Stalled, 1990 Finish in Jeopardy," *Arms Control Today* 20, no. 7 (September 1990): 17, 21.

30. See Garthoff, *The Great Transition*, 463; Beschloss and Talbott, *At the Highest Levels*, 370–74; and Dunbar Lockwood, "Moscow Summit, START Signing Postponed," *Arms Control Today* 21, no. 2 (March 1991): 25, 28. Changes in the personnel on both sides had occurred in the interim period. Shevardnadze had resigned on 20 December. Bessmertnykh had assumed the post in January of 1991. Burt had also announced in January he would leave his position of chief START negotiator. He stayed on until March, then was replaced by his deputy Linton Brooks.

31. See Beschloss and Talbott, *At the Highest Levels*, 370–73, and 402; and Lockwood, "Moscow Summit, START Signing Postponed," 25.

32. On the SS-25 see R. Jeffrey Smith, "Arms Treaty Talks Settle Most Issues," *The Washington Post*, 15 July 1991, A1; and Beschloss and Talbott, *At the Highest Levels*, 405.

33. Membership included Bartholomew and James Timbie (State Department), Stephen Hadley (Defense Department), Doug MacEachin (CIA), Howard Graves, then General John Shalikashvili, then General Barry McCaffrey (JCS), and Vic Alessi (Energy Department). Beschloss and Talbott, *At the Highest Levels*, 365; and Baker, *The Politics of Diplomacy*, 660.

34. Doyle McManus, "U.S. Aides Can't Agree on START Treaty," *The Los Angeles Times*, 6 June 1991, A6; Thomas L. Friedman, "Baker and Russian May Meet on Arms Treaty," *The New York Times*, 6 June 1991, A11; and Beschloss and Talbott, *At the Highest Levels*, 403.

35. Thomas L. Friedman, "U.S. Arms Request Backed by Moscow," *The New York Times*, 9 July 1991, A1.

36. On these negotiations see Beschloss and Talbott, *At the Highest Levels*, 404–6; Thomas L. Friedman, "U.S. and Soviets Report Progress on Nuclear Pact," *The New York Times*, 14 July 1991, A1; and Thomas L. Friedman, "U.S. and Soviet Union Agree on All but Technical Issue for Strategic Arms Treaty," *The New York Times*, 15 July 1991, A1. See also Gerald Marsh, "The Ups and Downs of Downloading," *Bulletin of the Atomic Scientists* 47, no. 9 (November 1991): 21–23.

37. On these negotiations see Beschloss and Talbott, *At the Highest Levels*, 405–8; Smith, "Arms Treaty Talks Settle Most Issues," A1; and David Hoffman and John E. Yang, "U.S., Soviets Reach Pact Reducing Nuclear Arms," *The Washington Post*, 18 July 1991, A1. On the definition of a new type of missile see definition number 69 in the definitions Annex within the START treaty text. United States Arms Control and Disarmament Agency, *START: Treaty between the United States of America and the Union of Soviet Socialist Republics on the Reduction and Limitation of Strategic Offensive Arms*, 1991, 27; and "Strategic Arms Reduction Treaty (START): Analysis, Summary, Text," *Arms Control Today* 21, no. 9 (November 1991): 20. See United States Arms Control and Disarmament Agency, *START*. An excellent summary can be found in Pat Towell and Carroll J. Doherty, "START Sets Historic Terms for Nuclear Arms Curbs," *Congressional Quarterly* 49, no. 29 (20 July 1991): 1993–1998; "Strategic Arms Reduction Treaty: Analysis, Summary, Text," 1–24.

38. On these discussions see John E. Yang, "Bush Plan Emerged After Failed Coup," *The Washington Post*, 28 September 1991, A23; Andrew Rosenthal, "Arms Plan Germinated in Back Porch Sessions," *The New York Times*, 29 September 1991, A14; and Bush and Scowcroft, *A World Transformed*, 545.

39. These discussions are detailed in Powell, *My American Journey*, 541; Beschloss and Talbott, *At the Highest Levels*, 445; and Yang, "Bush Plan Emerged after Failed Coup," A23; and Rosenthal, "Arms Plan Germinated in Back Porch Sessions," A14.

40. Powell, *My American Journey*, 541; Rosenthal, "Arms Plan Germinated in Back Porch Sessions," A14; Bush and Scowcroft, *A World Transformed*, 546; and Yang, "Bush Plan Emerged after Failed Coup," A23.

41. Many of the new initiatives were unilateral and merely asked the USSR to match the U.S. actions. Bush stated that the U.S. would eliminate tactical nuclear weapons on surface ships and ground basing systems and asked the USSR to do the same. Bush also cancelled development of a new Short-Range Attack Missile (SRAM). The U.S. was going to take all

its strategic bombers off alert, ending the policy of keeping some on airborne patrol at all times. He asked the USSR to match this by putting all its mobile ICBMs in their garrisons on a permanent basis. ICBMs targeted for elimination under START were to be taken off alert. He also proposed that both the U.S. and USSR be limited to modernizing their ICBM forces with only one single-warhead ICBM. George Bush, "Address to the Nation on Nuclear Weapons Reductions," 27 September 1991, in U.S. President, *Public Papers of the Presidents of the United States* (Washington, DC: Office of the *Federal Register*, National Archives and Records Service, 1992), George Bush, 1991 Book 2, 1220–24. Scowcroft's influence can be seen in the proposal to limit new missiles to single-warhead capability.

42. See Bush and Scowcroft, *A World Restored*, 547; Jack Mendelsohn,"U.S., Soviets Continue Dialogue on Nuclear Cutbacks," *Arms Control Today* 21, no. 9 (November 1991): 17, 24; and "Arms Team to Visit Moscow," *The New York Times*, 3 October 1991, A8. The debate within the administration is detailed in R. Jeffrey Smith, "U.S. Considers 50% Cut in Strategic Nuclear Weapons, *The Washington Post*, 7 January 1992, A4; R. Jeffrey Smith, "Soviet Proposals Divide Bush Aides," *The Washington Post*, 25 October 1991, 1; Eric Schmitt, "Two Top Officials Reported to Differ On Arms Response," *The New York Times*, 26 October 1991, A5. Eric Schmitt, "U.S. Considers Move to Cut Multiple Warhead Missiles, Core of the Nuclear Force," *The New York Times*, 23 January 1992, A1; and R. Jeffrey Smith, "Bush Plans Steeper Arms Cuts," *The Washington Post*, 24 January 1992, A1. The text of the speech is reprinted in George Bush, "Address before a Joint Session of Congress on the State of the Union," 28 January 1992, U.S. President, *Public Papers of the Presidents of the United States* (Washington, DC: Office of the *Federal Register*, National Archives and Records Service, 1993), George Bush, 1992 Book I, 156–63.

43. See "START II: Analysis, Summary, Text," in *Arms Control Today* 23, no. 1 (January/ February 1993): 1–8.

44. Policy initiatives that might commit the U.S. to the expenditure of resources are different from those that only require the expenditure of rhetoric. Whether the former could so easily be slipped passed the bureaucracy is a question for further research.

45. On the political challenges to verification in START and the Senate INF debate see Graham Kinahar, "Ratification of START: Lessons from the INF Treaty," *Journal of Social, Political and Economic Studies* 14, no. 4 (winter 1989): 387–415; and Adam Garfinkle, "STARTing Over," *The National Interest* 20 (summer 1990): 71–76.

46. Friedman, "U.S. and Soviet Union Agree On All but Technical Issue for Strategic Arms Treaty," A1.

47. Author's interview with James Baker, 10 July 2001; and author's interview with Brent Scowcroft, 16 July 2001.

48. One danger here is that as crises arise the subordinates simply do not have the bureaucratic muscle or decision-making authority to get some issues on the agenda of the informal process. Issues may remain within the formal process, while the most important decision makers never address it within the informal settings that can make the difference. For example, as Saddam Hussein's attitude toward Kuwait grew more belligerent in 1990, the policy was still addressed by the formal part of the Bush administration, within the NSC/DC and within the State Department and NSC staff. Not until after the invasion took place did the informal small group begin to deal with the issue seriously. On pre-crisis U.S. policy toward Iraq see Baker, *The Politics of Diplomacy*, 269–74.

49. This conclusion was confirmed in the author's interview with James Baker, 10 July

2001, and the author's interview with Brent Scowcroft, 16 July 2001. Both men felt that the Bush administration was unusual in that respect.

50. See Woodward, *The Commanders*; and Christopher Madison, "Scrambling Vicar," *National Journal* 23, no. 16 (20 April 1991): 924–28. Baker and Powell had been reported to be more willing than the rest of the Gang of Eight during the Gulf War to continue sanctions for a greater period of time, rather than initiate military action against Kuwait.

51. On groupthink see Irving Janis, *Groupthink*. On the relationship between leadership and groupthink see Paul Kowert, *Groupthink or Deadlock* (Albany: State University of New York Press, 2002).

Chapter Seven

1. Iran-Contra can be placed on this list. One of the key problems in Iran-Contra was the ease with which NSC staffers felt they could simply shut out Secretary of State George Shultz and Secretary of Defense Caspar Weinberger from the decision making. This may have developed in part because of the fierce fighting between the hardliners and pragmatists. Excluding key decision makers who opposed specific policies from any meetings that considered those policies had become standard operating procedure.

2. See James MacGregor Burns, *The Deadlock of Democracy* (Englewood Cliffs: NJ, Prentice-Hall, 1962); Jon R. Bond and Richard Fleisher, *The President in the Legislative Arena* (Chicago: University of Chicago, 1990); and Jon R. Bond and Richard Fleisher, ed., *Polarized Politics* (Washington, DC: Congressional Quarterly Press, 2000).

3. Bert Rockman, "The Style and Organization of the Reagan Presidency," 5.

4. Quoted in I. M. Destler, *Presidents, Bureaucrats, and Foreign Policy*, 90.

5. Henry Kissinger, *White House Years*, 31.

6. This point is stressed in other analyses as well. See Rockman, "The Style and Organization of the Reagan Presidency," *The Reagan Legacy*, ed. Jones, 19–20; and James J. Best, "Presidential Learning: A Comparative Study of the Interactions of Carter and Reagan," *Congress and the Presidency* 15, no. 1 (spring 1988): 26. Rockman states that presidents learn to whom they should listen and whom they should ignore by the midpoint of their first term.

7. As told to John Kenneth Galbraith and quoted in Galbraith, *Ambassador's Journal* (Boston: Houghton-Mifflin Company, 1969), 7.

8. The use of the term *structure* rather than *system* here reflects a difference between the formal interagency process or system and the informal and confidence structures. The interagency structure could also be called a process or a system since it has well-defined procedures, staffing requirements, and committee relationships. The term structure is used for the latter two since these have ill-defined or completely informal and ad hoc procedures, staffing requirements, and participation. The confidence structure may simply be as informal as the president and one of his senior advisers engaging in frequent brainstorming sessions on a regular, though nonplanned basis.

9. Brzezinski attempted to bring Turner close to the president. These efforts failed. Turner remained more distant from the president than other senior advisers. Author's interview with Zbigniew Brzezinski, 11 June 2001; and author's interview with David Aaron, 11 July 2001.

10. Bob Woodward, *Veil*, 1987.

11. Kennedy's quick disillusionment with DCI Allen Dulles and the Joint Chiefs of Staff

is one example, as is Secretary of State Alexander Haig's activities during the assassination attempt on President Reagan in March of 1981.

12. David Aaron, deputy ANSA in the Carter administration, suggests that those auditions take a great deal of time, if they ever end at all. Author's interview with David Aaron, 11 July 2001.

13. See Robert Gallucci, *Neither Peace nor Honor* (Baltimore: The Johns Hopkins University Press, 1975), 7.

14. John P. Burke and Fred Greenstein, *How Presidents Test Reality*, 1989.

15. See John L. Hirsch and Robert B. Oakley, *Somalia and Operation Restore Hope* (Washington, DC: United States Institute of Peace Press, 1994).

16. A look at the difficulties of reorganizing to deal with the new threats is found in William W. Newmann, "Reorganizing for National Security and Homeland Security, *Public Administration Review* 50 (special issue): 126–37.

17. John Kingdon, *Agendas, Alternatives, and Public Policies* (New York: Harper Collins, 1984), 174–80.

18. Kenneth N. Waltz, *Theory of International Politics* (New York, Random House, 1979); Colin Elman, "Horses for Courses: Why Not Neorealist Theories of Foreign Policy?" *Security Studies* 6, no. 1 (autumn 1996): 7–53; and Kenneth N. Waltz, "International Politics Is Not Foreign Policy," *Security Studies* 6, no. 1 (autumn 1996): 54–57.

19. A major debate about the merits of rational choice models vs. more traditional models that include historical, cultural, leadership, and decision-making factors is under way in the field of international relations. See Stephen Walt, "Rigor or Rigor Mortis: Rational Choice and Security Studies," *International Security* 23, no. 4 (spring 1999): 5–48; Bruce Bueno de Mesquita and James D. Morrow, "Sorting through the Wealth of Notions," *International Security* 24, no. 2 (fall 1999): 56–73; Lisa L. Martin, "The Contributions of Rational Choice," *International Security* 24, no. 2 (fall 1999): 74–83; Emerson M. S. Niou and Peter C. Ordeshook, "Return of the Luddites," *International Security* 24, no. 2 (fall 1999): 84–96; Robert Powell, "The Modeling Enterprise and Security Studies," *International Security* 24, no. 2 (fall 1999): 97–106; Frank C. Zagare, "All Mortis, No Rigor," *International Security* 24, no. 2 (fall 1999): 107–13; and Stephen Walt, "A Model Disagreement," *International Security* 24, no. 2 (fall 1999): 115–30.

20. Marie T. Henehan, *Foreign Policy and Congress* (Ann Arbor, MI: University of Michigan Press, 2000).

21. Peter J. Katzenstein, *Cultural Norms and National Security* (Ithaca: Cornell University Press, 1996); Alexander Wendt, *Social Theory of International Politics* (Cambridge: Cambridge University Press, 1999); Jack Snyder, *Myths of Empire* (Ithaca, NY: Cornell University Press, 1991); Thomas J. Christensen, *Useful Adversaries* (Princeton, NJ: Princeton University Press, 1996); and Fareed Zakaria, *From Wealth to Power* (Princeton, NJ: Princeton University Press, 1998). For a general overview of the state of realism and neorealism see Jeffrey W. Legro and Andrew Moravcsik, "Is Anybody Still a Realist," *International Security* 24, no. 2 (fall 1999): 5–55.

22. The earlier study is contained in William W. Newmann, "An Evolutionary Model of Foreign Policy Decision Making" (Ph.D diss., Graduate School of Public and International Affairs, University of Pittsburgh, 1999).

This research was conducted using primary and secondary sources. The primary sources include memoirs, archival material, and interviews, the National Security Archive at George Washington University, the Jimmy Carter Presidential Library, and George Bush Presidential Library internet-based resources (http://bushlibrary.tamu.edu). Interviews were conducted with the following officials:

Zbigniew Brzezinski, Assistant to the President for National Security Affairs, Carter Administration, 11 June 2001

David Aaron, Deputy Assistant to the President for National Security Affairs, Carter Administration, 11 July 2001

David Newsom, Undersecretary of State for Political Affairs, Carter Administration, 6 July 2001

James A. Baker, Secretary of State, Bush Administration, 10 July 2001

Brent Scowcroft, Assistant to the President for National Security Affairs, Bush Administration, 16 July 2001

Presidential directives from the Reagan and Bush administrations cited in the endnotes were found in Simpson, Christopher, ed., *National Security Directives of the Reagan and Bush Administrations*. Boulder: Westview Press, 1995. They are not listed individually in the bibliography unless taken from other sources.

Material from the following newspapers and weekly periodicals has also been used in this book. These sources are cited within the text as necessary: *New York Times, Washington Post, Los Angeles Times, Wall Street Journal, Boston Globe, Time, Newsweek,* and *U.S. News and World Report*.

General sources on the presidency, decision making, and national security

Aberbach, Joel D., and Bert A. Rockman, "Mandates or Mandarins? Control and Discretion in the Modern Administrative State." In *The Managerial Presidency*, edited by James P. Pfiffner, 158–79. Pacific Grove: Brooks/Cole Publishing, 1991.

Allison, Graham. "Conceptual Models and the Cuban Missile Crisis." *American Political Science Review* 63, no. 3 (September 1969): 698–718.

———. *Essence of Decision*. Boston: Little, Brown, and Company, 1971.

Allison, Graham, and Morton Halperin. "Bureaucratic Politics: A Paradigm and Some Policy Implications." *World Politics* 24 (supplement, 1972): 40–79.

Allison, Graham, and Peter Szanton. *Remaking Foreign Policy*. New York: Basic Books, 1975.

Allison, Graham, and Philip Zelikow. *Essence of Decision*. 2d ed. New York: Addison Wesley Longman, 1999.

Ambrose, Stephen. *Eisenhower: The President*. Vol. 2. New York: Simon and Schuster, 1984.

Art, Robert. "Bureaucratic Politics and American Foreign Policy: A Critique." *Policy Sciences* 4, no. 4 (December 1973): 467–90.

Auger, Victor A. "The National Security Council System after the Cold War." In *US Foreign Policy after the Cold War,* edited by Randall B. Ripley and James M. Lindsay, 42–73. Pittsburgh: University of Pittsburgh Press, 1997.

Axelrod, Robert, ed. *The Structure of Decision.* Princeton: Princeton University Press, 1976.

Ball, Desmond. "The Blind Men and the Elephant: A Critique of Bureaucratic Politics Theory." *Australian Outlook* 28, no. 1 (April 1974): 71–92.

Baldwin, David, ed. *Neorealism and Neoliberalism.* New York: Columbia University Press, 1993.

Barber, James David. *The Presidential Character.* Englewood Cliffs: Prentice-Hall, 1992.

Best, James J. "Presidential Learning: A Comparative Study of the Interactions of Carter and Reagan." *Congress and the Presidency* 15, no. 1 (spring 1988): 25–48.

Bond, Jon R., and Richard Fleisher. *The President in the Legislative Arena.* Chicago: University of Chicago Press, 1990.

Bond, Jon R., and Richard Fleisher, eds. *Polarized Politics.* Washington, D.C.: Congressional Quarterly Press, 2000.

Bose, Meena. *Shaping and Signaling Presidential Policy: The National Security Decision Making of Eisenhower and Kennedy.* College Station, TX: Texas A & M Press, 1998.

Brady, Linda P. "The Situation and Foreign Policy." In *Why Nations Act,* edited by Stephen Salmore and Charles Hermann, 173–90. Beverly Hills: Sage Publications, 1978.

Braybrooke, David, and Charles Lindblom. *A Strategy of Decision.* New York: Free Press, 1963.

Breslauer, George, and Philip Tetlock, eds. *Learning in U.S. and Soviet Foreign Policy.* Boulder: Westview Press, 1991.

Brzezinski, Zbigniew. "The NSC's Midlife Crisis." *Foreign Policy* 69 (winter 1987/88): 80–99.

Buchanan, Bruce. "Constrained Diversity: The Organizational Demands of the Presidency." In *The Managerial Presidency,* edited by James Pfiffner, 78–104. Pacific Grove: Brooks/Cole Publishing, 1991.

Burke, John. *The Institutional Presidency.* Baltimore: The Johns Hopkins University Press, 1992.

Burke, John, and Fred Greenstein. *How Presidents Test Reality.* New York: Russell Sage Foundation, 1989.

Burns, James MacGregor. *The Deadlock of Democracy.* Englewood Cliffs: Prentice-Hall, 1962.

———. *Presidential Government.* Boston: Houghton Mifflin, 1966.

Burns, Tom, and G. M. Stalker. *The Management of Innovation.* London: Tavistock Publications, 1961.

Bush (G. W.) Administration. *Executive Order Establishing Office of Homeland Security.* 8 October 2001. http://www.whitehouse.gov/news/releases/2001/10/print/20011008-2.html

Bush (G. W.) Administration. *Homeland Security Presidential Directive-1, Organization and Operation of the Homeland Security Council,* 29 October 2002. http://www.fas.org/irp/offdocs/nspd/hspd-1.htm

Campbell, Colin. *Managing the Presidency.* Pittsburgh: University of Pittsburgh Press, 1986.

Chandler, Alfred. *Strategy and Structure.* Cambridge: MIT Press, 1962.

Child, John. "Organizational Structure, Environment, and Performance: The Role of Strategic Choice." *Sociology* 6, no. 1 (January 1972): 1–22.

Clark, Keith C., and Laurence J. Legere. *The President and the Management of National Security.* New York: Praeger, 1969.

Corwin, Edward S. *The President: Office and Powers*, 4th ed. New York: New York University Press, 1967.

Cyr, Arthur. "The National Security Assistant: Helmsman, Captain, or First Mate." *Atlantic Community Quarterly* 20, no. 1 (spring 1982): 74–85.

Daalder, Ivo H., and I. M. Destler, moderators. *National Security Council Project: Oral History Roundtables: The Role of the National Security Adviser*. College Park, MD and Washington, D.C.: Center for International and Security Studies at Maryland, School of Public Affairs, University of Maryland and The Brookings Institution, 1999. http://www.brookings.edu/dybdocroot/fp/projects/nsc/transcripts/19991025.htm. Accessed 20 March 2002.

———. *National Security Council Project: Oral History Roundtables: Arms Control Policy and the National Security Council*. College Park, MD, and Washington, D.C.: Center for International and Security Studies at Maryland, School of Public Affairs, University of Maryland and The Brookings Institution, 2000. http://www.brookings.edu/dybdocroot/fp/projects/nsc/transcripts/20000325.htm. Accessed 20 March 2002.

———. *National Security Council Project: Oral History Roundtables: The Bush Administration National Security Council*. College Park, MD, and Washington, D.C.: Center for International and Security Studies at Maryland, School of Public Affairs, University of Maryland and The Brookings Institution, 2000. http://www.brookings.edu/dybdocroot/fp/projects/nsc/transcripts/19990429.htm. Accessed 20 March 2002.

Destler, I. M. *Presidents, Bureaucrats, and Foreign Policy*. Princeton: Princeton University Press, 1972.

———. "Comment: Multiple Advocacy: Some 'Limits and Costs.'" *American Political Science Review* 66, no. 3 (September 1972): 786–95.

———. "National Security Advice to U.S. Presidents: Some Lessons from Thirty Years." *World Politics* 29, no. 2 (January 1977): 143–76.

———. "A Job That Doesn't Work." *Foreign Policy* 38 (spring 1980): 80–88.

Dickinson, Mathew J. *Bitter Harvest*. Cambridge: Cambridge University Press, 1997.

Elman, Colin. "Horses for Courses: Why Not Neorealist Theories of Foreign Policy?" *Security Studies* 6, no. 1 (autumn 1996): 7–53.

Etheredge, Lloyd. *Can the Government Learn?* New York: Pergamon Press, 1985.

Fenno, Richard. *The President's Cabinet*. Cambridge: Harvard University Press, 1959.

Fleisher, Richard, and Jon R. Bond. "Are There Two Presidencies? Yes, But Only for Republicans." *Journal of Politics* 50, no. 3 (August 1988): 747–67.

Fleisher, Richard, Jon R. Bond, Glen S. Krutz, and Stephen Hanna. "The Demise of the Two Presidencies." *American Politics Quarterly* 28, no. 1 (January 2000): 3–25.

Ford, Gerald. *A Time to Heal*. New York: Harper and Row, 1979.

Galbraith, John Kenneth. *Ambassador's Journal*. Boston: Houghton Mifflin and Co., 1969.

Gallucci, Robert. *Neither Peace Nor Honor*. Baltimore: The Johns Hopkins University Press, 1975.

Garrison, Jean A. *Games Advisers Play: Foreign Policy in the Nixon and Carter Administrations*. College Station, TX: Texas A&M University Press, 1999.

Gelb, Leslie, and Anthony Lake. *Our Own Worst Enemy*. New York: Simon and Schuster, 1984.

George, Alexander. "The Operational Code: A Neglected Approach to the Study of Political Leaders and Decision Making." *International Studies Quarterly* 13, no. 2 (June 1969): 190–222.

———. "The Case for Multiple Advocacy in Making Foreign Policy." *American Political Science Review* 66, no. 3 (September 1972): 751–85.

———. "Case Studies and Theory Development: The Method of Structured, Focused Comparison." In *Diplomacy: New Approaches in History, Theory, and Policy*, edited by Paul Gordon Lauren, 43–68. New York: Free Press, 1979.

———. "Assessing Presidential Character." *World Politics* 26, no. 2 (January 1974): 234–82.

———. *Presidential Decision Making in Foreign Policy*. Boulder: Westview Press, 1980.

George, Alexander, and Timothy J. McKeown. "Case Studies and Theories of Organizational Decision Making." In *Advances in Information Processing in Organizations*, vol. 2. Edited by Robert F. Coulam and Richard A. Smith. Greenwich: JAI Press, 1985.

George, Alexander, and Eric Stern. "Presidential Management Styles and Models." In *Presidential Personality and Performance*, edited by Alexander L. George and Juliette L. George, 199–280. Boulder: Westview Press, 1998.

Gore, William. *Administrative Decision Making*. New York: John Wiley and Sons, 1964.

Greenstein, Fred. *The Presidential Difference*. New York: The Free Press, 2000.

Hagan, Joe. "Does Decision Making Matter? Systemic Assumptions vs. Historical Reality in International Relations Theory." *International Studies Review* 3, no. 2 (summer 2001): 5–46.

Hall, David K. "The 'Custodian-Manager' of the Policy-Making Process." *Commission on the Organization of the Government for the Conduct of Foreign Policy (Murphy Commission)*, vol. 2, appendix D, chapter 12, June 1975, 100–118.

Halperin, Morton. "The Decision to Deploy the ABM: Bureaucratic and Domestic Politics in the Johnson Administration." *World Politics* 25, no. 1 (October 1972): 62–95.

———. *Bureaucratic Politics and Foreign Policy*. Washington, D.C.: Brookings Institution Press, 1974.

Halperin, Morton, and David Halperin. "The Key West Key." *Foreign Policy* 52 (winter 1983/84): 114–28.

Halperin, Morton, and Arnold Kanter. "The Bureaucratic Perspective." In *Readings in American Foreign Policy*, edited by Halperin and Kanter, 1–42. Boston: Little, Brown, 1973.

Hammond, Paul Y. *Organizing for Defense*. Princeton: Princeton University Press, 1961.

Haney, Patrick J. *Organizing for Foreign Policy Crises*. Ann Arbor: University of Michigan Press, 1997.

Hart, John. *The Presidential Branch*, 2d ed. Chatham, NJ: Chatham House, 1995.

Heclo, Hugh. "The Changing Presidential Office." In *The Managerial Presidency*. Edited by James A. Pfiffner. Pacific Grove, CA: Brooks/Cole Publishing, 1991.

Henderson, Phillip G. *Managing the Presidency: The Eisenhower Legacy from Kennedy to Reagan*. Boulder: Westview Press, 1988

Hermann, Charles, ed. *International Crises*. New York: Free Press, 1972.

Hermann, Charles F., Janice Gross Stein, Bengt Sundelius, and Stephen G. Walker. "Resolve, Accept, or Avoid: Effects of Group Conflict on Foreign Policy Decision." *International Studies Review* 3, no. 2 (summer 2001): 133–68;

Hermann, Margaret, and Thomas Preston. "Presidents, Advisers, and Foreign Policy: The Effects of Leadership Style on Executive Arrangements." *Political Psychology* 15, no. 1 (1994): 75–96.

Hess, Stephen. *Organizing the Presidency*. Washington, D.C.: Brookings Institution Press, 1988.

Hilsman, Roger. "The Foreign Policy Consensus: An Interim Research Report." *Journal of Conflict Resolution* 3, no. 4 (December 1959): 361–82.

———. *The Politics of Policy Making in Defense and Foreign Affairs*. New York: Harper and Row, 1971.

Holsti, Ole. "Theories of Crisis Decision Making." In *Diplomacy: New Approaches in History, Theory, and Policy*, ed. Paul Gordon Lauren, 99–136. New York: Free Press, 1979.

———. "Crisis Decision Making." In *Behavior, Society, and Nuclear War*, edited by Philip E. Tetlock et al., 8–84. New York: Oxford University Press, 1989.

Hoopes, Townsend. *The Devil and John Foster Dulles*. Boston: Little, Brown, 1973.

Hoyt, Paul D. "The Political Manipulation of Group Composition: Engineering the Decision Context." *Political Psychology* 18, no. 4, (1997): 771–90.

Hoyt, Paul D., and Jean A. Garrison. "Political Manipulation within the Small Group: Foreign Policy Advisers in the Carter Administration." In *Beyond Groupthink*. Edited by Paul 't Hart, Eric K. Stern, and Bengt Sundelius. Ann Arbor: University of Michigan Press, 1997.

Janis, Irving. *Groupthink*. 2d ed. Boston: Houghton Mifflin, 1982.

Janis, Irving, and Leon Mann. *Decision Making*. New York: Free Press, 1977.

Johnson, Richard T. *Managing the White House*. New York: Harper and Row, 1974.

Kahneman, Daniel, Paul Slovic, and Amos Tversky, eds. *Judgment under Uncertainty*. Cambridge, MA: Cambridge University Press, 1982.

Keohane, Robert , ed. *Neorealism and Its Critics*. New York: Columbia University Press, 1986.

Kingdon, John. *Agendas, Alternatives, and Public Policies*. New York: Harper Collins, 1984.

Kissinger, Henry A. *White House Years*. Boston: Little, Brown, 1979.

Kohl, Wilfred. "The Nixon-Kissinger Foreign Policy System and U.S.-European Relations: Patterns of Policy Making." *World Politics* 28, no. 1 (October 1975): 1–43.

Kowert, Paul. *Groupthink or Deadlock*. Albany: State University of New York Press, 2002.

Krasner, Stephen. "Are Bureaucracies Important? (Or Allison Wonderland)." *Foreign Policy* 7 (summer 1972): 159–79.

Lake, David, and Robert Powell, eds. *Strategic Choice and International Relations*. Princeton: Princeton University Press, 1999.

Lawrence, Paul, and Jay Lorsch. *Organizations and Environment*. Cambridge: Harvard University, 1967.

Leites, Nathan. *A Study of Bolshevism*. Glencoe, IL: Free Press, 1953.

Lepgold, Joseph, and Alan C. Lamborn. "Locating Bridges: Connecting Research Agendas on Cognition and Strategic Choice." *International Studies Review* 3, no. 3 (fall 2001): 3–29.

Levy, Jack S. "Learning and Foreign Policy: Sweeping a Conceptual Minefield." *International Organization* 48, no. 2 (spring 1994): 279–312.

Light, Paul Charles. *The President's Agenda*. Baltimore: The Johns Hopkins University Press, 1982.

Lindblom, Charles. "The Science of Muddling Through." *Public Administration Review*, 19, no. 2 (spring 1959): 79–88.

Lowenthal, Mark. "The National Security Council: Organizational History." Congressional Research Service Background Paper. In U.S. Senate. Committee on Foreign Relations. *The National Security Advisor: Role and Accountability: Hearing before the Committee on Foreign Relations*. 96th Cong., 2d sess., 17 April 1980, 53–105.

Lowi, Theodore. *The Personal Presidency*. Ithaca: Cornell University Press, 1985.

March, James, and Herbert Simon. *Organizations*. New York: John Wiley and Sons, 1958.

March, James, and Johan P. Olsen. *Ambiguity and Choice in Organizations*. Bergen, Norway Universitetsferlaget, 1976.

Moe, Terry M. "The Politics of Bureaucratic Structure." In *Can the Government Govern*, edited by John E. Chubb and Paul E. Peterson, 267–329. Washington, D.C.: Brookings Institution Press, 1989.

———. "The Politics of Structural Choice: Toward a Theory of Public Bureaucracy." In *Organization Theory: From Chester Barnard to the Present and Beyond*, edited by Oliver Williamson, 116–53. New York: Oxford University Press, 1995.

———. "The Presidency and the Bureaucracy: The Presidential Advantage." In *The Presidency and the Political System*, 5th edition, edited by Michael Nelson, 437–68. Washington, D.C.: Congressional Quarterly Press, 1998.

Moe, Terry M., and Scott A. Wilson. "Presidents and the Politics of Structure." *Law and Contemporary Problems* 57, no. 2 (spring 1994): 1–44.

Neustadt, Richard. *Presidential Power and the Modern Presidents*. New York: Free Press, 1990.

Newmann, William W. "Reorganizing for National Security and Homeland Security. *Public Administration Review* 62 (special issue.): 90–101.

Nichols, David. *The Myth of the Modern Presidency*. University Park: The Pennsylvania State University Press, 1994.

Odeen, Philip. "Organizing for National Security." *International Security* 5, no. 1 (summer 1980): 111–29.

Pearlmutter, Amos. "The Presidential Political Center and Foreign Policy." *World Politics* 27, no. 1 (October 1974): 87–106.

Ponder, Daniel F. *Good Advice*. College Station: Texas A&M University Press, 2000.

Porter, Roger. *Presidential Decision Making: The Economic Policy Board*. Cambridge: Cambridge University Press, 1980.

Prados, John. *The Keepers of the Keys*. New York: William Morrow and Co., 1991.

Preston, Thomas. "'Follow the Leader': The Impact of U.S. Presidential Style upon Advisory Group Dynamics, Structure, and Decision." In *Beyond Groupthink*. Edited by Paul 't Hart, Eric Stern, and Bengt Sundelius, 191–248. Ann Arbor: University of Michigan Press, 1997.

———. *The President and His Inner Circle*. New York: Columbia University Press, 2001.

Preston, Thomas, and Paul 't Hart. "Understanding and Evaluating Bureaucratic Politics: The Nexus between Political Leaders and Advisory Systems." *Political Psychology* 20, no. 1 (1999): 49–98.

Reedy, George. *The Twilight of the Presidency*. New York: New American Library, 1970.

Report of the President's Special Review Board (The Tower Commission Report). New York: Bantam Books, Times Books, 1987.

Rhodes, Edward. "Do Bureaucratic Politics Matter? Some Disconfirming Findings from the U.S. Navy." *World Politics* 47, no. 1 (October 1994): 1–41.

Rockman, Bert. "America's Departments of State: Irregular and Regular Syndromes of Policy Making." *American Political Science Review* 75, no. 4 (December 1981): 911–27.

———. "The Style and Organization of the Reagan Presidency." In *The Reagan Legacy*. Edited by Charles O. Jones (Chatham, NJ: Chatham House Publishers, 1988).

Rosati, Jerel. "Developing a Systematic Decision-Making Framework: Bureaucratic Politics in Perspective." *World Politics* 3, no. 2 (1981): 234–53.

Rossiter, Clinton. *The American Presidency*. Rev. ed. New York: Harcourt, Brace, and World, 1960.

Rourke, Francis. *Bureaucracy and Foreign Policy*. Baltimore: The Johns Hopkins University Press, 1972.

Schilling, Warner, Paul Hammond, and Glenn Snyder. *Strategy, Politics, and Defense Budgets*. New York: Columbia University Press, 1962.

Seidman, Harold. *Politics, Position, and Power*. New York: Oxford University Press, 1986.

Selznick, Philip. *Leadership in Administration*. Evanston: Row, Peterson, and Co., 1957.

Shoemaker, Christopher. *The National Security Council Staff: Structure and Functions*. Association of the U.S. Army Land Warfare Paper 3, December 1989.

Simon, Herbert. "A Behavioral Model of Rational Choice." *Quarterly Journal of Economics* 69, no. 1 (February 1955): 99–118.

———. *The New Science of Management Decision*. New York: Harper and Row, 1960.

———. *Administrative Behavior*, 2d ed. New York: MacMillan, 1961.

Snow, Donald, and Eugene Brown. *Beyond the Water's Edge*. New York: St. Martins, 1997.

Steiner, Miriam. "The Search for Order in a Disorderly World: Worldviews and Prescriptive Decision Paradigms." *International Organization* 37, no. 3 (summer 1983): 373–414.

Stern, Eric, and Bertjon Verbeek, ed. "Whither the Study of Governmental Politics: A Symposium." *Mershon International Studies Review* 42, Supplement 2 (November 1998): 205–56

Szanton, Peter. "Two Jobs, Not One." *Foreign Policy* 38 (spring 1980): 89–91.

Thompson, James D. *Organizations in Action*. New York: McGraw-Hill, 1967.

Thompson, Robert J. "Contrasting Models of White House Staff Organization: The Eisenhower, Ford, and Carter Experiences." *Congress and the Presidency* 19, no. 2 (autumn 1992): 113–36.

U.S. Senate Committee on Foreign Relations. *The National Security Adviser: Role and Accountability: Hearing before the Committee on Foreign Relations*. 96th Cong., 2d sess., 1980.

U.S. Senate Committee on Armed Services. *Defense Organization: The Need for Change*. 99th Cong., 1st sess., 1985. S. Rept.

Walcott, Charles E., and Karen M. Hult. *Governing the White House*. Lawrence: University Press of Kansas, 1995.

Waltz, Kenneth N. "International Politics Is Not Foreign Policy." *Security Studies* 6, no. 1 (autumn 1996): 54–7.

———. *Theory of International Politics*. New York: Random House, 1979.

Welch, David. "The Organizational Process Model and the Bureaucratic Politics Paradigm." *International Security* 17, no. 2 (fall 1992): 112–46.

Weko, Thomas J. *The Politicizing Presidency*. Lawrence: University Press of Kansas, 1995.

Wildavsky, Aaron. *The Beleaguered Presidency*. New Brunswick, NJ: Transaction Books, 1991.

Woodward, Joan. *Management and Technology*. London: Her Majesty's Stationary Office, 1958.

Zegart, Amy B. *Flawed by Design*. Stanford: Stanford University Press, 1999.

The Carter Administration

Andrianopolous, Gerry Argyris. *Kissinger and Brzezinski*. New York: St. Martin's Press, 1991.

Ball, Desmond. *Politics and Force Levels: The Strategic Missile Programs of the Kennedy Administration*. Berkeley: University of California Press, 1980.

———. "U.S. Strategic Forces: How Would They Be Used." *International Security* 7, no. 3 (winter 1982–83): 31–60.

———. *Targeting for Strategic Deterrence*. Adelphi Papers 185. London: International Institute for Strategic Studies, 1983.

———. "Counterforce Targeting. How New? How Viable?" In *American Defense Policy*, edited by John Reichart and Steven Sturm, 227–33. Baltimore: The Johns Hopkins University Press, 1984.

———. "The Development of the SIOP, 1960–1983." In *Strategic Nuclear Targeting*, edited by Desmond Ball and Jeffrey Richelson, 57–83. Ithaca: Cornell University Press, 1986.

Berger, Marilyn. "Vance and Brzezinski: Peaceful Coexistence or Guerilla Warfare." *The New York Times Magazine* (13 February 1977): 19, 21, 23, 24–25, 38, 41.

Bonafede, Dom. "Carter Staff Is Getting Itchy to Move to Washington." *National Journal* 8, no. 44 (30 October 1976): 1542–47.

———. "Brzezinski: Stepping Out of His Backstage Role," *National Journal* 9, no. 24 (15 October 1977): 1596–1601.

Bowie, Robert R., and Richard H. Immerman, *Waging Peace: How Eisenhower Shaped an Enduring Cold War Legacy.* New York: Oxford University Press, 1998.

Brodie, Bernard, ed. *The Absolute Weapon*. New York: Harcourt, Brace, 1946.

Brown, Harold. *Report of Secretary of Defense Harold Brown to Congress on the FY 1980 Budget, FY 1981 Authorization Request, and FY 1981–1984 Defense Programs.* Washington, D.C.: Government Printing Office, 25 January 1979.

———. "The Flexibility of Our Plans." *Vital Speeches of the Day* 46, no. 24 (1 October 1980): 741–44.

———. *Report of the Secretary of Defense Harold Brown to the Congress on the FY 1981 Budget, FY 1982 Authorization Request, and FY 1981–1985 Defense Programs.* Washington, D.C.: Government Printing Office, 29 January 1980.

———. *Report of Secretary of Defense Harold Brown to Congress on the FY 1982 Budget, FY 1983 Authorization Request, and FY 1982–1986 Defense Programs.* Washington, D.C.: Government Printing Office, 19 January 1981.

Brzezinski, Zbigniew. *Power and Principle*. New York: Farrar, Straus, Giroux, 1983.

Burt, Richard. "Zbig Makes It Big." *The New York Times Magazine* (30 July 1978): 8–10, 18, 20, 28.

Caldwell, Dan. *The Dynamics of Domestic Politics and Arms Control.* Columbia: University of South Carolina Press, 1991.

Carter Administration. *Presidential Directive/NSC-1 (PD-1), Establishment of Presidential Review and Directive Series/NSC.* 20 January 1977.

———. *Presidential Directive/NSC-2 (PD-2), The National Security Council System.* 20 January 1977.

———. *Presidential Directive/NSC-18 (PD-18), U.S. National Strategy.* 24 August 1977. Washington, D.C.: National Security Archive.

———. *Presidential Directive/NSC-53 (PD-53), National Security Telecommunications Policy.* 15 November 1979. Washington, D.C.: National Security Archive.

———. *Presidential Directive/NSC-59 (PD-59), Nuclear Weapons Employment Policy.* 25 July 1980. Washington, D.C.: National Security Archive.

———. *Presidential Review Memorandum/NSC-10 (PRM-10), Comprehensive Net Assessment and Military Force Posture Review.* 18 February 1977. Washington, D.C.: National Security Archive.

———. *Presidential Review Memorandum/NSC-10 (PRM-10), Military Strategy and Force Posture Review: Final Report.* June 1977. Washington, D.C.: National Security Archive.

Carter, Jimmy. *Why Not the Best?* Nashville: Broadman Press, 1975.

———. "Making Foreign and Defense Policy: Openness, Coherence, and Efficiency." *National Journal* 8, no. 43 (23 October 1976): 1528–9.

———. *Keeping Faith*. New York: Bantam, 1982.

Davis, Lynn E. *Limited Nuclear Options: Deterrence and the New American Doctrine*. Adelphi Papers 121. London: International Institute of Strategic Studies, 1976.

Davis, Vincent. "The President and the National Security Apparatus." In *Defense Policy and the Presidency: Carter's First Years*, edited by Sam Sarkesian, 53–110. Boulder: Westview Press, 1979.

Dockrell, Saki. *Eisenhower's New Look National Security Policy, 1953–1961*. New York: St. Martin's, 1996.

Drew, Elizabeth. "A Reporter at Large: Brzezinski." *The New Yorker* 54, no. 11 (1 May 1978): 90, 95–118, 121–30.

Dumbrell, John. *The Carter Presidency*. Manchester: Manchester University Press, 1993.

Edwards, John. *Superweapon: The Making of the MX*. New York: W. W. Norton and Co., 1982.

Fallows, James. "The Passionless Presidency." *The Atlantic Monthly* 243, no. 5 (May 1979): 33–48.

———. "Zbig without Cy." *The New Republic* 182, no. 19 (10 May 1980): 17–19.

Freedman, Lawrence. *The Evolution of Nuclear Strategy*. New York: St. Martin's, 1983.

Garthoff, Raymond. *Détente and Confrontation*. Washington, D.C.: Brookings Institution Press, 1985.

Gelb, Leslie. "Muskie and Brzezinski: The Struggle over Foreign Policy." *The New York Times Magazine* (20 July 1980): 26–27, 32, 34–35, 38–40.

Germond, Jack, and Jules Witcover. *Blue Smoke and Mirrors*. New York: Viking Press, 1981.

Gervasi, Tom. *The Myth of Soviet Military Supremacy*. New York: Harper and Row, 1986.

Gottemoeller, Rose. *Evolution of U.S. Organizational Setup for Dealing with SALT*. Santa Monica: The Rand Corporation, November 1978.

Hargrove, Erwin. *Jimmy Carter as President*. Baton Rouge: Louisiana State University Press, 1988.

Holloway, David. *The Soviet Union and the Arms Race*. New Haven: Yale University Press, 1983.

Huntington, Samuel. "The Renewal of Strategy." In *The Strategic Imperative*, edited by Samuel Huntington, 1–52. Cambridge: Ballinger, 1982.

Hyland, William. *Mortal Rivals*. New York: Random House, 1987.

Jervis, Robert. *The Illogic of American Nuclear Strategy*. Ithaca: Cornell University Press, 1984.

Jones, Charles O. *The Trusteeship Presidency: Jimmy Carter and the United States Congress*. Baton Rouge: Louisiana State University Press, 1988.

Kaufmann, William. *The McNamara Strategy*. New York: Harper and Row, 1964.

Kirschten, Dick. "Beyond the Vance-Brzezinski Clash Lurks an NSC Under Fire." *National Journal* 12, no. 20 (18 May 1980): 814–18.

Korb, Lawrence. "National Security Organization and Process in the Carter Administration." In *Defense Policy and the Presidency: Carter's First Years*, edited by Sam Sarkesian. Boulder: Westview Press, 1979.

Labrie, Roger, ed. *The SALT Handbook*. Washington, D.C.: The American Enterprise Institute, 1979.

Lake, Anthony. "Carter's Foreign Policy: Success Abroad; Failure at Home: Interview with

Anthony Lake," interview by Kenneth Thompson, *The Carter Presidency*, ed., Kenneth Thompson, 145–57. Lanham: University Press of America, 1990.

Mlyn, Eric. *The State, Society, and Limited Nuclear War*. Albany, NY: SUNY Press, 1995.

Moens, Alexander. *Foreign Policy under Carter*. Boulder: Westview Press, 1990.

Mulcahy, Kevin V. "The Secretary of State and the National Security Adviser: Foreign Policy Making in the Carter and Reagan Administrations." *Presidential Studies Quarterly* 16, no. 2 (summer 1986): 280–299.

Newhouse, John. *Cold Dawn: The Story of SALT*. New York: Holt, Rinehart, and Winston, 1973.

Nolan, Janne. *Guardians of the Arsenal*. New York: Basic Books, 1989.

Perle, Richard. "Arms Control." In *Staying the Course: Henry M. Jackson and National Security*, edited by Dorothy Fosdick, 89–100. Seattle: University of Washington Press, 1987.

Powers, Thomas. "Choosing a Strategy for World War III." *Atlantic Monthly* 250, no. 5 (November 1982): 82–110.

Prados, John. *The Soviet Estimate*. Princeton: Princeton University Press, 1986.

Richelson, Jeffrey. "PD-59, NSDD-13, and the Reagan Strategic Modernization Plan." *Journal of Strategic Studies* 6, no. 2 (June 1983): 125–146.

Rosati, Jerel. *The Carter Administration's Quest for Global Community*. Columbia: University of South Carolina Press, 1987.

Sagan, Scott. "SIOP-62: The Nuclear War Plan Briefing to President Kennedy." *International Security* 12, no. 1 (summer 1987): 22–52.

Schlesinger, Arthur. "The Great Carter Mystery." *The New Republic* 182, no. 15 (12 April 1980): 18–21.

Slocombe, Walter. "The Countervailing Strategy." *International Security* 5, no. 4 (spring 1981): 18–27.

Smith, Gaddis. *Morality, Reason, and Power*. New York: Hill and Wang, 1986.

Spencer, Donald. *The Carter Implosion*. New York: Praeger, 1988.

Szulc, Tad. "The New Brinksmanship." *The New Republic* (8 November 1980): 18–21.

Talbott, Strobe. *Endgame*. New York: Harper and Row, 1980.

Terriff, Terry. *The Nixon Administration and the Making of U.S. Nuclear Strategy* (Ithaca: Cornell University Press, 1995).

Thompson, Kenneth, ed. *The Carter Presidency*. Lanham, MD: University Press of America, 1990.

Treaty between the United States of America and the Union of Soviet Socialist Republics on the Limitation of Strategic Offensive Arms. Washington, D.C.: Government Printing Office, 18 June 1979.

U.S. Senate Committee on Armed Services. *DOD Authorizations for Appropriations for FY 1982, Part 7: Hearing before the Armed Services Committee*, 97th Cong., 1st sess., February–March 1981.

U.S. Senate Committee on Armed Services. *Nominations of Harold Brown and Charles W. Duncan, Jr.* 95th Cong., 1st sess., 11 January 1977.

U.S. Senate Committee on Foreign Relations. *Hearing before the Committee on Foreign Relations, United States Senate, on Presidential Directive 59*, 96th Cong., 2d sess., 16 September 1980.

Vance, Cyrus. *Hard Choices*. New York: Simon and Schuster, 1983.

Wohlstetter, Roberta. *Pearl Harbor: Warning and Decision*. Stanford: Stanford University Press, 1962.

Wolfe, Thomas. *The SALT Experience*. Cambridge, MA: Ballinger, 1979.

The Reagan Administration

Anderson, Martin. *Revolution*. Stanford: Hoover Institution Press, 1990.

Arkin, William. "Going with Small ICBMs." *Bulletin of the Atomic Scientists* 40, no. 5 (May 1984): 7–8.

Arnson, Cynthia. *Crossroads*. 2d ed. University Park: The Pennsylvania State University Press, 1993.

Ball, Desmond. "The Carter Administration's Decision on MX Basing." In *American Defense Policy*, 5th ed., edited by John Reichart and Steven Sturm, 234–41. Baltimore: The Johns Hopkins University Press, 1982.

———. "The Development of the SIOP, 1960–1983." In *Strategic Nuclear Targeting*, edited by Desmond Ball and Jeffrey Richelson, 57–83. Ithaca, NY: Cornell University Press, 1986.

Barnett, Lawrence I. *Gambling with History*. Garden City: Doubleday and Co., 1983.

Baucom, Donald R. *The Origins of SDI, 1944–1983*. Lawrence: University Press of Kansas, 1992.

Beschloss, Michael, and Allen Weinstein. "The Best National Security System: An Interview with Zbigniew Brzezinski." *Washington Quarterly* 5, no. 1 (winter 1982): 71–82.

Cannon, Lou. *President Reagan: The Role of a Lifetime*. New York: Touchstone, 1991.

Carnesale, Albert, and Charles Glaser. "ICBM Vulnerability: The Cures Are Worse than the Disease." *International Security* 7, no. 1 (summer 1982): 71–93.

Carter, Ashton, and David Schwartz, eds. *Ballistic Missile Defense*. Washington, D.C.: Brookings Institution Press, 1984.

Chayes, Antonia Handler, and Paul Doty, eds. *Defending Deterrence*. Washington, D.C.: Pergamon-Brassey's, 1989.

Cole, Paul M., and William J. Taylor, Jr. *The Nuclear Freeze Debate: Arms Control Issues for the 1980s*. Boulder: Westview Press, 1983.

Crocker, Chester. *High Noon in Southern Africa*. New York: W. W. Norton, 1992.

Dalby, Simon. *Creating the Second Cold War*. London: Pinter Publishers, 1990.

Deaver, Michael. *Behind the Scenes*. New York: William Morrow and Co., 1987.

Destler, I. M. "The Evolution of Reagan Foreign Policy." In *The Reagan Presidency: An Early Assessment*, edited by Fred Greenstein. 117–58. Baltimore: The Johns Hopkins University Press, 1983.

Destler, I. M., Leslie Gelb, and Anthony Lake. *Our Own Worst Enemy*. New York: Simon and Schuster, 1984.

Draper, Theodore. *A Very Thin Line*. New York: Simon and Schuster, 1991.

Edwards, John. *Superweapon: The Making of the MX*. New York: W. W. Norton, 1982.

Endicott, John. "The National Security Council: Formalized Coordination and Policy Planning." In *National Security Policy*, edited by Robert Pfaltzgraff and Uri Ra'anan, 177–200. Hamden, CT: Archon Books, 1984.

Fitzgerald, Frances. *Way Out There in the Blue*. New York: Simon and Schuster, 2000.

Frye, Alton. "Strategic Build-Down: A Context for Restraint." In *The Nuclear Controversy*, edited by William P. Bundy, 211–26. New York: Meridian Books, 1985.

Garthoff, Raymond. *The Great Transition*. Washington, D.C.: Brookings Institution Press, 1994.

Gates, Robert. *From the Shadows*. New York: Touchstone, 1996.

Gordon, Michael. "Administration Debates Arms Cuts with Congress as Well as the Soviets." *National Journal* 15, no. 32 (6 August 1983): 1624–29.

———. "The Aspin Paradox: A 'Liberal' Who Helped Keep the MX Alive." *National Journal* 16, no. 27 (7 July 1984): 1296–99.

————. "In the Great Nuclear Strategy Debate, The Issue Is Where Do We Stand." *National Journal* 14, no. 20 (15 May 1982): 856–60.

Gray, Colin, and Jeffrey G. Barlow. "Inexcusable Restraint: The Decline of American Military Power in the 1970s." *International Security* 10, no. 2 (fall 1985): 27–69.

Greenstein, Fred. "Reagan and the Lore of the Modern Presidency: What Have We Learned?" In *The Reagan Presidency: An Early Assessment*, ed. Fred Greenstein, 159–87. Baltimore: The Johns Hopkins University Press, 1983.

Haig, Alexander. *Caveat*. New York: MacMillan, 1984.

Halloran, Richard. *To Arm a Nation*. New York: MacMillan Publishing Company, 1986.

Hill, Dilys M., and Phil Williams. "The Reagan Presidency: Style and Substance." In *The Reagan Presidency*, edited by Dilys M. Hill, Raymond Moore, and Phil Williams, 3–25. London: MacMillan, 1990.

Holland, Lauren H., and Robert A. Hoover. *The MX Decision*. Boulder: Westview Press, 1985.

Johnson, Michael. "Debunking the Window of Vulnerability." *Technology Review* 85, no. 1 (January 1982): 59–65, 70.

Kampelman, Max M. *Entering New Worlds*. New York: Harper Collins, 1991.

Kegley, Charles W., and Eugene R. Witkopf. "The Reagan Adminstration's World View." *Orbis* 26, no. 1 (spring 1982): 223–44.

Kent, Glenn A., and Edward L. Warner. "Key Aspects of a Compulsory Double–Build Down Approach." The Rand Corporation (14 September 1983), mimeo.

Kent, Glenn, with Randall DeValk and Edward L. Warner. *A New Approach to Arms Control*. Santa Monica: The RAND Corporation, June 1984.

Kirschten, Dick. "Clark Emerges as a Tough Manager, Not a Rival to the Secretary of State." *National Journal* 14, no. 29 (17 July 1982): 1244–48.

————. "Decision Making in the White House: How Well Does It Serve the President." *National Journal* 14, no. 14 (3 April 1982): 584–89.

————. "His NSC Days May Be Numbered, but Allen Is Known for Bouncing Back." *National Journal* 13, no. 48 (28 November 1981): 2114–17.

————. "Inner Circle Speaks with Many Voices, but Maybe That's How Reagan Wants It." *National Journal* 15, no. 22 (28 May 1983): 1100–3.

————. "Reagan's Cabinet Councils May Have Less Influence Than Meets the Eye." *National Journal* 13, no. 28 (11 July 1981): 1242–47.

Komer, Robert. "What 'Decade of Neglect.'" *International Security* 10, no. 2 (fall 1985): 70–83.

Korb, Lawrence, and Linda Brady. "Rearming America: The Reagan Administration Defense Program." *International Security* 9, no. 3 (winter 1984/85): 3–18.

McFarlane, Robert. *Special Trust*. New York: Cadell and Davies, 1994.

————. Interview with Robert McFarlane. By Ivo Daalder and I. M. Destler. *National Security Council Project: Oral History Roundtables: The Role of the National Security Adviser*. College Park and Washington, D.C.: Center for International and Security Studies at Maryland, School of Public Affairs, University of Maryland and Brookings Institution, 1999, 39–50. http://www.brookings.edu/dybdocroot/fp/projects/nsc/transcripts/19991025.htm. Accessed 20 March 2002.

McNeill, John H. "U.S.-USSR Nuclear Arms Negotiations: The Process and the Lawyer." *American Journal of International Law* 79, no. 1 (January 1985): 52–67.

Meese, Edwin, III. "The Institutional Presidency: The View from the White House." *Presidential Studies Quarterly* 13, no. 2 (spring 1983): 191–97.

Meese, Edward. *With Reagan*. Washington, D.C.: Regnery Gateway, 1992.

Melbourne, Roy. "The Odyssey of the NSC." *Strategic Review* 11, no. 3 (summer 1983): 51–64.

Menges, Constantine. *Inside the National Security Council*. New York: Simon and Schuster, 1988.

Meyer, David S. *A Winter of Discontent*. New York: Praeger, 1990.

Meyer, Stephen M. "Verification and the ICBM Shell Game." *International Security* 4, no. 2 (fall 1979): 40–68.

Morrison, David. "ICBM Vulnerability." *Bulletin of the Atomic Scientists* 40, no. 9 (September 1984): 22–29.

Mulcahy, Kevin V. "The Secretary of State and the National Security Adviser: Foreign Policy Making in the Carter and Reagan Administrations." *Presidential Studies Quarterly* 16, no. 2 (summer 1986): 280–99.

Posen, Barry, and Stephen Van Evera. "Defense Policy and the Reagan Administration." *International Security* 8, no. 1 (summer 1983): 3–45.

Prados, John. *Keeper of the Keys*. New York: William Morrow and Co., 1991.

Reagan, Ronald. *An American Life*. New York: Simon and Schuster, 1990.

Record, Jeffrey. "Jousting with Unreality." *International Security* 8, no. 3 (winter 1983/84): 3–18.

Report of the President's Special Review Board (Tower Commission Report). New York: Times Books and Random House, 1987.

Rich, Jonathan. "Midgetman: Superhero or Problem Child." *Arms Control Today* 14, no. 4 (May 1984): 1, 6–9.

Richelson, Jeffrey. "PD-59, NSDD-13, and the Reagan Strategic Modernization Plan." *Journal of Strategic Studies* 6, no. 2 (June 1983): 124–46.

Risse-Kappen, Thomas. *The Zero Option: INF, West Germany, and Arms Control*. Boulder: Westview Press, 1988.

Rochan, Thomas R., and David S. Meyer, eds. *Coalitions and Political Movements*. Boulder: Lynne Rienner Publishers, 1997.

Rockman, Bert. "The Style and Organization of the Reagan Presidency." In *The Reagan Legacy*, ed. Charles O. Jones, 3–29. Chatham, NJ: Chatham House Publishers, 1988.

Rosenfeld, Stephen. "The Guns of July." *Foreign Affairs* 64, no. 4 (spring 1986): 698–714.

Rowny, Edward L. *It Takes One to Tango*. Washington, D.C.: Brassey's, 1992.

Sanders, Jerry W. *Peddlers of Crisis*. Boston: South End Press, 1983.

Scheer, Robert. *With Enough Shovels*. New York: Random House, 1982.

Schieffer, Bob, and Gary Paul Gates. *The Acting President*. New York: Dutton, 1991.

Schneider, Barry, Colin Gray, and Keith B. Payne, eds. *Missiles for the Nineties*. Boulder: Westview Press, 1984.

Scott, James. *Deciding to Intervene*. Durham: Duke University Press, 1996.

Scoville, Herbert. *MX: Prescription for Disaster*. Cambridge: MIT Press, 1981.

Shimko, Keith. *Images and Arms Control*. Ann Arbor: University of Michigan Press, 1991.

Shultz, George. *Turmoil and Triumph*. New York: Charles Scribner's Sons, 1993.

Smith, Hedrick. *The Power Game*. New York: Ballantine Books, 1988.

Speakes, Larry. *Speaking Out*. New York: Avon Books, 1989.

Stein, Jonathan. *From H-Bomb to Star Wars*. Lexington, MA: Lexington Books, 1984.

Szulc, Tad. "The Vicar Vanquished." *Foreign Policy* 43 (summer 1981): 173–86.

Talbott, Strobe. *Deadly Gambits*. New York: Alfred A. Knopf, 1994.

Taubman, Philip. "The Shultz-Weinberger Feud." *The New York Times Magazine* (14 April 1983): 50, 91, 94–95, 98, 108.

Thompson, Kenneth W., ed. *Foreign Policy in the Reagan Administration*. Lanham: University Press of America, 1993.

Towell, Pat. "Reagan Cites Soviet Power: Embraces Nuclear Reduction and Says Talks May Begin Soon." *Congressional Quarterly* 40, no. 14 (3 April 1982): 725–26.

———. "START Talks Resume with New U.S. Offers." *Congressional Quarterly* 41, no. 40 (8 October 1983): 2099–2100.

Tyroler, Charles II. *Alerting America: The Papers of the Committee on the Present Danger.* Washington, D.C.: Pergamon-Brassey's, 1984.

U.S. Office of Technology Assessment. *Ballistic Missile Defense.* Washington, D.C.: Government Printing Office, 1984.

U.S. Office of Technology Assessment. *MX Missile Basing.* Washington, D.C.: Government Printing Office, 1981.

U.S. President. *Public Papers of the Presidents of the United States.* Washington, D.C.: Office of the *Federal Register*, National Archives and Records Service, 1982. Ronald Reagan, 1981.

U.S. President. *Public Papers of the Presidents of the United States.* Washington, D.C.: Office of the *Federal Register*, National Archives and Records Service, 1983. Ronald Reagan, 1982.

U.S. President. *Public Papers of the Presidents of the United States.* Washington, D.C.: Office of the *Federal Register*, National Archives and Records Service, 1984. Ronald Reagan, 1983.

U.S. Senate Committee on Armed Services. *Defense Organization: The Need for Change.* 99th Cong., 1st sess. staff report, 15 October 1985.

U.S. Senate Committee on Armed Services. *Department of Defense Authorization for Appropriations for Fiscal Year 1986: Hearings before the Senate Armed Services Committee.* 99th Cong., 1st sess., Part 7, February / March 1985.

U.S. Senate Committee on Foreign Relations. *International Security Policy: Hearing before the Senate Committee on Foreign Relations.* 97th Cong., 1st sess., 27 July 1981.

Walker, Paul, and John Wentworth. "Midgetman: Missile in Search of a Mission." *Bulletin of the Atomic Scientists* 42, no. 9 (November 1986): 20–26.

Waller, Douglas C. *Congress and the Nuclear Freeze.* Amherst: University of Massachusetts Press, 1987.

"Weapons in Space, vol. 1: Concepts and Technologies." *Daedalus* 114, no. 2 (spring 1985).

"Weapons in Space, vol. 2: Implications for Security." *Daedalus* 114, no. 3 (summer 1985).

———. *Report of Secretary of Defense Caspar W. Weinberger to Congress on the FY 1983 Budget, the FY 1984 Authorization Request, and the FY 1983–1987 Defense Programs.* Washington, D.C.: Government Printing Office, 8 February 1982.

———. *Report of Secretary of Defense Caspar W. Weinberger to Congress on the FY 1984 Budget, the FY 1985 Authorization Request, and the FY 1984–1988 Defense Programs.* Washington, D.C.: Government Printing Office, 1 February 1983.

Weinberger, Caspar. *Fighting for Peace.* New York: Warner Books, 1991.

Winik, Jay. *On the Brink.* New York: Simon and Schuster, 1996.

Woodward, Bob. *Veil.* New York: Pocket Books, 1987.

Woolsey, R. James. "The Politics of Vulnerability, 1980–1983." In *The Nuclear Controversy,* edited by William P. Bundy, 211–26. New York: Meridian Books, 1985.

The Bush Administration

Adelman, Kenneth. *The Great Universal Embrace.* New York: Simon and Schuster, 1989.

"Agreement on Notification of Strategic Exercises," as printed in *Arms Control Today* 19, no. 8 (October 1989): 25.

Baker, James A. *The Politics of Diplomacy.* New York: G. P. Putnam's Sons, 1995.

Beatty, Jack. "Reagan's Gift." *The Atlantic Monthly* 263, no. 2 (February 1989): 59–62, 64–66.

Beschloss, Michael, and Strobe Talbott. *At the Highest Levels*. Boston: Little, Brown, 1993.

Bolton, John R. "The Making of Foreign Policy in the Bush Administration." In *The Bush Presidency*, edited by Kenneth W. Thompson, 109–18. New York: University Press of America, 1997.

Bunn, Matthew, and Lee Feinstein. "Baker and Shevardnadze Clear START Road Blocks." *Arms Control Today* 20, no. 2 (March 1990): 21–22, 26.

Bush, George, and Brent Scowcroft. *A World Transformed*. New York: Alfred A. Knopf, 1998.

Campbell, Colin. "The White House and the Presidency under the 'Let's Deal' President." In *The Bush Presidency: First Appraisals*, edited by Colin Campbell and Bert Rockman, 185–222. Chatham, NJ: Chatham House, 1991.

David, Charles-Phillipe. "Who Was the Real George Bush? Foreign Policy Decision Making under the Bush Administration." *Diplomacy and Statecraft* 7, no. 1 (March 1996): 197–220.

Deibel, Terry L. "Bush Foreign Policy: Mastery and Inaction." *Foreign Affairs* 84 (fall 1991): 3–23.

Dowd, Maureen, and Thomas Friedman. "The Fabulous Bush and Baker Boys." *The New York Times Magazine* (6 May 1990): 34–36, 58–62, 64, 67.

Duffy, Michael, and Dan Goodgame. *Marching in Place*. New York: Simon and Schuster, 1992.

Fitzwater, Marlin. *Call the Briefing*. New York: Times Books, 1995.

Flournoy, Michelle A. "START Ends Temporarily as Reagan Team Puts Last Touches on Negotiating Position." *Arms Control Today* 18, no. 10 (December 1988): 28.

Franklin, Daniel P., and Robert Shephard. "Is Prudence a Policy? George Bush and the World." In *Leadership and the Bush Presidency*, edited by Ryan Barrilleaux and Mary E. Stuckey, 165–76. Westport: Praeger, 1992.

Garfinkle, Adam. "STARTing Over." *The National Interest* 20 (summer 1990): 71–76.

Garthoff, Raymond. *The Great Transition*. Washington, D.C.: Brookings Institution Press, 1994.

———. *Policy versus the Law: The Reinterpretation of the ABM Treaty*. Washington, D.C.: Brookings Institution Press, 1987.

Gates, Robert. *From the Shadows*. New York: Touchstone, 1996.

Halverson, Thomas E. "First Bush Defense Budget Reveals Program Cuts, Strategic Decisions." *Arms Control Today* 19, no. 4 (May 1989): 21, 27.

Hirsch, John L., and Robert B. Oakley. *Somalia and Operation Restore Hope*. Washington, D.C.: United States Institute of Peace Press, 1995.

Hutchings, Robert L. *American Diplomacy and the End of the Cold War*. Baltimore: The Johns Hopkins University Press; Washington, D.C.: The Woodrow Wilson Center Press, 1997.

"Joint Statement on Arms Control," as printed in *Arms Control Today* 19, no. 8 (October 1989): 22.

Kampelman, Max. "START: Completing the Task." *Washington Quarterly* 12, no. 3 (summer 1989): 5–16.

Kegley, Charles. "The Bush Administration and the Future of American Foreign Policy: Pragmatism or Procrastination." *Presidential Studies Quarterly* 19, no. 4 (fall 1989): 717–732.

Kinahar, Graham. "Ratification of START: Lessons from the INF Treaty." *Journal of Social, Political, and Economic Studies* 14, no. 3 (winter 1989): 387–415.

Kolb, Charles. *White House Daze*. New York: Free Press, 1994.

Lockwood, Dunbar. "Bush-Gorbachev Concur: START to Be Finished by Year's End." *Arms Control Today* 20, no. 5 (June 1990): 28–29.

———. "Moscow Summit, START Signing Postponed." *Arms Control Today* 21, no. 2 (March 1991): 25, 28.

———. "START Talks Stalled, 1990 Finish in Jeopardy." *Arms Control Today* 20, no. 7 (September 1990): 17, 21.

Madison, Christopher. "No Sharp Elbows." *National Journal* 22, no. 21 (26 May 1990): 1277–81.

———. "Scrambling Vicar." *National Journal* 23, no. 16 (20 April 1991): 924–928.

Mandelbaum, Michael. "The Bush Foreign Policy." *Foreign Affairs* 70, no. 1 (1990/91): 5–22.

Marsh, Gerald. "The Ups and Downs of Downloading." *Bulletin of the Atomic Scientists* 47, no. 9 (November 1991): 21–23.

Mendelsohn, Jack. "U.S., Soviets Continue Dialogue on Nuclear Cutbacks." *Arms Control Today* 21, no. 9 (November 1991): 17, 24.

Morocco, John D. "Cheney Endorses MX Rail Garrison, Calls for Few Cuts in USAF Budget." *Aviation Week and Space Technology* (24 April 1989): 22.

Morrison, David C. "After the Bombs Drop." *National Journal* 21, no. 7 (18 February 1989): 405–6.

Munro, Neil. "Report: Defer MX, Field Midgetman and B-2 Bomber." *Defense News* 4, no. 6 (6 February 1989): 1.

Newhouse, John. "The Tactician." *The New Yorker* 66, no. 12 (7 May 1990): 50–52, 54, 58, 60–82.

NSR-14 National Security Review 14, see "Review of United States Arms Control Policies," 3 April 1989, George H. W. Bush Presidential Library. Available at http://bushlibrary. tamu.edu; and Gordon, "U.S. Is Considering a Tactical Shift on Strategic Arms," 1. Accessed 17 July 2001.

Oberdorfer, Don. *From the Cold War to a New Era*, updated ed. Baltimore: The Johns Hopkins University Press, 1998.

Peele, Gillian. "The Constrained Presidency of George Bush." *Current History* 91, no. 564 (April 1992): 151–5.

Pfiffner, James P. "Establishing the Bush Presidency." *Public Administration Review* 50, no. 1 (January/February 1990): 64–73.

———. "Presidential Policy Making and the Persian Gulf War." In *The Presidency and the Persian Gulf War*, edited by Marcia Lynn Whicker et al., 3–24. Westport: Praeger, 1993.

Powell, Colin. *My American Journey*. New York: Random House, 1995.

———. Interview with Colin Powell. By Ivo Daalder and I. M. Destler. *National Security Council Project: Oral History Roundtables: The Role of the National Security Adviser*. College Park and Washington, D.C.: Center for International and Security Studies at Maryland, School of Public Affairs, University of Maryland and The Brookings Institution, 1999, 51–61. http://www.brookings.edu/dybdocroot/fp/projects/nsc/transcripts/19991025.htm. Accessed 20 March 2002.

Prados, John. *Keeper of the Keys*. New York: William Morrow and Co., 1991.

Report of the President's Special Review Board (Tower Commission Report). New York: Times Books and Random House, 1987.

Rowny, Edward. *It Takes One to Tango*. Washington, D.C.: Brassey's, 1992.

Rubin, James P. "As START Resumes, Bush Pushes Early Verification." *Arms Control Today* 19, no. 6 (August 1989): 24–25.

Safire, William. "Bush's Cabinet: Who's Up, Who's Down." *The New York Times Magazine* (25 March 1990): 30–33, 63–67.

Schneider, William. "For Bush, a Prudent Foreign Policy." *National Journal* 21, no. 20 (20 May 1989): 1278.

————. "The In-Box Presidency." *The Atlantic Monthly* 265, no. 1 (January 1990): 34–37, 40–43.

Shogan, Robert. *The Riddle of Power.* New York: E. P. Dutton, 1991.

Simpson, Christopher, ed. *National Security Directives of the Reagan and Bush Administrations.* Boulder: Westview Press, 1995.

Snow, Donald M., and Eugene Brown. *Beyond the Water's Edge.* New York: St. Martins, 1997.

Solomon, Burt. "Bush's Passion for Friendship Abets His Diplomatic Policy." *National Journal* 22, no. 49 (8 December 1990): 2986–87.

START: Treaty between the United States of America and the Union of Soviet Socialist Republics on the Reduction and Limitation of Strategic Offensive Arms. Washington, D.C.: Government Printing Office, 1991.

"Strategic Arms Reduction Treaty (START): Analysis, Summary, and Text." *Arms Control Today* 21, no. 9 (November 1991): supplement.

Talbott, Strobe. "Why START Stopped." *Foreign Affairs* 67, no. 1 (fall 1988): 49–69.

Thompson, Kenneth W., ed. *The Bush Presidency.* New York: University Press of America, 1997.

Towell, Pat, and Carroll J. Doherty. "START Sets Historic Terms for Nuclear Arms Curbs." *Congressional Quarterly* 49, no. 29 (20 July 1991): 1993–1998.

U.S. President. *Public Papers of the Presidents of the United States.* Washington, D.C.: Office of the *Federal Register*, National Archives and Records Service, 1992. George Bush, 1991.

————. *Public Papers of the Presidents of the United States.* Washington, D.C.: Office of the *Federal Register*, National Archives and Records Service, 1993. George Bush, 1992–93.

U.S. Senate Committee on Armed Services. *NATO Defense and the INF Treaty.* 100th Congress, 2d sess., parts 1–5, 1988.

U.S. Senate Committee on Foreign Relations. *INF Treaty.* 100th Congress, 2d sess., parts 1–6, 1988.

Walcott, Charles E., and Karen M. Hult. *Governing the White House.* Lawrence: University Press of Kansas, 1995.

Welch, David. "The Organizational Process Model and the Bureaucratic Politics Paradigm," *International Security* 17, no. 2 (fall 1992): 120–22.

Woodward, Bob. *The Commanders.* New York: Simon and Schuster, 1991.

125–28, 131–33, 135–37; Commission on
Strategic Forces of, 119–21, 123, 142, 178;
on Eureka, 104–5, 110, 112–13, 115–19,
123–27, 135–36; leadership style of, 13,
55–56, 57–58, 115, 135, 137; learning experience of, 128, 137, 204; on nuclear war,
109; on nuclear weapons freeze, 112; on
weapons, 107–8, 111, 112, 113–18, 122,
125, 128–34, 136

Reagan administration, 7, 9–11, 13–15, 77–78,
103–37; on ABM treaty, 141; arms control policy in, 103–5, 116, 128; committees and advisers in, 63–65; Dam
Group, 123, 181; decision making in,
109, 134–36, 175, 186–91; environment
of, 105–9, 117, 128–29; evolution of,
134–35; informal processes of, 73–74;
interagency process of, 104–5, 109–10,
118, 123, 128–32, 176, 180–81; organizational dynamics of, 68–70, 110–12, 118,
129–30; political pressures in, 136; presidential choice and strategy of, 118, 123,
124–28, 130–34; on SALT, 105–6, 108, 111;
Scowcroft commission of, 116–17,
119–21, 123, 124, 178; on START, 104–5,
109–10, 112–16, 118–21, 123–27, 131–37,
152–59; START II genesis and, 159–64;
structure of, 193–98; troika in (Meese,
Baker, Deaver), 88, 101–2, 123
Reedy, George, 22
Republican Party, 68–69
Ridge, Tom, 2
Rockman, Bert A., 26, 46, 186
Roosevelt, Franklin Delano, 195
Rosati, Jerel, 28, 30
Rostow, Eugene, 111, 114
Rourke, Francis, 21, 28
Rowny, Edward, 111, 124
Rudman, Warren, 122
Rusk, Dean, 51, 190
Russia, 160, 163. *See also* USSR

Scowcroft, Brent, 23, 125–26, 132–33, 138–39,
144; as ANSA, 51, 59, 65–66, 71, 169, 196;
in Breakfast Group, 150, 151, 164, 167;
Chairman of President's Commission
on Strategic Forces, 116–17, 119–21, 123,
124, 178; at Malta Summit, 148–49, 150,
153, 155, 157–58; in START, 159, 161–63,
164, 170, 177. *See also* Gang of Eight
secretary of state, 65–66, 68, 169. *See also*
State Department

Seidman, Harold, 42
Senate, U.S., 122, 143, 178. *See also* Congress,
U.S.
Senior Arms Control Policy Group
(SACPG), Reagan administration,
124–25, 181
senior interagency groups (SIGs), Reagan
administration, 61; Foreign Policy
(SIG-FP), 109–10, 112; Interagency
Group (SIG-IP), 74
Shevardnadze, Eduard, 147–48, 151, 153–54
Shultz, George, 58, 69, 70, 103, 123, 126; in in-
teragency process, 132–33, 135; in NST,
141
Simon, Herbert, 18, 19, 39
Single Integrated Operating Plan, 10
Slocombe, Walter, 84
Solidarity movement (Poland), 69
Somalia, 68, 165, 208
Soviet Union. *See* USSR
standard weapons stations (SWS), 125–26
Special Coordination Committee (SCC),
SALT, 60, 83–84, 86, 87, 92
State Department, 99, 109, 113–14, 144, 162,
184, 211; exclusion of, 88, 90, 97–98, 181;
on warheads, 162
Strategic Arms Limitation Talks (SALT), 10,
175, 182, 187–88; Carter administration
on, 80–86, 88–89, 100; deep cuts proposals, 80–89; Reagan administration
on, 105–6, 108, 111
Strategic Arms Reduction Talks (START),
166, 182–83, 187, 190; Bush administration on, 143–48, 152–59, 160–64, 168;
Eureka proposals, 104–5, 112, 115–16,
135, 190; Reagan administration on,
104–5, 109–10, 112–16, 118–21, 123–27,
131–37; START I, 170, 174, 177, 206–7;
START II, 77–78, 139, 143–48, 152–59,
162, 168, 177, 180–81
strategic defense, 128–34, 137, 177
Strategic Defense Initiative (SDI), 104, 128,
129, 141
structural contingency theory, 34
Sununu, John, 149, 161–62. *See also* Gang of
Eight
survivability, 167, 183–84. *See also* vulnerability, window of

telemetry encryption, 154–55, 158
Teller, Edward, 129, 130
terrorism, 1, 207